For B.H.

for

all best wishes

Human Possibilities

Human Possibilities

*Mind Exploration in the USSR
and Eastern Europe*

Stanley Krippner, Ph.D.

ANCHOR PRESS/DOUBLEDAY
GARDEN CITY, NEW YORK
1980

For the Pecks:
Richard, Donna, Mason, and Laura

The Anchor Press edition is the first publication of *Human Possibilities*.
Anchor Press edition: 1980

We gratefully acknowledge permission to reprint excerpts from *The Power of the Mind*, by Suzy Smith, Copyright © 1974 by Suzy Smith. Reprinted by permission of Chilton Book Company.

ISBN: 0-385-12805-3
Library of Congress Catalog Card Number 80–953

Contents

	Preface	vii
1	Search for the New	1
2	Psychokinesis in Leningrad	32
3	Soviet Parapsychology: The Tip of an Iceberg?	54
4	Fasting in Moscow and Other Soviet Therapies	81
5	Hypnosis, Hypnoproduction, and Creativity	103
6	Suggestopedia in the Classroom	122
7	Around a Language in Fifty Days	147
8	The Electrical Photographs of Semyon Kirlian	166
9	Problems of the Unconscious	194
10	Self-regulation in Kazakhstan	233
11	Acupuncture by Laser Beams	268
12	Personality, Bioplasma, and Holographic Patterns	298
	Afterword by Martin Ebon	332
	Index	335

Preface

Many people will not be pleased with this book. It is not a sensational account of psychic wonders. It is not a revelation of the latest horrors of psychological warfare. It is not a comprehensive cataloguing of the latest developments in Soviet social science. Then what does *Human Possibilities* attempt to do? It is an account of my trips to the USSR and Eastern Europe and the people I have met who are engaged in what Americans would call "mind research" or "consciousness studies"—and what many foreign scientists would refer to as "hidden reserves" or "latent human possibilities." This movement is a vital and growing one, but it is also controversial and fragile. Its growth could accelerate—or it could be stifled, depending on the social and political conditions that determine the milieu in which the mind researchers operate. I only hope that my account is accurate enough and honest enough to bring a description of the efforts of these pioneers to a wider audience.

In reading about these efforts, one may find it useful to set aside prejudices and preconceived ideas, and attempt to deal with Soviet and Eastern European concepts within their own framework. I recall the statement of one Soviet researcher who told me, "Your government claims to be interested in human rights. We, too, are interested in human rights—the right to hold a job, the right to have enough to eat and to have a place to live, the right to a sound mind and a healthy body, the right to a supermemory, the right to learn other languages. Any idiot can stand on a street corner and mouth unpopular ideas. But what kind of right is that compared to these others?" This manifesto was repeated, with variations, many times during my trips to Communist nations and eloquently presents an important perspective from which the potentials of humanity can be understood and developed.

In the preparation of this manuscript, I have been assisted in various ways by Ivan Barzakov, Christopher Bird, Fred Blau, Mary Lou Carlson, Jonathan Cohen, Henry S. Dakin, John Gryl, Lelie Krippner, Nancy Rollins, Christopher C. Scott, Saul-Paul Sirag, Hadley Smith, Mark Smith, William Strachan, Charles T. Turley, and Rhea A. White. A. J. Lewis and Scott Hill provided the translations of some materials that are referred to in Chapters 10 and 11.

To document my information, I have supplemented each chapter with a reading list. Furthermore, I have noted the year of publication in the text to assist readers in their search for corroboration and additional detail. For example, the reference to Uznadze (1967) in Chapter 4 simply refers the reader to the list of references where he or she will find the listing: Uznadze, D. N. *The Psychology of Set.* New York: Consultants Bureau, 1967. In some instances, I have referred to books and articles written in Russian or another foreign language. In this case, I inform the reader of the situation by the use of brackets—for example, Krokhalev, G. P. [Objectifying optical hallucinations.] *Psychotronik*, 1979, *1*, 8–18. This citation also demonstrates the standard form of describing scientific articles—the author's and article's names followed by that of the journal, the year of publication, the volume number (in italics), and the page numbers. Many readers will care very little about such details, but in a field so controversial it is wise to document as many of one's reports as possible. In addition, page numbers are given for direct quotations from English-language books and other selected publications.

For those interested in overviews of Soviet psychology and psychiatry, I would suggest the following books:

Cole, M. (ed.). *Soviet Developmental Psychology.* White Plains, N.Y.: Sharpe, 1977.

Cole, M., and Maltzman, I. (eds.). *A Handbook of Contemporary Soviet Psychology.* New York: Basic Books, 1969.

Corson, S. E. (ed.). *Psychiatry and Psychology in the USSR.* New York: Plenum Press, 1976.

Peat, R. *Mind and Tissue: Russian Research Perspectives on the Human Brain.* Claremont, Calif.: Khalsa Publications, 1976.

Razran, G. *Mind in Evolution: An East-West Synthesis of Learned Behavior and Cognition.* Boston: Houghton Mifflin, 1971.

Rollins, N. *Child Psychiatry in the Soviet Union: Preliminary Observations.* Cambridge, Mass.: Harvard University Press, 1972.

The research discussed in *Human Possibilities* finds a very small place in the above volumes but they do give the context in which new developments can be more fully appreciated.

And what about future developments? No single source is adequate, but occasional translations appear in the *International Journal of Paraphysics* (Downton, Wilshire, England). *The Brain/ Mind Bulletin* (P.O. Box 42211, Los Angeles, Calif. 90042) summarizes current research in consciousness, including some data from the USSR and the other Warsaw Pact nations.

My greatest debt is to the mind pioneers themselves. Communication by mail is often difficult. For example, Victor Inyushin had twice sent me official invitations to visit Kazakh State University. These letters were never received, nor was the travel schedule I sent Inyushin prior to my 1979 arrival; he was in another part of Kazakhstan when I came to Alma-Ata. Nor was A. S. Romen in Alma-Ata when I arrived. He had sent me letters at three different addresses; all were returned from the USA as "undeliverable." However, upon hearing of my arrival, Inyushin and Romen immediately returned to Alma-Ata and extended their warmest hospitality to me and my colleagues.

Once contact was made, the mind researchers and I discovered more connecting us than dividing us. We spoke a common language—that of human beings, their nature, their needs, and their potentials. Time and time again the desire was expressed to work together on common problems. However, the fear was expressed that these discoveries could be perverted for destructive purposes in a world where the chances for peace are questionable. Science does not work in a vacuum; the future of international relations will, for better or for worse, determine the future of the scientific cooperation so earnestly desired by those of us exploring the human possibilities discussed in this book.

CHAPTER 1

Search for the New

> However bizarre from the standpoint of "common
> sense" the transformation of imponderable ether into
> ponderable matter and vice versa may appear . . .
> this is but another corroboration of dialectical mate-
> rialism.
>
> V. I. Lenin
> (1968, pp. 261–62)

An Invitation from the Academy

On June 23, 1971, I checked into Moscow's Intourist Hotel.
Shortly after reaching my room, the telephone rang. It was
Larissa Vilenskaya, a Soviet engineer and parapsychologist, wel-
coming me and my assistant to the USSR. She surprised us by an-
nouncing, "We have arranged for Dr. Krippner to give an address
at the Academy of Pedagogical Sciences on Monday. This will be
the first lecture on parapsychology ever delivered at the Academy.
We have invited over two hundred psychologists, psychiatrists,
physicists, engineers, space scientists, and cosmonauts in training."

I explained to Vilenskaya that our flight to Leningrad was
scheduled for early Monday morning. She insisted that we change
it; after acknowledging my pleasure concerning the invitation, I
went to the hotel lobby and told the Intourist travel official that I
would like a later flight. She was pessimistic, explaining, "Once
flight plans are made they are rarely changed. On the few occasions when a change is permitted, one must pay a fine." I agreed

to pay the fine, handed her the tickets, and agreed to make another inquiry the following day.

At dinner that evening, I told Richard Davidson, my assistant (a student from New York University), how surprised I was to receive the Academy's invitation. Before leaving New York City, I had studied how Soviet psychology was organized. The institution's full name was the Academy of Pedagogical Sciences of the USSR and of the Russian Soviet Federated Socialist Republic. It was concerned with problems of educational theory, history, and methodology, as well as with educational psychology and developmental physiology. Several months earlier, three of my friends from Esalen Institute had visited Moscow and had met V. N. Pushkin, a psychologist working at the Academy, who had a special interest in parapsychology.

The Academy of Pedagogical Sciences contained several institutes, the best known being the Institute of General and Educational Psychology, the Institute of Defectology (devoted to the study of handicapped children), and the Institute of Developmental Physiology and Physical Education. I told Davidson that the Academy was among the most prestigious institutions in the Soviet Union, the Academy's members being referred to as "academicians," a title held in even greater esteem than "professor."

The following morning, we returned to the Intourist desk to make inquiries regarding our requested change of flight plans. The official located our revised tickets and returned them to us with a smile, commenting, "No fine." A few minutes later we were in Red Square and had met Edward Naumov, director of the Department for Technical Parapsychology, and Larissa Vilenskaya, his assistant. Naumov told me that my scheduled address at the Academy would be of great assistance in legitimizing Soviet parapsychology, a goal he had been working toward for many years.

Naumov described for us the terminology he had proposed to make parapsychological (or "psi") phenomena palatable to Soviet scientists. He used the term "biological information" instead of extrasensory perception or ESP—the knowledge obtained without the apparent use of the recognized senses. Telepathy, the extrasensory perception of another person's thoughts, was referred to as "biological communication"; clairvoyance, ESP of distant objects or events, was termed "biological location." A special type of "biological location" was the "biophysical effect," better known as dowsing and reportedly used in both the USA and the USSR to locate underground oil, metal, or water.

"Proscopy"—ESP of future events—was known to us as precognition, while "biological energy" referred to psychokinesis or PK, an organism's influence on the environment without apparent utilization of the body musculature. Altogether, these were termed "psychoenergetic phenomena"—interactions between organisms and their environment (including other organisms) that cannot be explained by traditional scientific models of the universe.

I had been engaged in the study of psi (which comprises both ESP and PK) for several years, publishing my first paper on the subject in 1961. In 1964, I became director of the Dream Laboratory at Brooklyn's Maimonides Medical Center, where our primary research project was the study of telepathic effects in dreams. It was this work that had attracted the attention of the Soviets, had stimulated the correspondence that led to my visit to Moscow, and was to be the topic of my talk at the Academy.*

My personal interest in Soviet parapsychology had been a longstanding one. In 1966, I had been asked to write a book review of *Mysterious Phenomena of the Human Psyche* by L. L. Vasiliev. In my review, I noted:

> A distinguished Soviet physiologist, Vasiliev has specialized in the biophysiology of the nervous system. . . . There may be some connection between Vasiliev's parapsychological interests and the fact that he seems to have held no academic positions in the Soviet Union from 1938 (the year of the greatest Stalinist purge) to 1943. His recent book, however, should advance the cause of parapsychology in the U.S.S.R. because it places psychical research squarely within the framework of Marxian doctrine. [p. 290]

It seemed to me that Naumov's proposed terms were also designed to work within the structure of dialectical materialism. If ESP is "biological information" and PK "biological energy," there is no reason why the material aspects of these unusual phenomena could not be measured and applied. Indeed, one possible application noted by Naumov was "bioenergetic healing," and we had a

* These experiments are summarized in *Dream Telepathy* (Ullman, Krippner, and Vaughan, 1974).

lengthy discussion about the work of various "healers" we had known.

Naumov and Vilenskaya asked us about the funding situation for American parapsychology. We told them that only a few laboratories were fairly well assured of constant funding, those of the American Society for Psychical Research, the University of Virginia, and the Foundation for Research on the Nature of Man —an institution organized when J. B. Rhine, the great pioneer of experimental parapsychology, reached retirement age at Duke University. As for the Maimonides Dream Laboratory, we confessed that we never knew from year to year whether we would have the money to continue. Naumov was incredulous. "Don't your people realize the importance of parapsychology in what it has to teach us about human possibilities?" he asked. He then added, "This is extremely important work that you are doing for it opens the door to creativity and human potential. Your country is a nation of businessmen. Aren't they aware that it is good business to support humanitarian efforts?"

We concluded our tour of Red Square and returned to our room, spending several hours writing the first draft of the address scheduled for the Academy. Later that evening, we walked down the streets of Moscow, noting how much cleaner they were than the streets of any American metropolis we had ever visited. Suddenly, a middle-aged woman approached Davidson and berated him in Russian for what was, for her, his outrageous appearance —faded blue jeans held to his body by a colorful fabric belt, a blue work shirt with a missing button, and long, dark, curly hair that reached to his shoulders. But this was the only person who accosted us—it appeared that the streets of Moscow were much safer at night than the streets of New York City.

Seven Steps in the Sports Cinema

Over the next few days, we had several meetings with Victor Adamenko, a biophysicist who had been a boyhood friend of Semyon Kirlian, the inventor who—with his wife, Valentina—had developed the type of high-voltage photography that bears his name. Adamenko had also been involved in devising PK training programs. It was said that he had trained his wife to move objects at a distance.

We held lengthy conversations with G. S. Vassilchenko, a pioneer in the use of acupuncture for sexual dysfunction; Vladimir Raikov, a psychoneurologist who was using hypnosis to enhance creativity; Nikolaus Minayev, an engineer who claimed to be using counselors gifted with psi ability in his job-placement activities in the Ministry of the Coal and Mining Industry; and Yuri Nikolayev, a psychiatrist who had originated a treatment program for schizophrenics based on a three- or four-week fast. We met other interesting scientists and researchers at a reception arranged for us by Naumov at the Sports Cinema, a Moscow movie theater. Presented at the reception was a special showing of *Seven Steps Beyond the Horizon,* a Soviet documentary that had run for over two years in Moscow theaters (Skurlatov, 1969). The film dealt with seven unusual "human possibilities": Raikov's use of hypnosis to develop people's creative skills, a person with the ability to drive a car blindfolded, a guitarist who could improvise songs immediately after being given a topic, a chessmaster who could play a dozen games simultaneously with a dozen opponents, a young man with the ability to perform rapid mental calculations, a demonstration of dowsing—the "biophysical effect"—and an exhibition of "skin vision"—the "dermo-optical effect."

The segment on "skin vision" began by depicting blindfolded subjects identifying the color of cards that they were touching. I told Davidson that the blindfolds were inadequate. Over the years, I had seen many "clairvoyants" name colors, letters, and words simply by looking down their nose through the tiny opening that invariably appears when a blindfolded person squints, wrinkles the brow, and wiggles the nose. I also noted that one of the most celebrated practitioners of the "dermo-optical effect" had been accused of cheating and later worked with a circus. An adequate blindfold would need to extend to the waist to prevent conscious or unconscious visual clues.*

One scene in the film showed a blind girl correctly identifying colors, a feat that I suspected was due to the detection of subtle temperature differences between black cards, which absorb heat,

* A carefully controlled series of experiments with "skin vision" was described by Yvonne Duplessis at the Third International Congress on Psychotronic Research, Tokyo, 1977.

and white cards, which reflect heat. A final sequence demonstrated the accurate identification of colors and letters that were enclosed in metal containers—an impressive feat, but one that would need to be supplemented by a written scientific report describing the experimental conditions before anyone could make a judgment on its validity.

This same reservation would have to be made in regard to the other wondrous "steps beyond the horizon" in the film. Nevertheless, several of them were indeed provocative. In one segment, a young man was offered lists of numbers that he would immediately add correctly without the aid of pencil and paper. He could also take the seventeenth root of a number that had seventy or eighty digits. In addition, a woman read him a poem of some dozen lines; when she finished, he would tell her how many letters were in the poem—and presumably was correct.*

The film segment that showed a blindfolded man driving an automobile appeared to me to be an exercise in "muscle reading." I was told that the driver was Bronislav Drozhzhin, a stage entertainer. It is true that he correctly followed a curved pattern of circles and twists in an open field and that he drove through a city in busy traffic. However, there was always someone in the car with him, usually in direct physical contact. Even though he may not have intended to give clues, the passenger's change in body tension could have been picked up by Drozhzhin and interpreted as a desire to change direction. Further, there was no assurance that the blindfold was eliminating all visual clues. Nevertheless, the demonstration was remarkable even though it did not seem to involve ESP.

Touring in a Zil

Not all of our time was spent in professional activity. Davidson and I attended the Bolshoi opera's production of *Sadko*. We were impressed by the wide range of Soviet society represented in the

---

* Unusual feats of memory have been studied by several Soviet psychologists including A. R. Luria (1976), whose book *Mind of a Mnemonist* provided a remarkable description of the mental procedures used by an individual exhibiting "supermemory."

audience—students, workers, professionals, etc. And one day Naumov suggested that we take an all-day excursion to Peter Tchaikovsky's home in Klin. When we expressed our enthusiasm, Naumov suggested that we rent a car large enough for five people plus a driver. Upon arriving at the rental office, we were told that we were very fortunate: the only car large enough for our purposes was a Zil limousine, the automobile formerly reserved for use by governmental officials. It had just been made available for rental by tourists.

As we drove through the streets of Moscow, it was apparent not everyone realized that we had rented the car. Police officers and soldiers snapped to attention and saluted. As the limousine drove by, they stared incredulously at shaggy-haired Richard Davidson sitting in the Zil's back seat.

Upon returning to Moscow, Naumov directed our driver to stop at the Academy of Pedagogical Sciences. There was a great flurry of excitement as our Zil stopped before the main entrance; I suspected that the professors were under the impression that an official visitor had arrived. We were received with great cordiality by Dr. Pushkin and his colleagues.

I was taken to the hall where my speech was scheduled for Monday. I observed a large picture of V. I. Lenin on one wall and I. P. Pavlov, the distinguished Russian psychologist and Nobel laureate, on the other. On reflection, I suspected that Naumov had invited a few extra "translators" along on the trip to make sure we would have to order a Zil, thus giving the impression that my visit may have been semi-official in nature.

At the end of the day, Naumov, Vilenskaya, Davidson, and I discussed what steps could be taken to strengthen international cooperation in parapsychology. Naumov proposed an international conference, the first to be held in Moscow since 1966. At the end of the evening, we had drawn up a list of possible participants. I agreed to invite the Americans on the list, while Naumov assumed responsibility for contacting the others.

Later that evening, Vladimir Raikov appeared and took us to a party that had been arranged in our honor. Several artists were present as well as some students who had been subjects in his hypnosis experiments. I presented Raikov with a copy of *Psychedelic Art,* a book by Robert Masters and Jean Houston, which contained a chapter by me describing artists I had interviewed who had been influenced by LSD experience or other altered states of consciousness.

I recalled a recent article in a United Nations publication by a Soviet medical official (Babaian, 1971). He wrote:

> Drug addiction is not a serious social and health problem in the USSR. . . . There are isolated cases of the use of narcotic substances obtained from some wild varieties of hemp. During the last decade, there was not a single case of heroin addiction in the USSR. There is practically no cocaine addiction. In the Soviet Union, not a single case has come to light of addiction to LSD, amphetamines, and other psychotropic substances. This is mainly due to the favorable social conditions which have been established in our country. [p. 2]

A Bouquet of Peonies

On Sunday evening, Davidson and I attended the Bolshoi Ballet and saw Maya Plisetskaya dance the role of Carmen. Following the performance, there was thunderous applause and the dancers were presented with bouquets of peonies.

We awakened early the next morning and observed the ever-present cadre of women with brooms sweeping the streets, preparing their city for the coming day. Adamenko and his wife, Alla Vinogradova, met us at our hotel and took us to the Academy. On the way, they discussed their practice sessions; Vinogradova was learning how to move objects without touching them.

Upon our arrival at the Academy, we were greeted by Pushkin. Also present were Yuri Kamensky and Karl Nikolaev, the Soviet Union's celebrated telepathy team. Kamensky, a biophysicist, had served as a telepathic "transmitter" in a number of experiments, while Nikolaev, an actor, had served as the "receiver." Nikolaev apologized for not seeing me earlier in my stay but explained that he had been touring the country in a new political play based on the assassination of Martin Luther King. I suggested that a copy be sent to New York City to see if a producer would be interested in presenting it to an American public. Nikolaev appeared embarrassed; he observed that the play was somewhat anti-American. I rejoined, "That should guarantee its success. Most political plays in the USA are anti-American."

I had brought with me several copies of *Psychic Discoveries Behind the Iron Curtain* by Sheila Ostrander and Lynn Schroeder. This book, published in 1970, was an account of parapsychological activity in the USSR and Eastern Europe, based on interviews with Naumov and other investigators. Naumov did not take the unflattering title very seriously, noting that, although there was an "Iron Curtain" in former years, there was now an active information exchange. I commented that if Soviet journalists were to write about psi research in the USA, they could retaliate by naming the book *Psychic Discoveries in Imperialist America.*

Davidson and I barely had time to cover the blackboard with statistics and diagrams before it was time for me to deliver my lecture. I had written out every word of it so that the interpreter could translate each sentence into Russian as I went along.

I began my talk by mentioning Dr. Joseph Wortis, my colleague at Maimonides Medical Center who had been vilified by American reactionaries in the 1950s because of his visits to the USSR and his interest in Soviet psychiatry and psychology. I then spoke of my long personal relationship with Dr. Gardner Murphy, one of the first American parapsychologists to visit the Soviet Union—a trip he made in 1960 following a summer at the University of Hawaii, where I had served as his teaching assistant. I then noted that one needed to go back to the writings of I. P. Pavlov to appreciate our work at Maimonides. I said, "Learning theorists have maintained that there are two forms of conditioning —'classical' and 'operant.' In classical conditioning, as demonstrated by the eminent psychologist Pavlov in his laboratories, a conditioned stimulus is presented along with an innate unconditioned stimulus that normally elicits a certain innate unconditioned response. After a time, the conditioned stimulus elicits the same response as the unconditioned stimulus."

I was referring here to Pavlov's work with dogs. As the dogs were presented with food and began to salivate, Pavlov would ring a bell. Eventually, the dogs would salivate upon hearing the bell, even when no food was present. I continued, "In operant or instrumental conditioning, a reinforcement is given whenever the desired conditioned response is elicited by a conditioned stimulus. In classical conditioning, the stimulus and response must have a direct or innate relationship to begin with. In operant learning, the reinforcement strengthens any immediately preceding response. Therefore, a given response can be reinforced by a variety of rewards, and a given reward can reinforce a variety of responses. Operant learning can take place either for responses mediated by the cerebrospinal nervous system or by the autonomic 'vegetative' nervous system."

I then described biofeedback of autonomic system responses as an example of operant conditioning. In our experiments at Maimonides, I observed, biofeedback involved individuals placed in a closed feedback loop where information concerning one of their bodily processes was continually made known. When people are given this information about a bodily process, they often can learn to control that function (Krippner and Davidson, 1972).

I described how we had given special attention to the training of control over the "alpha rhythm," which occurs when people are in a state of relaxed alert wakefulness with little visual imagery or cognitive activity. In experiments conducted by Davidson and supervised by Charles Honorton at our laboratory, a circuit was activated by one alpha wave that triggered a pleasant-sounding tone in the subject's room. During these biofeedback sessions, subjects were asked to guess the markings on hidden decks of ESP cards. The subjects knew that the markings could be stars, squares, crosses, circles, or wavy lines, but they had no idea of the order in which the markings would occur.

During the study, subjects attempted to block alpha waves as well as to produce alpha waves. The highest number of correct ESP guesses was made during the shift from alpha production to alpha blocking or vice versa. This finding confirmed a prediction Gardner Murphy had made in an important article that appeared in a 1966 issue of the *Journal of the American Society for Psychical Research*. Murphy hypothesized that ESP activation would be more often associated with a shift from one state of consciousness to another than with a steady state.

I then described one of our dream telepathy experiments; two subjects attempted to dream about images being transmitted by two thousand people attending a rock concert about forty-five miles from Maimonides. The concerts featured the Grateful Dead, a band with a keen interest in both ESP and altered states of consciousness.

I held up several Grateful Dead albums as I described the rock group (and left them with my hosts when my presentation was completed). I spoke of the "target pictures" and how they were projected on a movie screen at 11:30 P.M. during each of the six concerts. The audience was given the name of one of the subjects —but not of the other. It was the former subject whose dreams showed a statistically significant relationship with the target pictures. On February 19, 1971, a slide of a painting by Scralian, "The Seven Spiral Chakras," was randomly selected as the target picture and was projected on the movie screen at 11:30 P.M. The painting shows a man deep in meditation; all of his "chakras," or energy centers, are vividly illuminated. The subject dreamed:

> I was very interested in . . . using natural energy. . . . I was talking to this guy who said he'd invented a way of using solar energy and he showed me this box . . . to catch the light from the sun which was all we needed to generate and store the energy. . . . I was discussing with this other guy a number of other areas. . . . He was suspended in midair. . . . I was thinking about rocket ships . . . an energy box and . . . a spinal column. [Ullman, Krippner, and Vaughan, 1974, p. 175]

Knowing that there were space scientists and future cosmonauts in the audience, I summarized an ESP experiment carried out during the Apollo 14 moon flight by Edgar Mitchell, the sixth American astronaut to walk on the moon. Knowing that A. S. Presman and other specialists on the body's electromagnetic fields were present, I concluded with the statement that perhaps the most important advances in this area will be made by those neurophysiologists and biophysicists who are studying the electromagnetic fields of living organisms and those scientists who are attempting to interpret electromagnetic and quantum phenomena. Therefore, it is necessary for those of us who perform experiments in this area to maintain contacts, exchange information, and work together for the benefit of all peoples everywhere.

There was a volley of warm applause. My lecture had lasted for two hours. Not one of the approximately three hundred people in the audience had left—and the program was still not over. Raikov came to the stage and held up the copy of *Psychedelic Art* I had given him. He said it was important to point out that I was known not only for my efforts in parapsychology, but also for my explorations in hypnosis and other areas of "human possibilities"—a term that was frequently used to denote research into altered states of consciousness, creativity, and a wide variety of human potentials.

A journalist by the name of Viktor Popovkin then took the floor. He praised my lecture, saying that it put the lie to those individuals who claimed that parapsychology was unscientific. As he began to attack one of the critics by name, Naumov stopped him by waving his hands and exclaiming, *"Nyet, nyet, nyet.* We have gathered today in the spirit of cooperation and should not allow negative thoughts to interrupt the display of good will."

Without a break, the audience sat through a documentary film on psi research from West Germany and a Soviet film portraying Alla Vinogradova's attempts at psychokinesis. Victor Adamenko then gave a lecture on skin electricity, acupuncture, and PK.

As the program ended, a woman came to the stage with a large bouquet of peonies; as she gave them to me, she noted how I had come to the USSR in the spirit of friendship. Naumov, usually reserved and dignified, gave me a bear hug and declared the day "a victory for parapsychology." Pushkin called my address "a historic event which marks the end of an era in which parapsychology was isolated from the mainstream of science."

Larissa Vilenskaya accompanied us to the airport, where we caught our flight to Leningrad. We spent two days sightseeing and were paid a visit by Nina Kulagina's husband. He informed us that his wife was at a rest home, recovering from a heart attack. Well known for her attempts to move objects at a distance through PK, Kulagina had been observed by several of my colleagues on their forays to the USSR.

On our return to Moscow from Leningrad we were met at the airport by Vilenskaya, who told us that my address at the Academy had received unanimously positive reactions. She also presented me with a gift—a copy of *The Man with a Shattered World,* by A. R. Luria. Dr. Luria was the Soviet Union's most prominent psychologist and a pioneer in the rehabilitation of individuals who had suffered brain injuries as a result of strokes, accidents, or war injuries. His book was the story of one such patient and how he was rehabilitated. The gift became a cherished souvenir of an exciting and productive trip, and a reminder of the work I had to do for the 1972 conference.

Cultivation of the Hidden

Upon my return to the United States, I researched the development of Soviet psychology, discovering that a physiology laboratory had been established in the Russian Academy of Sciences in 1864. In 1925, this laboratory, then directed by I. P. Pavlov, was transformed into the Institute of Physiology of the USSR Academy of Sciences. In 1943, the first psychologist was admitted to the Academy of Sciences and, in 1945, a Sector of Psychology was established within the framework of the Academy's Institute of Philosophy. In 1952, there was a heated debate between J. F. Dorofeev and A. J. Shinkarenko over the meaning of the term "consciousness" in the texts of Marx and Lenin. After Stalin's death, less emphasis was placed on the Marxist interpretation of psychology, and more articles began to appear reflecting a diversity of interests (Brozek, 1970; Brozek and Mecacci, 1974; Wortis, 1962). By 1968, psychology was finally recognized as an independent scientific discipline in which higher degrees could be granted.

The problems of education and child development were assigned to the Academy of Pedagogical Sciences, where I had given my lecture on parapsychology. At the end of 1971, an Institute of Psychology was organized within the USSR Academy of Sciences —a major event because one of its stated functions was to intensify research on the neurological basis of mental processes. B. F. Lomov was named director of the Institute; I had met him at the 1971 International Congress of Applied Psychology in Liège, Belgium, and knew of his reputation as an expert in the field of engineering psychology.

Another Soviet psychologist who had attained prominence was A. N. Leontiev. I was intrigued by his papers on the "new consciousness" of the Soviet citizen that was being formulated by an improvement in living conditions. Leontiev had won the Lenin Prize and was regarded as the leading ideologist of Soviet psychology.

Leontiev, Lomov, and Luria were the three most prominent psychologists in the USSR when I began to write letters of invitation for Naumov's proposed 1972 meeting. I addressed a special letter to Luria, telling him of my interest in his work on rehabilitation and asking him if I could make contact with him or his associates during my forthcoming trip to Moscow. Similar letters were addressed to other Soviet psychologists by Carmi Harari, an officer of the Association for Humanistic Psychology; several members of the Association had decided to attend Naumov's meeting on their way to the Twentieth International Congress of Psychology in Tokyo. I decided to travel with this group to both meetings and the arrangements were put in the hands of an American travel agent.

In the meantime, several of my assistants at Maimonides had built Kirlian photography devices and began to take intriguing pictures. James Hickman, Ronny Mastrion, and Daniel Rubin constructed three different types of devices and were sharing their results with Thelma Moss and William Tiller, the two most prominent West Coast investigators of the Kirlian effect. We all decided that the time was ripe for a public meeting regarding these developments, and on May 25, 1972, we convened the first Western Hemisphere Conference on Kirlian Photography, Acupuncture, and the Human Aura. Moss, Tiller, Hickman, Mastrion, Rubin, and others presented their work. A paper from Victor Adamenko was translated and read. I chaired the conference and opened it by reading a congratulatory letter from Semyon Kirlian:

> On the opening of the first conference on the Kirlian effect, I personally greet you, all the conferees, and everyone in attendance. . . . From the conference, I hope there will develop significant creative solutions for the blessing of mankind and the affairs of the world. In conclusion, I ask you to please keep in mind the contributions of Valentina Khrisanova Kirlian, who devoted all of her conscious energies to the search for the new and the cultivation of the hidden.

Daniel Rubin and I edited the papers from the conference, naming our book *The Kirlian Aura* and dedicating it to Valentina Kirlian, who had died in 1971.

In the meantime, the letters written by Harari and me to the Soviet psychologists went unanswered. When our group left for Moscow in July 1972, we had no idea if there would even be a meeting. The itinerary prepared for us by the travel agency included Iran, India, Nepal, Thailand, Hong Kong, and Japan, where we would all participate in the Twentieth International Psychology Congress. My paper on the Maimonides experiments had been accepted, as was Adamenko's paper on Vinogradova's ability to move distant objects. It would be the first time that presentations on psi research had been scheduled for an International Congress of Psychology. Richard Davidson, now a graduate student at Harvard University, preceded us; with him was Robert Harris, my stepson, who planned to take photographs of the Moscow conference.

When our group arrived in Moscow, Naumov appeared worried. He remarked that he had received neither approval nor disapproval for the meeting, so he and Vilenskaya had decided to proceed as if it would actually take place. Naumov also revealed that a group of government officials and psychologists had examined the book, *Psychic Discoveries Behind the Iron Curtain,* labeling it "anti-Soviet." There was only one dissenting opinion, according to Naumov; V. P. Zinchenko, a prominent psychologist, did not think it was worthwhile to make an issue out of the volume.

Naumov stated that he had been interviewed concerning his role in the preparation of the book. Naumov claimed that some of the information he gave the two journalists had been passed on in confidence because he was unsure as to its accuracy. One example concerned an unfounded rumor that the U. S. Navy had sponsored telepathy tests from an atomic submarine, the *Nautilus,* to psychic sensitives on land. Ostrander and Schroeder (1970) quote Naumov as saying:

> "If your Navy didn't do the *Nautilus* experiment, then Soviet scientists were the first in the world to test ESP from a subma-

rine! . . . We didn't use human subjects. We used a mother rabbit and her newborn litter. . . .

"Scientists placed the baby rabbits aboard the submarine. They kept the mother rabbit in a laboratory on shore where they implanted electrodes deep in her brain. When the sub was deep below the surface of the ocean, assistants killed the young rabbits one by one.

". . . at each synchronized instant of death, her brain *reacted.*" [p. 32]

Not only was the story about the *Nautilus* highly suspect, but also the rabbit's reactions were gross distortions of an experiment which had been conducted on land in Novosibirsk.* Some of the mother rabbit's reactions did synchronize with the stressing (not killing) of the infants, but they hardly produced the dramatic results reported in the book.

Naumov asked me not to discuss his troubles with the other participants, as he did not want to cast a shadow on their visit to Moscow. Besides, there was some good news: We had all been invited to visit the Gannushkin Institute for Schizophrenics by Yuri Nikolayev. We made the trip the following day, heard about the patients' fasting regimen, and had an opportunity to interview several individuals who were recovering from schizophrenia following several years of torment.

An "Unofficial Gathering"

On July 18 we assembled at the May Day Club for "The International Meeting on the Problem of Bioenergetics and Related Areas." It was described as an "unofficial gathering," so as not to violate any regulations.

The schedule was packed. Naumov traced the history of Soviet parapsychology, going back to V. M. Bekhterev, who is remembered for his attempts to make objective studies of individuals by recording their gestures, facial expressions, and vocalizations,

* This account of the submarine experiment was given to James Hickman by the Soviet investigator V. P. Kaznacheev during Hickman's visit to Novosibirsk in 1979.

which he then related to the stimuli that preceded them. Bekhterev took a mechanistic view of personality, positing that mental and physiological phenomena represent a single neural process. In his book *General Principles of Human Reflexology,* Bekhterev suggested that the complex behavior of humans consisted of the compounding of these associated motor reflexes, and that thought processes depended on the inner activities of the musculature of speech. Bekhterev also conducted several ESP tests with dogs, reportedly obtaining favorable results.

During the 1920s, Bekhterev's theory of reflexology was as influential in the USSR as was the work of Pavlov. After Bekhterev's death in 1927, however, the influence of his work declined. The Second All-Union Conference of Marxist-Leninist Research Institutes concluded that reflexology was a revisionist trend that deviated from the Marxist-Leninist position. However, Bekhterev had come back into favor in recent years and his parapsychological interests were well known. In addition, he had encouraged the parapsychological work of L. L. Vasiliev (1965) and B. B. Kazhinsky (1962). Kazhinsky's interest in psi was stimulated by an incident occurring one night in 1919 when he claimed to have been awakened by the sound of a spoon stirring up against a glass. There was no accounting for it until he learned that a close friend had died that night of typhoid just as his mother had stirred up his medicine with a spoon.

Films were then presented that appeared to show Nina Kulagina and Alla Vinogradova moving small objects across a table without touching them. Adamenko discussed his work with Vinogradova, and also presented a stunning color film of the Kirlian effect in which moment-by-moment changes in the flare patterns surrounding a leaf could be observed.

The next speaker was Victor Inyushin, a biophysicist from Kazakh State University in Alma-Ata. He discussed his concept of "biological plasma" or "bioplasma," a "fifth state of matter," along with solids, liquids, gases, and plasmas. Inyushin presented data from acupuncture, bioluminescence, and Kirlian photography to support his claim that "bioplasmic emission" from living objects could explain many psi phenomena.

Several Americans spoke on the topic of unconventional healing, an area of great interest to the Soviet participants. At the end of the day, the managers of the May Day Club informed us that we could not hold any more meetings in their auditorium; the police had arrived to investigate the proceedings, and the managers were hesitant to take further risks. As a result, we decided to hold the next day's meetings in a hotel suite.

We then assembled at the Sports Cinema for an evening of films, most of which I had seen in 1971. There were two additions —one presenting time-lapse photography of such plants as the Venus flytrap, and the other a film portraying the use of dowsing for land mines by Czech soldiers in a mock battlefield and by American soldiers in Vietnam. The military men in the film were shown holding dowsing rods at arm's length; the rods would sometimes turn downward sharply, and a close examination of the ground area would often result in the location of a land mine.

On Wednesday morning, we gathered at the Ukraine Hotel. There were some sixty participants from ten countries, and the room was packed. Our Intourist guide was with us, and complained that we had ignored the sightseeing agenda that had been arranged for us. I surmised that our travel agent had neglected to tell Intourist that we had our own agenda for Moscow, an oversight that was to have unfortunate consequences.

Papers were presented on a variety of topics. G. S. Vassilchenko described his use of acupuncture with people suffering from sexual dysfunction. He also noted that laser beams were more effective than needles in stimulating the appropriate acupuncture points. O. W. Markley of the Stanford Research Institute described clairvoyance experiments with Ingo Swann (1975), an artist and psychic sensitive who specialized in "remote viewing"— reportedly identifying distant geographical sites that were randomly selected just as the experiments began. Parapsychologists from Austria, Switzerland, and West Germany presented conflicting reports on their visits to the Philippines where they saw psychic healers appear to extract material from the bodies of sick people. Some of the observers dismissed the effect as sleight of hand, while others thought that parapsychological phenomena were at work, in at least some cases.

James Hickman, one of my assistants, presented a film he had produced at New Mexico State University. It consisted of several hundred colorful Kirlian photographs accompanied by a sound track of such songs as "Casey Jones" by the Grateful Dead, and "Back in the U.S.S.R." by the Beatles. The final frame of Hickman's film portrayed a dove—and the word "peace" in both Russian and English. The film was enthusiastically received; one of the Soviet participants called it "the best combination of art, science, music, and politics I have ever seen on film."

A Soviet psychiatrist, Ilmar Soomere, reported on several hundred cases of spontaneous ESP phenomena he had collected over an eight-year period. Soomere noted that more instances of ESP took place in dreams than in the waking state. When the dream was precognitive and concerned someone's death, the dreamer was more likely to awaken immediately than if it concerned another type of event, in which case the dream was often recalled in the morning. Soomere also found an association between spontaneous cases of ESP and the lunar cycle, with significantly fewer instances of clairvoyance, telepathy, and precognition occurring on nights of the full moon. Soomere also noted sex differences: About 60 percent of his cases were reported by men, and approximately 40 percent by women. The peak ages for both sexes were between the ages of twenty-one and twenty-five.

Carmi Harari led the group in an "encounter session"—apparently the first of its kind held in the USSR. Following the exercises in awareness, spontaneity, and expression of personal feelings, one Soviet psychiatrist told Harari, "I learned more about myself today than in all my years of psychiatric training." The ever-present Intourist guide was the only person who did not participate in the "encounter session"; observers saw her open her purse and turn on a small tape recorder.

Before the session ended, Hickman, Adamenko, and I left for a meeting with Licensintorg, the Soviet patent bureau, where we discussed the possibility of obtaining the Soviet data on Kirlian photography. The data, which covered a thirty-year span, could be ours, they informed us, for a few thousand dollars. (Upon arriving back in the United States, I found no business or agency willing to invest that amount of money for the purpose.)

I rejoined the group at the Ukraine Hotel that evening for a party hosted by the Association for Humanistic Psychology. Some eighty people arrived, drank toasts, sang Russian folk songs, and enjoyed each other's company.

The Moving Tubes

July 21 was our last full day in Moscow. I had been invited to the offices of *Technology for Youth,* a popular science magazine with a circulation of five million. Just as I was about to leave, I was told that the Intourist officials wanted to see me. I sent another psychologist to take my place and proceeded to the magazine office.

Hickman showed the staff of *Technology for Youth* his film and gave them several Kirlian photographs. One of the Soviet technicians inspected Hickman's color photograph of a leaf and called it "the best example of Kirlian photography I have seen outside the Soviet Union." The leaf was featured in a subsequent issue of the magazine; we could not bring ourselves to tell them that the Kirlian photograph depicted a marijuana leaf—with a corona that turned out to be a patriotic red, white, and blue.

Adamenko then showed the editorial staff his film of Alla Vinogradova, after which he introduced her to the group. Vinogradova sat on a chair near a Plexiglas table. Adamenko placed a Havana cigar tube on the surface of the table. Vinogradova rubbed her hands briskly, then put her right hand to the side of the tube. It began to move across the table without any physical contact with Vinogradova's hand. When it reached the table's far side, she shifted her hand to that side and the tube moved back.

Adamenko then removed the cigar tube and substituted a heavier tube made from aluminum. She picked it up and rubbed it for a few seconds—suggesting to me that she was simply producing an electrostatic charge that would cause her hand to repel the tube. As expected, the object moved across the table.

The next object placed before Vinogradova was a Ping-Pong ball. In this instance, Vinogradova moved her hand in a circular motion a few inches above the object; the ball obediently followed her hand. Next, Adamenko placed a Marlboro cigarette on the table. Vinogradova could not move it, even after rubbing it lightly. She asked for another one, and an onlooker opened his pack of Philip Morris cigarettes. It moved easily and she commented that it was more "tightly packed" than the Marlboro.

Vinogradova moved a film cylinder, which rolled fairly well across the table, despite its uneven surface. She then placed it on its end and "pushed" it about an inch. Adamenko commented that it requires about ten times as much effort to "push" an object without touching it as it does to "roll" it.

Adamenko placed a lightweight steel tube on the table. After Vinogradova had propelled it back and forth, Adamenko placed a small light bulb on the tube. The bulb lit for an instant, again suggesting that an electrostatic effect was involved, rather than PK.

Two tubes were then placed on the table. Vinogradova placed her hand above both of them. Adamenko pointed to one of the tubes and, with only a slight hand movement, Vinogradova was able to move the specified tube while the other one remained still. This control of the apparent electrostatic effect was quite impressive. Furthermore, Vinogradova was able to terminate movement in one tube and initiate it in another tube whenever someone requested a shift.

Vinogradova announced that it might be possible for someone else to move the tube. I leaped from my chair, sat down at the table, and—using the identical hand motions I had observed during the demonstration—rolled the tube across the table without touching it. After about thirty seconds, the tube slowed down and then stopped. Vinogradova rubbed her hands and initiated movement in the tube again. Two other observers then took turns rolling it without touching it.

I told Adamenko that if one rubs a smooth table surface with a cloth, static electricity is generated. If a cylinder is placed on the table, the object will be repelled by a person's hand.* Adamenko replied that it is true that objects will move on a surface that has been electrostatically charged by means of friction. But for heavy

* Upon returning to the United States, Hickman and I rubbed the top of a Plexiglas table with a cotton cloth. A tube was then placed on the table; the tube was easily moved when one's hands passed near it.

objects to be moved, or for objects to be moved selectively, a special distribution of the surface electrical field has to be created. This effect, Adamenko continued, may involve PK. In any event, selective movement indicates that a subject is ready to attempt PK, moving objects in ways that cannot be explained by electrostatic effects. For example, a small flame placed on the table could prevent the accumulation of an electrostatic effect. So could proper grounding of the subject, or the use of objects and table surfaces that are resistant to an electrostatic buildup.

Adamenko also told me that he could not attend the Tokyo conference, where he was to read the paper describing his work with Vinogradova. He gave me a copy of his paper as well as the film so that I could make the presentation for him. The paper was titled, "Objects Moved at a Distance by Means of a Controlled Bioelectric Field." Nowhere in the manuscript was there any claim that the effects were due to PK.

The Tokyo Congress

An Intourist representative roused us at 4:00 A.M. the next morning, an hour or so earlier than our schedule had indicated. On the way to the airport, the psychologist who had visited Intourist on my behalf told me that they had indicated their "extreme displeasure" with the conduct of our group.

And why not? Intourist had arranged a series of sightseeing excursions for us and were offended when we announced that we had made our own plans for the week. Our travel agency had not informed Intourist of our conference—a meeting that involved renting a Soviet clubhouse, bringing eighty people to a hotel suite, discussing a number of exotic topics with Soviet citizens—even exposing them to an "encounter session." A few years later, Melov Sturva (1978), a Soviet journalist, observed "encounter sessions" at Esalen Institute in California, describing them as "99 percent brazen charlatanism and 1 percent pseudoscience."

Upon our arrival at the airport, several armed guards, police officers, and Intourist officials escorted us to a special area. All of our suitcases were opened. Personal letters were confiscated. All

of my notes were taken, as well as reprints given to me by
Adamenko, Inyushin, and Naumov. As they inspected my suitcase, I handed them Adamenko's film, saying it was documentary
material for the Tokyo Congress. Perhaps they thought I had
brought it from the United States, because they handed it back
and dug into my suitcase in a search for less obvious items.

Harari and I were taken into private rooms and given special
attention. My coat, belt, and shoes were removed. I was frisked as
if I were suspected of carrying a weapon. As Harari and I finally
boarded the plane I mused, "Last year I left Moscow with a bouquet of peonies and a hero's farewell. Today I leave bereft of my
scientific notes, having been treated like a felon. It helps one to
retain one's modesty knowing that you can be applauded today
and disgraced tomorrow."

Upon registering for the International Congress of Psychology
in Tokyo, the secretaries were amazed that I had been asked to
read a Soviet paper. It was the first time in memory that an American scientist had read a paper from the USSR at an international
conference. Nevertheless, Adamenko's contribution was well received by the participants, as was my own presentation on ten
years of ESP research at the Maimonides Dream Laboratory.

Our next stop was Honolulu and the annual convention of the
American Psychological Association. Gardner Murphy received
the APA gold-medal award for his contributions to psychology;
his work in parapsychology was included in the citation. At lunch
we reminisced about our summer together at the University of
Hawaii thirteen years earlier—and how my last task as his assistant had been to buy him an English-Russian dictionary before he
left for the USSR.

Fiction or Reality?

When Harari and I arrived back in New York City, we sent cordial letters to Intourist thanking them for their help during our
visit to Moscow and apologizing for our travel agency's ineptitude
in neglecting to inform them of our scheduled meetings. The letters were never answered; about that time, there was a shakeup in

Intourist that resulted in an almost total change of administrative officials.

However, I did receive a letter from the Institute for Soviet-American Relations. It was dated April 1972, but did not reach me until August. It said that the facilities of the House of Friendship were booked during July. Enclosed was a letter from A. R. Luria also dated April 1972, unaccountably handwritten in English.

Luria noted that he had received letters from Harari and myself concerning the organization of a series of informal meetings on parapsychology in Moscow. Luria stated that "the Psychological Society of the USSR cannot support this project" because "parapsychology is not a branch of scientific psychology." Luria mentioned Naumov, stating that he was "unknown" to the Psychological Society and in no case was a psychologist.

If we had received these letters earlier, we never would have jeopardized Naumov's safety by pushing ahead with the meetings. Indeed, we began to wonder if we had been used as ploys by Naumov's enemies and became critically concerned about his safety.

We heard very little from Naumov during the following year. And then, in 1973, my Soviet colleagues sent me a photocopy of the first article on parapsychology to be published in *Questions of Philosophy,* the official publication of the prestigious USSR Academy of Sciences. The article was signed by V. P. Zinchenko, A. N. Leontiev, B. F. Lomov, and A. R. Luria; it was titled "Parapsychology: Fiction or Reality?"

The article was astonishing. After pointing out the poor work done by certain investigators and the fraud that exists among many "psychic sensitives," the authors concluded almost casually:

Obviously, some so-called parapsychological phenomena actually do happen. . . . Certainly the time has come to bring order into the scientific research and study of the phenomena described in parapsychology. Much of the research in the field of parapsychology is being done by physicists and engineers. Therefore, it would be expedient to assess, at the Institute for Biophysics in the U.S.S.R. Academy of Sciences . . . the direction . . . of the "biophysical effect" [dowsing]. The electromagnetic fields generated by living organisms could be likewise assessed as a possible means of "biological communication" [telepathy]. . . . If attention is paid to these phenomena from the point of biophysics and information theory, these efforts will help to demystify them.

The psychological institutes of the U.S.S.R. Academy of Sciences and of the U.S.S.R. Academy of Pedagogical Sciences . . . should also give consideration to the possibility of mounting programs for strictly scientific research into these phenomena. Evidently it would be advisable to organize a laboratory within one of the psychological institutions which would study persons who really do possess unusual abilities. [pp. 135–36]

Three of the four people who signed this report were the leading psychologists in the Soviet Union. With this article, the USSR became the first country in the world whose psychological "establishment" endorsed the study of ESP and PK. As some of us told the American Psychological Association's newsletter, the *APA Monitor,* when they asked for our comments:

Imagine B. F. Skinner, Harry Harlow, and Albert Bandura [the APA president] publishing an official APA policy statement on parapsychology in *Science,* urging the nation's best research centers to study ESP. The equivalent has just taken place in the Soviet Union. [Asher, 1974, p. 1]

The *APA Monitor* gave front-page space to this event, one of the most important developments to date in parapsychological research.

There were other points of interest in the Soviet article. It was noted that the first parapsychological paper to be accepted for delivery at an International Congress of Parapsychology occurred in 1972 when "a report by the American parapsychologist, S. Krippner, was presented." A claim was also made that "the American federal government spends between one-half and one million dollars a year on parapsychological research." One researcher friend of mine exclaimed, "If that's true, no parapsychologist that I know has ever seen it!"

There were also oblique references to Naumov that indicated to me that his fate was sealed. *Psychic Discoveries Behind the Iron Curtain* was denounced as a "low-level work" used to advertise "anti-Sovietism." It also noted:

There also exists a category of rather clever persons who often have no serious background of any kind. These are the very people who assume the role of propagandists and impresarios for those who actually possess unusual abilities. . . . Some of these "experts" declare themselves to be leaders of groups . . . which have never existed in our country. The "Institute of Technical Parapsychology" is an example of such an organization. It is necessary to put an end to the activity of poorly qualified but militant parapsychological "experts" who take upon themselves the role of . . . propagandists and who issue numerous reports and give lectures on parapsychology for audiences which even include scientists. These lectures offer an unscrupulous mishmash of fantasy and fact. [p. 132]

Shortly after the publication of this article, I received word of Naumov's arrest. I was also given three agencies in Moscow to which letters of protest were to be directed. Many of us wrote the letters. But parapsychologists, needless to say, have very little political clout as a scientific group. On March 29, 1974, the New York *Daily News* announced:

A Soviet specialist in telepathy and clairvoyance has been sentenced to two years at hard labor for refusing to break his contacts with his Western colleagues, dissident sources claimed today. The informants said . . . Edward K. Naumov was convicted following a fifteen-day trial in a Moscow court.
The sources said Naumov was charged with misusing funds of a club that invited him to lecture on parapsychology. . . . According to the informants, the charge was fabricated after Naumov ignored secret-police demands that he stop meeting with foreign specialists visiting Moscow.

The story was published in American newspapers under the heading, "Hard Labor for Mentalist," revealing the misunderstanding among many journalists of psychical research. A "mentalist," of course, is a stage performer—a role that Naumov never assumed.

My interpretation of Naumov's demise was that the Soviet scientific "establishment" had finally decided to give parapsychology the stamp of approval, albeit a cautious one. Apparently, parapsychology was not to be considered an independent discipline; its phenomena would be assigned to different scientific institutes for investigation. We all suspected that his

"Department of Technical Parapsychology" (not "Institute," as claimed by the four psychologists) had conducted little scientific research. However, he was just about the only person we could contact if we wanted information on psychoenergetics in the USSR.

Also, Naumov may have been considered too friendly to foreigners by the secret police. Unlike the Soviet dissidents, Naumov never criticized the Soviet system or veered from Marxist doctrine. However, in July 1974, at the very time Nixon was again meeting with Brezhnev in Moscow, I received an account of Naumov's trial from Lev Regelson, a Soviet physicist living in Moscow. (Later that same year, this letter was published in the *Journal of the Society for Psychical Research*.) Regarding the charge that Naumov had misused the funds a club paid him for his lectures, the physicist wrote:

> One cannot take seriously the procurator's claim that Naumov's receiving payment for a lecture . . . constitutes complicity in "financial gain." . . .
>
> What is Naumov really guilty of? . . .
>
> Here is what he had dared to do: for many years he has maintained free, personal, human contacts with many foreign scholars, contacts which were not sanctioned from above; he carried on an extensive correspondence with them and made use of the material he received for disseminating information on parapsychology in the U.S.S.R.
>
> On his personal initiative he organized international meetings and scientific symposia, became a member of international societies, presented himself as the representative of Soviet parapsychology at a time when this science was not officially recognized in the U.S.S.R. He created an undesirable precedent, made of himself a "dangerous" example, by taking seriously all this talk about peaceful coexistence and international scientific cooperation. In his wake other Soviet parapsychologists began to do similar things. . . . Although all these actions could not be brought to trial according to law, at the same time they could not be permitted to go unpunished. And so they were. Naumov has been sent to prison, the other parapsychologists so far only relieved of their jobs. [pp. 522–23]

The letter ended by noting that Naumov had been beaten and that, after sentencing, he was subjected to a "senseless and cruel three-hour interrogation" despite the fact that he was ill with pneumonia.

Naumov, through his efforts, had brought the emerging Soviet interest in psychoenergetics to the attention of the world. He had also played a role in forcing the ruling scientists to take a position on the subject, a position that was more positive than that taken by official scientific bodies in any other major country.

In June 1975, I received word that Naumov had been released from prison and told that he must abandon independent parapsychological research; any future work could be done only in official laboratories. However, he had been vindicated, in a sense, because a higher court had declared him completely innocent of the fraud charges. Naumov's early release must have been welcome, but he must also have felt disappointment at having the gates of autonomous ESP and PK experimentation closed to him. Possibly in the future, Naumov's efforts will be appreciated. In the meantime, perhaps, official research in Soviet parapsychology will proceed with the funding and recognition it deserves. The article in *Questions of Philosophy* is a visionary document. It remains to be seen if that vision will be incarnated.

References

Adamenko, V. G. Objects moved at a distance by means of a controlled bioelectric field. In *Abstracts, Twentieth International Congress of Psychology.* Tokyo: International Congress of Psychology, 1972.

Asher, J. Soviet psychologists reverse stand, urge new action on psychic research. *APA Monitor,* Apr. 1974.

Babaian, E. A. The Soviet perspective. *UN Bulletin on Narcotics,* 1971, *23,* 1–2.

Bekhterev, V. M. *General Principles of Human Reflexology.* New York: Arno Press, 1973. (Originally published in 1917.)

————. "Direct influence" of a person upon behavior of animals. *Journal of Parapsychology,* 1949, *13,* 166–76. (Originally published in 1920.)

Brozek, J. Soviet psychology's coming of age. *American Psychologist,* 1970, *25,* 1057–58.

Brozek, J., and Mecacci, L. New Soviet Research Institute of Psychology: A milestone in the development of psychology in the USSR. *American Psychologist,* 1974, *29,* 475–78.

Duplessis, Y. [Dermal-optical sensitivity and a possible extension.] *Proceedings, Third International Congress on Psychotronic Research.* Tokyo: International Association for Psychotronic Research, 1977.

Honorton, C.; Davidson, R.; and Bindler, P. Feedback-augmented EEG alpha, shifts in subjective state, and ESP card-guessing performance. *Journal of the American Society for Psychical Research,* 1971, *65,* 308–23.

Kazhinsky, B. B. [*Biological Radio Communication.*] Kiev: Academy of Science of the Ukrainian Soviet Socialist Republic, 1962.

Krippner, S. Book review. *Journal of the American Society for Psychical Research,* 1966, *60,* 290–94.

————. Experimentally induced paranormal effects in dreams and other altered conscious states. In *Abstracts, Twentieth International Congress of Psychology.* Tokyo: International Congress of Psychology, 1972.

————. *Song of the Siren.* New York: Harper/Colophon, 1975.

Krippner, S., and Davidson, R. The use of convergent operations in bio-information research. *Journal for the Study of Consciousness,* 1972, *5,* 64–76.

Krippner, S.; Davidson, R.; and Peterson, N. Psi phenomena in Moscow. *Journal of Contemporary Psychotherapy,* 1973, *6,* 79–88.

Krippner, S., and Rubin, D. (eds.). *The Kirlian Aura.* Garden City, N.Y.: Anchor Books, 1974.

Lenin, V. I. *Collected Works.* Vol. 14. Moscow: Progress Publishers, 1968. (Originally published in 1928.)

Leontiev, A. N. On the biological and social aspects of human development: The training of auditory ability. In M. Cole & I. Maltzman (eds.), *A Handbook of Contemporary Soviet Psychology.* New York: Basic Books, 1969.

Lomov, B. F. Present status and future development of psychology in the USSR in the light of decisions of the 24th Congress of the Communist Party of the Soviet Union. *Soviet Psychology,* 1972, *10,* 329–58.

Luria, A. R. *Mind of a Mnemonist.* Chicago: Contemporary Books, 1976.

————. *The Man with a Shattered World.* New York: Basic Books, 1972.

Masters, R. E. L., and Houston, J. *Psychedelic Art.* New York: Grove Press, 1968.

Mitchell, E. D. An ESP test from Apollo 14. *Journal of Parapsychology,* 1971, *35,* 89–107.

Murphy, G. Research in creativeness: What can it tell us about extrasensory perception? *Journal of the American Society for Psychical Research,* 1966, *60,* 8–22.

Naumov, E. K., and Vilenskaya, L. V. *Bibliographies on Parapsychology (Psychoenergetics) and Related Subjects.* Springfield, Va.: National Technical Information Service, 1972. (Originally privately published in Moscow, 1971.)

Ostrander, S., and Schroeder, L. *Psychic Discoveries Behind the Iron Curtain.* Englewood Cliffs, N.J.: Prentice-Hall, 1970.

Pavlov, I. P. *Lectures on Conditioned Reflexes.* New York: International Publishers, 1941. (Originally published in 1928.)

Regelson, L. An appeal to Soviet and foreign public opinion. *Journal of the Society for Psychical Research,* 1974, *47,* 521–24.

Skurlatov, A. P. [Can you do anything? Preview of the film *Seven Steps Beyond the Horizon.*] *Technika Moledezi,* May 1969.

Sturva, M. [The quest for identity: The American romance with pseudopsychiatry. *Literary Gazette,*] Jan. 25, 1978.

Swann, I. *To Kiss Earth Goodbye.* New York: Hawthorn, 1975.

Ullman, M.; Krippner, S.; and Vaughan, A. *Dream Telepathy.* Baltimore: Penguin, 1974.

Vasiliev, L. L. *Mysterious Phenomena of the Human Psyche.* New Hyde Park, N.Y.: University Books, 1965. (Originally published in 1959.)

Wortis, J. A. A "thaw" in Soviet psychiatry? *American Journal of Psychiatry,* 1962, *119,* 587.

Zinchenko, V. P.; Leontiev, A. N.; Lomov, B. F.; and Luria, A. R. [Parapsychology: Fiction or reality? *Questions of Philosophy,*] 1973, *27,* 128–36. Translation available in S. Krippner (ed.), *Psychoenergetic Systems.* New York: Gordon & Breach, 1979.

CHAPTER 2

Psychokinesis in Leningrad

> . . . We can interpret the brain's transformation of
> psychic into physicochemical energy as "miniature"
> PK over the neurons proper; the neurons, in turn, set
> muscles into motion. . . . This transformation can
> be assumed to be one of the basic phenomena of life.
>
> Victor Adamenko (1979)

A colleague of mine arrived for the 1972 Moscow meetings with a copy of *World* magazine in his hand. It contained a book review of Arthur Koestler's *The Roots of Coincidence,* written by Martin Gardner, one of parapsychology's most vitriolic critics. In his book, Koestler had spoken highly of our work at Maimonides. However, Gardner (1972) observed:

> Perhaps the most respected of recent work is that being done by Stanley Krippner and Montague Ullman in the Dream Laboratory at the Maimonides Medical Center in Manhattan (see their book, *Dream Studies and Telepathy,* 1970). . . .
>
> How trustworthy is Krippner? To answer indirectly, let us now turn to "Parapsychology in the U.S.S.R.," a magazine article by Krippner and his assistant. On the first page is a photograph of Ninel Kulagina, identified as a "noted Russian sensitive," causing a "plastic sphere" to float in the air. . . .
>
> Krippner well knows that Mrs. Kulagina is a pretty, plump, dark-eyed little charlatan who took the stage name of Ninel because it is Lenin spelled backward. She is no more a sensitive than Kreskin, and like that amiable American television humbug, she is pure show biz. [p. 68]

Gardner's attack was one of the most absurd I had seen, and one unworthy of the intelligence he had displayed in his "Mathematical Games" columns in *Scientific American*. Apparently Gardner was familiar with the monograph Ullman and I had written in 1970, but had found nothing in it to criticize, so moved on to an easier target—an article in *Saturday Review* that Richard Davidson and I had written upon our return from the Soviet Union. By incorrectly placing the Maimonides Dream Laboratory in Manhattan rather than Brooklyn, Gardner revealed that he had not done his homework very well.*

Gardner's reference to the photograph of Kulagina omitted the key words "seemingly" and "supposedly," which I had inserted as a cautionary measure. And his notation that Kulagina had taken a stage name was preposterous because she had never appeared on stage. For Gardner to state that "Krippner well knows that Mrs. Kulagina is a . . . charlatan" was an outright lie. I knew no such thing; although I had never examined her myself, I had spoken to scientists from six nations who had worked with her and found no suggestion of trickery.

Gardner, in his book review, also cited a May 1968 dispatch from Moscow that claimed that Kulagina had been employing concealed magnets to fool "Soviet scientists and newsmen into thinking she possessed the ability to move objects by staring at them." And a month later *Pravda* had printed another attack on Kulagina, accusing her of performing "tricks," labeling her a "swindler," and calling her performance "a public fraud" (Chijov, 1968).

The *Pravda* article asked, "How could certain editorial staff use up a fairly substantial space in its newspapers with fancy tricks, with the presentation of a kind of scientific sensation, to introduce its readers widely and favorably to material that is itself nothing but fake wonder in a sieve?"

American parapsychologist J. G. Pratt was in Moscow when the article appeared. He was attending an international parapsychol-

* It is also possible that Gardner had been misled by his cohort James Randi, who for years told people that he had unmasked a case of fraudulent "skin vision" at Maimonides. We discovered that the incident had taken place at the New York State Department of Mental Hygiene in Manhattan, and eventually I received a letter of retraction from Randi (Krippner, 1977).

ogy conference arranged by Edward Naumov in the House of Friendship. In his opening remarks, Naumov spoke about the article that had appeared in *Pravda* that morning. Pratt (1973) recalled that Naumov

> . . . reacted vigorously to this article. It was clear, both from his manner and from what he said, that he regarded the appearance of the story as most unfortunate for our plans, but he was determined to go on with the meeting. The publication largely wrecked the formal plans for the program, because it discouraged some of the Russians from taking an active part and it put those who did so under considerable strain. [p. 71]

Furthermore, the effect of *Pravda*'s critical piece on Kulagina was to force the House of Friendship to withdraw permission for Naumov to show a film of Kulagina at work. The film was eventually presented at the Czechoslovakian Embassy, but a note of caution had been injected into the proceedings. In fact, the *Pravda* article was probably written to dampen the enthusiasm of the conference participants. Naumov told Pratt that some two hundred titles had been submitted by Soviet scientists for presentation at the 1968 meeting. Because of pressures exerted on him to keep the conference small, he only scheduled fifteen of the Soviet papers, as well as fifteen presentations by foreign visitors.

Nevertheless, the Kulagina film had an electrifying effect. Many scientists outside the USSR learned about Kulagina for the first time when the film was shown. The interest generated by that film led to intermittent efforts on the part of some Western parapsychologists to make firsthand observations of her. These efforts resulted in a slowly accumulating body of evidence that supported the largely unpublished claims made by Soviet and Czechoslovakian investigators.

The Growing Controversy

Over the next few years, several foreign parapsychologists visited Leningrad, observed Kulagina's attempts to demonstrate PK, and discussed the phenomena with G. A. Sergeyev (the Soviet scientist from Leningrad's A. A. Uktomskii Physiological Institute who had worked with her). These investigators included J. G. Pratt (a psychologist with the University of Virginia), Montague Ullman (a psychiatrist and my colleague at the Maimonides Medical Center), H. H. J. Keil (a psychologist with the University of Tasmania), Benson Herbert (director of the Paraphysical Laboratory in Downton, England), and Zdeněk Rejdák (the leading Czechoslovakian investigator of psi phenomena). All of these researchers have published scientific reports of their observations.

In addition, four of them authored a monograph on Kulagina published by the Society for Psychical Research. In this monograph, Keil, Herbert, Ullman, and Pratt (1976) state that "all our observations suggest that the investigations carried out by our Russian colleagues were carefully controlled, skillfully executed, and at times involved laboratory facilities of a high order of sophistication" (p. 200). It is, of course, unfortunate that this Soviet material remains largely unpublished, especially the investigations by Sergeyev, of which we only have secondhand knowledge with the exception of brief accounts he published in a 1971 English journal (Sergeyev, 1971) and a Czechoslovakian book on psi (Sergeyev, 1970).

L. L. Vasiliev (1976), holder of the Order of Lenin and the founder of modern Soviet parapsychology, initiated work with Kulagina, but after his death, investigations generally were carried out by scientists on a part-time basis. Kulagina's husband, V. V. Kulagin (1971), in an article published in the *Journal of Parapsychics,* referred to these investigations as somewhat chaotic in nature because they were carried out by different scientists from various institutions with the use of different recording equipment.

Kulagina was hospitalized in 1964 following an emotional breakdown. In a discussion with Thelma Moss (1971), Kulagina indicated that she first discovered her unusual abilities during her hospitalization when she noticed she had picked out the correct threads for embroidery without looking. As investigations of the "dermal-optical effect" (or "skin vision") were being pursued at that time, Kulagina told a physician about her success during a medical consultation. This led to Vasiliev's taking an interest in her as a subject for his experiments in "skin vision" when she was dismissed from the hospital in 1965.

Rejdák (1968, 1970) recalled that Vasiliev discovered Kulagina's PK abilities upon asking her to try to move a compass needle. When Kulagina was able to do this successfully, she was quite surprised, as she had never attempted this feat before. However, Kulagina and Vasiliev may have been aware of her PK abilities before the compass demonstration. Kulagina told Moss that during the "skin vision" experiments some objects on the table began to move; when she deliberately attempted these movements, the objects continued in motion.

Kulagina has been accused of fraud, but no direct evidence exists that she has ever used deception in her PK demonstrations. Her critics ignore the fact that she participated in the defense of Leningrad during World War II, often working under fire. During the time she worked with Vasiliev, Kulagina is said to have been involved in a court case, receiving a short jail sentence (Ryzl, 1969). It is not clear whether she was unable to repay some money or whether she had engaged in black-market operations. According to one account, she attempted to buy a refrigerator on the black market. Critics of Kulagina (for example, Chijov, 1968) claim that suspect dealings in one area justifies the inference of fraudulent PK. Personally, I agree with the observations of Keil, Herbert, Ullman, and Pratt (1976):

> While it is not entirely clear what led to Kulagina's difficulties with the law it must be remembered that transgressions that would be minor in the West can be more serious and therefore have graver consequences in the U.S.S.R. From the evidence available it would be unreasonable to suggest a character defect. [p. 211]

During my visits to the USSR, my assistants and I were frequently approached to see if we would like to exchange money at black-market rates—or to sell blue jeans or popular music records. We always declined, not only out of respect for the Soviet economy but also because we feared what would befall the Soviet citizens who approached us if any of them were apprehended.

A second source of critical comment has been based on the strong magnetic field detected around Kulagina's body. It has been claimed (for example, Chijov, 1968) that Kulagina was concealing magnets. Vladimir Lvov (1968) snidely remarked in the *Evening Leningrad* that Kulagina "performs her dexterous tricks with the help of magnets concealed in intimate places both higher and lower than the waist." However, Zdeněk Rejdák informed me (during a 1973 meeting in Prague) that before his investigations, he would examine Kulagina for hidden magnets by passing metallic detectors around her hands and other parts of her body. Furthermore, many of the objects moved by Kulagina were nonmetallic.

A third criticism involves the possible employment of legerdemain. In addition to the *Pravda* attack of 1968, there have been frequent critical remarks by Alexander Kitaigorodsky, a Soviet physicist and mathematician. For example, Kitaigorodsky (1966) once attributed all PK effects to fraud or "accidental events" and, in 1972, claimed that Kulagina "moves pitchers and water glasses across a table with simple devices that go unnoticed by enraptured journalists." These devices purportedly include threads, hair, or wire attached to the objects to be moved and manipulated by Kulagina's knees below the table surface. Again, Rejdák told me he had investigated this possibility and found it without basis.

Vladimir Lvov is the best-known Soviet critic of parapsychology. His 1974 book *Fabricated Miracles* denounces me and my work at Maimonides as well as most of my Soviet friends. Kulagina is ridiculed, and considerable attention is given to a study commission report signed by S. V. Gorvatsevich, M. G. Boguslavsky, A. I. Kartashev, L. B. Langans, and N. A. Smirnov. Lvov (1974, p. 248) claims that Kulagina, who was studied by the Commission in a Leningrad laboratory, failed to stop the pendulum of a clock or move heavy weights across a table. This is quite true, but Lvov omitted a section of the report (in Demikov, 1974) that read:

> As to experiments with the movement of light objects, an aluminum tube with a diameter of 20 millimeters and a height of 46 millimeters, a glass, matches, etc., the Commission confirms that the motion took place. The aluminum tube moved 90 millimeters, and the glass about the same distance. The aluminum tube moved under a transparent cover as well as without a cover. Observations by the members of the Commission were made both at a close distance, and at a far distance with television cameras.

Another article (Kolodny, 1971) indicates that this study was sponsored by the Institute of Meteorology, which concluded that "the Committee at the present time cannot give an explanation of the observed phenomena of the transference of objects." Measures were taken to confirm the absence of electrostatic or magnetic fields as well as air currents. Like the criticisms of Martin Gardner, those of Vladimir Lvov tend to disintegrate on close inspection.

In March 1974, *Time* magazine ran a cover story, "The Psychics," which was highly critical of parapsychology and in which I counted no fewer than six major errors. For example, it stated:

> Ninel Kulagina . . . took the stage name of Ninel because it is Lenin spelled backward. . . . Ninel has been caught cheating more than once by Establishment Soviet scientists. [p. 71]

I wrote *Time,* asking for the names of the "Establishment Soviet scientists" who had discredited Kulagina. I also asked for proof that she had appeared on the stage taking the name of "Ninel." In reply, *Time* wrote to me, stating that:

> . . . all the research for our cover story has been mislaid and although we have searched everywhere for it, we unfortunately have been unable to locate it. . . . The researcher . . . recalls she took the quotation from an article by [Martin Gardner] . . . [and] also talked to Gardner on the phone. . . . [Storfer, 1974]

This bizarre episode demonstrates how easily falsehood can be perpetuated once it appears in print. Distortions and lies have lives of their own and continue to rear their ugly heads for extended periods of time before they expire.

Movement of Resting Objects

When Kulagina first began her PK work, she tended to move objects away from her (Kulagin, 1971). Later, she was able to move objects toward her, and this type of movement became predominant (Keil et al., 1976, p. 205). Circular movements have also been observed (Keil and Fahler, 1975). The surfaces on which the resting objects were moved varied from glass and Plexiglas to wooden tabletops, sometimes covered with a tablecloth. Little difference has been reported in the way objects move in relation to these various surfaces.

Kulagina has found it relatively easy to move long objects in an upright position, such as cigar containers, tall glass objects, and cigarettes standing on end. It has been noted that cigarettes are moved with a high degree of stability; that is, they seldom fall over, except when moving toward the edge of a tabletop. In an attempt to simulate such a movement by legerdemain it was found that placing a steel pin inside a cigarette made it possible to move the cigarette with a magnet held under the tabletop. However, it was not possible to keep the cigarette in an upright position for more than fifty millimeters, a shorter distance than that observed by the investigators who worked with Kulagina.

When Kulagina moves objects, continuous sliding movements last for only a few seconds. She has moved objects over distances as long as forty centimeters, but not as one continuous movement. The complete movement cannot be attributed to an initial momentum applied during the first part of the movement, which then continues to propel the object the rest of the way; the movements are slow enough to require a force as long as a movement occurs (Keil et al., 1976, p. 205).

The size of objects moved by Kulagina has varied from a single match to a large vase. She has been able to move, along a predetermined course, one match from a group of matches thrown on the table (Rejdák, 1969). Pratt and Keil (1973) observed Kulagina's attempt to move an object within a sealed ten-centimeter Plexiglas cube; instead, they reported that the entire cube began to move. Pratt and Keil also placed aquarium gravel on a table and asked Kulagina to move a cylinder about two inches in diameter through it. As the cylinder moved through the gravel, it pushed the tiny stones aside as if there were no PK force acting on the gravel itself.

On one occasion, Kulagina attempted to move an ink blob on a piece of paper. Initially, the ink was elongated in the direction of movement and then gradually changed into a two-centimeter-long, thin line, which separated from the original blob (Kulagin, 1971).

Sometimes Kulagina has been observed to move more than one object simultaneously. Keil and Fahler (1975) noted that sometimes one object moved until it contacted another object, and then began to push that object. Herbert (1970) reported that sometimes small objects were moved as one group, while Pratt and Keil (1973) saw two objects moving in the same direction. In addition, there are reports of two or more objects moving in different directions (Keil et al., 1976, p. 206).

Altering Moving Objects

Kulagina is reported to have achieved 10 complete 360-degree turns of a compass needle (Rejdák, 1969), stopping a pendulum and initiating its swinging again in a different plane (Kulagin, 1971), and accelerating the movement of a Ping-Pong ball suspended on a light suspension spring from the top of a Plexiglas cube (Keil and Fahler, 1975). In the latter instance, Kulagina was seen to depress the ball about 15 millimeters to the bottom surface and propel the ball toward her body. The spring became noticeably extended and when Kulagina relaxed, the ball jumped back into its original position.

Herbert (1973) prepared a hydrometer floating in a saturated saline solution in such a way that it was surrounded by an earthed metal-wire screen and monitored by a sensitive electrostatic probe. This apparatus was brought to Kulagina, who had never worked with such a device. After examining it, she sat in a chair separated from the table with the device about four feet away. While she stared in the direction of the hydrometer, it floated away from her to the opposite wall of the chamber, a distance of over six centimeters. After remaining stationary for two minutes, the hydrometer floated toward Kulagina until it reached the wall of the container nearest to her. During these movements, the electrostatic probe registered no change. Subsequent tests failed to detect any means by which the movements of the hydrometer could have been produced by ordinary means.

Kulagina has also worked with scales, reportedly moving the

pans of a scale that was in balance—and then preventing further movement when 10 grams of weight were added to a pan (Kulagin, 1971). When she relaxed, the heavier pan descended at once.

When I was in Moscow in 1971, Naumov gave me a photograph of Kulagina suspending what seemed to be a Ping-Pong ball between her two hands. G. A. Sergeyev told Keil that he had observed this phenomenon (Keil et al., 1976, p. 209). However, not enough details are available of this purported feat to enable one to make a reasonable evaluation of the claim.

Altering Biological Systems

Sergeyev also is said to have supervised Kulagina's work with frog hearts on March 10, 1970 (Keil et al., 1976, p. 209; Ullman, 1971). A frog's heart sometimes beats for several hours after it is taken from the frog's body. In this instance, the beating heart was placed in a glass jar in front of Kulagina. She concentrated on the heart, giving it commands to go faster or slower; cardiograms showed that the heart responded to her commands. About twelve minutes after the experiment began, she stopped the heart entirely. The cardiograph registered a sudden increase in electrical activity just before the heart stopped, as if by an electrical shock. The heart could not be restarted by electrical impulses (Herbert, 1973). Unfortunately, no firsthand report is available of this experiment that would allow an informed judgment to be made on the adequacy of the controls.

Kulagina has told some investigators that she has revived fish in an aquarium when they appeared to be dead (Keil et al., 1976, p. 209). Furthermore, Kulagina reportedly has been able to induce extreme heat by placing her hand on a person's forearm. Herbert (1973) reported heat to the point of unbearable pain; Keil and Fahler (1975) also felt heat and pain. Both Herbert and Fahler had "burn marks" on their arms that were visible for several hours. These effects (including the "burn marks") are similar to those produced in other situations by suggestion and hypnosis; therefore, additional tests need to be made before the matter is settled. Indeed, when Kulagina placed her hand on Fahler's arm, a mercury thermometer was placed between them. It showed no change. Sergeyev had hypothesized there would be no change (Keil et al., 1976, p. 211), but it can also be argued that the impression of heat was due to suggestion.

Photographic Effects

Sergeyev also has claimed that Kulagina has been able to influence unexposed film that had been enclosed in double light-sealed envelopes (Keil et al., 1976, p. 211; Kulagin, 1971; Vilenskaya, 1977). In 1971, I was given copies of some of these attempts; the pictures show fuzzy white crosses—purportedly where Kulagina focused on the film—moving her eyes up, down, and sideways. I was told by Naumov that her gaze functions like a laser beam. Further, he noted that her heartbeat increased and the electrical field around the body decreased. In 1970, Pratt was unable to duplicate these results using Polaroid film, but Herbert obtained fogging effects on photographic enlargement paper in 1972 (Rogo, 1978, pp. 108–9, 113).

Naumov also gave me photographs that depicted bright white discs on black backgrounds. He told me that these had been obtained by placing a thirty-five-millimeter negative film in an opaque cover around Kulagina's head while she attempted PK. Keil, Herbert, Ullman, and Pratt (1976, p. 212) note, "The effects obtained were clearly visible flashes and suggest discharges of a high order of magnitude." No details are available as to how often Kulagina produced these effects or the existing conditions. However, Vilenskaya (1977) suggested it involved "electromagnetic oscillations from Kulagina's eyes."

Because a Soviet report claimed that an exposure track on film was observed after Kulagina's PK, Pratt and Keil (1973) placed a roll of unexposed Polaroid film on top of a cylinder that she was about to attempt to move. Although the cylinder moved in an unexplained manner, the film was not affected. However, the original report mentioned that the film had been placed underneath the object rather than above it.

Measuring the Phenomena

According to the most reliable of the available reports, Kulagina has been able to move at least one hundred different kinds of objects (Keil et al., 1976, p. 212). Her success rate has been estimated at 90 percent and usually does not seem to depend on the nature of the materials, although plastic is said to be more difficult (Keil et al., 1976, p. 213) and gold somewhat easier than other materials (Rejdák, 1969). These differences may be due to the expectancy of the observers or of Kulagina herself, but no properly conducted comparative tests have been reported.

Herbert (1973) measured the force necessary to produce a sliding movement of a compass case apparently moved by psychokinetic means by Kulagina. He estimated that Kulagina had exerted a force of 8,340 dynes acting upon a mass of 22.3 grams in a horizontal direction. Of course, when she moved objects weighing several hundred grams, the force exerted would have been much higher.

Sometimes Kulagina began to move objects a few minutes after beginning deliberate efforts, while at other times it took several hours. Hostile observers inhibited her abilities, but if Kulagina persisted, she usually was able to succeed even in these circumstances (Keil et al., 1976, p. 214). Kulagina also found it difficult to demonstrate PK in hot weather (Herbert, 1973) or during storms (Keil et al., 1976, p. 215), nor has she been successful when objects are placed in a vacuum (Kulagin, 1971).

Kulagina's heart rate increased during demonstrations, sometimes to 240 beats per minute. Ullman (1971) found that her pulse rate was 86 during rest, but 132 during a demonstration. Sergeyev (in Keil et al., 1976, p. 201) is said to have reported that a strong pulsing magnetic field has been measured around Kulagina's body when she is demonstrating PK. Furthermore, the voltage potentials measured at the front and the back of her scalp showed a difference about 10 times as great as in most other people. Electrodes attached to the occipital region of the skull (above the visual areas) recorded brain waves that had an amplitude estimated to be 50 times as great as those recorded while she was relaxed (Pratt, 1977, p. 893). Other brain-wave changes have been reported, but the conditions are inadequately described.

Loss of body weight has been reported to be as high as two thousand grams after one session, although a loss of seven hundred to one thousand grams per session is more typical (Pratt, 1977, p. 894). Extreme exhaustion and an increase in blood-sugar level followed some sessions (Kulagin, 1971). All of these changes varied from one session to the next and often were minimal when Kulagina was working under optimal conditions (Keil et al., 1976, p. 215; Kulagin, 1971).

Pratt (1977) has described the setting in which Kulagina usually attempts to demonstrate her ability to foreigners:

In a typical session, Kulagina sits in a straight chair before a table. At first she appears to be relaxed, though she may become nervous if she has come outside her own environment to meet strangers in an unfamiliar location. She takes some time to prepare herself mentally and emotionally for the effort to demonstrate her ability. . . . As part of her preparation, she sometimes breathes deeply several times. Then she holds one or both hands near (approximately ten to twenty centimeters) some small object that has been placed on the table before her. Usually, the object is one chosen by an observer and may be any object that he happened to have on his person. Sometimes two or more objects are placed on the table at the same time, and under informal conditions Kulagina may touch one of them briefly in order to separate it from the others or to put it in a position that she finds more comfortable for her effort to make it move.

It is by no means the case, however, that the subject always touches an object before she moves it. In many observations on record the experimenter has placed the objects on the table and immediately covered them with an inverted Plexiglas cube, and Kulagina has moved some of the objects under the cube without touching the cover. . . .

The movement of an object may come almost immediately after Kulagina shows by her behavior that she is beginning her effort to make it move. At other times movement is delayed for some seconds or up to a minute. If movement does not occur after such an interval of time Kulagina usually admits failure and stops the trial, during which she may have been under great physical strain from the effort to succeed. [pp. 892–93]

A report on Kulagina's inner experience during PK was contributed by two journalists, Henry Gris and William Dick (1978), following several trips to the USSR to interview Soviet parapsychological researchers:

> Kulagina found that to move items successfully with the power of her mind, she must cast all other thoughts from her head. She concentrated solely on the target object—to such an extent that only its image filled her mind. Just before the target object moved, she told the researchers, she would feel a sharp pain in her spine, and her eyesight blurred. [p. 31]

The journalists also noted that Kulagina suffered another heart attack following the death of her father. In a phone conversation, Kulagina is reported to have observed, "They tell me the experiments were very important," and vowed to continue her work.

PK in Moscow

Several films have been made of Kulagina that are helpful in allowing the viewer to understand the procedure she utilizes during her PK sessions. Naumov gave me one of these films; it depicts a session with Kulagina that he personally supervised. At the beginning of the film, one sees Naumov passing his hand between Kulagina and the table in an attempt to show that there are no threads attached to the objects she is about to move. Later in the film, as she is moving the needle of a compass that rests on a small table, Naumov places one hand over the compass to keep it from falling, while the other hand grips the table and turns it upside down. The viewer sees no hidden apparatus underneath, but does see Kulagina raising her hands and extending her fingers as if to indicate that there are no magnets hidden in her palms or between her fingers (Herbert, 1970).

One of the people who saw the Kulagina films was Alla Vinogradova, the wife of Victor Adamenko. A child psychologist and teacher, Vinogradova told me that she suspected that she could move objects without touching them as soon as she saw the film in 1969. She and her husband designed a training program based upon Adamenko's conjecture that PK occurs naturally in the brain as one's decisions set the neurons into action; externally observed, PK is a logical extension of this internal process. To enhance her motivation, she was hypnotized and given positive suggestions. To protect her health, she embarked on a program of physical exercise. To develop her confidence, Adamenko made her aware of her other psi abilities, such as purported precognitive dreaming. Gris and Dick (1978, p. 39) report that Vinogradova recalled a dream in which she saw herself and her family on a train, going to a funeral. Her brother was the only close relative who was not present; two days later he died unexpectedly.

Ullman (1974) also reported Vinogradova's claims of precognitive ability. Furthermore, he described her ability to slide objects weighing up to thirty grams and to roll objects of up to one hundred grams. Ullman further noted that objects influenced by Vinogradova become charged, even when she is grounded—indicating that her ability involves more than a production of static electricity. William Tiller (1972), a physicist from Stanford University, came to the same conclusion after seeing Vinogradova at work, but stated that "electrostatic phenomena clearly play a strong role in . . . her PK force. . . ."

Canadian parapsychologist A. R. G. Owen (1975), however, took issue with the claim that Vinogradova had demonstrated PK:

> Visitors who have returned recently from Russia say that some Soviet scientists are seeking to train . . . people to do voluntary psychokinesis, and claim some success with this venture. To give their trainees confidence the Russian workers let them practice a kind of "electrostatic pseudo-psychokinesis." Small cylinders of glass, cardboard, or metal (a cigar tube will do) are laid on a Plexiglas table. We have seen a film brought from Russia which shows a woman putting her hand some inches away from such a tube. The tube will then roll briskly on the tabletop following her hand, but without contact. . . . Anyone can produce this effect. . . . It is entirely due to static electricity. [pp. 153–54]

PK Grows in Brooklyn

Montague Ullman arranged a private showing of the Kulagina film at Maimonides in 1971. Among those present was Milbourne Christopher, the distinguished magician. He watched Kulagina's movements with great interest, observing that he could duplicate all of her effects by sleight of hand. Ullman and I pointed out that the film was only suggestive and in no way could be construed as evidential.

Another member of the audience was Felicia Parise, a laboratory technician at Maimonides. Following the film showing, Parise was convinced that she could produce similar effects.

Later in the week, Parise attempted to produce movement in small objects. Initially she tried to move the items by entering a relaxed, meditative state of consciousness. When that approach failed, she induced an agitated state and projected the anxiety onto the target object. That approach did not work either.

Parise had been a subject in several of our ESP dream experiments at Maimonides. In one of Parise's experimental sessions, she had dreamed of seeing her elderly grandmother sitting on the floor in a pool of blood. Returning home the morning after the dream session, she learned that her grandmother had fallen during the night, cutting her head as she fell. This was only one of several instances in which Parise appeared to have telepathic communication with her grandmother.

During Parise's initial PK attempts with small objects, her grandmother was again critically ill. Parise returned home after visiting her grandmother in the hospital. Parise was just about to focus her attention on a small plastic bottle when the phone rang; her grandmother had taken a turn for the worse and Parise was called back to the hospital. Parise reached for the plastic bottle to put it away—and the object suddenly moved away from her.

Over the next several months, Parise repeated this feat several times, once when she was observed by a student assistant at the Dream Laboratory. In that instance, Parise and the student were joking, and Parise instructed him to watch the plastic bottle. Immediately it moved two inches across the table. Later in 1971, Charles Honorton observed similar movements with the same bottle. He tried to move the bottle on the same Formica surface through other means. Honorton (1974) later recalled, "I tried pressing gently and firmly against the sides, top, and underside of the counter; I forcibly jarred the countertop; I moistened the counter and the bottle by spilling some of the alcohol solution. I was completely unsuccessful in getting the bottle to move." Honorton later took a carpenter's level to Parise's apartment and found that the surface over which the bottle had moved was not perfectly level. The bottle had been moving slightly uphill!

Over the next few months, Parise succeeded in deflecting the needle of a small compass. Honorton developed the habit of taking Parise's hands unexpectedly and passing them directly over the face of the compass to insure against concealed bits of metal. And on one occasion, the compass needle deflected ninety degrees after Parise had laughingly uttered the word "abracadabra."

Parise described the process as focusing her attention on the object to be moved until "that's the only thing there." She would pick a spot on the object and concentrate upon it until everything else disappeared. She would work up to an emotional excitement in which her desire to make the object move was stronger than anything else. She described how she would perspire freely during a PK session, how her eyes would water, and how her nose would tremble. After a successful session, Parise would often have difficulty speaking for a few moments.

Parise later tape-recorded an account of her PK development (in Smith, 1975). This document provides unique insights into her feelings during the period of time she was moving objects:

Dr. Ullman . . . invited the lab crew to view a film . . . of Nina Kulagina, who purports to move objects at will by the power of her mind. I cannot begin to tell you how impressed I was when I saw this film. There was no doubt in my mind then or now that this woman is 100 percent legitimate. And after viewing the film, I couldn't wait to go home and try the same thing.

When I went home that evening, I tried to move something with the power of my mind. I had no idea what Kulagina was thinking while she was moving objects. It was obvious from the film that she wasn't in any meditative kind of situation. She was trying very hard and focusing her attention on the object and nothing else. I just had to try to get into a similar state and find the right condition that was necessary for me to move objects. I happened to have a little plastic pill vial on my coffee table and I began to concentrate on it. I had no success at all for a long time, but was so interested that I kept on trying.

All during the months that followed, my personal life became one emotional crisis after another. I was very close to my grandmother and we had a very tight relationship. She was then dying at Maimonides Hospital, and I was there every day watching her and doing what I could for her. I can't tell you what this was doing to me. . . . I had never seen anyone die in such a slow and agonizing way and it was torturing to me. So it was a highly emotional time for me. Yet I could hardly wait each night to get home for a quiet period with my plastic bottle. That was the only time I could stop thinking about the heartache and tragedy that was coming on at the time. It became such an obsession that I took my plastic bottle to work and tried to move it during lunch hours and coffee breaks. This went on for several months.

Now, I have a plastic bottle that contains alcohol in which I put my artificial eyelashes at night when I take them off, to clean them and keep them safe until the next morning. This one night I removed my lashes as soon as I got home and laid the bottle on the kitchen table. The phone rang and it was my mother telling me that I'd better get back to the hospital because grandmother had taken a turn for the worse. I got very excited and dressed quickly to return to the hospital. When I ran into the kitchen to put the eyelash bottle away, it moved away from me. At this point I wasn't sure it had happened. I just knew I hadn't touched the bottle. Well, grandma died, and several weeks later I tried again to move this same bottle in the same place, and I was successful. I kept examining everything to make sure it wasn't being influenced to move by any other means. I didn't tell anybody because I couldn't believe it was happening. Although I had been deliberately trying to do this, I still wasn't sure. Eventually I became convinced this was really PK and I told Mr. Honorton what I was doing. He asked for a demonstration and the bottle moved.

Dr. Krippner suggested I try moving a compass needle, and so I did this and was successful with it. I tried several other things. . . . I avoided using metals and anything that was magnetic except the compass. I primarily stick to plastic, aluminum foil, cotton balls, corks, and a whole variety of things, but mostly plastic. For some reason, I have not been successful with wood.

Finally, I made a film, and then I continued to do PK for a year or two after that. [pp. 266–69]

Parise demonstrated before other parapsychologists such as J. G. Pratt, Graham Watkins, and Anita Watkins. Watkins and Watkins (1974) observed an interesting "lingering effect":

> About five minutes after the first indication of compass needle movement, Parise . . . walked to a far corner of the room. The compass needle, however, remained fifteen degrees off north, and was found to be totally unresponsive to either the knife blade or the bar magnet. We thought that perhaps the needle was jammed. To test this, the compass was moved to a position about four feet away from the point of concentration, and during the movement the needle gradually returned to north. In this position it was easily affected by the knife blade. The compass was then returned to the original spot on the chair, and again the needle moved fifteen degrees off north, and was incapable of being influenced by the metal blade. This procedure was repeated several times with the same results. The needle gradually returned to north over a period of about twenty-five minutes, and also gradually became more responsive to the knife blade. [pp. 132–33]

Watkins and Watkins (1974) also reported what occurred when a compass was placed on unexposed black-and-white film. Similar film was also placed at varying degrees around the compass. Parise's success in turning the needle was limited as compared to other demonstrations she had given, as the needle only turned about fifteen degrees. However, it was found that the film placed under the compass was almost totally exposed and that the other films were partially exposed. The exposure diminished with increasing distance from the compass.

Parise was filmed moving corks and aluminum foil that had been placed in a large jar; the camera operator, an amateur magician, examined the surroundings, inspected Parise, and failed to find anything suggesting chicanery. Later, I personally saw her deflect a compass needle by five degrees.

Parise's last observed session was in 1972, when Honorton saw her move a bottle more than six inches. Shortly afterward, she discontinued her PK work, stating: "It took all of my spare time. PK is something you have to do every day. It's more than just putting it on your schedule." Parise (1974) also admitted, "I am not the kind of person who can withstand constant criticism." She knew only too well that if she gained a reputation for PK ability, she would be subjected to the type of vilification that had been directed against Kulagina. Parise commented:

> I do not enjoy having to defend myself, nor having my integrity under fire. . . . I have tried to maintain a normal life style continuous with PK and have found it impossible to do so. . . . Now I would like to move on to something else. [Smith, 1975, p. 269]

References

Adamenko, V. G. Psi and physical fields. In W. G. Roll (ed.), *Research in Parapsychology, 1978*. Metuchen, N.J.: Scarecrow Press, 1979.

————. Controlled movement of objects. *Journal of Paraphysics,* 1972, *6,* 180–226.

Chijov, V. Wonder in a sieve. *Journal of Paraphysics,* 1968, *2,* 109–11. (Originally published in *Pravda,* June 24, 1968.)

Demikov, V. I. [By a stroke of the pen. *Journalist,*] Nov. 1974.

Gardner, M. Arthur Koestler: Neo-Platonism rides again. *World,* Aug. 1, 1972.

Gris, H., and Dick, W. *The New Soviet Psychic Discoveries.* Englewood Cliffs, N.J.: Prentice-Hall, 1978.

Herbert, B. Kulagina ciné films: Summary. *Journal of Paraphysics,* 1970, *4,* 160–64.

————. Alla Vinogradova: Demonstration in Moscow. *Journal of Paraphysics,* 1972, *6,* 191–208.

————. Spring in Leningrad: Kulagina revisited. *Parapsychology Review,* 1973, *4,* 5–10.

Honorton, C. Apparent psychokinesis on static objects by a "gifted" subject. In W. G. Roll, R. L. Morris, and J. D. Morris (eds.), *Research in Parapsychology, 1973*. Metuchen, N.J.: Scarecrow Press, 1974.

Keil, H. H. J., and Fahler, J. A strong case for PK involving directly observable movements of objects recorded on ciné film. In J. D. Morris, W. G. Roll, and R. L. Morris (eds.), *Research in Parapsychology, 1974.* Metuchen, N.J.: Scarecrow Press, 1975.

Keil, H. H. J.; Herbert, B.; Ullman, M.; and Pratt, J. G. Directly observable voluntary PK effects: A survey and tentative interpretation of available findings from Nina Kulagina and other known related cases of recent date. *Proceedings of the Society for Psychical Research,* 1976, *56,* 197–235.

Kitaigorodsky, A. [Parapsychology: For and against.] *Nauka i Zhirn,* Mar. 1966.

———. [*Not Believable, Not Fact.*] Moscow: Molodaya Gvardiya, 1972.

Koestler, A. *The Roots of Coincidence.* New York: Random House, 1972.

Kolodny, L. When apples fall. *Journal of Paraphysics,* 1971, *5,* 54–62.

Krippner, S. Editorial. *Psychoenergetic Systems,* 1977, *2,* 5–11.

Krippner, S., and Davidson, R. Parapsychology in the U.S.S.R. *Saturday Review,* Mar. 18, 1972.

Kulagin, V. V. Nina S. Kulagina. *Journal of Paraphysics,* 1971, *5,* 54–62.

Lvov, V. [Telekinesis explained. *Evening Leningrad,*] Apr. 17, 1968.

———. [*Fabricated Miracles.*] Leningrad: Lenizdat, 1974.

Moss, T. Searching for psi from Prague to Lower Siberia. *Psychic,* June 1971.

———. Psychic research in the Soviet Union. In J. White (ed.), *Psychic Exploration: A Challenge for Science.* New York: G. P. Putnam's Sons, 1974.

Owen, A. R. G. *Psychic Mysteries of the North.* New York: Harper & Row, 1975.

Parise, F. Interview with H. H. J. Keil, 1974.

Pratt, J. G. *ESP Research Today: A Study of Developments in Parapsychology Since 1960.* Metuchen, N.J.: Scarecrow Press, 1973.

———. Soviet research in parapsychology. In B. B. Wolman (ed.), *Handbook of Parapsychology.* New York: Van Nostrand Reinhold, 1977.

Pratt, J. G., and Keil, H. H. J. Firsthand observations of Nina S. Kulagina suggestive of PK upon static objects. *Journal of the American Society for Psychical Research*, 1973, *67*, 381–90.

Rejdák, Z. Telekinesis or fraud? *Journal of Paraphysics*, 1968, *2*, 68–70.

————. The Kulagina ciné films: Introductory notes. *Journal of Paraphysics*, 1969, *3*, 64–67.

————. [The psychokinetic phenomena of Nina Kulagina.] *Zeitschnift für Parapsychologie und Grenzgebiete der Psychologie*, 1970, *12*, 106–10.

Rogo, D. S. *Minds in Motion*. New York: Taplinger, 1978.

Ryzl, M. ESP in Eastern Europe and Russia. *Psychic*, June/July 1969, and Aug./Sept. 1969.

Sergeyev, G. A. KNS phenomenon. *Journal of Paraphysics*, 1971, *5*, 47–50.

————. [Some methodological parapsychological problems.] In Z. Rejdák (ed.), [*Telepathy and Clairvoyance*.] Prague: Svoboda, 1970.

Smith, S. *The Power of the Mind*. Radnor, Pa.: Chilton, 1975.

Storfer, B. Personal communication. Aug. 1974.

Tiller, W. A. The psychokinetic phenomena of Alla Vinogradova. *Journal of Paraphysics*, 1972, *6*, 77–81.

Ullman, M. Fragments of a parapsychological journey. *Newsletter, American Society for Psychical Research*, October, 1971.

————. PK in the Soviet Union. In W. G. Roll, R. L. Morris, and J. D. Morris (eds.), *Research in Parapsychology, 1973*. Metuchen, N.J.: Scarecrow Press, 1974.

Ullman, M., and Krippner, S. *Dream Studies and Telepathy*. New York: Parapsychological foundation, 1970.

Vasiliev, L. L. *Experiments in Distant Influence*, New York: E. P. Dutton, 1976. (Originally published in 1962.)

Vilenskaya, L. Personal communication. Oct. 1977.

Watkins, G. K., and Watkins, A. Apparent psychokinesis on static objects by a "gifted" subject: A laboratory demonstration. In W. G. Roll, R. L. Morris, and J. D. Morris (eds.), *Research in Parapsychology, 1973*. Metuchen, N.J.: Scarecrow Press, 1974.

CHAPTER 3

Soviet Parapsychology: The Tip of an Iceberg?

Biological researchers have shown that organisms are
capable of active interaction with the real physical
time in which they exist. They can slow down or accelerate time—compress or condense it.

A. P. Dubrov (1974)

In 1973, I went to Prague, Czechoslovakia, to attend the First International Congress on Psychotronic Research. Zdeněk Rejdák,
who organized the conference, described psychotronics as the
scientific study of interactions among consciousness, energy, and
matter. Rejdák chaired the Committee of Applied Cybernetics of
the Czechoslovakian Scientific Technical Association and had
been able to win official recognition for psychotronics. I was
asked to co-chair the anthropology sessions.

The Congress convened on Peace Square in the Railway
Workers' House of Culture. There were approximately 250 participants, among them a few Soviet delegates as well as a number of
Czechoslovakian scientists. As a result of Rejdák's (1974) patient
fostering of psychotronics over the years, some provocative work
was reported.

Devices and Distances

Julius Krmessky (1976) taught physics at the State Pedagogical Institute in Bratislava, Czechoslovakia, until his retirement. He discussed the devices he had built to study PK, among them a simple mobile sealed under glass and shielded by wood and metal. By staring at the mobile, Krmessky claimed he was able to produce movement. He made the same claim for a small object floating on water in a sealed glass container.

Before coming to Prague, I had seen a film in which Krmessky attached a white file card to an inverted test tube suspended over a long, upturned needle. Seated several feet away, Krmessky stared at the card. As it turned, it tripped a switch, and a light bulb was illuminated. Krmessky produced movement in one of his simpler devices at the conference; however, it was not sealed and one could not rule out wind currents and floor vibrations as the sources of the object's movement. Nevertheless, Krmessky's devices were ingenious and deserving of attention.

Another demonstration was given by Robert Pavlita and his daughter, Jana Pavlitova. An engineer, Pavlita had directed a development program for the Czechoslovakian textile industry, inventing a series of automatic machines to cut and fold material. Upon retirement, he devoted himself to PK experiments, a topic that had been his hobby for years.

Pavlita called his devices "psychotronic generators" because he claimed they could store and utilize "psychic energy." One of the "generators" resembled a microphone; Jana Pavlitova touched her forehead with the device in a rhythmical manner for about three minutes. The "generator" was then placed before a solid semicircular copper screen. A light metal cone was placed on top of the "generator." Pavlitova then touched the table lightly with the fingers of her left hand; it began to revolve from left to right. When Pavlitova removed her fingers, the cone's motion stopped; when she again touched the table, the cone resumed its movement (Krippner and Hickman, 1974).

Again, the large crowd and the possibility of floor vibrations or air currents made an evaluation impossible. However, I saw Pavlita at his home on a visit to Czechoslovakia in 1974. He and Pavlitova demonstrated ten devices, allowing me to observe carefully and take photographs. Later, I published my impressions, noting that there were alternative explanations such as hidden magnets, electrostatic effects, or even PK coming directly from Pavlita rather than being "stored" in the devices. I concluded, "only future research will indicate whether the psychotronic generators are the scientific breakthrough that his supporters suspect" (Krippner, 1977, p. 430). Despite this cautionary position, I was criticized by some parapsychologists and nonparapsychologists for even suggesting that the "generators" might be taken seriously. Michael Rossman (1979), one of those who did not scoff, devoted a chapter to the "psychic arms race" in his book *New Age Blues,* in which he speculated on the military uses of such devices. Several years earlier, a more detailed report had been prepared by the U. S. Army Medical Intelligence Information Agency (Maire and LaMothe, 1975); it took a sober look at the generators and suggested that they should be carefully investigated. John Chamberlain (1976) also speculated on a variety of destructive mind-altering procedures, from beaming microwaves at embassies to aiming "psychotronic energy" toward pilots of airplanes.

On a positive note, Josef Wolf (1975), an anthropologist at Charles University in Prague, took the position that psychotronic abilities support the concept of human freedom and of the person's refusal to be subordinated to technology. Wolf observed that psychotronics will someday take a place with biological and psychological approaches to the study of personality, proving to be especially useful in the prevention and treatment of psychosomatic illness.

Jiri Bradna (1973), a physiologist and neurologist with an international reputation, described his experiments with the electromyograph (EMG), an apparatus that measures muscle tension. By attaching the EMG to humans, animals, and birds, Bradna claimed to have charted PK influence over long distances. The muscular activity of his pigeons reportedly was associated with the movement of philodendron plants at a distance. Bradna claimed that a human "transmitter" could project muscle tension to a human "receiver," and displayed EMG charts that recorded the distant influence. Bradna told us that his data suggested that the optimal germination time for seeds is related to the time at which the influence of humans was strongest on the plants from which the seeds were produced. To explain his findings, he hypothesized the existence of "bioenergetic fields" that surround living organisms.

V. A. Patrovsky (1973), an engineer, presented data for a series of experiments in which plant growth apparently was stimulated by using water that had been treated either with electricity or with magnets. Both types of water produced faster plant growth than did ordinary water. When Patrovsky had psychic sensitives move their hands around the containers of water, the plants also showed accelerated growth. Patrovsky claimed he could produce similar effects by having the psychic sensitives gaze intently at the water. Patrovsky's work is specific and detailed enough to allow for replications; for example, he reported that plant growth was accelerated by fields produced by direct current but not by alternating current.

One of the psychic sensitives who worked with Patrovsky was Josef Zezulka, Prague's best-known folk healer. Zezulka read a paper at the Congress presenting a holistic approach to healing that would take into account the three components of personality: the psychological, the somatic, and the "vital force." Psychotronics, he maintained, could be used to treat imbalances in each of these areas.

An American participant, Shelby Parker, who used a cane, complained of severe pain in her hip one morning before our session convened. Zezulka offered to treat her ailment. In front of our entire session, he performed a "laying on of hands" that Parker described as extremely effective in reducing her discomfort. Over the following year, Parker arranged a series of long-distance attempts at healing with Zezulka; when the series was completed, she no longer used a cane, and the pain had disappeared (Krippner and Villoldo, 1976, pp. 191–93). How much of Parker's improvement was due to her contact with Zezulka is difficult to assess. I spent additional time with Zezulka when I visited Czechoslovakia in 1974; he continued to stress his availability for scientific research and, in 1975, sent a paper to the Second International Congress on Psychotronic Research (held in Monaco), which proposed that the healer works by removing "body plasma" that has been "spoiled" by the disease and then filling the patient with "vital power." Through these practices, Zezulka proposed that "healership" could be revived and scientific methods could be used to study its effectiveness.

In 1975, Zdeněk Rejdák organized a seminar on unorthodox healing in Prague under the auspices of the Committee of Applied Cybernetics. The participants concluded that these healers sometimes have the capacity to transfer energy that has healing characteristics to indisposed individuals. It was also observed that unorthodox healing should be seen as an auxiliary to traditional medicine and complementary to it.

The Soviet Participants

Until I reached the Prague Congress, I had no idea who would attend from the USSR. Upon arriving, I was delighted to discover that the Soviet participants included A. G. Bakirov, a mineralogist, Y. A. Kholodov, a biophysicist, A. P. Dubrov, a biologist, and Tofik Dadashev, a stage performer and "mentalist."

Dadashev had toured the Soviet Union many times, appearing to "read the minds" of members of his audience as well as identifying objects (while blindfolded) and providing information about volunteers (Tserkover, 1979). In *The New Soviet Psychic Discoveries* (Gris and Dick, 1978) an account is given of his Prague appearance:

> Tofik baffled them all. . . . Commanded silently by an English scientist to walk up to a certain man in the second row and to identify him as John, Tofik, who was on stage, smiled, came down, unhesitatingly walked up to the man and said in Russian, "You are John." [p. 25]

What I recall occurring was somewhat different. Lois Bird, an American psychologist, silently requested Dadashev to identify a conference participant. Dadashev was blindfolded and, in an attempt further to rule out visual clues, a black hood was placed over his head and tied at the throat.

Dadashev, his hands stretched out before him, walked through the aisles that separated the conference tables. Bird initially followed him, then was instructed to go to the stage and concentrate. Dadashev stopped near a woman, told her to stand, then asked her to sit down. Dadashev then summoned the man in the next chair to lead him to the stage. The man was Cleve Backster, the American polygraph expert, and the person selected by Bird.

When I have seen American "mentalists" perform, they usually have the person who has made the selection lead them by the hand, or by a handkerchief held by both persons. The task then becomes one of "muscle reading," in which the "mentalist" knows by the involuntary tightening and loosening of muscles when they have reached the selected individual. Dadashev had no physical contact with Bird. However, it is quite possible that Bird could have emitted clues while she was trailing Dadashev on the auditorium floor. In addition, she could have directed her attention toward Backster from the stage, and her unconscious signaling (through gestures and glances) could have been picked up by the audience—and perceived by Dadashev. Further, Dadashev's blindfold and hood could have been translucent, permitting him to observe visually any hint given by Bird. Why did he select the wrong person and ask her to stand? It could have been to develop suspense. Or it could have been that Dadashev had correctly identified the row and needed additional feedback before the right person was apparent. At that point, he could have perceived additional clues from Bird and the audience confirming his choice.

Dadashev's performance was impressive and I hoped that he would be studied scientifically between his stints as an entertainer. Nevertheless, I knew enough about stage performers and their techniques to consider alternative explanations and to leave open the question of Dadashev's psi ability.

The Biophysical Effect

A. G. Bakirov (1973; Bakirov et al., 1976) discussed the "biophysical effect," a term that the Soviets find less controversial than "dowsing," a practice that is thousands of years old. Bakirov, a professor of mineralogy and geology at Tomsk Polytechnical Institute, admitted that he has used rods and other instruments himself, attempting to find underground deposits. He claimed that Soviet dowsers had located underground ore deposits, had made accurate geological maps from helicopters, and were attempting to develop dowsing as an early-warning system for earthquakes.

Conferences on the biophysical effect had been held in Moscow in 1968 and 1971, the latter attracting more than 100 scientists from 40 research institutes throughout the country. Participants from all over the USSR gave reports attesting to the dowsers' success. For example, in one region 1,120 water wells had been found by dowsers by 1973 as compared with 158 sites located by traditional methods. Reputedly, only about 7 percent of the dowsers' wells were dry as compared with 13 percent of the other wells (Williamson, 1979).

Another seminar on dowsing was held in the USSR in 1979. Among the topics discussed was a study indicating that an electromagnetic field accompanied underground water if it filtered at a rate of at least one millimeter per second. This information, if true, would support the interpretation of dowsing that holds that dowsers are sensitive to electromagnetic fields (Bird, 1979).

It occurred to me that dowsing would be a splendid skill for intensive study. What materials would work best in a dowsing rod —metal, plastic, or wood? Could some types of ores be detected more easily than others? Could dowsers be used to find oil, coal, and other energy resources? Dowsing, like healing, presents an extremely practical application of psi; however, the data supporting both phenomena too often come from anecdotal reports rather than from experimental laboratories.

Bakirov suggested that some human biological system may have evolved a remarkable sensitivity to very small changes in electromagnetic fields. I immediately recalled the work of A. S. Presman, whose important volume *Electromagnetic Fields and Life* had been published in English in 1970. When I met Presman in Moscow in 1971, he told me of this book and I immediately purchased a copy

In his book, Presman took issue with the traditional view that electromagnetic fields do not affect the nervous system of living organisms. Instead, he presented evidence from plant and animal research, space research, physiology, psychology, and the study of "internal clocks" to demonstrate significant effects. He concluded that organisms can be affected by electromagnetic fields in the environment, around other organisms, and within themselves.

Presman discussed parapsychology in his book, suggesting that emotional factors might be able to enhance ESP test scores and observing that electromagnetic fields may play a role in psi phenomena. In our conversation, he speculated that psi might be an archaic human trait that began to disappear once its usefulness was minimized by language, weapons, and other forms of communication and protection.

A few years later, Presman's work was applied to dowsing by Zaboj Harvalik (1978), a Yugoslavian-born physicist who directed research for the U. S. Army Engineering Laboratories in Virginia. He asked dowsers in a laboratory to indicate when they had the same feeling that accompanied their hunch that they were standing near water. Harvalik, from time to time, exposed the dowsers to an electromagnetic field. At these times, they would usually respond with a signal, such as letting a forked stick drop.

Harvalik then tried shielding different portions of their bodies against the electromagnetic field. When the kidney was shielded, the dowsing responses failed to occur; nor did they occur when the head was shielded. Harvalik concluded that magnetic sensors exist in the human body, probably in the kidney area and in the vicinity of the pineal gland in the brain, the latter operating as a discriminator and processor. Many underground water, oil, and ore deposits are associated with electromagnetic fields, making it possible for identification to occur. An earlier study (Rocard, 1969) had produced similar results; however, the fields were not detected in studies with nondowsers (Whitton and Cook, 1978) nor with a dowser who did not use a "divining rod" (Foulkes, 1971).

These data may help to demystify dowsing and support the Soviet approach of studying psi phenomena without being accused of dabbling in religion or occultism—a charge frequently levied by critics.

Bodily Fields and the "Head State"

A. S. Presman is often regarded as one of the Soviet Union's three pioneering researchers on field effects. The other two, Y. A. Kholodov and A. P. Dubrov, attended the Prague Conference. Kholodov (1964, 1967) spoke on his monumental work involving the effect of electromagnetic fields on the brain, as well as his observation that living organisms produce their own electromagnetic fields. Kholodov had experimented with birds, rabbits, and fish, discovering that certain portions of their brains were more easily stimulated by electromagnetic fields than were other portions. Further, the motor activity of the organisms increased when a constant electromagnetic field surrounded them. If the electromagnetic field was too strong, the brains of the animals, birds, and fish were frequently damaged.

L. L. Vasiliev had discussed Kholodov's work with J. G. Pratt (1973) in a 1963 interview:

. . . the receiving organ in telepathy may be the brain structure itself. In this instance, it would be more correct to say "extra-receptor perception." . . .

I think that . . . it is wrong to think of the process as "extrasensory" at all. The concept of ESP fits only if we are concerned with different conscious and unconscious effects on the brain structure. . . .

In one experiment that has been done, a magnet was brought near the wall of an aquarium. At the same time an impulse current was put through the water. The fishes reacted to the current by quick movements. After many repetitions, the magnetic field alone can bring about the quick movement of the fish. This reflex is maintained even after cutting the sensory nerves to the brain. It stops only when a definite part of the fish's brain is destroyed.

The conclusion reached from this experiment is that the magnetic field influences the brain directly. Here is an "extrasensory" action of the magnetic field. . . . I want this method to penetrate parapsychology. [pp. 67–68]

Kholodov's work is highly regarded in more orthodox fields because Soviet scientists recognize that both water and organisms are sensitive to magnetic fields. In animals, the most obvious trend in evolution is that of "cephalization" or the "head state"—the increasing centralization of nervous-system processes in the head, and the growing complexity and size of the brain. At the same time that this anatomical centralization occurs, there is also a metabolic tendency toward a higher efficiency of energy production in the body. This change of efficiency apparently represents an increase of structure in the cell, and structure in general corresponds to the electrical potential of the cell. It has been known since the end of the 1800s that a magnet will delay a nerve's response to an electrical stimulus, as if its structure had been momentarily frozen. If the magnetic field is thought of as stabilizing the "head state," it is possible that the earth's magnetic field might have been an important factor in evolution, supporting or promoting cephalization.

Kholodov has found that higher organisms tend to be more sensitive to magnetism than lower ones, and that the most sensitive tissue is nervous tissue, especially in the brain and the glial cells. He observed that glial cells, thought to be involved in memory processes, enlarge under the influence of magnetic stimulation, and it has been discovered recently that the testes are also exceptionally sensitive to magnetism.

Many fish that are not considered "electrical" generate a very weak electromagnetic field around themselves and are able to use this field to detect small objects in the surrounding water. Similarly, sharks can detect incredibly weak fields, such as those created by a minnow buried under sand, even at considerable distances. It is apparently the electrical field of a wound that attracts them rather than just the smell of blood.

The same increase in the efficiency of energy production that has been thought to occur in the brain in evolution and that has been observed in the state of mental alertness, has been found to occur in many tissues under the influence of an electromagnetic field. High-efficiency energy production will have survival value in many ways, but if efficient metabolism is the key to cephalization, and if the brain is sensitive to this kind of stimulation, it is clear to some Soviet scientists that magnetism has been an environ-mental support for brain evolution.

Of Time and Change

Soviet astronomer and physicist N. A. Kozyrev (1968) has spec-ulated that planets and stars, including the sun, are evolving to-ward higher energy states rather than dying down; such an evolu-tionary process would include changes in electromagnetic fields.

Kozyrev has proposed that time is a participant in physical processes rather than an abstract framework in which events hap-pen. As such, time would be a source of energy and order. He first made this proposal in relation to some problems of stellar energy but has also suggested that biological structures and "time-energy" may interact. Thus Kozyrev's theory fits nicely with the known facts suggesting electromagnetism as a link between cosmic evolution and the evolution of life forms.

There is a practical problem that grows out of the suspected in-teraction of brain and solar magnetism—namely, the fact that sunspots are followed by magnetic disturbances on the earth that result in high rates of nervous and emotional diseases, accidents, suicides, and heart attacks. In some parts of the USSR, there are nationwide medical and safety alerts on the days following sudden bursts of solar activity.

Since it is a fundamental principle of Soviet medicine that the brain must be considered as a possible factor in all diseases and recovery processes, the electromagnetic environment is considered to be of great importance in health. In addition to the brain, it affects white blood cells, the liver, the kidneys, and other parts of the body. It is suspected that the body's immune system, which helps to resist disease, is sensitive to electromagnetic fields and that it may be damaged if the fields are too strong (Schiefelbein, 1979).

Most American scientists, basing their opinions on studies in which animals exposed to radio waves showed no gross tissue changes, have refused to be concerned about harm from the very low-energy waves of radio, television, and microwave ovens because there was no known mechanism by which they could act on living tissue. The energy involved, they asserted, was insufficient to cause a nerve to fire, so it could not possibly act on the brain. However, the Soviet researchers tend to think of nerves as complexes of water and molecules rather than as bags full of chemicals; they have looked for more subtle effects and found them. For example, they found that microwaves could affect epilepsy in animals. As a result of such studies, Soviet workers are protected, not only from high-energy X rays and nuclear radiation, but from electromagnetic radiation as well (Peat, 1976). Soviet physiologists hypothesize that nerve-cell firing is only one way in which the nervous system operates; there are other processes in the brain that may be sensitive to microwaves.

Chemical changes play the main roles when electromagnetic fields affect an organism. The major effect of electromagnetic fields is on the central nervous system, but in contrast to ordinary nerve-cell functioning, this effect is realized primarily through chemical changes in the glial cells—those cells that run alongside the central nervous system and that seem to be centers of electrical activity. In addition, the effect is propagated by a nonpulsed slow system. For example, in tests on lobsters, it was shown that slow changes in the membrane potential of one giant cell affected the discharge frequency of small cells located some distance away. This effect was achieved without the participation of nervous impulses.

I was reminded of Kholodov's work when I read about the role of glial cells in a direct-current electrical system in the body, which appears to be important in assisting recovery from injury and which correlates with many acupuncture points and meridians (Becker et al., 1976). I also learned of Karl Pribram's (1971) discovery of "slow-wave potentials"—slow impulses of electrical activity occurring between nerve cells. These slow potential energy alterations can be detected within the cell even in the absence of nerve impulses and can be influenced by extremely small amounts of energy. Thus they just might provide a clue by which we can conceptualize how ESP and PK can interact with the physical properties of the brain. Kholodov did not mention acupuncture, ESP, or PK, but his discoveries may someday help us to understand these phenomena.

There has been considerable confirmation (Becker, 1969; Brenner, Williamson, and Kaufman, 1975) for Kholodov's claim that the brain has its own electromagnetic field. These fields can even be detected outside the scalp and can serve as indicators of brain activity (Wortz, 1977). A. P. Dubrov (1974) advanced an even more intriguing idea—that all living organisms emit gravitational waves. Physicists recognize four forces in nature: electromagnetism, gravity, the strong nuclear force, and the weak nuclear force. That the brain emitted an electromagnetic field had been a startling discovery; Dubrov's proposal seemed far more outrageous.

Dubrov cited data from his experiments with polarizing microscopes (which divide light into its components for easier observation) to support his claim that high-frequency oscillations, or rhythmic movements of the cell's molecules, can generate "biogravitational" waves and propagate them over long distances. He observed that photons as well as ultrasonic sound can be observed emanating from cells as they divide. He then made an association between these rhythmic events to biogravitational waves, proposing that the human brain could coordinate these waves to produce observable effects.

What might some of these effects be? Dubrov suggested the movement of distant objects, air ionization during mental activity, the exposure of distant film, organic interaction with time, and the altering of molecular movement. In other words, human consciousness could coordinate the organism's gravitational waves emitted by dividing cells and produce any number of psi phenomena. He professed that his theories could explain the energy emission during the transformation of cell particles from a liquid state to a crystalline state in the process of mitosis on cell division. Earlier Soviet researchers had referred to this phenomenon as "mitogenic radiation," but it was dismissed as nonsense by most biologists in other parts of the world.

The Toth Incident

Four years later, mitogenic radiation again was in the news. On June 11, 1977, Robert Toth, an American journalist, was arrested in Moscow under bizarre circumstances. Earlier that day, Toth had received a telephone call from V. G. Petukhov, a biophysicist who directed the biophysics laboratory in the Institute of Medical and Biological Preparations, a center where Edward Naumov had conducted psi research in 1976. Petukhov offered Toth one of his research reports from the laboratory—a report said to demonstrate the existence of "psi particles" that are supposedly emitted during mitogenic radiation. Toth met Petukhov, was given the document, and was immediately arrested by the Soviet secret police. In a note to the U. S. Embassy, the Soviet Foreign Ministry said that the journalist had been engaged in "the collection of secret information of a political and military character." After several days of interrogation, Toth was released. Petukhov was praised for having helped the police "expose an archintelligence agent from one of the imperialist countries."

After leaving Moscow, Toth (1977) described an earlier conversation with Petukhov:

> His thesis . . . was that the psi particle is emitted when cells divide, that it can be detected and measured, and that this radiating particle can carry information. This would explain the basis for telepathy. . . . I told Petukhov that when he proved his theory, I would be interested in doing an article about it.
>
> About a month ago he phoned me and, when we met . . . he said his tests had been successful, that he intended to write up the experiments into scientific papers . . . for possible publication in the West. Soviet authorities would not let him publish his work, he said.
>
> So Saturday morning he phoned and asked to meet me. . . . He handed me the documents, more than twenty sheets including charts and photos of graphs, which I then held for about thirty seconds. . . . [p. 15]

In commenting on the case, Martin Ebon (1977) suggested that Toth had been lured into a clumsy Soviet encounter. Indeed, Toth had been charged by Tass, the Soviet news agency, with acting for "American special agencies." The Soviet press service accused Toth of having tried to turn Petukhov "into a regular and clandestine source of secret materials from a laboratory of an institute of a secret character." By taking Toth to a police station and interrogating him for a total of twelve hours on successive days, the Soviet authorities publicized the fact that parapsychological studies were being undertaken, secretly, at various research centers.

Perhaps the Soviet strategy was to determine what degree of publicity would be given the incident. Their answer was unambiguous; the incident became front-page news. I was interviewed about Soviet parapsychology and mitogenic radiation, as were several of my colleagues.

It should also be noted that in 1976, Toth had written an article concerning the possible use of radiation devices against the U. S. Embassy in Moscow. Therefore, the Soviets may have had a score to settle with Toth. This charge was echoed by Robert Beck in 1978; he claimed that Soviet technicians also have transmitted extreme low-frequency electromagnetic signals, capable of producing mood alterations in humans, to North America. The possible military uses of electromagnetic fields were described by J. L. Wilhelm in 1976. If any of this is true, it would represent a perversion of Kholodov's historic work.

The Mitogenic Rays

In 1979, I received a report that purported to be a summary of the document given to Toth by Petukhov. It paid tribute to A. G. Gurvich (1945), who studied plant roots, claiming to find that mitogenic rays, emitted by dividing cells, were transmitted through the root, stimulating other cells to divide. If another plant was growing nearby, cell division in that plant was also stimulated, because the mitogenic rays had the ability to extend beyond the root itself. He proposed that mitogenic radiation resembled a chain reaction; a mitogenic ray striking a cell could stimulate cell division and/or enable that cell to emit a radiation.

Since Gurvich's time, technology has advanced to the point where the mitogenic rays could be measured by photomultiplier tubes—extremely sensitive devices which detect tiny units of light (or photons) through an amplification process (or multiplier). Mitogenic radiation, it was claimed, ranged from about nineteen hundred to three thousand angstroms (a unit of length equal to one hundred-millionth centimeter used in discussing light waves). Experiments were conducted with a psychic sensitive with reputed PK ability. The tests attempted to study mitogenic rays. When the sensitive was relaxed, the photomultiplier tube detected very little ultraviolet radiation. But when he began to concentrate on manifesting PK by influencing another person, the rays sharply increased. The report conjectured: "Ultraviolet radiation may serve as a trigger mechanism for a general improvement in the bioenergetic reactions of another organism." It continued:

> It is not excluded that there may be forms of radiation as yet unknown, the clarification of whose physical nature may be achieved only in the course of further research. The solution might lie outside of traditional atomic and molecular radiation.

The report cited a monograph by N. I. Kobozev (1971) that hypothesized the existence of "superlight elementary particles." Kobozev claimed to have demonstrated that these particles would have to be infinitesimally smaller than an electron. The report concluded:

> It is just these particles that could be the source of the ultraviolet radiation so necessary for the Gurvich mitogenic effect; particles with a mass from 4 times 10^{-4} to 6 times 10^{-4} . . . [appear to] give off ultraviolet light . . . , covering the entire range of mitogenic radiation and, consequently, perhaps its source. In any case, the analysis carried out makes one consider adopting the particles as the source of mitogenic radiation and on this basis studying the Gurvich effect more closely.

Visitors to the USSR in 1977 had told me that Edward Naumov was searching for a "superlight particle" responsible for psi and mentioned Petukhov as one of his collaborators. However, if this report was indeed the document that caused Toth so much trouble, it was hardly worth the effort because the experiment it describes is only one step toward the discovery of the conjectured "psi particle."

In the meantime, other documents were sent to me listing some of the laboratories in which one or more researchers supposedly are attempting to identify the "psi particle." The centers cited were:

1. The Adjunct Laboratory of Medical and Biological Problems (Moscow).
2. The Institute of Problems of Transmission of Information (Moscow).
3. The Institute of Reflex Therapy (Moscow).
4. The Interdepartmental Commission for the Coordination of Work on the Biophysical Effect (Moscow).
5. Special Department No. 8, Institute of Automation and Electricity, Siberian Academy of Sciences (moved from Novosibirsk to Moscow in 1969).
6. Department of Cybernetics, Physical Engineering Institute (Moscow).
7. The Institute of Psychiatry and Neurology (Kharkov).
8. Laboratory of Biological Cybernetics, Department of Physiology, Leningrad University (Leningrad).

My conversations with scientific workers who have emigrated from the USSR suggest that this list is accurate. However, emigrés are not always infallible sources of information; to justify their decision to leave their country, they often give interviewers information that will please them even if it distorts an actual situation. Even so, and if the list represents only a partial compilation of Soviet parapsychological laboratories, it is possible that the Soviet efforts surpass those of any other nation.

Death of an Embryo

The best-known series of experiments that relate to mitogenic radiation involve tissue cultures (Kaznacheev et al., 1976). The basic experiment reportedly has been repeated hundreds of times and received a special diploma from the USSR State Committee for Inventions and Discoveries. The report acknowledges its debt to Gurvich and his discovery of electromagnetic radiation within the ultraviolet spectrum. It then describes the process by which tissue from a chicken embryo was divided and placed in two isolated metal containers. These containers were equipped with quartz windows that permitted optical contact between tissue cultures. Containers with glass windows were used for tissue cultures in a "control group."

The containers were placed on a revolving drum; their temperatures were kept constant and were monitored by thermostats. One of the two tissue cultures was then infected with a toxic virus or a poisonous chemical, or was exposed to lethal radiation. The embryo cultures were examined at the end of the second day and at twelve-hour intervals thereafter.

Not all the cultures were infected; these embryos showed no evidence of tissue degeneration. In the other cases, all embryos began to die; calculations were made of the percentage of cells that were found to be dead following each examination. For the tissues in containers with glass windows, only the infected cultures died. In the case of those with quartz windows, a "mirror effect" was observed; cells began to die in the noninfected containers. This "mirror effect" occurred whether the lethal agent had been a virus, a chemical, or radiation.

In the case of viral infection, the tissue began to degenerate within thirty-six hours. The noninfected tissue began to discolor twelve hours later. When photomultiplier tubes were employed, it was discovered that ultraviolet radiation emanated from the diseased tissue, passed through the quartz window, and infected the other tissue. Ultraviolet rays cannot pass through glass, hence the differential effect.

The ultraviolet radiation followed a pattern, first surging, then stopping, then surging again, then stopping. These four phases appeared to correspond to the stages the tissue went through when infected by the virus. First the cell wall was penetrated, then the cell shed its protein sheath, then new viruses were produced that finally burst from the cell, spreading the infection. The radiation resembled a "code" that had a lethal effect upon the noninfected tissue culture.

There are several implications of this experiment. Can mitogenic radiation, if it exists, be harmful as well as helpful? Could a healthy "code" be devised to halt the progress of a disease? Could a "code" be devised to protect an organism from a disease during an epidemic? Is the purported mitogenic effect a fluorescence (emitting radiation while it is absorbing radiation from another source) or a catalyst that accelerates an ongoing reaction without undergoing changes itself? Are there therapeutic effects in light that need to be explored?

I have been contacted by American scientists who hoped to repeat the experiments. However, from reading the reports, they found several questions unanswered. What amount of tissue was used? Were the chambers closed at the top? Is it necessary to rotate the cultures? If so, at what speed should they be rotated? What precautions were taken in introducing toxic materials to prevent contamination of the other preparation? What method was used to determine the number of cells killed? How was the "mirror" tissue examined? Were there variations in the various experiments? How close were the tissue cultures to the windows? How could such weak rays penetrate living tissue, creating profound effects? Unfortunately, this lack of detail permeates most of the Soviet articles in mitogenic radiation, psychoenergetics, and parapsychology. After reviewing the Soviet literature, one study team concluded that "most of the published material we have received is confusing, inaccurate, and of little value from a scientific point of view" (Wortz et al., 1979, p. 258).

In 1969, I spoke at a parapsychology symposium at UCLA. A paper had been sent from the USSR and was read in the absence of its author, I. M. Kogan, the engineer who chaired the Bioinformation Section of the Popov Society's Moscow Board. Kogan speculated that extremely low-frequency carrier waves might be responsible for ESP. Kogan's (1966, 1967, 1968) work involved three types of experiments: (1) clairvoyance without hypnosis over short distances, (2) telepathy over short distances in which subjects were aroused from hypnosis, and (3) telepathy over long distances. Kogan's main interest was the quantification of information obtained through psi. His major finding was that the information "bit" rate decreases from 0.1 "bit" for laboratory experiments to 0.005 "bit" for experiments conducted between cities. Kogan's work was hailed as the most sophisticated to be published in a Soviet journal.

However, a close analysis by F. A. Blau (1979) produced sobering results. Some details were incorrect, while others were incomplete. For example, it was stated that the distance between

Moscow and Tomsk is four thousand kilometers; actually it is approximately three thousand kilometers. In one paper, Kogan noted that "many" experiments were conducted, but does not give the number. More important is Kogan's observation that "results of data processing have been confined to successful experiments" (1968, p. 125). In one of these experiments, there were three telepathic receivers, but only one is discussed by Kogan, leaving open the possibility that the high score might have been due to chance, not psi. Questions could also be raised as to Kogan's rationale in determining information content; in an experiment in which a telepathic receiver was attempting to determine whether a comb or a glass was being transmitted, Kogan alleged that there are twenty-eight units of information but did not discuss how these units were determined. The Kogan experiments were among the few Soviet reports to be published in scientific journals rather than in popular magazines; thus their inadequacies were major disappointments.

It is necessary for published parapsychological experiments to adhere to key hallmarks of the scientific method (Tart, 1975, Chapter 1):

1. The procedures need to be public; the methods and the results must be both communicable and communicated. Secret research that is not made public does not deserve to be considered a part of science.
2. The report must contain a detailed description of what was done and how it was done so that another scientist can repeat the procedure. [Much of the criticism of mitogenic radiation research concerned the lack of specific details concerning the experiments.]
3. The definitions need to be precise. All variables must be well defined, and the techniques by which they were measured must be specific. For example, there are many types of hypnosis, and an investigator must describe what type of hypnotic induction was used and how its effects were measured.
4. The findings need to be replicable. Another scholar can test the finding by seeking to reproduce it. If the data were incorrectly collected, if the variables were inadequately measured, or if the procedures were adversely influenced by experimental bias, the findings will not be amenable to replication.

A Religion Without a Cross?

The lack of scientific rigor in Soviet parapsychology is due to several factors. It had to operate underground during the years of the Stalinist repression. When it surfaced, it was still surrounded by controversy. Proper scientific publishing outlets were not available, and the popular press did not print articles that adhered to scientific standards (Pratt, 1977).

The controversy over psi continues. The article in *Questions of Philosophy* by four distinguished Soviet psychologists was an important event, as it called for a high standard of investigating ESP and PK. Furthermore, the article made several procedural suggestions for accomplishing this goal. But Vladimir Lvov (1976), the outspoken critic of parapsychology, complained:

> There are . . . people historical experience does not benefit . . . for example, the four psychologists . . . who published a collective article. . . . They stated, "In what is called parapsychology, one has to distinguish on the one hand, opinions described by mystics and charlatans as to 'supernatural' phenomena really existing but not yet fully explained scientifically satisfactorily. . . ." It is a hundred years since adherents of the "secret psychism" of those days wrote about table-lifting and communication with the dead. Thus the authors of this article in *Questions of Philosophy* repeated the same errors. More regrettable is their proposal to attract attention of serious scientific organizations to those phenomena described in parapsychology and earlier shown by psychiatrists as various forms of paranoid delirium.

The other Soviet antagonist, Alexander Kitaigorodsky (1977), complained:

> Recently, I read an article about parapsychology in one of our most highly respected journals written—much to my amazement—by psychologists. Think of it: Scholars . . . telling us about circus tricks!
> . . . Where does parapsychology belong? The answer is that it should be relegated to the intellectual junkheap. . . .

Criticism was also forthcoming from *Hung Chi,* the monthly theoretical publication of the Chinese Communist Party (Chen, 1975):

Lenin said that matter acts upon our sensory organs in order to create impressions. Without impressions, it is impossible for us to recognize the shape of an object or the nature of a movement. Lenin's traitorous sons and grandsons in the Soviet Union have come to disregard these truths entirely. The Kremlin has fostered a parapsychology fad that has created a religion without a cross in the U.S.S.R. Because religion has become threadbare today, the revisionist scientists of the Soviet Union have transplanted the psyche of the church into the scientific laboratory.

However, Soviet parapsychologists frequently cite V. I. Lenin to support their position that psi phenomena should be studied and that they will be found to have a material base. In his book *Materialism and Empiro-Criticism,* Lenin (1968) quoted Marx's colleague, Friedrich Engels, to the effect that "Consciousness and thinking, however suprasensuous they may seem, are the products of a material . . . organ, the brain" (p. 87). Lenin continued:

It is, of course, sheer nonsense to say that materialism ever maintained that consciousness is "less" real, or necessarily professed a "mechanical," and not an electromagnetic, or some other, immeasurably more complex, picture of the world of *moving matter.* [p. 280]

Parapsychologists have also observed that Pavlov (1925) was open-minded on the topic. He once wrote, "In some cases where ordinary conscious activity undergoes changes, the differentiation ability becomes sharper. In the peculiar state of so-called clairvoyance, this ability comes with infinitesimal subtlety" (p. 520).

Vasili Kasatkin conducts dream research at Leningrad's Neurological Surgical Institute, where he uses his patients' dreams to help diagnose the onset and course of their illnesses. He claims that Pavlov once dreamed about his son, Volodya, returning from World War I, although he had not heard from the young man for many months. Nevertheless, Pavlov told his wife to set up a samovar to welcome Volodya—and by the time the tea was ready, their son returned (Gris and Dick, 1978, p. 211).

The most unusual dreamlike report to come out of the Soviet

Union in recent years involves Lenin. The Twenty-second Congress of the Communist Party was held in Moscow during 1961 and is best remembered for Nikita Khrushchev's stirring speech, "The Crimes of the Stalin Era." Some days after Khrushchev's denunciations, Darya Lazurkina rose to speak. She had known Lenin as a girl and had survived two decades in the labor camps of the Gulag, having been a victim of a Stalinist purge. Lazurkina told the Congress, "Lenin was my heart; he sustained and advised me." Her voice trembling, Lazurkina continued to relate how the previous day, apparently in a dream, Lenin had appeared to her, saying, "It is unpleasant for me to lie next to Stalin in the mausoleum, he caused so much harm." Stalin's body was soon removed and was buried without ceremony behind the Kremlin. Lazurkina's remarks were published in the official transcript of the Congress (Ebon, 1962).

On the last day of the 1973 Prague Conference, I was elected vice president for the International Association for Psychotronic Research. Since then, I have frequently heard this question asked: What is one to make of the enigma of Soviet parapsychology? There is some evidence that parapsychological research is an ongoing enterprise, although little of it is published. The data that are reported typically are incomplete and presented in popular magazines rather than in scientific journals. Furthermore, their authors seem to be working on a part-time basis with little official support. Is this work the tip of the iceberg? Or is the reputed massive parapsychological effort a mirage—one encouraged by Soviet officialdom to produce fear and anxiety in other nations? Is there really something to hide, or are the Soviets overly concerned that they might be accused of betraying Marxism if they revealed the extent of their psi research? J. G. Pratt (1973), until his death in 1979, the most knowledgeable American parapsychologist in this area, wrote that many Western observers have dismissed Soviet parapsychology as "much ado about nothing." Pratt stated that they are incorrect, noting:

> The fact that a stirring of scientific interest in ESP has occurred at all where it was so unexpected would even by itself be a matter of major importance. [p. 56]

And there the matter stands until further information is available.

References

Bakirov, A. G. The geological possibilities of biophysical method. *Proceedings, First International Conference on Psychotronic Research*. Prague: Cerven, 1973.

Bakirov, A. G., et al. [Yes, the biophysical method does exist. *Geology of Ore Deposits*,] July–Aug. 1976.

Beck, R. C. Extreme low frequency magnetic fields entrainment: A psychotronic warfare possibility? *Association for Humanistic Psychology Newsletter*, Apr. 1978.

Becker, R. O. The effect of magnetic fields upon the central nervous system. In M. F. Barnothy (ed.), *Biological Effects of Magnetic Fields*, Vol. 2. New York: Plenum Press, 1969.

Becker, R. O., et al. Electrophysiological correlates of acupuncture points and meridians. *Psychoenergetic Systems*, 1976, *1*, 105–12.

Bird, C. *The Divining Hand: The 500-year-old Mystery of Dowsing*. New York: E. P. Dutton, 1979.

Blau, F. A. Personal communication, Oct. 1979.

Bradna, J. Interpersonal relations and energetic transfer. *Proceedings, First International Conference on Psychotronic Research*. Prague: Cerven, 1973.

Brenner, D.; Williamson, S. J.; and Kaufman, L. Visually evoked magnetic fields in the human brain. *Science*, 1975, *190*, 480–82.

Chamberlain, J. Soviet "ultimate weapon"? New Haven *Register*, June 21, 1976.

Chen, C. [The miraculous use of telepathy.] *Hung Chi*, Jan. 1975.

Dubrov, A. P. Biogravitation and psychotronics. *Impact of Science on Society*, 1974, *24*, 311–19.

————. The interaction of biological objects with time and space. *Psychoenergetic Systems*, 1976, *1*, 209–14.

————. *The Geomagnetic Field and Life: Geomagnetobiology*. New York: Plenum Press, 1978.

Ebon, M. Russia explores inner space. *Tomorrow,* Winter 1962. Account taken from [*Proceedings, Twenty-second Congress of the Communist Party of the Soviet Union,*] Vol. 3. Moscow: State Publishers of Political Literature, 1962, p. 121.

———. Moscow's ESP dilemma. *The Humanist,* Sept./Oct. 1977.

Foulkes, R. A. Dowsing experiments. *Nature,* 1971, *229,* 163–68.

Gris, H., and Dick, W. *The New Soviet Psychic Discoveries.* Englewood Cliffs, N.J.: Prentice-Hall, 1978.

Gurvich, A. G. [*Mitogenic Radiation.*] Moscow: Medgiz, 1945.

Harvalik, Z. V. Anatomical localization of human detection of weak electromagnetic radiation: Experiments with dowsers. *Physiological Chemistry and Physics,* 1978, *10,* 525–34.

Kaznacheev, V. P., et al. Distant intercellular interactions in a system of two tissue cultures. *Psychoenergetic Systems,* 1976, *1,* 141–42.

Kholodov, Y. A. Effects on the central nervous system. In M. F. Barnothy (ed.), *Biological Effects of Magnetic Fields,* Vol. 1. New York: Plenum Press, 1964.

———. *The Effect of Electromagnetic Fields on the Central Nervous System.* Springfield, Va.: Clearinghouse for Federal Scientific and Technical Information, 1967. (Originally published in 1966.)

Kitaigorodsky, A. [Just a vaudeville act. *Literary Gazette,*] May 25, 1977.

Kobozev, N. I. [*Research in the Thermodynamics of Information and Thought Processes.*] Moscow: Moscow State University, 1971.

Kogan, I. M. [Is telepathy possible? *Radio Engineering,*] 1966, *21,* 75.

———. [Telepathy: Hypotheses and observations. *Radio Engineering,*] 1967, *22,* 141.

——— [Information theory analysis of telepathic communication. *Radio Engineering,*] 1968, *23,* 122.

Kozyrev, N. A. *Possibility of Experimental Study of the Properties of Time.* Washington, D.C.: Joint Publications Research Service, U. S. Department of Commerce, 1968.

Krippner, S. A firsthand look at psychotronic generators. In

J. White and S. Krippner (eds.), *Future Science.* Garden City, N.Y.: Anchor Books, 1977.

Krippner, S., and Hickman, J. L. West meets East: A parapsychological détente. *Psychic,* June 1974.

Krippner, S., and Villoldo, A. *The Realms of Healing.* Millbrae, Calif.: Celestial Arts Press, 1976.

Krmessky, J. How to look for energies with PK mobiles. In S. Ostrander and L. Schroeder (eds.), *The ESP Papers.* New York: Bantam Books, 1976.

Lenin, V. I. *Collected Works,* Vol. 14. Moscow: Progress Publishers, 1968. (Originally published in 1928.)

Lvov, V. [Myths and realities in the Soviet Union.] *Le Monde,* Aug. 4, 1976.

Maire, L. F., and LaMothe, J. D. *Soviet and Czechoslovakian Parapsychology Research.* Washington, D.C.: U. S. Army Medical Intelligence Information Agency, 1975.

Patrovsky, V. Magnetized water and plant growth. *Proceedings, First International Congress on Psychotronic Research.* Prague: Cerven, 1973.

Pavlov, I. P. *Complete Collected Works,* Vol. 5. Moscow: Progress Publishers, 1925.

Peat, R. *Mind and Tissue: Russian Research Perspectives on the Human Brain.* Claremont, Calif.: Khalsa Publications, 1976.

Pratt, J. G. *ESP Research Today: A Study of Developments in Parapsychology Since 1960.* Metuchen, N.J.: Scarecrow Press, 1973.

————. Soviet research in parapsychology. In B. B. Wolman (ed.), *Handbook of Parapsychology.* New York: Van Nostrand Reinhold, 1977.

Presman, A. S. *Electromagnetic Fields and Life.* New York: Plenum Press, 1970.

Pribram, K. H. *Languages of the Brain.* Englewood Cliffs, N.J.: Prentice-Hall, 1971.

Rejdák, Z. What is psychotronics? *Journal of Paraphysics,* 1974, *8,* 26–29.

Rocard, Y. Actions of a very weak magnetic gradient: The reflex of the dowser. In M. F. Barnothy (ed.), *Biological Effects of Magnetic Fields,* Vol. 1. New York: Plenum Press, 1969.

Rossman, M. *New Age Blues.* New York: E. P. Dutton, 1979.

Schiefelbein, S. The invisible threat. *Saturday Review,* Sept. 1979.

Tart, C. T. (ed.). *Transpersonal Psychologies.* New York: Harper & Row, 1975.

Toth, R. C. Newsman's Soviet arrest over ESP secrets. San Francisco *Chronicle,* June 13, 1977.

Tserkover, E. The talents of Tophik Dadashev. *International Journal of Paraphysics,* 1979, *13,* 56–58.

Whitton, J. L., and Cook, S. A. Can humans detect weak magnetic fields? *New Horizons,* 1978, *2* (4), 1–6.

Wilhelm, J. L. *The Search for Superman.* New York: Pocket Books, 1976.

Williamson, T. Dowsing achieves new credence. *New Scientist,* Feb. 1979.

Wolf, J. The integral study of the person, culture and society in anthropology. *Psychoenergetic Systems,* 1975, *1,* 87–89.

Wortz, E. C. Cited in: Soviet remote sensor reportedly detects EEGs from a distance. *Brain/Mind Bulletin,* May 2, 1977.

Wortz, E. C., et al. An investigation of Soviet psychical research. In C. T. Tart, H. E. Puthoff, and R. Targ (eds.), *Mind at Large.* New York: Praeger, 1979.

Zezulka, J. One healer's views. *Proceedings, Second International Congress on Psychotronic Research.* Paris: Institut Métaphysique International, 1975.

CHAPTER 4

Fasting in Moscow and Other Soviet Therapies

> . . . the Soviet psychotherapist is concerned with the active mobilization of the personality and its compensatory powers on the basis of . . . creating new, powerful dynamic structures which, insofar as they are the more powerful, are capable . . . of extinguishing and destroying the pathologically dynamic structures that have given rise to the illness.
>
> N. V. Ivanov
> (In Ziferstein, 1976, p. 173)

In 1971, our laboratory at the Maimonides Medical Center was provided with an Electrosone 50 device. This machine was an experimental model developed by the National Patent Development Corporation, which had obtained patent rights from the USSR. The original Soviet version was a device to induce "electrosleep," an alteration in consciousness purportedly therapeutic for patients with insomnia and anxiety problems (Khromchenko, 1970). According to a report in *Soviet Life* (March, 1980) it has also been used to stabilize arterial pressure, improve blood circulation in the brain, prevent fatigue, and improve workers' efficiency.

I volunteered to be the first person in the laboratory to experience electrosleep. Electrodes were attached above my eyebrows and on the mastoid bones behind my ears. As the Electrosone 50 was activated, a mild current flowed over my head and I felt very relaxed. Soon I began to visualize colorful images: a jungle scene in which a butterfly was perched on top of a puma, a mountain covered with snow and gnarled pine trees, a picnic on Mount Olympus attended by gods and goddesses. By the time the electrodes were unfastened, I had decided to use the Electrosone 50 in an experiment (Krippner and Brown, 1973).

Field Dependence, Field Independence

We enlisted the services of thirty college students, who were randomly assigned to an experimental group or to a control group. There were eight female and seven male experimental subjects; the control subjects consisted of seven females and eight males. All subjects were administered a test to see if they were "field dependent" (susceptible to an embedding context and open to external suggestions) or "field independent" (not dependent on a context and not easily influenced by external suggestions). Group scores averaged about the same, but subjects who scored above the average were classified "field dependent," while those falling below the average score for their group were placed in the "field independent" category (Witkin et al., 1962).

The Electrosone 50 is a low-voltage unit that operates on batteries with a peak output of 50 volts. Four electrodes are attached to it and, after their placement on the subject's head, are held in place with a sleep mask. A mild current is passed through the electrodes and flows across the subject's head. For our experimental subjects, we used a pulse frequency of 100 cycles per second and a pulse duration of 0.1 to 0.3 millisecond for a duration of 20 minutes. For our control subjects, we simply did not turn on the current.

Before the experiment began, all subjects signed a consent form and were told:

This is the Electrosone 50, a machine that has been found to produce relaxation among subjects in other experiments. You will receive either a very low or a high current with this machine. However, I cannot tell you at this time which type of current you will receive. After all the subjects have participated in this study, you will be told. If you received the very low current, you will have an opportunity to return to the laboratory for a session at the higher current.

The subjects were also taught our 5-point state report scale in which "0" represents no change in consciousness and "4" indicates that one has become oblivious to the external surroundings. All subjects were asked for a state report before the electrodes were attached and at the end of the 20-minute session. The subjects in the experimental group gave an average initial report of 0.7 and a second report of 2.2 following 20 minutes with Electrosone 50. The reports of the control group were almost identical (0.4 and 2.3) despite the fact that the machine had not been turned on.

Field-independent subjects in the experimental group had an average post-Electrosone 50 score of 2.6, while the field-dependent individuals averaged 1.4. In the control group, the field-independent group averaged 3.1, while the field-dependent group again averaged 1.4. The latter difference was significant, a surprising development to those who thought that the suggestibility of the field-dependent group would enhance their state reports. However, this state report is based on the degree of concentration a subject can place on internal events—a trait in which the field-independent group excels.

Thus we obtained evidence that one does not have to be field dependent to enjoy an alteration in consciousness. Indeed, for changed mental states demanding inner attentiveness, the field-independent person may excel. As for the control condition, it again demonstrated the effectiveness of the placebo effect: If you give a person a piece of candy and a suggestion that it is really a powerful medicine, the illness may vanish.

The Powerful Placebo

The importance of the placebo effect in medicine and psychotherapy cannot be overemphasized. Its effectiveness rests solely in its ability to mobilize the patient's expectancy of assistance. A physician might use a sugar pill rather than a drug in treating a patient's problem to avoid the possibility of addiction or the drug's aftereffects. The word "placebo" comes from the Latin phrase "I shall please," and the patient's hope and expectations are so powerful that they can often stimulate self-healing if the placebo serves as an effective trigger. In one study of patients who had been hospitalized with bleeding peptic ulcers, 70 percent showed excellent results lasting at least a year when the physician gave them an injection of distilled water, telling them it was a new medicine that would cure them (Volgyesi, 1954). With psychiatric patients, placebos are very effective; in five separate studies involving a total of 56 patients, an average of 55 percent showed symptomatic improvement from placebos (Frank, 1973, p. 141).

The study of brain neurotransmitters has been helpful in determining a mechanism by which placebos might work. For example, pain travels in nerve cells in the form of electrical impulses. To cross the synapse, or gap between two cells, the electrical message changes into a chemical carrier called a neurotransmitter, which travels on to the next nerve. It then changes back into an electrical message and continues its journey. However, the brain may produce enkephalin—an opiumlike neurotransmitter that can block the pain by keeping the neurotransmitter from jumping the gap.

A number of studies have been reported that suggest that placebos may activate enkephalin and other bodily healing mechanisms (Levine, 1979, p. 5). Over the centuries, physicians and psychotherapists have used remedies and treatment procedures that, from the view of modern Western medicine, were useless. Nevertheless, they may have worked anyway because of the faith placed in them by the patient.

The role of the placebo reminded me of the studies initiated by D. N. Uznadze (1967) on the concept of "set." Uznadze used this term to describe psychoneurological changes that play an important role in the dynamics of succeeding conscious experiences. Sets are held to be the most important elements of unconscious activity and form the most important components of goal-directed behavior. Many sets are "nonfixed"—adequate to a given situation but short-lasting. Other sets are "fixed" and firmly es-

misinterprets the data (e.g., becomes convinced that Mr. Katz next door is a member of the KGB . . .), and hooks up the wrong emotion to the data (e.g., giggles when told that his mother has died). [p. 15]

The Fasting Treatment

During 1971, I met Yuri Sergeyvitch Nikolayev, a Soviet psychiatrist who had initiated a remarkable treatment program for schizophrenics. Nikolayev (1970) invited me to his clinic when I returned in 1972, and I was permitted to bring along our group from the Association for Humanistic Psychology (Krippner, 1974). A psychiatrist friend of mine, Allan Cott (1971), had been to the clinic during the previous year and was favorably impressed with Nikolayev's procedures.

We gathered at the Fasting Treatment Unit of the Moscow Psychiatric Institute at the P. B. Gannushkin Memorial Hospital to meet the staff and the patients. We were told that since the Institute opened in 1948, some eight thousand patients had been treated. According to Nikolayev's follow-up studies, 64 percent of them made considerable improvement; 47 percent maintained their improvement without symptom recurrence over a six-year span.

The Fasting Treatment Unit accommodates forty male and forty female patients at any one time. It occupies one floor of the Moscow Psychiatric Institute, a three-thousand-bed psychiatric research center that has five hundred physicians on its staff.

Most of Nikolayev's patients request admission to the unit. Others are referred, and the remainder are transferred from other units when all conventional treatments have failed. All patients must agree to adhere to the required routine of the treatment but may leave at any time. If a patient breaks the routine, the treatment is terminated. Many patients who break the posttreatment regimen relapse; for the remainder, the maximum effects of the procedure occur three or four months after the treatment has been initiated.

Nikolayev, in his initial address to our group, commented that the basic principles of his method were to create a rest for the central nervous system, free the organism from all poisonous substances, organize the natural defense forces of the system, and restructure the personality of his patients so that they change their habits after treatment. Therefore, the arriving patient is placed on a fast for approximately thirty days, the exact time depending on the patient's condition and progress. Although the patients can drink as much distilled water as they like, they can have no food.

Nikolayev hypothesized that some types of schizophrenia are caused by allergies and related conditions that produce toxins in the body. These toxins can be eliminated through fasting and a daily enema with a magnesium solution. The patients receive a daily massage, supportive counseling, the option of an afternoon nap, and are encouraged to walk outdoors for long periods of time in the Institute's beautiful park. Breathing exercises and a minimum of three hours of physical exercise are required each day.

In most instances, the patients' delusions and hallucinations begin to disappear, their emotionality becomes more appropriate to their observable behavior, and they start to relate to other people. They discuss their personality changes with other patients in regularly scheduled periods of group therapy. In some cases, acupuncture, hypnosis, and autogenic training (a form of relaxation therapy) are utilized as well. Nikolayev observed that relationships with other patients form an important part of the therapy; he noted, "Sometimes patients treat each other more skillfully than do the psychiatrists."

During the fast, Nikolayev's patients appear to change dramatically in appearance. During the first few days of fasting, a patient's appetite is very intense. Then the appetite diminishes, the tongue becomes coated, and the body develops acidosis—a condition of drastically reduced alkaline content in the body. Depression is not uncommon at this stage of the treatment, but once it disappears, the patient feels stronger and in a better mood. The patient's tongue clears, the acidosis diminishes, and the skin color improves, as does the muscle tone. By the end of the fourth week, Nikolayev's patients have lost between 18 and 26 percent of their body weight, a few losing as much as 50 percent.

Once Nikolayev and his staff feel that the toxins have been

eliminated from the patient's body, the fast is terminated. Strained fruit and vegetable juices gradually are introduced; vitamins and minerals, in their natural forms, are given in large quantities. For example, rose hip tea is served because it is rich in vitamin C. Buttermilk and salt-free salads follow. Bread is not added until the second week; meats, fish, and eggs are added even later. Whenever a particular food becomes associated with the recurrence of symptoms, that food is removed from the patient's diet permanently. As a result, many of the patients are never allowed to resume consumption of white sugar. Some are forbidden to eat salt, red meat, or white bread; others are told that they have allergies to strawberries or cucumbers. Any of the forbidden foods, it is claimed, will bring back the patients' schizophrenic behaviors.

A diet rich in fruit and vegetables is worked out for each departing patient. Alcohol and tobacco are to be avoided even if they are not on the allergy list. Most patients quickly regain the weight they lost during the fast. However, they are advised to take occasional fasts of three to five days each, not exceeding ten days in one month. Even these fasts are terminated when the patient's appetite is restored and when the symptoms have disappeared.

Studies at the Department of Hematology and Genetics of the Moscow Psychiatric Institute have shown that some types of schizophrenics have a higher protein level than nonschizophrenics; but after the controlled fasting, their protein level is normal. If the protein level rises again, short fasts will reduce it (Cott, 1971, p. 5). Other schizophrenics may suffer from hypoglycemia, a condition in which body sugar is not utilized effectively. Controlled fasting is said to correct this problem as well. Although Nikolayev uses drugs with some patients at the beginning of their therapy, fasting is frequently recommended for those who have adverse reactions to drugs. Nikolayev had just started to use large doses of vitamins and minerals with some patients during my 1972 visit. These nutrients were administered during the postfast period and appeared greatly to assist the recovery of several patients.

Nikolayev emphasized that his entire program was grounded in I. P. Pavlov's concept that the central nervous system can be returned to health by various types of inhibition—for example, fasting, resting, massage, walking in the park. He noted that Pavlov's work resembled that of Hans Selye (1956), the Canadian physician who coined the term "nonspecific stress" to describe a condition of tension in living matter that manifests itself by changes in the body's organs and glands. Selye came to the conclusion that many illnesses are diseases of adaptation rather than the primary results of infection. In other words, the body is affected by stress before it is infected; the stressful condition leaves the body vulnerable to infection and other ills. Nikolayev told us that Selye's ideas could also be applied to the onset of schizophrenia and its treatment, a treatment that restores the central nervous system to health rather than merely treating symptoms.

Case Studies

Following Nikolayev's tour and discussion, he introduced a few patients who told us their stories through interpreters. It was obvious that "schizophrenia" was even more of an umbrella category in the USSR than in the USA; nevertheless, the patients were quite disturbed and many had undergone other treatment programs without success. One young man reported the onset of schizophrenia at the age of sixteen. He lost his time and space orientation, his language became irrational, and he began to think about committing suicide. His aberrant behavior was reported and he was hospitalized. At the time of our visit, he was in his twenty-eighth day of fasting. He told us that his schizophrenic symptoms had disappeared and that he would be breaking the fast in two days.

Another patient had suffered from schizophrenia for four years. He had lost interest in his university studies and felt so isolated that he could not hold a conversation or even answer simple questions. After fifteen weeks of the treatment, he felt vastly improved, was beginning to talk with his fellow patients, and was planning to resume his education.

A fifty-six-year-old schizophrenic man had also suffered from a disease of the skin as well as high blood pressure. In the first week of his fast, his skin cleared up. He broke the fast after twenty days, then resumed the fast for nine days. His blood pressure dropped and his schizophrenic symptoms disappeared.

Nikolayev told us that many of his patients suffer from a type of schizophrenia that is characterized by a fear of offending bodily gases and odors. These patients are convinced that everyone near them can hear the sounds and smell the odors. These patients are difficult to help because they tend to avoid people, but the fasting procedure has assisted many of them to overcome their fears.

One patient told us that he had walked over two hundred miles to reach the clinic for help. In another case, the patient did not have schizophrenia at all; he weighed five hundred pounds, and the members of his village sent him to Nikolayev telling him to return only when he had lost enough weight not to be a disgrace to his community.

As other patients told their stories, several members of the group commented that Nikolayev had turned our visit to good advantage. This opportunity to discuss their progress with outsiders was therapeutic in its own right. It was also observed that Nikolayev's program was holistic; perhaps the group therapy, occupational therapy, and exercise contributed as much to a patient's recovery as the fast did. And what of the placebo effect? Any patient willing to give up food for a month could be expected to have faith in the procedure and to be highly motivated to recover. Faith and hope can stimulate physiological and psychological changes even among seriously disturbed patients (Shapiro and Morris, 1978, p. 395). However, Nikolayev claimed that infants and young children benefit from fasting for various disorders; for them, the placebo effect probably would not operate. What is needed is additional inquiry as to the effects each portion of the program might have upon a patient's recovery.

The American research in schizophrenia indicates that psychotherapy for schizophrenics tends to be ineffective unless it is combined with the use of such drugs as chlorpromazine, thioridazine, or stelazine (Hollon and Beck, 1978). A member of our group asked if the fasting treatment was being used in the United States. Nikolayev referred to a successful project inaugurated by Allan Cott (1974), the New York psychiatrist who had visited him in Moscow. Nikolayev pointed out that the New York City program charged its patients one hundred dollars per day; the Moscow treatment was free of charge.

In 1977, Frank Ervin and Robert Palmour reported that they had isolated a chemical from the blood of schizophrenics that may be at the root of their illness. The American scientists described the substance as a "brain opiate" and named it leuendorphin. Of ten patients undergoing hemodialysis, or blood purification with a kidney machine, seven showed a pronounced remission of symptoms. This study, if replicated, would lend further support to Nikolayev's theories.

The Soviet System

I later learned that the Soviet structure of psychiatric services is much simpler than is the American system, with its mix of private and public facilities. The Soviet health-care system provides geographically placed "health dispensaries" that are free and readily available to patients (Bieliauskas, 1977; Holland, 1976). From there, patients are often referred to more specialized clinics, such as neuropsychiatric dispensaries that provide for care of patients who do not need to be hospitalized. Some of these patients are hospitalized, in which case they will be assigned to a different physician. However, they usually return to their former therapist once they are switched from inpatient to outpatient status.

The neuropsychiatric dispensary can also function as a day-care hospital and as an occupational therapy center. Its patients may be suffering from alcoholism, mental retardation, speech and language difficulties, epilepsy, and other neurological problems, as well as emergencies that may arise in the course of childhood, adolescence, or marriage. This single-care system leads to efficient and rapid detection of mental illness as well as assured follow-up of the patient. It is unlike the American system, which has no central authority and no mechanism to insure continuity of care when a patient moves from one facility to another (Holland, 1976, pp. 137–38).

When E. Fuller Torrey (in Hines, 1971) visited Leningrad on behalf of the U. S. National Institute of Mental Health, he observed a psychiatric ambulance service that could be dispatched to a patient within a few minutes at any time of the day or night. A psychiatrist and two assistants staffed the ambulance and gave immediate assistance; Torrey noted that Soviet police were never used in handling psychiatric emergencies. By giving the patients immediate treatment in the same location where the crisis took place and by calming patients before they went to the hospital, the average period of hospitalization was decreased.

On the other hand, there is less emphasis on the mental patient's legal rights in the Soviet Union. There is no legal review of patients who are admitted, either voluntarily or involuntarily, to ordinary mental hospitals. Soviet citizens who are accused of a crime, but are suspected of being mentally ill, are handled through a judicial psychiatric system that functions quite separately from the usual procedure. These patients would not be admitted to a regular mental hospital but would go directly to a judicial or legal unit (Holland, 1976, p. 138).

Several Soviet psychiatrists have attempted to correct some of the system's problems. Alexander Voloshanovich (1978) checked the records of twenty-seven persons who claimed they had been wrongly committed to mental institutions and found "not a single case of definite mental illness." E. P. Kazanetz (1979), of Moscow's Serbski Institute of Forensic Psychiatry, reviewed over seven hundred patient records from Gannushkin Hospital. In his opinion, retaining an individual in a psychiatric hospital long after a single psychotic episode can result in an unnecessary restriction of that patient's social and vocational rights and responsibilities. He found the term "schizophrenia" to be applied very broadly and to have been incorrectly used in cases that a close examination revealed to be situational stresses, somatic disturbances, or temporary disorders of mood and feeling. He concluded that his results pointed out "the necessity for revising many long-standing diagnoses of schizophrenia. . . ."

Concepts of Mental Illness

Both Soviet and American psychiatrists share the concept that schizophrenia and manic-depressive psychosis have both biological and environmental roots. However, Soviet therapists are more likely to take careful genealogical histories and pay attention to the neurological status of their patients.

One of my colleagues at Maimonides Medical Center's Department of Psychiatry was Joseph Wortis (1950), who had published the first comprehensive book on Soviet psychiatry in English. Wortis' good relationship with the Soviet psychiatrists was one of the factors responsible for his appearance before a congressional investigative committee in the 1950s, as a suspected "fellow traveler" and Communist "sympathizer." Wortis' son was a classmate of mine at the University of Wisconsin, and I was able to read the transcript of the hearing. It was a war of wits; the congressmen came out second best.

In his book, Wortis discussed Pavlov's influence on Soviet psychiatry. Pavlov (1951) had defined "higher nervous activity" as that occurring in the brain's cortex and subcortex; the activity ensures for the organism an adaptation in its complex relations with the outside world. The remainder of the brain and spinal cord control the integration of the various parts of the organism through "lower nervous activity." Mental illness is typically a breakdown in the responsiveness of the higher nervous activity. The breakdowns may occur in various areas of conditioned reflex activity, giving rise to a number of pathological symptoms.

Two systems of higher nervous activity signals were effective in producing conditioned reflexes, the cortical "first signal system" (direct sensations of objects in the environment) and the subcortical "second signal system" (abstractions of reality, expressed primarily through speech). The signals of the first system often come into play when the second system breaks down during sleep, hypnosis, or schizophrenia—producing dreams, fantasies, or hallucinations. On the other hand, an obsessive-compulsive individual would demonstrate a predominance of the verbal, intellectual second signal system over the sensory, concrete, emotional first signal system. Pavlov felt that the nervous system could be inhibited. In hysteria, the cortex cells become fatigued and their activity is inhibited or stimulated. The subcortical centers then take control and violent discharges or hysterical fits often result.

In the USSR today, the use of prolonged sleep therapy (up to one hundred hours) is explained as providing protection to the nerve cells that have been traumatized by excessive stimulation. Drugs are carefully selected by psychiatrists on the basis of whether excitation or inhibition should be produced. During psychotherapy, most Soviet therapists carefully avoid repeating their patients' negative statements for fear that the unhealthy attitude will be reinforced in the patient's higher nervous activity. Instead, the therapist gives a positive suggestion, using the therapist's authority to initiate a new attitudinal pattern.

Soviet psychotherapy is also influenced by the writings of Karl Marx and V. I. Lenin; both pointed out that the social structure in which individuals are born and reared is crucial in determining the way in which their neurophysiological functioning develops. A. R. Luria (1976) added, "The basic categories of human mental life can be understood as products of social history . . ." (p. 164).

A third basic theoretical aspect is the study of a patient's intrapsychic conflicts, the role of the unconscious, and the process of "uncovering" these influences during treatment (Ziferstein, 1976). An example of the latter process is "rational psychotherapy," a system that aims to restructure the interpersonal relations of patients, helping them to resolve their real-life problems constructively. A related procedure, "dynamic psychotherapy," involves a review of the traits a person may wish to change with a re-examination of relevant past experiences. Rapport with the patient is obtained by demonstrating interest and concern; the therapist then helps the patient interpret his or her past experiences, indicating how what is learned can be helpful in designing a more realistic and mature posture in life.

Soviet psychiatrists who follow those approaches play an active role in treatment. One example of this activity is the therapist's frequent manipulation of the patient's environment, career, residence, or job placement. Work becomes a healing force; group therapy may be utilized. Since the collective is considered to be a central factor in the security system of individuals, the satisfaction of their material and emotional needs, and the furthering of their growth and development, Soviet psychotherapists call upon the various collectives in society to help in therapeutic work. For example, case histories of patients are obtained not only from their families but also from members of their trade unions. The collectives of fellow patients and of the staff are consciously employed as an encouraging and supportive—but also pressuring, corrective, and reality-testing—medium.

Occupational therapy is not confined to basket weaving, as in many American hospitals. Sometimes mental patients constitute complete production units; I was told of one unit in Leningrad that has six full-size looms and manufactures snowsuits. The patients receive full industrial-scale pay for their work. Some chronic psychotic patients are kept in country work villages, but most patients are released and are said to be better able to support themselves than when they entered.

In this regard, N. V. Ivanov (1961), as chief of the Psychiatry Department of the Kirov Institute of Medicine, compared the retroactive emphasis of foreign group therapy with the Soviet attempt to condition the nervous processes of the patient and to develop new connections and structures in the nervous system. "Collective psychotherapy" (which incorporates people from the patient's social group in the therapy sessions) is practiced in connection with individual psychotherapy. Sometimes dream interpretation, psychodrama, family therapy, and conjoint marital therapy are utilized as well as electrosleep, hydrotherapy, physical therapy, and acupuncture. One observer (Ziferstein, 1976), following a visit to the Bekhterev Institute in Leningrad, commented:

> . . . I was able to observe how, consciously and unconsciously, the staff used the collective as a therapeutic instrument. The patient's time was almost totally occupied with a variety of activities involving constant interaction with fellow patients and staff. The emphasis was always on the collective as an inspirational, encouraging, supportive, pressuring, corrective, and reality-testing medium. [p. 174]

I had seen many of these procedures firsthand at Nikolayev's unit in Gannushkin Hospital. I had also seen medicine men, spiritists, and other folk healers use the group as a therapeutic instrument in American Indian tribes and in Latin American healing circles.

Even Soviet research specialists interact with the patients. In accordance with the principle of studying the personality while influencing it, Soviet psychotherapy researchers take an active role in treatment. They may intervene directly in patients' life situations by manipulating their environment, occupation, or residence. They actively strive to maintain a positive therapeutic climate by giving the patients emotional support, warmth, and help. They try to re-educate patients, guiding them toward the development of moral fiber, social consciousness, and collectivism (Ziferstein, 1972).

American experimenters usually maintain a distance from their subjects, fearing that they may influence their behavior. But Soviet researchers often intervene deliberately, hoping to facilitate psychotherapy. An early psychological discovery was that when a person enters a room where a dog is attached to recording devices, the dog's respiration becomes slower and deeper. People were found to respond in the same way to the approach of another person. This response, named "the effect of the person," alters during development as culture inhibits the organism's capacity to make adaptations and changes.

Soviet psychotherapists usually combine psychotherapy with physiotherapy. Patients are examined in a search for neurological and somatic causes of a mental illness, such as infection, trauma, malnutrition, or toxic manifestations.

Because of Pavlov's formulation that mental illness is a manifestation of "protective inhibition" in which the weakened nerve cells attempt to protect themselves from the danger of being destroyed as a result of excessive stimulation, Soviet psychotherapists for many years have used various techniques for inducing prolonged sleep in order to reinforce the already existing protective inhibition and to give the weakened cortical cells rest and an opportunity to recover. With the advent of modern drug therapy, prolonged sleep is not used as frequently. However, drugs are used less often than they are in the USA; deep rest (sometimes facilitated by low-frequency sound waves) and nutrition are still utilized to help patients regain their "energy potential." This is especially important for psychotic patients, who Pavlov thought went into a state of partial inhibition to restore themselves and to prevent complete exhaustion or even death.

Because of their Pavlovian orientation to the psychiatric patient as someone suffering from a weakening of the cortical nerve cells, Soviet psychotherapists prescribe various tonics, medications, physical exercises, hydrotherapy, and acupuncture. Electricity is a popular treatment; mentally ill patients are often placed in cages that are charged with a low-voltage current producing an electrical field believed to stimulate the nervous system.

Acupuncture and Sex Therapy

I had observed acupuncture at work during a trip to Hong Kong in 1972. However, it had already been well established in the USSR. In the July 1972 issue of *Zdorovye,* a popular Soviet health magazine, V. G. Vogralik produced data on acupuncture treatment from Gorky Medical Institute. He revealed that in a 15-year study of 1,146 patients, acupuncture had been utilized for such ailments as bronchial asthma, chronic itching, stomach ulcers, spastic constipation, and high blood pressure. A "cure" reportedly had been effected for 726 patients, while the condition of another 221 was considered "greatly improved." Vogralik observed that acupuncture facilities existed in 37 Soviet cities and that further expansion was being implemented by the Ministry of Public Health.

Both in 1971 and 1972, I learned about acupuncture from G. S. Vassilchenko (1956, 1969), a physician and one of the Soviet Union's leading sexologists. He discussed the sexology seminars he had been organizing in Moscow for physicians from various parts of the Soviet Union. At these seminars, the participants would study diagnostic and therapeutic techniques for sexual dysfunction from Vassilchenko and other specialists associated with the Institute of Psychiatry of the Russian Federation Ministry.

Vassilchenko noted that the most frequent problems he was called upon to deal with were impotence, exhibitionism, premature ejaculation, and frigidity. The therapeutic procedures he utilized varied from case to case but included acupuncture, medication, diet, and "structural analysis," an eclectic type of psychotherapy that involved common-sense advice with guided imagery and the taking of a careful psychological history and physical examination.

Vassilchenko also described his work with children, especially those suffering from bed-wetting problems. He had found that stimulation of an acupuncture point at the base of the spine was often helpful in these cases—to what extent the placebo effect entered into the success he did not say. However, he did not typically use the Chinese needles, preferring procedures the parents could carry out in his absence, such as massage, ointments, and lotions.

I recalled Vassilchenko's pioneering work in 1979, when *Sex in the Soviet Union* was published. Its author, Mikhail Stern, was the director of the Vinnitsa Health Center in the Ukraine for three decades before he left the USSR. His center specialized in treating cases of sexual dysfunction, many of them, according to Stern, arising from an almost complete absence of sex education in the schools and books on the subject for adults. In addition, many couples are deprived of opportunities for intimacy because of overcrowded housing. Stern claimed that alcohol and sex often influence the male-female relationship and recalled that Russian mothers traditionally told their daughters, "If he doesn't beat you, he doesn't love you."

Stern claimed that most Soviet men suffer from impotence at some point in their lives and that a large number of women experience some form of frigidity. Often, a distressed individual will turn to a governmental sex manual for help. However, the advice is often inadequate; one Soviet sex guide recommends mineral-water douches and vacations in warm climates as cures for frigidity.

Before he left us one day, Vassilchenko remarked that his goal was the establishment of sexology as an independent professional discipline in the USSR. If he were able to accomplish this task, we knew it would be an important landmark in Soviet medicine.

References

Bieliauskas, V. J. Mental health care in the U.S.S.R. *American Psychologist*, 1977, *32*, 376–79.

Cott, A. Controlled fasting treatment of schizophrenia in the U.S.S.R. *Schizophrenia,* 1971, *3,* 1–10.

———. Controlled fasting treatment for schizophrenia. *Journal of Orthomolecular Psychiatry,* 1974, *3,* 301–11.

Ervin, F., and Palmour, R. Leu-endorphin levels in blood samples of schizophrenic patients. A paper presented at the annual meeting of the Society for Neuroscience, Anaheim, Calif., 1977.

Frank, J. D. *Persuasion and Healing,* rev. ed. Baltimore: The Johns Hopkins University Press, 1973.

Hines, W. Psychiatric care in the USSR. New York *Post,* May 5, 1971.

Hoffer, A., and Osmond, H. *How to Live with Schizophrenia.* New Hyde Park, N.Y.: University Books, 1966.

Holland, J. A comparative look at Soviet psychiatry: Training, concepts and practice. In S. A. Corson (ed.), *Psychiatry and Psychology in the USSR.* New York: Plenum Press, 1976.

Hollon, S. D., and Beck, A. T. Psychotherapy and drug therapy: Comparison and combinations. In S. L. Garfield and A. E. Bergin (eds.), *Handbook of Psychotherapy and Behavior Change: An Empirical Analysis,* 2nd ed. New York: John Wiley & Sons, 1978.

Ivanov, N. V. [*Problems of Psychotherapy of Functional Disorders in the Sexual Sphere in Medical Practice.*] Moscow: Russian Federated Soviet Socialist Republic Ministry of Health, 1961.

Kazanetz, E. P. Differentiating exogenous psychiatric illness from schizophrenia. *Archives of General Psychiatry,* 1979, *36,* 740–45.

Khromchenko, M. [Medicinal electrosleep.] *Ogonyek,* 1970, *20,* 20–21.

Krippner, S. Can fasting cure mental illness? *Fate,* Jan. 1974.

Krippner, S., and Brown, D. P. Field independence/dependence and Electrosone 50 induced altered states of consciousness. *Journal of Clinical Psychology,* 1973, *29,* 316–19.

Krippner, S., and Davidson, R. Acupuncture and hypnosis in the U.S.S.R. *Journal of Paraphysics,* 1972, *6,* 82–92.

Levine, J. D. Cited in: Growing convergence between "faith

healing" and modern medicine. *Behavior Today,* Apr. 16, 1979.

Luria, A. R. *Cognitive Development: Its Cultural and Social Foundations.* Cambridge, Mass.: Harvard University Press, 1976.

Natadze, R. G. Experimental foundations of Uznadze's theory of set. In M. Cole and I. Maltzman (eds.), *A Handbook of Contemporary Soviet Psychology.* New York: Basic Books, 1969.

Nikolayev, Y. S. [*The Treatment of Neuropsychiatric Diseases by Gradual Fasting.*] Moscow: State Scientific Institute of Psychiatry, 1970.

Pavlov, I. P. Physiology of the higher nervous activity. In *Complete Works,* Vol. 3, Bk. 21. Moscow: USSR Academy of Sciences, 1951.

Selye, H. *The Stress of Life.* New York: McGraw-Hill, 1956.

Shapiro, A. K., and Morris, L. A. The placebo effect in medical and psychological therapies. In S. L. Garfield and A. E. Bergin (eds.), *Handbook of Psychotherapy and Behavior Change,* 2nd ed. New York: John Wiley & Sons, 1978.

Stern, M. *Sex in the Soviet Union.* New York: New York *Times* Books, 1979.

Torrey, E. F. Schizophrenia: Sense and nonsense. *Psychology Today,* Nov. 1977.

Uznadze, D. N. *The Psychology of Set.* New York: Consultants Bureau, 1967.

Vassilchenko, G. S. [*Pathogenic Mechanisms of Impotence.*] Moscow: Medguiz, 1956.

————. [*Regarding Some Human Neuroses and Their Pathogenic Treatment.*] Moscow: Medicina, 1969.

Volgyesi, F. A. "School for patients," hypnosis-therapy and psychoprophylaxis. *British Journal of Medical Hypnosis,* 1954, *5,* 8–17.

Voloshanovich, A. Cited in: News roundup. *Behavior Today,* Sept. 4, 1978.

Witkin, H. A., et al. *Psychological Differentiation: Studies of Development.* New York: John Wiley & Sons, 1962.

Wortis, J. *Soviet Psychiatry.* Baltimore: Williams & Wilkins, 1950.

Ziferstein, I. Group psychotherapy in the Soviet Union. *American Journal of Psychiatry,* 1972, *129,* 595–99.

————. Psychotherapy in the USSR. In S. A. Corson (ed.), *Psychiatry and Psychology in the USSR.* New York: Plenum Press, 1976.

CHAPTER 5

Hypnosis, Hypnoproduction, and Creativity

The possibilities of the human organism are indeed unbounded. Scientists have only begun their task.

Vladimir Raikov (1966)

Hypnosis has been practiced under various labels in different places since time immemorial. Tribal medicine women, witch doctors, and faith healers have used it in various forms to heal the sick. The Ebers papyrus, over three thousand years old, describes how Egyptian soothsayers employed hypnotic procedures similar to those practiced today (Kroger, 1977, p. 1).

In modern times, Franz Anton Mesmer gained notoriety during the eighteenth century by treating a large number of sick people, attributing their cures to a rebalancing of their "universal fluids" brought about by the "magnetic passes" he performed around their bodies. A French commission (headed by America's Benjamin Franklin) investigated Mesmer in 1784, stating that the cures were due to imagination, not magnetism. The practice waxed and waned over the years, but obtained considerable attention in the USSR, where physiologist I. P. Pavlov suggested that hypnosis was a kind of limited sleep due to an inhibition of the brain's cortex. In recent years, American psychologists have placed more emphasis on the hypnotized subject's ability to role play, exercise imagination, and respond to the suggestions offered by the hypnotist.

Hypnosis and creativity appear to be interconnected because of the roles that imagination and fantasy play in both. Some research studies indicate that the greater the hypnotizability of a subject, the higher his or her ability for creative behavior (Bowers and Bowers, 1979).

The most celebrated use of hypnosis to stimulate creative behavior took place in Moscow at the turn of the century (Foley, 1963). Sergei Rachmaninoff was plunged into deep depression when his First Symphony was jeered by the audience and was received unfavorably by the critics. For nearly two years he lived by himself, seeing nobody, and writing virtually no new music. He doubted that he would ever compose again and his friends feared that he might become suicidal. Finally, they convinced him to see Nikolai Dahl, a physician who specialized in hypnosis.

Dahl treated Rachmaninoff thirty minutes each day over a period of three months. After some preliminary instructions, Dahl repeated over and over such statements as, "You will begin to write again. You will work with great facility. Inspiration flows freely in you, and nothing can block it." Dahl also taught Rachmaninoff self-hypnosis so he could practice it on his own.

Once he began to respond to Dahl's treatment, Rachmaninoff found that creative inspiration would often emerge spontaneously. He would frequently go on strolls in the countryside, and music would come to him as he gazed at the trees or watched a sunset. He later remarked that the music came from within him and demanded to be written down. In this manner, Rachmaninoff composed his celebrated Second Piano Concerto in C Minor. It was performed in Moscow in 1901 and was dedicated to Nikolai Dahl.

Hypnosis at a Distance

During our Moscow meeting in 1972, Edward Naumov had described the pioneering work of V. M. Bekhterev (a student of

Pavlov) who investigated telepathy at the University of Leningrad's Institute for Brain Research, which he headed. In 1922, a Commission for the Study of Mental Suggestion was formed; some of its work on telepathy was presented at the Second All-Russian Congress held in Leningrad in 1924. The Congress went on record as recognizing the importance of further research on telepathy. This resolution was implemented by the Society for Neurology, Reflexology, Hypnotism, and Biophysics, which functioned within Bekhterev's Institute for Brain Research. At a meeting held in 1926, L. L. Vasiliev reported on the biophysical foundations of "thought transmission."

The Society's directors instructed a group of its members to confirm and extend the work of Vasiliev; this directive led to the formation in 1926 of the Experimental Commission on Hypnotism and Psychophysics under the chairmanship of Bekhterev. Vasiliev continued his research after Bekhterev's death in 1927. In 1932, the Institute for Brain Research received an assignment to determine the physical basis of telepathy; Vasiliev headed this effort until 1938.

With the outbreak of World War II, Vasiliev's experiments were interrupted. Parapsychology fell under a cloud in the Stalinist repression that followed the war. Under the more favorable conditions of the Khrushchev period, Vasiliev resumed active work, writing two books that were translated into English: *Mysterious Phenomena of the Human Psyche* (1965) and *Experiments in Distant Influence* (1976).

Vasiliev attempted to determine whether electromagnetic radiation formed the basis of telepathic transmission. He selected subjects who were easily hypnotized and attempted to initiate and terminate hypnosis at a distance. To his surprise, he discovered that he was able to do this successfully, even if the subjects were in specially constructed rooms that would screen out electromagnetic radiation. For example, in 1933 and 1934, one man served as subject during 260 attempts to hypnotize him at a distance—or to bring him out of hypnosis. Vasiliev claimed that success was attained in 9 out of 10 attempts. An objective method was used for registering when sleep began and when it ended: The subject was given the task of pressing continuously upon a bulb of air that had a tube connected with a marker resting on moving paper, but when hypnotized, the subject automatically stopped pressing the bulb. The marker registered this fact on the paper. By 1936, the technique was improved by the addition of control trials; Vasiliev asserted that the subject's success continued. In evaluating Vasiliev's work, C. E. M. Hansel (1980) referred to the allocation of tests to experimental and control conditions as "excellent" but criticized the fact that recordings of data were made by someone who knew the nature of the experiment.

Seven Steps

In 1971, when I saw the Soviet film documentary *Seven Steps Beyond the Horizon,* I found the segment on hypnosis to be the most interesting. It featured Vladimir Raikov, a Moscow psychoneurologist and psychotherapist. To stimulate the creative potential of his hypnotized subjects, Raikov would tell them that they were historical figures possessing unusual talents in a special area. He told them they would enhance their skills in this field under hypnosis and that sometimes the improvement would carry over into their everyday life.

In one of the first sequences, a student was portrayed playing the piano. Her technical ability was adequate but she was nervous, unsure of herself, and played with little feeling or emotion. After she was hypnotized, she was told that she was Rachmaninoff. As she approached the keyboard again, her rendering of a Chopin selection was markedly improved; she played brilliantly, with verve and gusto. Her facial expressions and body movements were those of a different person—or at least of a different part of her personality.

Other students in the film were studying in scientific fields. Under hypnosis, the personality of a celebrated scientist in their field was evoked. Once they identified with that person, a curious phenomenon occurred: They gave Raikov and his assistant blank stares when they were asked questions about celebrated personalities from the 1960s. They could not identify cosmonauts or entertainers. They examined cameras and tape recorders but could not operate them. Their role playing appeared to be complete.

Most of the students had spent years immersed in the subject areas of their evoked personalities. However, there were two exceptions, a young man and a young woman who had no previous exposure to art, yet were drawing industriously under hypnosis. Raikov, an amateur artist himself, appeared to be giving them art lessons. Another factor that may have influenced the results is that the hypnotized students worked in small groups, which may have enabled them to learn from their observations of each other and to have those learnings socially reinforced.

"Raphael, 1500"

When Richard Davidson, my assistant, and I were in Moscow, Raikov visited us several times, often bringing his hypnosis subjects with him. One day he brought the young woman from the film, a former physics student at Moscow University who had switched to art after several sessions with Raikov. Under hypnosis, she had been told that she was Raphael, the Italian artist who lived during the Renaissance. Her ability had developed rapidly. In drawing upon her hidden reserves, she was assisted by Raikov's comments on artistic technique (during hypnosis) and by the artists she observed during the week, as well as by the paintings she studied. Her identification with the Italian genius was so intense that when asked (during hypnosis) to sign a painting, she immediately wrote "Raphael, 1500."

Davidson and I asked her why she left the field of physics, certainly a career choice with more opportunities than painting. She replied that she had never experienced the degree of satisfaction in science that would compare with what she felt when immersed in her artwork.

On another occasion a student from a musical conservatory played his violin for us. The student was then hypnotized with the suggestion that he was Fritz Kreisler. The student played again— in our opinion with more confidence and expertise. When the hypnotic experience was terminated, he told us that it only took a few seconds for him to "slip away"; from that point on, he had no memory of the experience. Nevertheless, he told us that his skill with the violin had improved as a result of his twenty-five hyp-noproduction sessions.

Davidson and I also met the young woman who had "become Rachmaninoff" under hypnosis. In her case, she had not made the transfer from her brilliant hypnotic performance on the piano to what she could do under ordinary circumstances. We heard her play the piano under both conditions and there was still a dra-matic difference. Raikov attributed this situation to a drinking problem—a condition quite common in the USSR. However, Raikov was helping the student overcome her dependence on al-cohol; to demonstrate this situation, he told her that we were her drinking companions. She looked at us with disdain and moved to another part of the room.

Another student told us that he had developed artistic ability after being told that he was Ilya Repin, a well-known Russian painter. Unlike the woman who "became Raphael," the latter-day Repin did not change his career plans. However, he did develop a modest ability in art and was able to paint for relaxation and as a hobby.

Like the other students, this one told us he had no memory of his experience as Repin. This phenomenon is not typical of most people who are hypnotized; usually they can remember what transpired with a high degree of accuracy. The frequency of "posthypnotic amnesia" indicated that Raikov's students had the capacity for extremely deep hypnotic experience, an ability that characterizes about 10 to 15 percent of the general population.

A Roll of the Eyes

Raikov hypnotized one of the students and told her that she was three days old. When she opened her eyes, they were unfocused and wandered aimlessly, as do those of an infant. Raikov said that this phenomenon demonstrates that hypnoproduction is more than role playing; actors asked to imagine that they were infants did not produce the unfocused gaze characteristic of Raikov's deeply hypnotized subjects.

This procedure gave me an idea: To examine the hypnotizability of Raikov's subjects, I would administer the "eye roll" test devised by Herbert Spiegel (1977), a psychiatrist I had met in New York City. Spiegel had postulated that hypnosis involves a capacity for attentive, responsive concentration that is inherent in the person. Thus it can be measured by an examiner using Spiegel's Hypnotic Induction Profile, a ten-minute test. A key task is to make this request to the subject:

> Now look toward me. As you hold your head in that position, look up toward your eyebrows—now toward the top of your head. [Spiegel and Spiegel, 1978, p. 45]

Almost without exception, Raikov's subjects were able to roll back their eyes so far that the pupils all but disappeared under the eyelids. This ability would indicate, to Spiegel, that the subject would be highly hypnotizable—so much so that "posthypnotic amnesia" might result.

Richard Davidson volunteered to be a subject for hypnoproduction. Raikov commanded, "Sit down, Richard, and relax." Raikov pushed Davidson's head back, pulled his neck and shoulders forward, and began to stroke his chest. In so doing, Raikov made what used to be called "magnetic passes" in the days when hypnosis was felt to influence "universal fluids." In fact, I was struck by Raikov's utilization of direct, authoritarian hypnotic induction procedures, rather than the indirect, permissive procedures preferred by most American hypnotherapists. However, the procedure appeared to work well for Raikov's subjects.

Raikov gave some simple suggestions that Davidson followed rather quickly. Then Raikov said, "I am holding a rose under your nose; nod your head if you can smell it." Davidson's head bobbed up and down; afterward he told me that the smell was remarkably vivid.

Raikov then attempted some age-regression techniques; Davidson did not respond. When Raikov told him he was three days old, Davidson opened his eyes but they remained focused. Raikov concluded, "I am sorry, Richard. You are not a candidate for hypnoproduction." I administered the eye-roll test to Richard; his pupils did not disappear, as did those of Raikov's subjects. If nothing else, Spiegel's Hypnotic Induction Profile attained a bit more confirmation and I suspected it measured one's psychophysiological "set" for hypnosis. In fact, I sent the entire test to Raikov after I returned to the United States; he wrote back saying he had found the technique quite useful.

Limitations of Hypnoproduction

Raikov admitted that he is quite selective in those people he uses in his hypnoproduction experiments. In the first place, only a minority of people are able to go deeply enough into hypnosis for the procedure to be effective. Raikov told me that arts and humanities students are more likely to become candidates for hypnoproduction than engineering and education students. In the second place, Raikov noted that there are dangers in this technique if unstable people are hypnotized or if the hypnotist has not had adequate training.

When Raikov was developing this procedure, he and his associates tested twenty young students, finding no observable artistic ability. The students were then taken through from five to twenty hypnoproduction sessions. The pictures they drew and painted demonstrated individual differences but remarkable improvements as the sessions proceeded (Tsipko, 1967). What is needed now is a similar research program in which some students are not hypnotized at all but are merely encouraged to imagine that they are Raphael, Repin, or Rembrandt, as well as a third group, which is simply told to draw during their sessions with the help of neither hypnosis nor imagination. Raikov (1978) has reported a similar study involving anesthesia. Hypnotized subjects who were told they were cosmonauts with their legs jammed into a space capsule, did not report feeling a needle that pierced their skin. Nonhypnotized subjects who imagined the same situation did feel the needle prick, and often complained about the pain.

In future studies, the long-term effects of hypnoproduction would need to be recorded. I have known of instances in which an alteration of consciousness has brought about dramatic changes in behavior but only temporarily. I met an aspiring orchestra conductor who underwent a controlled psychotherapeutic LSD session. During the session and for a period of time following, his conducting was brilliant, his ability to coordinate the orchestra superb. After a few months, however, his lack of confidence reasserted itself and his performance diminished. I have noted similar declines in the ability of people to cope with alcoholism, drug addiction, and sexual dysfunction following a promising beginning in the context of LSD-type drugs, meditation training, or other therapeutic processes involving the alteration of consciousness.

In some of these cases, the old habits simply were so strong that they prevented change from taking place. In others, the phenomenon of statebound learning probably interfered; what was learned in an altered state of consciousness did not transfer easily to behavior in one's ordinary state of consciousness. A fictional instance of statebound learning occurs in the film *City Lights*. Charlie Chaplin saves a drunken millionaire from attempted suicide and becomes his friend. When sober, however, the millionaire does not remember Chaplin. But when the millionaire is drunk again, he spots Chaplin and treats him like a long-lost friend. He takes Chaplin home with him, but in the morning, when he is again sober, he forgets that Chaplin is his friend and guest—and has his butler throw Chaplin out. Later, while intoxicated, the millionaire spots Chaplin on the street and greets him warmly. Less dramatic examples of statebound learning occur in laboratory experiments and in real-life situations (Fischer, 1971).

Engels' Experiment

Friedrich Engels witnessed an intriguing experiment that involved statebound learning and hypnosis. During the winter of 1843–44, Engels watched a demonstration by Spencer Hall in Manchester, England. Hall was a hypnotist who traveled about the country in the company of several clergymen and a young girl. The girl was his hypnosis subject and, with her, Hall endeavored to prove the existence of God, the immortality of the soul, and the falsity of materialistic philosophy.

Once the audience had gathered and the demonstration had begun, Hall hypnotized the girl and directed the audience's attention to her skull. Claiming that each part of the brain corresponded to a particular function, Hall touched the area supposedly associated with maternal feelings; the girl fondled and kissed an imaginary baby. At the conclusion of his act, Hall touched the top of the skull—home of the trait of veneration. The subject then fell to her knees and folded her hands in prayer. Hall said that he had proved the existence of God!

Engels and his friends were curious as to whether they could reproduce Hall's effects. A twelve-year-old boy volunteered as subject and was easily hypnotized. Engels (1940) describes their results:

> To set [the] cranial organs into action was the least that we achieved; we went much further. We could not only exchange them for one another, or make their seat anywhere in the whole body, but we also fabricated any amount of other organs; organs of singing, whistling, piping, dancing, boxing, sewing, cobbling, tobacco-smoking, etc., and we could make their seat wherever we wanted. . . . We discovered in the great toe an organ of drunkenness which only had to be touched in order to cause the finest drunken comedy to be enacted. But it must well be understood, no organ showed a trace of action until the patient was given to understand what was expected of him; the boy soon perfected himself by practice to such an extent that the merest indication sufficed. [pp. 299–300]

Engels noted that the cranial "organs" produced in this way retained their identity for later occasions as long as the conditions were not altered in some way. Their subject even developed a "double memory"—one for the waking condition and one for hypnosis. In other words, the boy could not recall while awake what he knew under hypnosis—a typical effect of statebound learning.

Raikov feels that one reason his subjects usually are able to avoid statebound learning is because hypnoproduction is an active process. Once they begin to role play the celebrated individual from the past, the subject is active and independent, not passively following a procedure dictated by the hypnotist. Although deeply hypnotized, Raikov's subjects (usually in groups) draw, paint, play musical instruments, solve mathematics problems, perform tests of attention, and even learn the words of a foreign language.

This procedure creates an active posthypnotic momentum; specific posthypnotic suggestions are rarely needed.

For example, after several attempts at drawing under hypnosis, the students develop a desire to draw at home. Subjects often report that they are seeing objects in the environment in brighter colors, developing greater three-dimensional vision, and appreciating the aesthetic aspects of their surroundings to a greater extent. They typically take a greater interest in the fine arts, visit museums more frequently, and study art prints and monographs about famous painters. Conservatory students, after playing while hypnotized, report that they frequently are able—on their own—to give more complex interpretations of a musical composition than they did before hypnoproduction.

In addition to finding their creativity enhanced, many of Raikov's subjects report that they have achieved greater control over such bodily processes as heart activity, body temperature, and the ability to eliminate headaches. Others claim they can work longer without becoming fatigued, while some subjects say that they can control or change their emotional reactions and moods. A few individuals note that they can predetermine their dreams. Others claim they can prevent or terminate influenza and the common cold.

Three Elements

Raikov told me that there are three elements in hypnoproduction, the first being a demonstration of what a person could do with the help of hypnosis. Even if subjects do not remember their experiences, the pictures they have drawn give testimony to their work, as do the mathematical and scientific problems they have solved and tape recordings of the music they have played.

The second element is the mobilization of effort resulting from imagining oneself as a highly talented creator. The image of that person sets a goal and channels the students' efforts in an attempt to meet that goal. Of course, the reverse would also hold true; Raikov has used the image of an unsuccessful person in a small number of hypnoproduction sessions, and a sharp reduction of intellectual activity occurred. In either case the subject's concept of his or her own capability was affected.

The third element of hypnoproduction involves enhancement of the pleasure a subject takes in performing the suggested activity. Facilitating a positive emotional state usually assists in transferring the skill from hypnosis to ordinary consciousness.

Raikov (1977) studied the brain-wave recordings of his subjects during hypnoproduction. Typically, there was no change during hypnosis because most hypnotized people are alert and attentive, just as they are in ordinary consciousness. However, when Raikov told his subjects, "You feel very good," or "This activity is bringing you pleasure," bursts of high-amplitude theta waves often occurred on the electroencephalogram (or EEG).

Raikov also reported low-amplitude delta brain-wave activity from four of the six most easily hypnotizable subjects in one of his studies. Delta activity is even slower than theta and is most typically observed when subjects are asleep. Raikov observed that the four subjects in question had normal brain-wave activity during ordinary, waking consciousness, thus the appearance of delta during hypnosis was remarkable.

Raikov's EEG results are so unusual that they need to be replicated by other experimenters using his technique. It could be that there are many types of hypnosis, and that most of them produce no EEG change. Raikov claims that when the subject receives the hypnotist's suggestion, his or her vigilant consciousness is blocked, excluding contact with the hypnotist. It is then possible for the subject to imagine the person he or she is to become, investing that image with emotion and motivation. Raikov (1977) continues:

> The hypnotized person knows nothing of his own individuality, and does not identify his relatives, friends, and even himself when he looks in a mirror. He adjusts his life experience, knowledge, and memory to the hypnotic image of himself as another person, and interprets his surroundings from the position of that image. [p. 218]

Raikov (1975b) concludes that hypnoproduction is based on an alteration in the nervous system itself. This change is accompanied by a reprogramming and reoperating of the control and analysis systems that process information. In this instance, they utilize information of a hypnotic nature rather than analyzing ordinary reality.

Raikov suspected that if this were true, it would be possible to transform nighttime sleep to hypnoproduction. He waited for about ninety minutes, after a subject had completed the first "sleep cycle" and was about to start dreaming. But before the dreams could occur, Raikov successfully initiated hypnoproduction. This was possible, according to Raikov, because the control system of ordinary consciousness had already been switched off.

There are obvious comparisons between hypnoproduction and dreams, especially those dreams in which the dreamer appears to be immersed in a new reality or in which the dreamer solves creative problems. An example of the former is Robert Louis Stevenson, who regularly used his dreams as bases for short stories and novels. Perhaps the best example of a dream Stevenson utilized in this manner is one in which he imbibed a potion that drastically altered his personality. This dream stimulated the writing of *The Strange Case of Dr. Jekyll and Mr. Hyde,* Stevenson's most famous short story.

An example of creative problem-solving in a dream occurred in nineteenth-century Russia. In 1869, D. I. Mendeleev was exhausted following his unsuccessful struggle to categorize the elements (oxygen, hydrogen, copper, mercury, neon, etc.) based upon their atomic weights. He fell into bed and later dreamed. He subsequently reported, "I saw in a dream a table where all the elements fell into place as required. Awakening, I immediately wrote it down on a piece of paper. Only in one place did a correction later seem necessary" (Kedrov, 1957). In this manner, Mendeleev's Periodic Table of the Elements was created.

The "Hidden Observer"

At one point, I. P. Pavlov had called hypnosis "partial dreaming," noting that both involved a partial inhibition of the brain's cortex. V. M. Bekhterev (1926) described hypnosis as a more active process than that proposed by Pavlov. Bekhterev observed that hypnosis involved an energetic focusing of the subject's perception with a consequent inhibition of ordinary consciousness and suspected that the electrochemical processes of the nervous system played a decisive role in shifting the subject's reality.

There are times in hypnoproduction when the subject's knowledge about himself is not completely blocked out by hypnosis. In these cases, the subject has a dual self-awareness—that is, of himself as well as of Raphael or Rachmaninoff. Raikov (1975b) refers to this phenomenon as a "splitting" of consciousness. This account reminded me of E. R. Hilgard's (1977) work with what he called "divided consciousness." In Hilgard's experiments, subjects were deeply hypnotized and had their arms submerged in ice water for long periods of time. Hilgard asked the subjects if they felt any pain, and they usually responded that they did not. But Hilgard then established a communication channel with another aspect of the psyche, "the hidden observer," which was able to make its feelings known through finger signals, gestures, or automatic writing. Typically, the "hidden observer" would complain that it *did* feel pain and was quite aware of what was taking place under hypnosis.

For most of Hilgard's subjects the "hidden observer" represented a central core of the self, contributing to the subjects' feelings of unity and integration. Perhaps this "hidden observer" is present even as Raikov's subjects enact their roles in hypnoproduction. If so, it might further assist the subjects' development of their latent potentials and hidden possibilities.

The presence of a "hidden observer" may also prevent the subject from suffering adverse effects from hypnoproduction. When I first met Raikov in Moscow, he admitted that his work was controversial. Critics have claimed that there is a danger that his subjects might suffer dissociation or even the multiple-personality syndrome popularized in the United States by such books as *Sybil* and *The Three Faces of Eve*. However, a study by Reima Kampman (1976) of the University of Oulu, Finland, produced data to the contrary. Kampman screened some 450 students, selecting 78 who could enter deep hypnosis. These individuals were given such suggestions as, "Go back to an age preceding your birth; you are somebody else, somewhere else." Of the 78 students, 32 were able to create a secondary personality in hypnosis. Psychiatric interviews revealed that these students were mentally healthier than those unable to produce secondary personalities. Kampman (1976) concluded that "the sounder the subject's ego, the easier it is to undergo a split reaction under the control of the observing ego without the risk of getting into areas of irreversible regression. Thus, responding to suggestions to develop multiple personalities would be a creative activity of the ego" (p. 224). In other words, the better the "hidden observer" is able to function, the more creatively the subject can respond to suggestions involving a secondary personality.

Eliciting Hidden Reserves

I saw Raikov again in 1972 when I returned to Moscow. We kept in touch through the mail and I showed a film portraying Raikov's work at a convention of the International Society of Hypnosis in 1976. I also assisted Raikov's efforts to publish his work in the *American Journal of Clinical Hypnosis* and the *International Journal of Clinical and Experimental Hypnosis*. In a 1976 issue of the latter publication, Raikov described his most ambitious project, a study of fifty university students who had experienced hypnoproduction. When in deep hypnosis, they were all capable, after being told they were newborn infants, of manifesting desynchronized eye movements, sucking and grasping reflexes, and other infantile behavior. Each subject participated in from five to twenty hypnoproduction sessions; five played chess, eleven studied mathematics, twenty-four memorized foreign words, fifteen played musical instruments, and twenty-seven drew pictures. (The total number exceeds fifty because some subjects attempted several tasks.) A control group was formed consisting of twenty-eight students of low hypnotic susceptibility and seventy-eight students who did not respond to hypnosis at all.

Personality-test data revealed that subjects who could accept suggestions to manifest a different personality in hypnosis were in

e.g. who have willingness (cooperation) or wants to be hypnosis - you have to have "want". This everybody can be hypnotized if he (she wants it.

better mental health than those in the control group. All subjects were followed up, some for eight years. Raikov found none of them to be harmed by their experiences in deep hypnosis.

The fifteen subjects who (as Rachmaninoff, Kreisler, etc.) played musical instruments were studying at the Moscow Conservatory. Their performances before, during, and after ten hypnoproduction sessions were tape recorded and indicated significant improvement when evaluated. Two types of experiments with mathematics were conducted; those students who made highest scores had experienced hypnoproduction, while those who did not improve were members of the control group.

During the course of the chess experiments, a former world champion, Mikhail Tal, visited the laboratory and played six games with one subject. During three of those games, the subject was hypnotized and was told he was Paul Morphy, another champion. Tal was aware of the difference, commenting, "In hypnosis he was a different man, energetic, strong, and daring . . . who can play chess on two classes higher." The control group showed no improvement.

The art experiment involved twenty-seven students who considered themselves unable to draw. Under hypnosis they were told they had become famous masters such as Raphael and Repin. The quality of their drawing improved, and the change was seen in the waking state as well. The control group showed no such improvement. Raikov (1976) noted there were individual differences in hypnoproduction because "a person's creative ability can be manifested in hypnosis only when the person has this ability in a latent state" (p. 259).

Raikov's use of hypnoproduction to stimulate creativity is done in his spare time, and is his avocation. He is a full-time psychotherapist at a psychoneurological clinic in Moscow. Even there he utilizes hypnosis, integrating it with other psychotherapeutic procedures such as autogenic training and guided imagery. In working with alcoholics, for example, he will have the patient role play his or her parents, friends, children, spouse, or others who reinforce the dependence on alcohol or desire to stop it. Not only can this procedure help develop insight, but also, according to Raikov, it can deepen the emotional determination to change one's behavior.

"Set" theorists hold that in the context of social life people develop the ability to "objectify," which, according to Uznadze (1958), constitutes the most characteristic feature of human beings. It is precisely because of the development of "objectification" that a conditioned set can lose its power. Therefore, people are not slaves of given situations; behavior is not irrevocably conditioned. Human beings can react to the environment after they have realized, thought over, and "objectified" a given situation. They can act, not impulsively as other animals do, but voluntarily according to their judgment. Such specifically human activity is designated by Uznadze as the "second plane" of the mind's operation—the higher level of behavior—and contrasted with impulsive action, the "first plane."

This ability to change one's behavior is important both in Raikov's use of psychotherapy and in his utilization of hypnoproduction. In each area where hypnoproduction was used, the subject's set was of critical importance. If the readiness for creativity is absent, even the best techniques cannot elicit one's hidden reserves. But when some motivation is present and when the subject's attitude is favorable, an image can be suggested that often has the ability to enhance creative performance. Raikov's work needs to be repeated elsewhere, for it appears to be a powerful tool in tapping hidden reserves and in manifesting new human possibilities.

[handwritten margin note: → subject must be cooperative and has "want"]

References

Bekhterev, V. M. [The hypnotic process.] *Vestnek Znanja,* 1926, *2,* 37–40.

Bowers, K. S., and Bowers, P. Hypnosis and creativity: A theoretical and empirical rapprochement. In E. Fromm and R. E. Shor (eds.), *Hypnosis: Developments in Research and New Perspectives,* 2nd ed. New York: Aldine, 1979.

Engels, F. *Dialectics of Nature.* New York: International Publishers, 1940.

Fischer, R. A cartography of the ecstatic and meditative states. *Science,* 1971, *174,* 897–903.

Foley, C. The legend of Rachmaninoff. *Music Guide,* 1963.

Hansel, C. E. M. *ESP and Parapsychology: A Critical Re-evaluation.* Buffalo, N.Y.: Prometheus Books, 1980.

Hilgard, E. R. The problem of divided consciousness: A neodissociation interpretation. In W. E. Edmonston, Jr. (ed.), *Conceptual and Investigative Approaches to Hypnosis and Hypnotic Phenomena.* New York: New York Academy of Sciences, 1977.

Kampman, R. Hypnotically induced multiple personality: An experimental study. *International Journal of Clinical and Experimental Hypnosis,* 1976, *24,* 215–27.

Kedrov, B. M. [On the question of the psychology of scientific creativity on the occasion of the discovery by D. I. Mendeleev of the Periodic Table of the Elements.] *Voprosy Psikologii,* 1957, *3*(2), 91–113.

Krippner, S. The psychedelic state, the hypnotic trance, and the creative act. *Journal of Humanistic Psychology,* 1968, *8,* 49–67.

Kroger, W. S. *Clinical and Experimental Hypnosis,* 2nd ed. Philadelphia: J. B. Lippincott, 1977.

McDonald, G.; Conway, M.; and Ricci, M. (eds.), *The Films of Charlie Chaplin.* New York: Citadel, 1965.

Pavlov, I. P. *Conditioned Reflexes and Psychiatry.* New York: International Publishers, 1941.

Raikov, V. L. [Creation by hypnosis.] *Nauka i Zhirn',* Sept. 1966.

———. [*The Psychological Study of Creative Activity.*] Moscow: Nauka, 1975a.

———. Theoretical substantiation of deep hypnosis. *American Journal of Clinical Hypnosis,* 1975b, *18,* 23–27.

———. The possibility of creativity in the active stage of hypnosis. *International Journal of Clinical and Experimental Hypnosis,* 1976, *24,* 258–68.

———. Theoretical analysis of deep hypnosis: Creative activity of hypnotized subjects into transformed self-consciousness. *American Journal of Clinical Hypnosis,* 1977, *19,* 214–20.

———. Specific features of suggested anesthesia in some forms of hypnosis in which the subject is active. *International Journal of Clinical and Experimental Hypnosis,* 1978, *26,* 158–66.

Schreiber, F. R. *Sybil.* Chicago: Henry Regnery, 1973.

Sizemore, C. C., and Pittillo, E. S. *I'm Eve.* Garden City, N.Y.: Doubleday, 1977.

Spiegel, H. The hypnotic induction profile (HIP): A review of its development. In W. E. Edmonston, Jr. (ed.), *Conceptual and Investigative Approaches to Hypnosis and Hypnotic Phenomena.* New York: New York Academy of Sciences, 1977.

Spiegel, H., and Spiegel, D. *Trance and Treatment: Clinical Uses of Hypnosis.* New York: Basic Books, 1978.

Thigpen, C. H., and Cleckley, H. *The Three Faces of Eve.* New York: McGraw-Hill, 1957.

Tsipko, A. Art instruction under hypnosis. *Sputnik,* May 1967.

Uznadze, D. N. [Experimental Research Studies on the Psychology of Set.] Tbilisi: Nauka, 1958.

Vasiliev, L. L. *Mysterious Phenomena of the Human Psyche.* New Hyde Park, N.J.: University Books, 1965. (Originally published in 1959.)

————. *Experiments in Distant Influence.* New York: E. P. Dutton, 1976. (Originally published in 1962.)

CHAPTER 6

Suggestopedia in the Classroom

Suggestion is the most simplified and the most typical conditioned reflex in man.

I. P. Pavlov (1941)

I first began to utilize educational hypnosis when I was a dormi-
tory counselor at Northwestern University in Illinois. Upon request, I would use hypnosis to improve study habits, increase concentration, reduce examination anxiety, and increase motivation.
Some students went very deeply into hypnosis; some did not. But
I soon discovered that most of the students could be assisted re-
gardless of the depth of their experience with hypnosis (Krippner,
1963).

I remember Clark, a student with a short attention span. After
studying for a few minutes, he would feel the need to open the
window, get a drink of water, or visit the candy-vending machine.
He would turn on his radio or record player, or remember a telephone call that had to be made. I hypnotized Clark several times,
attempting to replace these destructive habits with constructive
behavior patterns. He was told that he would be able to ignore the
room temperature while he was studying, as well as his own sensations of thirst or hunger and the appeals of the radio, record
player, and telephone. After a few weeks, Clark was spending sev-

eral consecutive hours on his studies each night and would even be able to resist other students when they tried to distract or interrupt him.

Between 1961 and 1964, I directed the Child Study Center at Kent State University. I hypnotized several children and adolescents with language disabilities, often developing their ability to see words in the "mind's eye," which improved their visual memory and spelling skills. In 1977, Ira Greenberg's book *Group Hypnotherapy and Hypnodrama* appeared, containing a chapter I had written on my work, "Individual Hypnosis, Group Hypnosis, and the Improvement of Academic Achievement."

When I worked at Maimonides Medical Center, I met Cecelia Pollack, who directed the Center's learning disabilities clinic. Pollack also used hypnosis, and we spent many hours discussing the potential that altered states of consciousness held for education. We were delighted when the Center's director, Montague Ullman, scheduled a lecture by Georgi Lozanov during the Bulgarian psychiatrist's visit to the United States in March 1971.

Lozanov had studied Yoga in India, taking a special interest in the "stotrayas" who claimed to be able to memorize the 10,550 verses of the *Rig-Veda,* an ancient Hindu hymn. In Bulgaria, he had investigated paranormal healing as well as hypnosis, and had invited dozens of Bulgarian psychics into his laboratory, studying their brain waves as they entered altered states of consciousness. He did the same with "lightning calculators," individuals who can work complex mathematical problems without pencil and paper. He reviewed Pavlov's work with conditioning as well as the Soviet work with "sleep learning" when he earned a doctorate in psychology at the Kharkov Medical Institute. He also continued to practice psychotherapy and observed his patients' progress over the course of treatment. He acted as an anesthetist in a hospital, using suggestions instead of drugs during operations. Eventually he concluded that there are a number of "laws of suggestion" that operate in human communication. These laws provide the basis of his science of "suggestology," a hybrid word formed from the Latin *suggestió* (suggestion) and the Greek *logos* (word or speech). The practical application of suggestology in education is referred to as "suggestopedia" (or "suggestopedy").

In his address at Maimonides, Lozanov described his work at

the Research Institute of Suggestology, founded in 1966. The main emphasis of his classes was the learning of languages; he reported instances of people developing a speaking vocabulary of a foreign tongue in a matter of weeks. Indeed, when suggestopedia was introduced in the USSR, *Pravda* ran a headline story, "Is it Possible to Learn a Language in a Month?" (Simurov, 1969). Later, suggestopedic classes were inaugurated in the United States, many of them organized by the Mankind Research Foundation* in Maryland, which bought the rights to Lozanov's foreign-language instructional methods from Technika, the Bulgarian foreign-trade office.

I saw Lozanov again in Los Angeles in May 1975. We both spoke at a conference entitled "Suggestology and Altered States of Consciousness" sponsored by Pepperdine University. The meeting was chaired by Elizabeth Philipov (1978, 1979), a professor at the university who had received her doctorate from U. S. International University in San Diego. Her dissertation involved the use of suggestopedia to teach Bulgarian; her data demonstrated that the process took only a third as long as traditional techniques. I met Donald Schuster at Pepperdine and heard him describe the experiments with suggestopedia he was carrying out at Iowa State University. In 1977, I had the opportunity to lecture at Iowa State and to meet Schuster's enthusiastic staff.

The Students at Yuri Gagarin

In December, 1978, I flew to Sofia for a meeting of "The Working Group on Suggestology as a Learning Methodology." The meeting was sponsored by the Bulgarian National Commission for UNESCO and the Bulgarian Ministry of Public Education (Schuster and Miele, 1978).

There were three other Americans present: Dr. Schuster from Iowa State University, Philip Miele from the New York Institute of Technology, and Dr. Pollack, my former colleague at Maimon-

* As of 1980, the Foundation's address was 1110 Fiddler Lane, Silver Spring, Md. 20910.

ides, now the director of the Intersensory Learning Clinic in Great Neck, New York. Most of us arrived on Sunday night; on Monday morning we were escorted to an experimental school—even before we had recovered from jet lag.

Upon entering the school, we noticed a large statue of Yuri Gagarin, the Soviet cosmonaut in whose honor the school is named. We were introduced to a class of some twenty second-grade students who had been studying English by means of suggestopedia. As the teacher walked to the front of the room, the class sang "Good morning, dear teacher" in splendid English. The teacher then drew back a curtain revealing a story, mounted on cardboard and written in English:

> This is a big family.
> A mother, a father,
> a brother, a sister,
> and little twin sisters too.
> George Smith is a doctor.
> Lillian Smith is a painter.
> Richard is a very good boy.
> Julia is a sweet girl.
> Nancy and Hattie are happy children,
> Fluffy is a greedy fat cat.
> Dixie, the parrot, is red, green, and yellow.
> These are Nancy's pets.

The teacher asked the pupils if they could read the story, and they answered negatively by shaking their heads. Nor could they read the words or letters in the story, with the exception of "a," "c," "e," and "k," the four letters that the English and Bulgarian alphabets have in common. The pupils were informed that by Friday they would be able to read the story for the visitors on their final trip to the school, following three days of practice sessions.

We were informed that the children were eight years old, having entered first grade when they were seven. About half the class wore blue scarves; I was told that these youngsters were members of a Communist youth group.

We then visited a "control" class of second graders that used traditional educational techniques. The class of thirty-seven children was much larger, but the teacher was equally dynamic and theatrical. Indeed, each of the teachers we observed appeared to be devoted to her pupils and eager to stimulate the maximum amount of learning possible. We were informed that once the comparisons between "experimental" and "control" classes have been made, the teachers in the traditional classes will have an opportunity to undertake the three-month training program in suggestopedia.

I inspected one of the readers the pupils were using and was impressed with the variety of the stories it contained. There were beautifully illustrated stories about Sputnik, space exploration, Lenin, and Soviet-Bulgarian friendship. There were folk tales, stories about families, and a brief biography of Georgi Dmitrov, Bulgaria's first postwar Premier who was laid to rest, after his death in 1949, in a handsome mausoleum built in his honor.

The pupils enjoyed playing a word game that involved pictures of a snowman. They listened to classical music and were asked what images the music elicited. "Falling snowflakes," volunteered one child; "skaters" said another. In other words, the traditional class used a wide variety of activities—but not the special combination of procedures that has been associated with suggestopedia.

For example, the walls of a suggestopedia classroom are filled with attractive posters. A colorful picture fills the top of the poster; on the bottom is the word that describes the picture. And hidden in the picture itself is the first letter of that word. The pupils' attention is not directed to the posters for several weeks. In the meantime, learning is taking place through "peripheral perception," a type of indirect learning involving unfocused awareness; this learning supplements the formal instruction carried out in the classroom. Lozanov told us that many of the children are able to read the Sofia newspapers after three months of suggestopedia.

The next group of pupils we saw were first graders studying mathematics through suggestopedia. They engaged in a number of arithmetic games involving pictures of Father Frost (a legendary character who brings cold weather, similar to "Jack Frost" in America and England), a mathematical train, and a dwarf who quizzed the children on the meanings of addition, subtraction, multiplication, and division signs. The class worked on problems involving the addition and subtraction of snowballs; music played in the background, and pupils were encouraged to utilize internal imagery.

A simple geometry task was handled well by the class members as they differentiated among acute, obtuse, and right angles. This was followed by simple algebra:

$$\text{If } 375-a=0, \text{ what is } a?$$
$$\text{If } 23+a=25, \text{ what is } a?$$

The children worked these problems in their copy books so that they would have a record of their responses. They also attempted such problems as:

$$(438+121)-438=?$$
$$865-(64-21)=?$$

We were told that the pupils were exposed to numbers during the first week of school. The activities were presented as games rather than as drudgery. Children were told not to be afraid of making mistakes, and the enthusiasm in the class was remarkable. Youngsters volunteered eagerly whenever there was an opportunity to write something on the chalkboard or to make an oral response.

On Television and Film

Later in the week, we again visited the Yuri Gagarin school for a televised performance of a suggestopedic operetta. Performed by members of the Bulgarian National Opera Company and a chamber orchestra, the operetta was written by a member of Lozanov's staff and based on a tale by the Brothers Grimm. Lozanov told us that the music, the words, the costumes, and the colors had been carefully chosen to "harmonize consciousness and facilitate learning." We were informed that fifteen experimental schools around the country were watching the televised performance.

The operetta told the story of an old miller and his three apprentices; to determine which one should inherit the mill, he sends them on a search for a horse. Two of the apprentices lure Hans, the third, into a cave and desert him as he dreams about a family of dwarfs:

How many of them are there?
Six dwarfs, wise and clever,
plus four so brave and bold,
makes ten—a familiar sum.
Add three more dwarfs, quite nimble,
quick and artful;
there are thirteen dwarfs in all.

At this point, the numbers flashed on the screen:

$$6+7=(6+4)+3=13.$$

Later, Hans meets thirteen kittens, and another equation is presented:

$$(6+4)+3=10+3=13.$$

When the kittens begin to leave, yet another set of operations is performed:

$$13-7=(13-3)-4=6.$$

Later, Hans discovers nine white and eight black horses:

$$9+8=(9+1)+7=17.$$

Hans selects nine horses to bring back to the old miller, and leaves eight.

$$17-9=(17-7)-2=8.$$

One of the kittens promises to meet Hans at the mill with the nine horses he has chosen.

The operetta's finale finds the two unworthy apprentices returning with an ancient donkey and a blind mule. Even so, they have done better than Hans, who returns empty-handed. As they ridicule the young apprentice, a beautiful woman arrives in a coach driven by nine white horses. The old miller is delighted. But Hans and his lady leave for

. . . a different world,
created by fables
and the dreams of poets.

The class observed the television screens with great interest. Whenever the teacher saw a youngster become distracted, she simply went over and sat by the child. We were told that class discussion would center on the arithmetic problems, the ethical dimensions of the plot, and the songs that the children would learn to read as well as to sing.

Back at our conference room in the Moskva Park Hotel, we were shown two films that demonstrated the use of suggestopedia in other classrooms. One film, made in 1978, depicted two firstgrade classes—one "experimental" and one "control." All of the students were individually tested and none knew how to read. Those students who did have some knowledge of letters and words were placed in a different class.

In the "control" class, children learned words, divided them into syllables, and analyzed the syllables. Other traditional instructional procedures were used; by the end of thirty-two days in the classroom, the "control" children had mastered a rudimentary Bulgarian vocabulary.

The walls of the "experimental" classroom were covered by the pictures containing hidden letters; a tree would, at its base, have the word "tree" spelled out—and also would have a large "T" painted into its trunk and branches. Reading was combined with arithmetic; mathematical sets and subsets were taught as soon as pupils learned the numbers. The teacher's suggestions were indirect; instead of commanding, "Pay attention," she would say, "I am going to tell a story, and everyone who likes a story can listen to me." A television program, "The Day," portrayed additional stories through which reading and arithmetic were taught indirectly. Lozanov uses the term "paraconscious learning" to refer to knowledge assimilated unconsciously or through "peripheral perception." Describing this unique process, Lozanov (1978) has observed:

> There is one category of stimuli which in absolute intensity should belong to the sensory, but which under specific conditions remain unconscious. This occurs most often when other stimuli remain on the "periphery" of the attention. [These] unconscious stimuli are called marginal subsensory stimuli. They are subsensory not in their absolute intensity but in their topicality in the given moment. . . . Peripheral subsensory stimuli play an important role in all interhuman relations. . . . Our studies have shown that this

peripheral unconscious information rests at the base of long-term memory. [pp. 96–97]

By the end of three days, some children were able to match the correct words with pictures identical to those on the walls—even though no formal instruction on those word-picture combinations had been given. At the end of twenty-seven school days, the pupils had a reading knowledge of Bulgarian that surpassed that of the "control" group, which had the benefit of five additional days of instruction.

The second film dealt with adults who were attempting to learn English. At the first meeting, the teacher created a congenial atmosphere, and the students selected new names for the duration of the course. Nikolas became Tom, Ivan became Edward, Donata became Daisy. The teacher then introduced the English vocabulary words, sometimes using pantomime and visual aids. She read the words three times, first in a conversational tone of voice, then in a whisper, then in a loud, bombastic manner. These steps were repeated, this time accompanied by a recording of classical music. But the students were told to listen to the music, not to the teacher.

The next day's class began with role playing. Students would use their new names to act out impromptu skits, utilizing props and costumes, and using the English words that they remembered. After three hours of these activities, the class was dismissed and its members were given some material in English to read before they went to bed.

On the third day, the new material was discussed in a group session. The teacher taught the group songs, games, and plays, using this vocabulary. And then the cycle repeated itself with the introduction of an additional list of new words. After twenty-three days, most of the students purportedly had learned two thousand English words and were able to put them into practice.

Even though this procedure had worked well, it has been superseded by a more integrated approach. Lozanov (1978) has observed:

. . . at the beginning, it was divided up into an "active" part and a "passive" or "concert" part. In the active part of the session, the teacher read the new words with a special three-stage intonation.

In the concert part of the session, the new material was read quietly, with . . . classical music . . . playing in the background. With this variant the students used to be trained in muscle relaxation.

On the basis of the results of our experimental research, the passive part of the session, with the muscle relaxation then practiced, was dropped and only the concert part of it retained. . . . The teacher must be able to modulate the tone and the pitch of his voice to be in harmony with the particular features of the music. In this form, the concert session has proved sufficient for attaining concentrative psychorelaxation even without resorting to exercises in muscle relaxation and rhythmical breathing.

The active session was dropped because it did not produce the same satisfactory results as the concert session. At the same time, it constituted a danger of insufficiently trained teachers intonating unsuitable material and creating some external conditions similar to those for inducing a light form of hypnosis, something which has to be avoided altogether in suggestopedy. For the same reasons, all monotonous sounds and utterances were eliminated from the sessions, as well as the shading of the light in the rooms with curtains. [pp. 268–69]

The practitioners present in Sofia appeared to be aware of these modifications; however, the popular press in the United States and elsewhere often describes suggestopedia as it was practiced in its earlier stages.

That night, our Bulgarian hosts took us to see a splendid production of *La Traviata* at the opera house. Much to our delight, we recognized the two leading male singers from the suggestopedic operetta.

Learning to Music

Back at the Moskva Park Hotel, the purpose of our meeting was explained by Guennadi Matkhanov, a Soviet member of the UNESCO Secretariat. We were to evaluate the educational potential of suggestology and the application of suggestopedia in primary education and adult language learning, and to analyze the applicability of suggestopedia for various types of educational systems. Also attending the conference was Zachari Zachariev, a Bulgarian member of UNESCO who was program director of language learning projects. In addition, we were greeted by Produn Stoyanov, First Deputy Minister of the Bulgarian Ministry of Public Education, who observed that "the social revolution in Bulgaria eliminated educational inequality long ago." He stated that these changes produced a climate favorable for the implementation of innovative educational procedures such as suggestology, which now is used with forty-five hundred children in fifteen schools. In addition, a number of centers use suggestopedia to teach foreign languages to adults. Stoyanov observed that a national program for aesthetic education has been introduced in Bulgarian schools.

Lozanov then presented a discussion of the theoretical foundations of suggestology. He observed that there were human possibilities yet to be appreciated by education—"the hidden reserves of the mind." Lozanov noted that long-term memory, stimulation of creativity, control of pain, bleeding, and other bodily functions were a few of these "hidden reserves"—human potentials that are ordinarily felt to be outside conscious control, or "paraconscious."

According to Lozanov, his work as a psychotherapist was of inestimable value in the development of suggestology. He observed the critical "therapeutic moments" and identified the status of the patient's psychology and physiology at those times. He then attempted to develop educational procedures that would elicit those same conditions. In doing this, he arrived at three fundamental principles of suggestology:

1. Interpersonal communication and mental activity are always conscious and "paraconscious" at the same time. Thus it is important to understand the holistic nature of personality; the conscious and "paraconscious" always work together as do interpersonal and intrapersonal processes.
2. We perceive the world globally rather than in bits and pieces. Every stimulus is coded, symbolized, associated, and generalized, becoming part of a larger pattern.
3. Every perception is complex. The brain works with the impressions of each moment; thus our world view is in a constant state of change. Further, the brain can assimilate a great deal

of information—much more than it has a chance to process in the typical educational institution.

Lozanov observed that psychotherapy and education both rest upon these principles. "We cannot heal without educating, we cannot educate without healing." One aspect of both therapy and education is the liberating effect of knowledge; rather than conditioning individuals, suggestopedic techniques make them aware of their potentials and give them more choices. Lozanov had a quick response to those who accused him of "brainwashing." He replied, "If we don't know the real effect of suggestive influences that are all around us—from television, cinema, music, and the environment—then we are being brainwashed. By becoming aware of suggestion, for the first time we are no longer victims of our own culture."

Therefore, Lozanov's teachers (or "suggestopedists") need to undergo a certain amount of training in psychotherapy. They learn how to "orchestrate" classroom instruction, combining all elements of suggestopedia harmoniously. It must be realized that students unconsciously "mirror" the words of the teacher with their hands, faces, and other parts of the body; this can be an important learning process. Teachers need to learn how to motivate students and keep them in a positive frame of mind. They must know when to be directive and when to be nondirective. They need to be aware of the importance of body language, facial expressions, gestures, and pantomime. And they must know the effects on learning of different types of music, and how to modulate their instruction according to the music.

Suggestopedic methods involve the simultaneous activation of concentration and relaxation, of logic and emotion, of the brain's left and right hemispheres, of the brain's higher and lower centers, and of the unification of conscious and "paraconscious" mental activity. Often, students are presented with new information—such as vocabulary words—while reading silently as the teacher dramatically intones the material. Then the teacher will present the material with a different intonation accompanied by background music—for example, Bach, Vivaldi, or Telemann. (The Sarabande from Bach's "Goldberg Variations" is often used—an aria that Bach reputedly composed to cure Count Kaiserling's insomnia.) This is often referred to as the "concert" phase of suggestopedia; Lozanov suggested that it activates the right hemisphere of the brain's cortex, which is ignored in most traditional education.

Suggestopedia also involves skits, plays, psychodrama, and other opportunities to utilize the new vocabulary in a lifelike situation. Lozanov has divided the material in foreign-language learning into segments that comprise the basic grammar of each language as well as at least two thousand words. He told us that students generally learn 90 percent of the vocabulary well enough to read it, and 60 percent well enough to speak it.

When Lozanov monitored the brain waves, muscle tone, and skin electricity of the students, he noted that they were in a state of alert calmness. It did not resemble hypnosis, nor did it resemble dreaming. Both hemispheres of the brain were active, and many students showed higher percentages of alpha waves than would be expected normally. Lozanov told us that students do not experience fatigue as the result of suggestopedic training. Furthermore, their mental health often improves; according to Lozanov, depression, anxiety, and nervousness frequently disappear.

The Iowa Version

Donald Schuster described his work with "suggestive-accelerative learning and teaching" (or SALT) at Iowa State University. He had not wanted to use the word "suggestology" to describe his procedures, as he had never been to Bulgaria but had devised his practices from a careful reading of Lozanov's articles and lengthy discussions with Lozanov and his teachers. However, after seeing suggestopedia firsthand, Schuster was pleased with how closely it resembled his Iowa version.

Schuster (1976b) had also studied the brain waves of students engaged in suggestopedic instruction. He discovered that the restful state produced was a by-product of suggestopedia, not a cause; alpha waves were not necessary for accelerated learning to take place.

He outlined three types of studies he had supervised at Iowa State: the case study, field research (in classrooms), and experimental research (in a laboratory classroom). Case studies included an art class taught by his wife, an eighth-grade science class, and foreign-language classes at the university level. All used SALT or suggestopedic approaches; all indicated that further study was desirable because of the promising results obtained (for example, Schuster and Prichard, 1978).

As an example of field research, Schuster (1978) described a three-year project in which the teachers were trained to use SALT in elementary and junior high-school classrooms. In their training, they were shown how to present material (reading, spelling, foreign languages, vocational courses) and were coached in emotional communication and in sensitively perceiving the optimal time for instruction. Teachers were urged to enhance their ability to trust, to maintain high expectations, to overcome biases, and to motivate students in nonmanipulative ways. They were helped to develop a self-accepting, assertive, dynamic style and given training in voice, stage presence, singing, nonverbal communication, and psychodrama. No teacher's class showed negative results in comparison with students taught conventionally. In two cases there were no differences between the SALT and "control" classes, but in one of those instances, the SALT teacher was ill for much of the school year. The other eight classes attained higher test scores than did students in the "control" classes, especially in spelling tests. In seven of those cases, the difference was statistically significant.

Schuster also reported several experimental studies. In one such study (Martin and Schuster, 1977) involving 128 subjects, it was discovered that there was an optimal level of stress for learning. Some students were chronically anxious; they learned better if they tensed their muscles while learning new words. Other students were basically relaxed; they learned better if they relaxed their muscles during the SALT sessions.

In another study (Benítez-Bordón and Schuster, 1976), SALT techniques were significantly more effective than traditional techniques in a Spanish instruction class. As the data were based on only a single class session, the experiment was considered a pilot study. When an entire course was taught utilizing SALT tech-

niques, it was found that students in the "experimental" section
learned Spanish in significantly less time than that required by
students in the two "control" sections (Schuster, 1976a). At the
beginning of the course, the students were told:

> This course will have a positive effect on you. You will find that it
> is a pleasant experience. . . . Learning Spanish is going to be a
> game and an enjoyable experience for you. Take your Spanish
> name given you and use it to project yourself into a situation such
> as in a Latin American country where you are speaking Spanish
> and having a lot of fun. . . . At this point, think about the first
> time in your life when you were learning to read, that you realized
> that you liked reading and enjoyed it. . . . Now take your
> Spanish name, change this same enjoyable English experience, and
> translate it into Spanish. Realize that it is fun in the same
> way. . . . Shortly we are going to be reading Spanish words to
> you, spelling them, translating them into English, and repeating
> them again in Spanish. Pretend that you are attending a concert
> and get into the same frame of mind. . . . Flow along with the
> material, get its true meaning, concentrate on the overall meaning,
> and let the details fall into place in your subconscious mind. . . .
> Feel yourself back in that first happy experience again. Your mind
> is clear, alert, you feel good and whole. Now you are back in
> school when you first learned to read and enjoyed it. Now use
> your Spanish name and see yourself reading and enjoying
> Spanish. . . . Your mind is inquiring, active, but you feel com-
> fortable and at ease. The material is interesting to learn. . . .
> Here we go.
>
> (One-half hour of a native Spanish person's speaking Spanish
> words and phrases with English translations on a cassette recorder
> followed. Then the material was reviewed and the instructions al-
> tered slightly.) Concentrate on the music; let the words sink in. If
> you find yourself dozing, return simply to the music and the
> words. Watch your breathing; say "in" to yourself mentally as you
> inhale and "out" as you exhale. At the end of this time you will be
> refreshed, relaxed, alert, and very much alive. You will feel
> confident in your usage of Spanish. When you want to use your
> Spanish, relax, remember this comfortable learning situation, and
> the words will come to you as desired. . . . [pp. 43–44]

The SALT students met once a week for a two-hour session; nineteen students completed the course. The "control" sections
consisted of two classes of sixteen students each. They met five

times per week (for a total of six hours) during a college quarter. Data from a student questionnaire did not reveal that the SALT students did any more homework than the other students; in fact, half of them reported that they devoted less time to studying than they did for their other courses.

Schuster told us that the use of imagery is a critical element of SALT. When students were told *not* to use imagery, their language scores dropped 50 percent. Their retention was excellent when they tried to see words in their "mind's eye" or when they were given specific instruction in this skill (Schuster, 1976a; Schuster, Stavish, and Burchinal, 1976). This report reminded me of my own work with children whose learning disabilities interfered with their reading and spelling competency. Often, developing their ability to visualize letters and words was the key to facilitating their mastery of written language.

Suggestopedia Around the World

Cecelia Pollack (1976, 1979) described her use of suggestopedic principles in private practice with learning-disabled students. In one instance, a youngster named Randy Smith was renamed "Dandy Learner." He was asked to imagine that he had a magic pen; Pollack took him through a guided imagery session (accompanied by a Bach selection) in which he directed this pen in his "mind's eye" to practice words he had failed in a spelling test. Later he was able to use pencil and paper to produce the same words, spelling eighteen of twenty correctly. Further, he remembered most of them on his next appointment with Pollack. She also reminded the group that Lozanov's basic principles—for example, that stimuli are coded, symbolized, and generalized—rested on the monumental work of I. P. Pavlov, the great Russian psychologist and physiologist who had noted that suggestion is the simplest and most typical conditioned reflex.

Gabriel Racle (1975, 1977) told us about his project, supported by the Public Service Commission of Canada, which used suggestopedia in his country's efforts to produce bilingual civil servants. The project was initiated in 1972 when a team of Canadian teachers arrived in Sofia to study the Lozanov method. Results of the first Canadian experiment were announced in 1973. English-speaking people learned French quite well in suggestopedic classes. Racle (1975) observed, "The students were satisfied, the teachers were satisfied, learning was well under way, and there were no major negative reactions. . . . The transfer from Bulgaria to Canada was possible" (p. 113).

Another experiment began in 1974, this time with both French and English courses. The students in the suggestopedic courses learned as well as students in traditional classes as measured by tests of speaking and listening vocabulary. However, in tests of speaking and listening communication, the suggestopedic students were clearly superior to the others, due, perhaps, to the emphasis on practical usage in suggestopedia. It was also observed that older students learned as well as younger students—while in the "control" classes, the younger people made superior scores.

Racle concluded that society imposes a large number of limitations upon learning. The limitations result from incompetent teachers, a boring routine at school, a fear of failure, and ignorance of the total capacity of humans—both physiological and psychological. Suggestopedic methods remove people's prior conditioning and foster personality development. Indeed, Racle noted, many of the students in the Canadian program lost such psychosomatic symptoms as headaches, stomach cramps, and anxiety following their training. A frequent comment from the students was, "We like the course because we are treated as adults."

Fanny Saféris (1979), a French psycholinguist, observed that the first suggestopedic course in France was offered in English to adults at the University of Paris in 1977. Since then, additional courses have been offered in various languages at several institutions of higher learning, including the Sorbonne. She noted that there are a number of highly sophisticated language instructional techniques in France, but none as satisfactory as suggestopedia in leading to the creative use of the new language.

Her colleague, Fauda Winnykamen of René Descartes University in Paris, injected a note of caution. She speculated that much of the suggestopedic effect could be explained by the teacher's confidence in the students and the elicitation of the students' confidence in their own capacities. Lozanov replied that he encourages teachers to build up this positive expectancy with students and that this is a vital part of the program.

Katja Piller discussed the four-year-old suggestopedia program at Polytechnical University in Budapest, Hungary. Some students have taken one language class in the morning and another in the afternoon, attaining success in learning both languages. Foreign-language courses have become so popular that some students must wait for a year before they can be admitted. Since 1974, some one hundred suggestopedic courses have been offered in English, German, Russian, and Spanish to Hungarian students at various technical institutes and universities. A samovar is an essential teaching device in the Russian classes for the skits and plays, and most classes take a trip to the USSR—at the university's expense—to put their Russian into practice.

Christer Landahl, a Swedish teacher, reported on the success of suggestopedic foreign-language courses for high-school students in Sweden. A program has also been activated to teach Swedish to immigrant workers in 250 suggestopedic sessions. In June 1978, Lozanov and his assistant, Evilina Gateva, came to Sweden and gave a three-day demonstration of how an Italian class would be taught with suggestopedic techniques; this stimulated international interest in the topic, as it was a featured attraction at the First European Congress of Hypnosis in Psychotherapy and Psychosomatic Medicine.

Klaus Jänicke, a professor at Karl Marx University in Leipzig, surveyed the scene in East Germany where seventy suggestopedic language courses have been offered in English, French, Russian, and Spanish. Jänicke claimed that, generally, in six weeks students learn over three thousand vocabulary words as well as the basic grammar of a language.

Both Landahl and Jänicke observed that a small number of students objected to the type of music used. I felt that this was inevitable because musical taste is highly personal and many young people have never developed a liking for classical music. Jänicke stressed the importance of music in relaxing the students while still facilitating the reception of information. Observing that the three dimensions of suggestopedia—the psychological, the educational, and the artistic—must always be integrated, Lozanov pointed out that music assists this integration. Landahl agreed, noting that music facilitates concentration among the students he has observed, and Schuster stressed that although research studies have demonstrated that the music is not important by itself it does assist learning in combination with other elements of the program.

Suggestopedia programs also have been established in both Austria and the USSR. There were no representatives at the conference to describe them, but frequent mention was made of the Ludwig Voltzmann Institute for Learning (in Vienna) and the Soviet suggestopedia classes (usually referred to as "accelerated learning") at Togliatti University, the Maurice Thorez Institute for Foreign Languages, the Pushkin Institute, and the V. I. Lenin State Pedagogical Institute.* V. M. Bekhterev had used suggestion in education in the 1920s, calling it "motivated self-suggestion."

Lozanov has emphasized the importance of motivation in suggestopedia, obtaining considerable support from the research studies of D. N. Uznadze's "set" theory in developing suggestology, noting that Uznadze linked motivation with "set." Lozanov (1978, p. 52) observed that every person has his or her own special "set," which determines the manifestation of various motivation trends in that person's activity, as well as the direction of conscious attention.

One's "set," or psychological orientation, however, is largely unconscious. Uznadze has maintained that "set" precedes consciousness. According to Uznadze, people live in a particular environment that provides them with the opportunity to satisfy many of their needs. The human organism reacts to different stimuli—if they correspond to a particular internal need. But before displaying a particular response, the organism has created a special psychoneurological disposition, which is an unconscious "set." If the external stimulus is subliminal and not strong enough to provoke a reaction, the individual still is affected and a disposition is created.

Sometimes, suggestopedia does not elicit an immediate response, but will help produce a "set" that will enable surprisingly strong responses (such as newly learned vocabulary words) to

* Vyschoslav Vyacheslavovich, a Soviet inventor, applied for a U.S. patent on August 4, 1975, for an "information conversion system for accelerated instruction." This system provides for multichannel recording of information and is claimed to be a mechanized form of suggestopedia.

emerge because of the "set" that was produced. On the other hand, suggestions may not be effective if they are incompatible with other aspects of "set"—for example, culture, ethics, interest, expectations. New stimuli are more likely to be incorporated if they are congruent with the pre-existing "set." One way of enhancing the effects of suggestopedia is to prepare the students carefully, creating receptive conditions that will be favorable to new learning (Philipov, 1979, p. 383; Zemke and Nicholson, 1977). Thus "set" both facilitates the new learning and is a precondition for it.

In 1975, I. Z. Velkovskiy reported a Soviet attempt to replicate Lozanov's work. Twelve students in Kharkov were enrolled in a foreign-language class to determine if they could master two thousand new words in one month. Velkovskiy, a member of the Kharkov Psychological Institute, enlisted a jury of educators and psychologists to evaluate the results. The students learned twenty-two hundred or more words in a month, and the experiment was considered a success. Velkovskiy (1975) added that "no overfatigue . . . appeared in any of the students attending the course, either during their lessons or during the normal hours of work" (p. 17). Further, "the effect of the course on persons with neurosis was typical of a successful course of psychotherapy, namely, the disappearance of headache, irritability, and depression, and the appearance of a good appetite, sound sleep, and cheerful self-confidence." Velkovskiy (1975) noted that Lozanov's emphasis on the "paraconscious" reminded some people of Sigmund Freud. However,

> None of the scientists in the USSR who have studied the theoretical principles formulated by G. Lozanov . . . have found any Freudian positions in them. . . . The evil of Freud's doctrine lies not in the recognition of the unconscious but in the idealistic . . . treatment of the unconscious. . . . However, there is not even a trace of that in the entirely materialistic ideas of G. Lozanov about the reserve capacities of the individual, which lie in the unconscious. . . . [p. 20]

Velkovskiy concluded that Lozanov's contribution "is a new milestone along the road of humanism" (p 21).

Another Soviet report was presented by G. A. Kitaygorodskaya in 1975. She described the courses in foreign languages at the Maurice Thorez Institute in Moscow; three thousand words have been taught over a ten-week period, with the students taking five one-hour lessons per week. There were thirty-minute homework assignments and an extra one or two hours of supplemental work per week in an "electronic hall" where films were shown. Kitaygorodskaya (1975) concluded, "It can be assumed that the suggestopaedic system can be used successfully in courses of instruction in widely differing subjects, provided all the principles of suggestopaedia are duly observed" (p. 24).

A New Challenge

On Friday, we returned to the Yuri Gagarin school. Each of the second graders was now able to read the story about the Smith family; about Fluffy, the "greedy fat cat"; and about Dixie, the red, green, and yellow parrot. One of the members of our group had brought several copies of a story of her own. It read, in part:

> This cat is on the mat.
> Nancy's brother is George's father.
> A dog sits in the little yellow bath.
> They paint the pets green.
> Julia's mother is bigger than Hattie's.

I showed a copy to several children. Some of them read it perfectly, despite the fact that many of the words were new to them and that the letters were formed somewhat differently than the renditions of the English alphabet they had studied that week. Other pupils were only able to identify an occasional word or phrase. However, none of the youngsters was reluctant to try; their eagerness to meet a new challenge and their lack of any fear of failure was even more impressive to me than their knowledge of the letters, sounds, and words.

I reminded our group that many educational techniques attract considerable attention when first introduced. Teachers are excited about novel approaches, and this excitement is transferred to their students. The students are highly motivated because they find themselves involved in an experimental program that is highly publicized. After a few years the excitement often wears off and achievement levels go down. In the United States, this was the fate of teaching machines in the early 1960s; once the enthusiasm receded, so did the test scores. Schools put the machines into storage, losing thousands of dollars in the process. I emphasized the need for long-range studies of suggestology to insure that it is the approach itself that yields outstanding results, rather than the enthusiasm surrounding the approach.

We concluded our meeting by unanimously adopting a resolution calling for more research, for an expansion of teacher training, for teacher certification, and for the creation of an international association for suggestology.* Our resolution noted that "suggestopedia is a superior teaching method" and we encouraged its use for increasing literacy in the developing countries. The representatives from UNESCO promised to do what they could to facilitate our suggestions.

Lozanov was pleased with the results of the conference. In his closing remarks he again observed that the concept of unused reserves was based on neurophysiology: "Each of us has more reserves of personality than science has considered possible."

References

Benítez-Bordón, R., and Schuster, D. H. The effects of a suggestive learning climate, synchronized breathing and music on the learning and retention of Spanish words. *Journal of Suggestive-Accelerative Learning and Teaching,* 1976, *1,* 27–40.

Block, A. B. The sputnik of the classrooms. *New West,* July 18, 1977.

Kitaygorodskaya, G. A. The suggestopaedic system of instruction and suggestopaedic courses. *Suggestology and Suggestopaedia* (Sofia), 1975, *1,* 22–25.

* Elizabeth Philipov, responding to this resolution, founded the International Academy for Holistic Learning Methods in 1979. The academy's central office is Vochtingstrasse 1, P.O. Box 1766, D-7400 Tübingen, West Germany.

Krippner, S. Hypnosis and reading improvement among university students. *American Journal of Clinical Hypnosis,* 1963, *5,* 187–93.

————. Individual hypnosis, group hypnosis, and the improvement of academic achievement. In I. A. Greenberg (ed.), *Group Hypnotherapy and Hypnodrama.* Chicago: Nelson-Hall, 1977.

Lozanov, G. *Suggestologia.* Sofia: Nauka i Iskutsvo, 1971.

————. The nature and history of the suggestopaedic system of teaching foreign languages and its experimental prospects. *Suggestology and Suggestopaedia* (Sofia), 1975, *1,* 5–14.

————. *Suggestology and Outlines of Suggestopedy.* New York: Gordon & Breach, 1978.

Lozanov, G., et al. (eds.). *Problems of Suggestology.* Sofia: Nauka i Iskutsvo, 1973.

Martin, D. J., and Schuster, D. H. The interaction of trait anxiety and muscle tension in learning. *Journal of Suggestive-Accelerative Learning and Teaching,* 1977, *2,* 63–67.

Miele, P. M. The power of suggestion: A new way of learning languages. *Parade,* Mar. 12, 1978.

Pavlov, I. P. *Lectures on Conditioned Reflexes.* New York: International Publishers, 1941. (Originally published in 1928.)

Philipov, E. R. Suggestopedia: The use of music and suggestion in learning and hyperamnesia. *Journal of Suggestive-Accelerative Learning and Teaching,* 1978, *3,* 65–107.

————. The role of suggestology in the arts of healing and learning. In H. A. Otto and J. W. Knight (eds.), *Dimensions in Holistic Healing.* Chicago: Nelson-Hall, 1979.

Pollack, C. Educational experiment: Therapeutic pedagogy. *Journal of Suggestive-Accelerative Learning and Teaching,* 1976, *1,* 95–99.

————. Suggestology and suggestopedia revisited. *Journal of Suggestive-Accelerative Learning and Teaching,* 1979, *4,* 16–31.

Racle, G. (ed.). *A Teaching Experience with the Suggestopaedic Method.* Ottawa: Public Service Commission of Canada, 1975.

Racle, G. Practical developments and theoretical concepts of suggestopaedia in language teaching in Canada. *Journal of*

Suggestive-Accelerative Learning and Teaching, 1977, *2,* 118–27.

Saféris, F. One year of suggestopedia in France. *Journal of Suggestive-Accelerative Learning and Teaching,* 1979, *4,* 52–56.

Schuster, D. H. A preliminary evaluation of the suggestive-accelerative Lozanov method in teaching beginning Spanish. *Journal of Suggestive-Accelerative Learning and Teaching,* 1976, *1,* 41–47. (a)

————. The effects of the alpha mental state, indirect suggestion, and associative mental activity on learning rare English words. *Journal of Suggestive-Accelerative Learning and Teaching,* 1976, *1,* 116–23. (b)

————. The effects of suggestive-accelerative teaching in elementary and junior high schools. *Journal of Suggestive-Accelerative Learning and Teaching,* 1978, *2,* 156–61.

Schuster, D. H., Benítez-Bordón, R., and Gritton, C. A. *Suggestive-Accelerative Learning and Teaching: A Manual of Classroom Procedures Based on the Lozanov Method.* Des Moines, Ia.: Suggestive-Accelerative Learning and Teaching, 1976.

Schuster, D. H., and Miele, P. Minutes of Conference for Suggestology, Dec. 11–16, 1978, Sofia, Bulgaria. *Journal of Suggestive-Accelerative Learning and Teaching,* 1978, *3,* 211–22.

Schuster, D. H., and Prichard, R. A. A two-year evaluation of the suggestive-accelerative learning and teaching (SALT) method in central Iowa public high schools. *Journal of Suggestive-Accelerative Learning and Teaching,* 1978, *3,* 108–22.

Schuster, D. H.; Stavish, M.; and Burchinal, M. The effects of imaging ability, prepared images and sex of subject on learning English words. *Journal of Suggestive-Accelerative Learning and Teaching,* 1976, *1,* 124–30.

Schwartz, I. E. [*Suggestion in Pedagogical Processes.*] Perm: Perm State Pedagogical Institute, 1971.

Simurov, A. [Is it possible to learn a language in a month?] *Pravda,* July 27, 1969.

Velkovskiy, I. Z. The ideas and method of G. Lozanov in the eyes of the psychotherapeutist-psychohygienist. *Suggestology and Suggestopaedia* (Sofia), 1975, *1,* 16–21.

Wolkowski, Z. W. Suggestology: A major contribution by Bulgarian scientists. *Frontiers of Science,* 1974, *2,* 8–12.

Zemke, R., and Nicholson, D. R. Suggestology: Will it really revolutionize training? *Training,* Jan. 1977.

CHAPTER 7

Around a Language in Fifty Days

We do not doubt that we . . . have made errors. But through our own experience we have become firmly convinced that there is no error about the main point —the right to existence of the science of suggestology. . . . We are far from saying that we can supply the ultimate answers to all the problems. We have only taken one of the possible roads to revealing a small part of man's possibilities.

Georgi Lozanov (1978, p. 11)

Early in 1979, I received an invitation to visit suggestopedia classes in Hungary. The letter was sent by the director of the Hungarian Scientific and Technical Societies, whose office is one of the locations in Budapest where foreign languages are taught with suggestopedic methods.

When I arrived in Budapest in May, I was met by an official car, which took me to my hotel and then to the offices of the Hungarian Societies. One of the teachers, Alexander Jarovinsky, introduced me to the teaching staff who had gathered to meet me and to discuss the direction that suggestopedia has taken in Hungary. I discovered that foreign-language classes are sponsored by the Hungarian Scientific and Technical Societies, by the Ministry of Culture, and by the Technical University. I had heard a report by Kathy Pillar at the Sofia conference describing the work she and her colleagues were doing at the Technical University, and in the next few days, I had the opportunity to visit classes arranged by the other two organizations.

An Imaginary Conference

The Hungarian Societies' staff members offer courses in English, Spanish, German, and Russian. (Four to eight years of Russian are required in all public schools, but students who enroll for the suggestopedic course typically are unable to converse in the language.) There is an introductory course of five weeks followed by a secondary course, which also lasts for five weeks. Students meet for four hours per day, five days a week. When I visited the English course, I learned that the students were completing the final week of the secondary course. I was given the lesson plans for both the courses and observed that they often centered around an imaginary conference held in London. For example, early in the course, students role play the process of checking into the hotel:

PETER: Excuse me, madam. Aren't you Linda King, the singer?
LINDA: Yes, I am a singer. Are you a delegate too?
PETER: Yes, I am. My name is Peter Reeves. How do you do? Happy to meet you.
LINDA: How do you do? Glad to meet you. Where are you from, Mr. Reeves?
PETER: I am from Leeds.
LINDA: What is your job?
PETER: I am an engineer in a factory.

A brief lesson on the verb "to be" followed, contrasting the positive form (for example, "I am happy," "You are on the list," "He is in London") to the negative form (for example, "She is not from Boston," "We are not neighbors," "They are not delegates"). This lesson takes two or three class sessions to complete, as do the other lessons.

Lesson two takes place on the second day of the imaginary conference. The delegates have a lively conversation during the refreshment break.

ALLAN: Hello everybody. Oh photos! You miss your families. I
    am still a bachelor and have only a mother and father.
IRENE: Have you no brothers or sisters?
ALLAN: No brothers. No sisters. No wives. I am a lucky fellow.

Grammar exercises centered on the verb "to have" in its positive
form (for example, "We have a lot of friends"); negative form
(for example, "We haven't many photos"); and interrogative form
(for example, "Have we many friends?").

By the third day of the conference, some of the delegates have
found a supermarket and have been invited to Upton's home.

UPTON: Will you have some gin?
ROBERT: Alcohol is our enemy.
UPTON: They say we must love our enemies.
ROBERT: Yes, but not swallow them.

The fourth lesson involves sight-seeing; by this time, the grammar
lessons have moved to comparison of adjectives ("better," "best,"
"worse," "worst," etc.).

In the fifth lesson Robert and Arthur are trying to cheer up
Linda:

ROBERT: Linda, don't always look on the black side of things. Do
    you know the difference between a pessimist and an optimist?
ARTHUR: The optimist says, "The bottle is half full." The pessi-
    mist says, "It's half empty."

One of the instructors brought this lesson to my attention when
we were touring Buda, the city that united with Pest in the nineteenth century to produce Budapest. In the middle of a historic
collection of stately buildings that were centuries old, a Hilton
hotel had been constructed. The instructor asked for my opinion,
stating that many of her friends considered it a monstrosity. Noting that the building architect had tried to keep the design simple
and had matched the color to the surroundings, I replied, "Well,
it could be worse." The instructor remarked, "You are like the
optimist who sees the bottle as half full."

Lesson six of the introductory course contains episodes concerning a soccer match, a performance of *Hamlet,* and an attempt
at letter writing. This gives class members a chance to write their

own letters and to share their experiences with sports and the theater—in the context of the imaginary conference.

By days seven, eight, and nine, it appears as if the delegates are spending more time sight-seeing and socializing than attending conference meetings. After dinner, Allan cannot find his wallet:

ALLAN: What shall I do now? I've left my money behind. I'll have to borrow some money to pay the bill.

PAUL: Sorry, I'm broke. I can't lend you a penny.

WAITER: Here is the bill, sir. And a letter for you.

ALLAN: The letter reads, "Cheer up. We'll never leave you in a tight corner."

FRIENDS: (They return the wallet, which they have hidden. They reveal the trick and burst out laughing.)

ALLAN: A friend in need is a friend indeed. Was that the idea?

Lesson ten concluded with the delegates at the airport making their farewells. The grammar has advanced to the use of relative pronouns (for example, "who," "whom," "whose"), and the use of the simple future tense (for example, "Our dreams will come true tomorrow"), present continuous tense (for example, "I'm going window shopping"), and the interrogative tense (for example, "When does he start?"). I was told that the final class session usually consists of an extended dramatization in which class members have an opportunity to converse spontaneously with each other, pulling together all the language skills they have learned over the past sessions. The lesson materials include songs (such as "Auld Lang Syne" and "Home on the Range"), humor, and information about the countries using the language being studied.

The new material is presented on alternate days, utilizing the typical suggestopedic methods. To produce a relaxing effect, the slow movements of baroque music are used. This type of classical music has a steady beat of about one beat per second, sixty per minute. Typical selections include the Bach and Telemann flute concertos, and the largo movements from the symphonies and concertos of Handel and Vivaldi. The tempo of a recording can be checked against a clock with a second hand to be sure it is about sixty beats per minute (Ostrander and Schroeder, 1979). The educators at Karl Marx University in Leipzig, East Germany, have observed that the best baroque selections for suggestopedia feature string instruments and have a slow, constant rhythm. The melodic structure is not distracting, and the harmonic patterns are based on specific ratios.

For best results, the material to be learned is presented in an eight-to-ten-second rhythm. Sometimes a follow-up session is made with romantic classical music and emotionally toned presentations by the instructor.

I was familiar with a hypnotic procedure developed by Linn Cooper and Milton Erickson (1959) that used rhythm. To establish this procedure, they set a metronome at sixty beats per minute and used ten-second activity cycles. The hypnotized subjects listened to the metronome click and experienced the beats as being slower than clock time. As a result, time seemed to expand. One subject, a fashion designer, was asked after ten seconds:

HYPNOTIST: How long did it seem that you were working?
DESIGNER: Maybe an hour. . . .
HYPNOTIST: What did you do?
DESIGNER: . . . First I thought about pleats. . . . I was sitting in an easy chair at home. I don't usually use pencil and paper. After I have the dress in mind, I may draw it. . . .
HYPNOTIST: Were you pleased with the dress?
DESIGNER: Yes.

Cooper and Erickson's work is still controversial as attempts to replicate it have not produced consistent results.

Under the London Subways

The class session I visited was held in the offices of the Hungarian Scientific and Technical Societies. A dozen students were seated in comfortable chairs arranged in a circle. Maps of several English-speaking countries festooned the walls of the classroom; also in view were other appropriate materials, including a map of the London subway system.

The class members as well as Peter Hargitai, the instructor, were dressed informally, many of them wearing sandals and blue jeans. There were equal numbers of men and women, all of whom appeared to be in their late twenties or in their thirties. Most of them were taking the secondary course for professional reasons, but a few were enrolled because of personal interest; all seemed highly motivated. A majority of the class members were engineers; in addition, there were a few people involved in management as well as one psychologist. I was told that the company allows the students to take time off for these courses and usually pays the two-hundred-dollar precourse fee.

The actual professions—and names—of the class members are disregarded during the classes in suggestopedia. Instead, the students took on the identities suggested by the teaching manual: Allan Black (a Canadian actor), Daisy Gray (an American playwright), Paul Norman (an Australian reporter), Linda King (a British singer), Robert Fox (a British physician), Irene O'Brien (an Irish writer), and Roland Roma (a British sociologist). The class added a few characters of their own, including Charley, the chess champion; all of these individuals purportedly had met in London at the international conference.

Indeed, on the day of my visit, the conference had ended and each class member offered a toast from an empty glass. Each toast was individual and many made use of idioms:

> Dear friends: The time has flown. The congress was very useful. I hope everyone will be very successful.
>
> The festival was very interesting and useful. I hope we shall met again. (At the prompting of the instructor, "met" was changed to "meet.") A friend in need is a friend indeed.
>
> I'm very sad today to leave you. Charley was the hero of the day. Last but not least, let me thank my teacher.

One of the class members was asked to name the student who offered the best toast. He designated Shirley, who was given some Hungarian candy as a prize. These frequent rewards were made in the spirit of fun rather than as serious competition, but they did serve the purpose of stimulating evaluation by one's fellow students

The use of idioms was further rehearsed as students were asked how they felt. Each class member attempted to make a response not used previously; one student was "as fresh as a daisy," while another was "as fit as a fiddle." The weather was discussed; original remarks were again requested.

Every half hour or so, Hargitai would direct the class members' attention to their song sheets and would turn on his tape recorder The group would sing "A Hundred Miles," "My Darlin' Clementine," or some other American song. I observed that Hargitai was supplied with a great variety of unusual materials as well as books and magazines printed in English. (*Time* and *Newsweek* were available at certain newsstands when I was in Budapest, a significant change from my previous visit in 1973.)

The next exercise involved activities at the airport as the "conference" participants began to leave London. Typical phrases and sentences that had been introduced in the previous day's "concert" session were put to use. Then the class was divided into pairs to practice the material relating to flight arrangements. I was told that this maneuver was one of the original facets of Lozanov's foreign-language instructional method. However, a few months earlier, when the Bulgarian teachers came to Budapest to give the Hungarian instructors an updated training course, they had modified the traditional method by placing more stress on individual monologues. The modification was a controversial one among the Hungarian teachers as it took time away from the practice in pairs, which allowed each student to use the new language more frequently in a social situation.

"Suggestopedic English"

"Suggestopedic English" was one of the issues I discussed at some length with the instructors in Budapest. They were a talented group, consisting of psychologists, linguists, teachers, and members of other professional groups. Most of them also had full-time jobs but taught one or two suggestopedic courses to supplement their income and to further their own knowledge about the process of language instruction.

The instructors agreed that the main concern of the students was to have a practical working knowledge of the foreign language and that the courses should be conducted in a spirit of excitement and good humor. However, some of them observed that the course materials were not complex enough for their students, many of whom would be using the new language for conversations with individuals who preferred to discuss abstract matters, theories, and ideas. The social situations in the text were often sentimental instead of intellectual, and the English used was somewhat old-fashioned and stilted. This led many instructors to supplement the text with current idioms, slang expressions, and jokes. One that I heard discussed in the class concerned an American visitor to London:

ENGLISHMAN: This is the National Gallery, one of our largest museums.

AMERICAN: Well, we have restaurants in America larger than that.

ENGLISHMAN: And this is a statue of Prince Albert, Queen Victoria's husband.

AMERICAN: We have statues of football players bigger than that.

(There is a break in the conversation as a fire engine races down the street.)

AMERICAN: That's a pretty big vehicle. What is it?

ENGLISHMAN: (Exasperated). Oh that's just a window cleaner who is late to work.

Another point of contention was the use of body language. One instructor had the students on their feet much of the time so that they would be encouraged to use gestures. I remarked that much of the meaning in a verbal communication is carried by nonverbal elements such as facial expressions, tone of voice, and bodily movement. There also were different opinions on whether mistakes should be corrected immediately or later, whether the speaking of Hungarian should ever be permitted in the class, and how much of the time should be taken by the instructor's comments.

One of the greatest concerns of some instructors was that their students might be obtaining too superficial a knowledge of the new language. One instructor said that "Suggestopedic English" does not enable students to do well at a professional congress; as a result a special "conference course" is sometimes taught for this purpose. But the opinion was also voiced that the potential is present to teach more thoroughly if the students are willing to work hard enough.

Another teacher surmised that suggestopedia teaches "around" the language rather than "through" it. The linguistic nature of a language is not adequately taught, grammar is given insufficient attention, and spelling is virtually ignored. Conversational vocabulary is given primary attention, with grammar emerging from it in a rather informal way. Thus suggestopedic courses do not prepare many students to take the state examination, which emphasizes knowledge of the language's structure.

I was sympathetic to these concerns because of my familiarity with the ongoing controversy in the area of reading instruction in America (Krippner, 1967). For several decades, the "synthetic" school has emphasized the learning of speech sounds and the letters to which they usually correspond. The child then learns how to combine these sounds and letters into words and, later, into sentences. The "analytic" school takes a different approach, encouraging the memorization of sentences and whole words, and only later helping the child to analyze the components of these larger units. The latter procedure is defended on the basis of enhanced pupil interest and motivation. However, most of the research tends to support the effectiveness of the "synthetic" approach, or an eclectic method that utilizes the best of both approaches (Chall, 1978).

I inquired as to the possibility of a more systematic introduction of a language's structural elements into the course through suggestopedia. I recalled that the children in Sofia learn grammar through suggestopedia and that there is nothing about a language's structure that would make it impossible to teach through Lozanov's approach.

In the meantime, it was advised that the suggestopedia courses be clearly identified as useful only for conversational English, French, German, or Russian. In this way, the courses would not be seen as competitive with the more traditional courses, which prepare students for the state language examinations.

I mentioned that some language instructors in the United States utilize a number of procedures that resemble suggestology. At Dartmouth College, for example, an "Intensive Language Model" initiates conversation in the new language on the first day of class. Each initial course requires two hours of drill a day as well as four hours of "language laboratory" work a week. During the first hour, the instructor might present a "microlog," a one-minute monologue that explains how to do something such as making a crepe. Then the instructor asks, "What are the ingredients?" or "How long does it cook?" During the second hour, smaller groups of students are drilled in the same lesson by apprentice teachers who attempt to elicit about sixty-five responses per student per hour. Drills may include imaginary telephone conversations, mock press conferences with "visiting dignitaries," and various word games. After ten weeks of instruction, the students go abroad for ten weeks to live with foreign families; they continue their intensive study, emphasizing grammar, under the supervision of a Dartmouth instructor. The course ends back at the college with a ten-week literature survey. In a report on the program, *Time* magazine (August 16, 1976) quoted an instructor as saying, "If you want to teach, you have to be willing to walk out of the class exhausted."

However, at least four principles set Lozanov's procedures apart from other approaches to learning:

1. His concept of "reserves of the mind."
2. His stress on unconscious functional organization to activate those reserves.
3. His identification of the barriers that resist activation.
4. His use of suggestion as a tool to bypass the barriers, change the unconscious organization of the psyche, and activate one's mental reserves.

None of the Hungarian instructors took issue with these basic maxims as have some Eastern European and Soviet educators (for example, Morgun, 1978) who emphasize fully conscious processes in the acquisition of a second language.

Holograms in the Brain

We also discussed matters of a more theoretical nature. Some of the instructors had read Karl Pribram's (1971) important book, *Languages of the Brain,* in its Russian translation. I had met Pribram at several conferences and was both impressed and intrigued by his work.

Other researchers have observed that memory is a result of biochemical changes in the brain; memory is stored in individual cells and is recalled when activated by the electrochemical activity of nerve cells. However, traces of the same memory have been shown to exist in more than one area of the brain. Further, when one area is damaged, another area often appears to take over and memory is not severely impaired (Goleman, 1979).

Pribram suggests that neurological data indicate that the brain often works in a manner resembling the mathematical transformation that occurs when a three-dimensional image is projected into space in holography. Laser beams consist of rays of focused monochromatic (that is, having only one frequency) light. (Ordinary light consists of diffused unfocused light rays of many different frequencies.) In holography, two laser beams are utilized—one, the "reference" beam, is focused on a photographic plate, while another beam of the same frequency is reflected off an object, such as a vase, and then strikes the photographic plate. The two beams form an "interference pattern" on the plate (resembling the wave pattern formed by two pebbles dropped in a calm lake). The interference pattern on the plate thus "stores" the image of the vase. When a laser light of the same frequency as the original is directed through the plate, the interference pattern is "reconstituted" to form a three-dimensional holographic image identical to the original vase. One can see a replica of the vase, projected away from the plate, that appears three-dimensional in that the viewer can see different sides of it from different positions. Furthermore, if a section of the plate is removed, that section will still be able to project an image of the vase, albeit one less distinct. According to Pribram, the hologram provides us with a model of how memory is stored in the brain and later reconstructed.

Pribram (1978) has suggested that the brain can also work in a manner resembling a computer, especially when electrochemical connections are made between nerve cells. He hypothesized that the left hemisphere of the human brain's cerebral cortex works in a way resembling a computer program. The right hemisphere, however, works with images that are compatible with the holographic model. Images, unlike computer programs, can be comprehended in their totality even after brief exposures and tend to be holistic rather than analytic. They are compatible with the visual arts, while the computer programs are related to linguistics. I observed that traditional language teaching may be oriented to the left-hemisphere, computer-programming components of the brain, while suggestopedia may be oriented to the brain's right-hemisphere, holographic-image components.

If this were true, even to a limited extent, there would be individual differences in people's receptivity to suggestopedia. There would also be some topics that would have to be adapted into an image rather than a program before they could be taught effectively through suggestopedia. Thus it seems that suggestopedic foreign-language instruction, which utilizes art, music, body language, dramatizations, and nonlinear presentation of information (as in the "concert" sessions and by incorporating subliminal perception), would be compatible with the brain's ability to store memory holographically.

One of the instructors told me that a recent series of language studies confirmed much of what I had proposed. M. L. Albert and L. K. Obler (1978) investigated the acquisition of a second language, finding that the right hemisphere played a major role. They proposed that a second language could be more easily learned if it were taught through nursery rhymes, music, dance, and techniques employing visuospatial skills. As the brain is dynamic and plastic throughout life, Albert and Obler hypothesized that the right hemisphere could play a critical role in learning a new language at any age level.

Forget That You Are Hungarian!

I also visited the suggestopedic class in English taught by Eva Füredi at the Fészek Club, an elegant building designated many years ago as "a club for actors, architects, artists, and other fools." The class, consisting of seven men and seven women, had been organized by the Hungarian Ministry of Culture. The class members, whose ages varied considerably, included actors, artists, art historians, journalists, writers, and workers in the television industry. The students were in the middle of the five-week secondary course.

The other class had commenced at 2:00 P.M.; this class started at 8:30 A.M. and continued for four hours. Peter Hargitai, the instructor in the first class I had observed, spoke with an American accent; Eva Füredi spoke with a cultured English accent, and the difference could be noted in the students' pronunciations.

The instructor pressed the lever on her tape recorder, the students turned to their song sheets, and merrily rendered a lyric by the Beatles: "Will you still need me, will you still feed me, when I'm sixty-four?" I was told that the previous class session had been a "concert" and that this was the "elaboration" on that material.

A unit on "Youngsters Will be Youngsters" in the Bulgarian-based materials was examined. Students took turns playing the roles of the parents and reading the dialogue. The instructor produced a rose, which was passed from student to student; upon receiving it, each student attempted to give a sentence in English with a grammatical construction resembling one in the unit. Each response differed:

The way my child sings makes me proud.
The way he drives makes me terrified.
The way she loves makes me depressed.

The class members then reverted to their constant roles, which were the same as those in the previous class. The instructor divided them into pairs and gave them an assignment: "Imagine you have just met on the street. One of you is on the way to a hotel and the other asks that person to stay at his or her flat instead." Later, several pairs were called upon to dramatize before the entire group. When the role playing was routine or insipid, the instructor exhorted, "Forget that you are Hungarian!"

The next unit was named "A Perfect Cup of Tea" and took place at an Englishwoman's country estate. Again, there was role playing with follow-up exercises. I noticed that the instructor introduced several supplementary exercises that stressed grammar and spelling; she took the position that those areas were only superficially treated in the Bulgarian materials. The instruction even used phonetic symbols to demonstrate the difference between voiced "th" words (as in "these" and "bother") and unvoiced "th" words (as in "thin" and "bathtub").

The next unit was "A Letter from Paul." After it was read,

Füredi had the students locate each verb in the letter and find its object. Then each class member wrote a telegram to an imaginary recipient. Füredi moved into the next unit, a discussion with "Dr. Fox," an English physician who transplants organs. I speculated on how frequently the students would come across an English medical specialist, a member of the British gentry with a country estate, or some of the other interesting but uncommon types portrayed in the lessons.

When Füredi reached the unit on Bulgarian history and folklore, she told me she had supplemented this with student projects. One class member described a Hungarian folk dance and demonstrated it with the class's help. Another student, a well-known actress, presented material on Arabian folk art, passing around souvenirs she had purchased when she was in the Middle East.

The class discussed the weather, corrected the instructor's rendition of a story whenever she made a mistake, participated in an imaginary press conference, and sang "Leaving on a Jet Plane" and "Black, Black Is the Color of My True Love's Hair." The instructor added exercises on grammar, pronunciation, and spelling. And then it was time for a coffee break; the class had reached its midpoint with two hours to go.

It can be seen that suggestopedia moves at a rapid and intense pace. Those teachers who deviate from the Lozanov material claim that the lessons are to serve as "frames" for the program, not as "pictures." Furthermore, they note that the Bulgarian material has changed considerably over the years. There are also individual differences on the part of the instructors. However, each of the students I observed was using English fairly competently, some more so than others. I was told that the critical test of their ability would come when all the classes had finished their fifty sessions. In addition, a four-week study program in Great Britain was planned, with courses using traditional approaches but of greater intensity. Some of the students hoped to try passing the state examination in English upon their return.*

* I returned to Budapest in February 1980, and was told that the British study program had been quite successful. In April 1980, an international conference on accelerated learning was held in San Francisco, arranged by Learning in New Dimensions (1746 California Street, San Francisco, Calif. 94109). Professor Artur Szentgyörgyvári, whom I had met in 1979, represented the Hungarian Scientific and Technical Societies.

Subsystems of Consciousness

Suggestopedia has gained the reputation of a type of instruction that takes place in an altered state of consciousness. After observing suggestopedia in Bulgaria and Hungary, it is apparent to me that this concept is an oversimplification. If we examine the literature on altered states, we find that suggestopedia is basically an educational procedure that only incidentally brings about a shift in some of the components of human consciousness.

I have held that it is useful to think of an altered state of consciousness as an overall pattern of experience and behavior in which a person feels that his or her consciousness is radically different from the way it functions ordinarily. This overall pattern has several components; Charles Tart (1975) has named them "subsystems" of consciousness and speculated that they are at least ten in number:

1. *Exteroception* (sensory perception of the external environment).
2. *Interoception* (sensory perception of one's bodily processes).
3. *Input processing* (the way that one makes sense out of one's perceptions).
4. *Emotions.*
5. *Unconscious processes.*
6. *Memory.*
7. *Sense of time and space.*
8. *Sense of one's identity.*
9. *Evaluation and decision making.*
10. *Motor output* (bodily responses and processes).

Suggestology, at its best, involves the entire organism in learning. Thus, it seems to me, suggestopedia could involve a change in several of these subsystems. Memory can be enhanced, according to the experiments conducted by Lozanov (1978) that demonstrated heightened foreign-language recall on the part of students taught through suggestopedia. Exteroception could shift if the subliminal perceptual cues are both available and attended to. Unconscious processes could be altered if the "paraconscious" participates in learning through art, music, utilization of both left and right hemispheres, and the other procedures I observed at work in the Bulgarian classrooms.

Sense of one's identity may be temporarily changed if the role playing is intense enough for a student to "forget that he or she is Hungarian" during an exercise. If students can identify with the English-speaking (or Russian-speaking or German-speaking) person inside of them, they are more likely to acquire knowledge of a language. If the role playing becomes intense, one's emotions can also undergo a change. Motor output could alter if body movement is encouraged during the dramatizations.

Perhaps a key to the effectiveness of suggestopedia is the extent to which the students' emotions are affected by the course. I have seen classes where participants go through the motions of the lesson in a lackluster way. It is difficult to see any alteration of consciousness in these individuals, and one wonders how effective the instruction will be. I have also observed classes where the students are deeply involved in the process, playing their roles with zest and gusto. It seems to me that these participants would benefit more fully from suggestopedia.

None of the suggestopedia classes I have observed were notable for inducing dramatic alterations in consciousness in their participants. Lozanov (1978) has addressed himself to this issue by noting that his experimental work with suggestopedia as well as the role that suggestive factors play in sleep learning, psychotherapy, and hypnosis "clearly show that reserve capacities are tapped mainly because of the unconscious" and because of the way it permits "suggestive factors to operate in human communication" (p. 182). Lozanov observed:

It is true that some altered states . . . do sometimes play a part in this process, but it is chiefly in exerting an influence as a suggestive placebo factor and less so as a state per se. [p. 182]

In other words, the relaxation encouraged in suggestopedia classes facilitate learning, but more importantly, they enhance motivation by building up the expectancy of students that something exciting is going to happen. Observers expecting to walk into a suggestopedia classroom and find participants manifesting dramatic alterations in consciousness, however, are likely to be disappointed.

Indeed, there may be a danger in learning a new language while one's consciousness is dramatically altered. Experiments in "state bound learning" indicate that procedures that are learned in an altered state of consciousness can be forgotten when one returns to ordinary consciousness (Overton, 1971). Lists of numbers learned when one is drugged may be forgotten when the effects of the drug wear off but can be recalled later when the drug is again administered. If suggestopedia involved a radical change in consciousness, the material a student learned might only be recalled when a similar state of consciousness was attained.

Before I left Budapest, some of the instructors told me that their vision was to organize a center of suggestology and suggestopedia. This center could coordinate the courses being offered by the Technical University, the Ministry of Culture, and the Hungarian Scientific and Technical Societies. It could also initiate research, conduct follow-up studies, and prepare materials more suitable for students with a Hungarian cultural background. If this goal is ever actualized, it would be a boon for suggestology specifically and for education in general. I was quite impressed by the instructors I met in Budapest. They were talented professionals in various fields as well as highly competent language teachers. Their enthusiasm, insights, and perspectives represent resources that deserve wider attention from those interested in human possibilities.

Upon my return to California, I investigated the suggestopedic classes that were being taught by Ivan Barzakov, a Bulgarian who once taught in the Sofia schools. In 1976, he was selected to demonstrate the method to international audiences, including the British Minister of Education. Barzakov's work proved to be interesting because of his insistence in maintaining the "purity" of Lozanov's ideas in their most updated form. Barzakov and his associate, Pamela Rand, have expanded suggestology to management training, self-instruction, stress reduction, communication skills, child-rearing, and personal development.* I was impressed

* Ivan Barzakov is director of Barzak Education Institute, 760 Market Street, Suite 315, San Francisco, Calif. 94102.

with how well Lozanov's method appeared to work in Hungary and Bulgaria, and how it became transplanted to the United States so easily. The ability to transcend various cultural differences is a mark of a theoretically sound educational system, and Lozanov's integration of psychology, psychiatry, learning theory, and aesthetics appears promising indeed.

References

Albert, M. L., and Obler, L. K. *The Bilingual Brain.* New York: Academic Press, 1978.

Chall, J. S. A decade of research on reading and learning disabilities. In S. J. Samuels (ed.), *What Research Has to Say About Reading Instruction.* Newark, Del.: International Reading Association, 1978.

Cooper, L. F., and Erickson, M. H. *Time Distortion and Hypnosis,* 2nd ed. Baltimore: Williams & Wilkins, 1959.

Goleman, D. Holographic memory. *Psychology Today,* Feb. 1979.

Krippner, S. The relationship of reading improvement to scores on the Holtzman Inkblot Technique. *Journal of Clinical Psychology,* 1967, *23,* 114–15.

Lozanov, G. *Suggestology and Outlines of Suggestopedy.* New York: Gordon & Breach, 1978.

Morgun, V. F. The problem of "suggestopedia" in light of the theory of staged formation of new acts and concepts. In A. S. Prangishvili, A. E. Sherozia, and F. V. Bassin (eds.), *The Unconscious: Nature, Functions, Methods of Study,* Vol. 3. Tbilisi: Metsniereba, 1978.

Ostrander, S., and Schroeder, L. *Superlearning.* Englewood Cliffs, N.J.: Prentice-Hall, 1979.

Overton, D. State-dependent learning produced by alcohol and its relevance to alcoholism. In B. Kissin and H. Begleiter (eds.), *The Biology of Alcoholism.* New York: Plenum Press, 1971.

Pribram, K. *Languages of the Brain.* Englewood Cliffs, N.J.: Prentice-Hall, 1971.

————. Consciousness: A scientific approach. *Journal of Indian Psychology,* 1978, *1,* 95–118.

Tart, C. T. *States of Consciousness.* New York: E. P. Dutton, 1975.

CHAPTER 8

The Electrical Photographs of Semyon Kirlian

> A living organism is an electrically sensitive body in-
> volved in ongoing information and energy exchanges
> with surrounding bodies and systems. Its complex
> electrical and biological self-regulating system inter-
> acts with the electrical and magnetic environment.
>
> I. F. Dumitrescu (1978b)

In 1975, I was invited to give two lectures in Poland on para-psychological topics. Zdeněk Rejdák flew to Warsaw from Prague to join me for the first presentation in which we discussed the International Association for Psychotronic Research and its efforts to demystify unusual phenomena. This lecture was given to the Committee of Applied Cybernetics of the Polish Society of Technology; the audience consisted of about fifty scientists and technicians, including Krysztof Borún and Stefan Manczarski, whose excellent book about parapsychological phenomena was published in Warsaw in 1977.

My second lecture was held at the Culture Center and was open to the general public; it attracted several hundred people. I spoke on our work in dream telepathy at the Maimonides Medical Center. Several of the questions raised concerned "out-of-body experience," which was translated as "experience in bilocation." I commented that most of these reports of an "energy body" probably were the results of a vivid imagination but that the few that involved "remote viewing"—accurate retrieval of distant information—required close attention. It was possible, I observed, that the clairvoyant subject had such a vivid impression of the distant material that the only way it would make sense was to imagine a physical "sensing" with eyes, ears, and other bodily organs. This phenomenon could easily lead to the feeling that one's "energy body" was in a different place than one's physical body.

After the lecture, I was ushered to the business office and, much to my surprise, was paid the princely sum of four hundred Polish zlotys (about twenty dollars). I also discovered that a lecture that debunked parapsychology had been held at the same time in another building. Was I offended? Not at all. I was only too happy to play a role in facilitating freedom of information and the public discussion of a controversial topic (for example, Musial and Wolniewicz, 1977).

"I Am You"

While in Poland, I observed ESP tests under hypnosis with a subject placed in a pulsed electromagnetic field using a process developed by Stefan Manczarski. L. E. Stefánsky, an engineer, told me that both the hypnotic induction and the electromagnetic field had been found to enhance ESP.

The subjects in the demonstrations I witnessed were Czestaw Klimuszko and Anna Bernat. Both attempted "psychic readings" on a photograph of a student whose body had been found but whose death had never been resolved. Klimuszko conjectured it was a case of suicide, while Bernat stated that the student had been murdered.

Both subjects claimed that they did better when hypnotized; indeed, the first Polish investigator to use hypnosis to facilitate ESP was Julian Ochorowicz, a physician whose work dates back to 1881 (Zielinski, 1968). However, Bernat used the technique devised in Czechoslovakia by Milan Ryzl (1962) for ESP development. Ryzl's procedure involved intensive hypnotic training, culminating in the subject's ability to experience very complex and very vivid visual imagery. Immediate feedback was given so that the subject would know which techniques were most effective. Bernat claimed to have studied Ryzl's work, developing her skills both with a hypnotist and through self-hypnosis.

During the demonstration, the hypnotist had planned to attempt telepathic communication with Bernat from a distant room. In hypnotizing her, he made the following suggestion:

I am you and you are me, and you will feel the same as I do.
Your own thoughts are disappearing. You will think my thoughts.

The hypnotist then went to another room, where he visualized his home. Bernat's description was fairly accurate, including such details as the color of the doors, a rose garden, wild vines, a pointed roof, and uniquely shaped windows. However, there was no way of knowing if Bernat could have had previous knowledge about the house or if she had picked up any clue as to the content of the hypnotist's image in her earlier conversation with him. Nevertheless, the demonstration was both provocative and impressive.

Body Radiation

Later in the week, I visited a biochemistry laboratory in Warsaw, where I observed blood extracts being studied with photomultiplier tubes. These devices are so sensitive that they can measure the emission of photons—tiny units of light that radiate from living organisms. As a result, weak electromagnetic radiation can be amplified and measured. The effects of different medications on cancer cells were being studied with this technique—the more effective the medicine, the fewer the photons emitted from the cancer cells. The enzymes in seeds also give off photons; thus the higher the count from the photomultiplier tubes, the higher the germination that could be expected from that group of seeds.

In an extension of the Soviet work on the "mirror effect" with chicken embryos, a Polish biochemist described the preparation of two frog hearts, which were then placed in different containers. If the containers were made from quartz or Plexiglas, the "mirror effect" would occur; shortly after one heart was injected with atropine, the other heart would "mirror" the increased heartbeat rate. If glass containers were used, this effect would not occur. Again, it was noted that the emission of ultraviolet light produced a "code" that stimulated the second heart to "mirror" the activity of the first.

The discussion of radiation from living organisms led to a discussion of the electrical photography techniques developed by Semyon Kirlian in the USSR. I had first read about this process in *Fate* magazine in 1962 (Leonidov, 1962) and had discussed it with Soviet investigators during both of my visits to Moscow. While in Warsaw, I saw a number of electrical photographs (or electrophotographs) taken by Edward Lepak, who had constructed a Kirlian device.

I was told that the first physician who had taken electrophotographs and used them diagnostically was Jacob Jodko-Narkiewicz. Born in 1848, the Polish physician first demonstrated his device in 1896. The Polish press published eight electrophotographs and headlined its stories "Photography Serves Physiology" and "Electrical Radiation of the Human Body." Some parts of the body showed a very bright radiance, while others showed little or none. Jodko-Narkiewicz argued that these differences were due to the state of health in different body organs or to the emotional interactions between the people being tested. When two friends had electric photographs made of their fingertips, the radiations were reported to be brighter than if two strangers were photographed together.

High-frequency Photography

Electrical photography was to be brought to international attention by Semyon Davidovitch Kirlian, who was born in 1896. As a young man, Kirlian was stimulated by a lecture given by Nikola Tesla, the Yugoslavian inventor of such devices as the first alternating-current generator and transformer as well as the "Tesla coil," an air-core transformer used to produce high voltages of high-frequency alternating currents. Kirlian was self-educated, having completed only four years of primary-school education.

With his wife, Valentina, Kirlian became involved in developing new photographic procedures. In 1939, while fixing medical equipment used in high-voltage, high-frequency electrical treatment, Kirlian noticed that the color of an electrical discharge between a glass-plated electrode and human skin changed abruptly. The Kirlians attempted to determine the cause of this effect by photographing the discharge without using a camera. They exposed a photographic emulsion to the field and, upon developing the film, found that it had recorded the electrical discharge. Semyon Kirlian placed his fingers on the film; he suffered a serious burn but obtained an intriguing picture of his hand (Edelson, 1977).

The Kirlians proceeded to discover that they could make photographic prints of any electrically conductive object using the corona discharge surrounding the object's surface—produced by a high-voltage, high-frequency field—as the only light source. The apparatus developed by the Kirlians consisted of a Tesla coil (which operated on several hundred thousand volts with low amperage) connected to two metallic plates or electrodes. When they placed an object on a photographic emulsion between the two plates, an image was obtained when the coil threw a spark. This spark is similar to the discharge of static electricity when one touches an uncharged or oppositely charged object after walking across a carpet on a dry day, but magnified literally thousands of times.

In 1949 the Kirlians received a patent for "a method of photography with the aid of high-frequency currents." Victor Adamenko lived in the city of Krasnador as a boy and recalls first seeing the electrophotographs in 1950. While still in school, he began to photograph coins and leaves using the Kirlian process. In 1964, the Kirlians asked Adamenko to join them in perfecting the procedure. Adamenko, who had moved to Moscow, visited the Kirlians in Krasnador several times each year; they received three patents for their work and published several papers together.

Adamenko came to believe that the electrophotographs were electron images that occur through a "cold electron emission" and that the high-frequency discharge was a low-temperature plasma. A plasma is a state in which ions (electrically charged particles), protons, and electrons exist as a kind of "soup" without a definite molecular configuration. Physicists view plasma as a fourth state of matter along with solids, liquids, and gases. Most plasmas exist at high temperatures (such as a candle flame), but the unusual characteristic of the high-frequency discharge occurring during electrophotography is not only its status as a low-temperature plasma, but also its reflection of the dynamics of the object being photographed. As a result, Soviet investigators began to use electrophotography for locating flaws in metal surfaces, detecting mineral traces in soil, and studying plant diseases.

The apparatus for electrophotography is basically a capacitive-discharge, high-frequency generator controlled by special timing circuits. The power source is connected directly to a metal electrode, which is covered by a smooth-fitting dielectric sheet such as Mylar or plate glass. (Dielectric refers to any nonconductor of direct electrical current.) Voltage and timing specifications are determined by the photographer according to the speed of the film as well as the object to be photographed. The electric discharge signaling interaction with the object usually consists of a bluish-white radiation with an intensity sufficient to expose the film and cause the image to be formed.

Electrophotographs of living tissue were made by using the tissue itself as one of the two electrodes needed. Electric-shock and tissue damage were minimized by using a low-amperage current and by controlling the output of the high-voltage power supply (such as a Tesla coil or Ouidin coil). Pictures had to be taken in a darkroom or by enclosing the film and object to be photographed in a nontransparent envelope, usually one constructed from a piece of dark cloth. The film was then removed from its packet and was placed, emulsion side up, on top of the dielectric. The object to be photographed rested directly on top of the emulsion.

There are various ways by which the image can be formed. The object can be placed upon a glass electrode, and the recording of the corona pattern can be made either by still photography or by using special low-light-level video cameras. The image can also be directly analyzed through spectral analysis with computer interface following separation into the individual electromagnetic frequencies. (Spectral analysis refers to the breaking down of light rays into their component parts—red, orange, yellow, etc.—us-

ing a spectroscope.) The corona image represents the surface to-
pography of the object as it rests on the emulsion side of the film.
Surrounding the border of the image on the photograph, a lumi-
nous band—the corona—is visible. Extending from the corona
are fine structures known as streamers.

On the electrophotographs, one sees an image of the object's
surface as well as the surrounding corona, which represents the
discharge of electrons from the object. There is very little emission from a dead leaf or from a corpse; therefore Adamenko came
to the conclusion that the electron discharge from a living organism was a reflection, to some extent, of the life process occurring
within that organism.

Adamenko also took the position that the information content

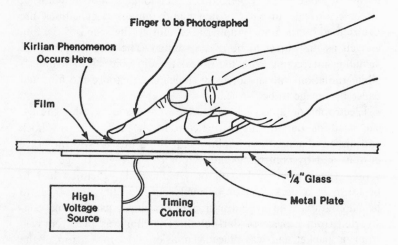

Fig. 1 Illustration of general components used in most high-voltage photography apparatus (adapted from Poock and Sparks,
1979, p. 190).

and quality of electrophotographs depend on the presence of an
electric field on the surface of the observed object; this is precisely
why a pulsed high-voltage generator is considered necessary. The
field around the object develops in the pauses between the pulses,
while during the pulse (or discharge) it decreases considerably. If
the discharge works continuously, the field is very small and the
corona contains little information.

Many physiological functions may alter and modulate the corona-discharge image, such as moisture, perspiration, surface temperature, electrical conductivity of the skin, or pressure exerted by the subject on the film. The photograph produced by the interaction of these factors reportedly provides information about the biological state of the organism being photographed. The Kirlians noted in 1961, "Having studied specimens with varying geometrical configurations . . . it is apparently possible to make judgments about the biological and pathological states of an organism and its organs."

The Air Force Translation

The Kirlians' first scientific report was published in the *Russian Journal of Scientific and Applied Photography and Cinemaphotography* in 1961. The article was initially translated by the Foreign Technology Division of the U. S. Air Force in 1962 and dispersed as an unclassified document in 1973; however, this translation aroused no great interest for ten years. Semyon Kirlian sent me a copy of the original article in 1972, which I had translated for presentation at the First Western Hemisphere Conference on Kirlian Photography in New York City. The proceedings of this conference were published in hardcover the following year (Krippner and Rubin, 1973) and in paperback a year later (Krippner and Rubin, 1974). In 1974, the International Kirlian Research Association* was formed in New York as a nonprofit organization with the purpose of correlating, standardizing, and promoting research in electrophotography (Bergman, 1979; Edelson, 1977; Graff, 1980).

In the meantime, several American technicians were attempting to construct their own devices. Henry Monteith (1974) took Kirlian-type photographs in early 1971. Later that same year, Thelma Moss and Kendall Johnson (1972) built a variant of the apparatus based on information Moss had brought back from the USSR in 1970. William Tiller (1975) visited the Soviet Union in

* As of 1980, the Association's office was located at 411 East Seventh Street, Brooklyn, N.Y. 11218.

1971 and developed a highly sophisticated electrophotography device upon his return. Much earlier work had, in fact, been carried out but had long been neglected due to a lack of interest. F. F. Strong, of Tufts University Medical School, had taken the first American electrophotographs in 1917 using voltage from a Tesla coil to photograph his hand by placing it directly on a sheet of film. In 1842, "electric patterns" of coins on a mica plate were obtained with the use of a condenser system in England, before either Jodko-Narkiewicz or the Kirlians were born (Moss, 1974).

What had happened to the Air Force translation from 1962 to 1972? Some intriguing information was obtained by Ronny Mastrion, a New York film maker who had built a Kirlian device with a car battery in 1971. The following year, Mastrion visited the offices of the Mankind Research Foundation, a group that had received a U. S. Government grant for research in electrophotography. Mastrion was shown a file of pertinent articles and was allowed to Xerox those he found of interest (Weberman, 1980).

Among the reports inspected by Mastrion was the Air Force translation of the Kirlians' 1961 article. Mastrion had no need for the article, as he had already read my translation; however, he copied the accompanying distribution list, which revealed that copies had been sent to the major Air Force commands as well as the U. S. Army and Navy. Between one copy and six copies had also been given to the Agency for International Development, the Atomic Energy Commission, the Central Intelligence Agency, the Defense Intelligence Agency, the National Aeronautics and Space Administration, and the National Security Agency. And, for some unexplained reason, the Rand Corporation (a "think tank" often contracted for secret government research) had received a *dozen* copies.

I recalled that a decade had elapsed between the time that the Kirlians had received their patent and the time that the first article about their work had appeared in the Soviet press (Belov, 1960). Adamenko (1979) has since written that information about electrophotography appeared in the press "only after an international agreement was reached on open discussions of work on thermonuclear reactions. . . ." Therefore, it appears that Semyon Kirlian's electrical photographs were seen as having possible strategic and security implications by governmental agencies in both the United States and the USSR.

Another piece of information emerged in 1975. An unclassified technical report from the Red River Army Depot in Texas revealed that electrophotography had been used for metal-fatigue assessment (Reeves, 1975). Upon hearing about this report, I recalled that the only representatives of the U. S. Government who had visited me after my trips to the USSR had been two scientists interested in the Soviet use of electrophotography to study metal defects in aircraft. They stated that electrophotography was one of the best procedures they had investigated to detect metal stress before it became critical enough to cause a serious accident.

A Healer's Hands

In the meantime, the media found electrophotography an interesting topic for discussion, even if the treatment was distorted. A number of people who claimed to see "auras," "halos," or "energy bodies" around living organisms stated that their claims were now vindicated by science.

The Universe Book Club, for example, announced *Psychic Discoveries Behind the Iron Curtain* as its November 1970 selection, with the claim that it described how "electrician Semyon Kirlian photographs the pulsing human aura previously seen only by clairvoyants." Ostrander and Schroeder (1970) proclaimed that the Kirlians "have made it possible for everyone to see at least part of the aura. They have photographed, it seems, the legendary energy body, our second, subtle body" (p. 216). Monteith (1974) asserted, "The Kirlian device also enables us to test many of the claims made by Hindus concerning the 'aura'" (p. 42). Actually, the Kirlians never made any such claim. On the topic of psychic phenomena, Semyon Kirlian took a skeptical position. However, Valentina Kirlian was more interested in the area and, in 1967, she persuaded her husband to participate in the first scientific study of a folk healer in the USSR.

Alexei Krivorotov, a retired colonel and the subject of the

study, became aware of his abilities in 1929, curing himself of migraine headaches after physicians had been unsuccessful. In that instance, he placed his right hand on his head, and continued to "lay on" hands when working with other people. When he "laid hands" on others, slight discharges of electricity were sometimes observed, and the people he treated commonly reported sensations of heat.

Krivorotov had been studied in 1956 at Republic Hospital in Tbilisi by a commission of seven physicians organized by the Georgian Republic Ministry of Health. For seven days he worked with thirty patients; to prevent Krivorotov from inadvertently engaging in psychotherapy, some of the selected patients did not speak either Georgian or Russian, the two languages in which Krivorotov was fluent. The commission found improvement in all patients and cures in several (Gris and Dick, 1978, p. 95).

The Kirlians photographed Krivorotov's fingertips before, during, and after the "laying on" of hands. After Krivorotov said that his hand was activated and in the condition required for the healing to be effective, the corona became modified and congregated with a dense pattern of short flares. After the healing session ended, Krivorotov's fingertips produced ordinary coronas, which were not remarkably different from those of ordinary subjects. Semyon Kirlian interpreted the corona change—and the effectiveness of the healing—on the basis of an electrostatic field that develops during the "laying on" of hands.*

In a 1974 study, Gregor Komitiani, a member of the Georgian Academy of Sciences, directed a similar investigation of Krivorotov using a photomultiplier tube; during a healing session, ultraviolet radiation coming from Krivorotov's hands increased dramatically. At one point, Krivorotov told the investigators that the apparatus would still register his influence once he removed his hands. They were skeptical, but they reportedly observed the photomultiplier tube detecting radiation for an hour. In addition, electrocardiograms and psychogalvanic skin responses were taken from both Krivorotov and his patients; during a healing session their responses gradually tended to resemble each other.

* H. E. Montandon (1977) failed to replicate these results in a carefully controlled study with American "healers."

Edward Naumov has suggested that the ultraviolet radiation generated by healers may be the same type of emanation as that detected by A. G. Gurvitch in his studies with mitogenic radiation —the emanations purportedly produced by cell nuclei during cell division. Victor Adamenko (1979) has voiced the opinion that the healer's electrostatic emanations and ultraviolet radiation are side effects of the healing phenomena, but Kirlian hypothesized that they were directly involved in healing itself.

For many years, Krivorotov has worked with his two sons— Victor, an artist, and Vladimir, a psychiatrist. Together they wrote an article, "Bioenergotherapy and Healing," which appeared in a 1974 issue of *Psychoenergetic Systems,* a journal that I edited. They spoke favorably of the Kirlians' work, stating:

> On the basis of the experiments carried out by the Kirlians, it can be suggested that bioenergotherapy . . . appears to be accompanied by complicated electrical manifestations resulting in action which takes place on the enervating systems of the human skin and tissue. Considerable amounts of some energetic processes appear to flow into the human organism, restoring a balance to all systems of the body. [Krivorotov, Krivorotov, and Krivorotov, 1974, p. 30]

I later discovered that Krivorotov had been called to Moscow to treat ailing government officials, and that he sometimes worked with sick persons at a distance. His success may have been responsible, in part, for the positive description of "paradiagnostics" in the "parapsychology" entry of Volume 19 of the official *Great Soviet Encyclopedia* (Zinchenko and Leontiev, 1974), where it is defined as "medical diagnosis without contact with the patient, based on clairvoyance."

The "Phantom Leaf"

Victor Adamenko took electrophotographs of Alla Vinogradova before, during, and after her attempts to move objects from a distance. The results resembled those of Krivorotov; when Vinogradova imagined that she was moving objects across a table, the corona became denser and the flares shorter than either before or after her attempts.

Adamenko is also responsible for the other Soviet attempt to explore paranormal phenomena with electrophotography.* In 1966, Adamenko (1979) cut away a small portion of a leaf and took an electrophotograph of the remainder. However, a shadow of the cutaway portion could be seen on the developed photograph, as if the entire leaf were still present. Valentina Kirlian congratulated Adamenko on the discovery of a new phenomenon, but Semyon Kirlian was skeptical about the photograph's validity. For Vladimir Lvov (1974), who referred to the Kirlians as "the amateur photographers from Krasnadov," there was no question as to the fraudulent nature of the "phantom leaf" effect:

> The very same plate is used twice. First the cutaway part of the leaf is photographed, producing an "aura," and later, when one part of the film is covered, the rest of the leaf is photographed. As to the "aura" itself, it has as much to do with "secret spirits" as to last year's snow.

However, the "phantom leaf" effect is not produced in this manner. John Hubacher and Thelma Moss (1976), in reporting on a dozen "phantoms," noted that the leaf was placed directly on the film after a section had been cut away. A thin glass plate was placed over the leaf to keep its surface flat. A heavy dielectric cube was placed on top of the plate to give the entire leaf uniform pressure. The stem of the leaf was touched with an electrode and, by pressing a button, electric current was pulsed through the leaf for three seconds. However, better results were obtained if a thin glass plate were placed between the leaf and the film, and if a metallic disc were used instead of the cube. With the latter technique, "phantoms" were obtained about 5 percent of the time.

Hubacher and Moss found that the "phantom" could be observed directly by using a transparent electrode and attaching it to

---

* In the only parapsychological study to be evaluated with statistics, three subjects with purported psi abilities attempted to alter the size of a leaf's corona. The leaf and the Kirlian device were in a distant room; nevertheless, one of the three subjects obtained a statistically significant effect (Krippner and Rubin, 1977).

the power source of the Kirlian device. I once watched Moss cut away a portion of a leaf, attach the remainder to the reverse of the transparent electrode by backing it with a glass plate covered with a copper disc, and turn on the electric power source. The "phantom" appeared vividly and pulsed for twenty seconds. The cutaway portion of the leaf was visible, then faded away, then reappeared, then faded away. Similar "phantoms" were reported from Brazil and from other parts of the United States.

When Hubacher and Moss attempted to follow the procedure suggested by Lvov, they obtained a much different picture, which could easily be differentiated from the other "phantoms." Yet another variant was obtained by pressing the cut leaf so as to release a fluid that might resemble the "phantom." These photographs did not resemble the pictures of the spontaneously occurring "phantom leaf."

Many explanations have been given for the "phantom leaf" effect. A team of Duke University investigators (Burton, Joines, and Stevens, 1975) suspected the effect might be due to the buckling of the film. William Tiller (1976) suggested it was due to the "vaporization of ionized tissue fluids at the freshly cut surface." Adamenko (1979) proposed the possibility of a "resonance of the ultrasonic vibrations in the discharge interval" analogous to a hologram. Mikol Davis and Earle Lane (1978) even suggested that the leaf's "energy body" has been captured. Until a definitive answer is forthcoming, the "phantom leaf" remains an enigmatic phenomenon.

Uncovering Nature's Secrets

In 1971, Valentina Kirlian died; Semyon Kirlian continued to work in the Agricultural Scientific Research Institute in Krasnador. In 1974 he wrote me a cordial letter thanking me for sending him a copy of the book I had dedicated to the memory of his wife. He added that he hoped electrophotography researchers would have success in "uncovering nature's secrets" and expressed the wish that "the results achieved be for the enrichment of all humanity."

In that same year, the Supreme Soviet of the Russian Soviet Federated Socialist Republic conferred on Kirlian the title of "Honored Inventor." A scientific conference on electrophotography was held in Moscow in 1976; it ended with a unanimous resolution to continue "research into the Kirlian effect in the USSR." In June 1978, the State Committee for Discoveries and Inventions awarded Kirlian and Adamenko a patent for an "electron telescope" they had created in 1966. Two months later, Semyon Kirlian died peacefully at his home in Krasnador.

In the meantime, William Tiller and one of his students had written articles pointing out that the same fingertip could produce different photographs if the variables were not carefully controlled (Boyers and Tiller, 1973, 1976). Yoshiaki Omura (1976), chairman of the Standards Committee of the International Kirlian Research Association, identified a number of interacting variables which are involved in electrophotographic effects. They include the condition of such factors as the electrode used, the insulating materials, the film and its manner of development, as well as electrical characteristics of the high-voltage source, exposure time, the surface photographed (for example, its heat, weight, pressure), grounding conditions, and environmental conditions (for example, air currents, ion content in a room, and even lunar pull and sunspots). When a living organism is photographed, several other factors assume importance: sweat or water vapor, hydration or dehydration, roughness or smoothness of the surface photographed, degree of lipid concentration, degree of deposited impurities, and the total area of the surface on which the corona discharge takes place. Finally, the experimenters themselves represent an important variable; their expectations and expertise may influence the results profoundly.

With all of these factors to consider, is there any possibility that electrophotography can achieve the standardization needed for practical use? Omura (1976) has sounded a note of optimism, stating, "If most of the major parameters influencing Kirlian photography are measured or controlled, there is a fairly good possibility that Kirlian photography can be used for evaluating the various conditions of the human body or animal including emotional

simpler than the complicated photography currently used to examine areas of the body that cannot be studied by X rays.

Electrophotography has been used in a pilot project in the USSR to discover whether a driver has been imbibing alcohol. In another pilot project, an inscription was photographed by the Kirlian process, then covered with black paper and photographed again. The latter shows the writing, although it was invisible to the human eye. It was suggested that "skin vision" may work on this basis, successful subjects obtaining a "trace" to which the skin is more sensitive than the eye (Vilenskaya, 1974).

An ambitious investigation was initiated at a hospital in Rostov-on-Don in 1973 (Dick and Gris, 1975). One hundred children were photographed at birth with Kirlian equipment; the program calls for a monthly progression of electrophotographs to be taken for several decades. The prediction of disease will be one major area of investigation; already there are some data indicating that scarlet fever can be detected in electrophotographs before it can be seen on the skin.

Thelma Moss and her associates (1979) photographed the tails of one hundred healthy rats, observing characteristically clear, bright coronas. However, the tails of one hundred rats infected with spinal tumors revealed irregular discharges. Moss was also able to correctly identify soybean seeds that had been chemically treated because their coronas were smaller and dimmer than those of healthy seeds.

Romanian Electronography

Research into the medical applications of the Kirlian process has been initiated not only in the USSR but also in Bulgaria, Czechoslovakia, East Germany, Hungary, Poland, and Romania. Perhaps the most widespread application of these procedures has been at the Labor Center for Hygiene and Preventive Medicine of the Romanian Ministry of the Chemical Industry in Bucharest. When I visited Bucharest in 1979, I spoke to I. F. Dumitrescu, the developer of "electronography," a variant of the Kirlian process. Dumitrescu (1978) described electronography as "a method of translating into images the electrical properties of an investigated organism." The organism can be continuously observed on a phosphorescent screen treated with liquid crystals, or by transforming the electrical images into a televised display (Krippner, 1979).

In diagnostic work, special attention is paid to the relationship between light and dark areas. According to Dumitrescu (1979), an inflammation manifests itself by the occurrence of a dark zone, while a malignancy manifests itself by intense bright zones, which differ from the zones of healthy tissues. It is felt that there is a shift toward the ultraviolet region of the spectrum with cancer patients. Using this technique, Dumitrescu claims a high success rate in the early detection of cancer. Between 1975 and 1978, over six thousand patients were diagnosed for cancer and other diseases through electronography (Dumitrescu, Golovanov, Golovanov, and Eugen, 1977).

In developing electronography, Dumitrescu and his colleagues investigated three principal variants: the charge source (primarily the wave characteristics of the electrical pulse transmitted to the plate electrode), the physical and electrical properties of the dielectric employed, and the specific characteristics of the apparatus. Dumitrescu has pointed out that each of these variables interacts with the conditions in the experimental environment, such as the atmosphere.

Dumitrescu took the position that electron discharge in electrical photography is the result of air ionization—the separation of electrons from molecules of air. These "excited" electrons eventually return to their normal state, releasing energy as they do. If the original charge (in effect, the pulse delivered to the plate electrode) is sufficiently great, large numbers of molecules are ionized and the discharge falls within the visible spectrum. This condition is referred to by Dumitrescu as a "breakdown," and the result is the sparking also evident in the Kirlian technique. The dependence of this effect upon pulse characteristics (especially the critical voltages) and the electrical characteristics of the surface of the object photographed (such as a subject's skin) has been the focus of most work in Kirlian photography. Dumitrescu has also emphasized this approach, especially the relationship between the frequency of the pulses used and the surface of what is being photographed. In particular, Dumitrescu notes that varying images are due to polarity changes in the pulse; he sees these variations as composite images that are virtually irreproducible. This is a major drawback of Kirlian photography.

Dumitrescu's most innovative contributions arise out of his work with pulses inferior to the critical "breakdown" voltage. At such amplitudes, no discharges are visible to the human eye, nor can any be recorded with conventional photographic techniques. However, by experimenting with unconventional photographic techniques, Dumitrescu claims to have recorded ionization which, he proposes, is mediated more directly—if not actually induced —by the physiological processes of the organism being studied. In this model, the electrical potential generated across the dielectric would seem to be *amplifying* rather than *initiating* the ionization and resulting discharge. In Kirlian photography, the subject simply modulates and amplifies a discharge initiated by a high-voltage power source; in electronography, a discharge is amplified and recorded that is produced by the organism itself. Therefore, electronography claims to present a more direct representation of the organism's condition than does Kirlian photography. Because the organism is basically responsible for the discharge, the images are more often reproducible than those obtained with the Kirlian technique.

Dumitrescu has invoked a variety of electronographic techniques to record such low-level discharges, exploiting the electrochemical consequences of ionization. Direct effects have been observed, as well as interference (or blocking) effects in which the effect of the subject upon a competing source of ionization is measured. Imaging devices range from phosphorescent and liquid-crystal screens to complex electronics that are able to detect electrostatic, magnetic, and thermal ionization effects.

Signal processing has also been attempted—replete with spectographic and computerized image analysis—and video display images have been utilized. Dumitrescu reports that modifications of the electromagnetic field surrounding the apparatus are useful both in resolving and in analyzing the image. In a similar fashion, he has made use of a variety of dielectric layers having a selective braking function and some auxiliary accelerating devices in vacuums, so that the electrons crossing the living organism are separated according to their energetic value. Finally, Dumitrescu has employed these techniques at microscopic levels in a process he has named "microelectronography." The general class of such low-level ionization effects produced by these recording techniques is referred to by Dumitrescu as "electroluminescence." All of these techniques, in a certain sense, are crude forms of electron photography, hence the term "electronography."

Dumitrescu reports that studies in electroluminescence reveal a region that he terms the "proximal electric medium." This is an area of ionization surrounding the living organism consisting of a series of layers with different electrical behaviors. Dumitrescu divides this medium into three strata: adherent ions structured near the organism due to electrostatic molecular and physiological behavior (such as respiration and perspiration), free ions more loosely associated with the surface of the organism, and miscellaneous other ionizing influences related to the organism. Images of this proximal electric environment are reportedly reproducible and are believed to reveal physiological as well as morphological information concerning surface structures of the subject.

In addition to this proximal electric effect, an internal effect is reported. This is based upon modifications in the basic techniques of electronography and indicate the electrical characteristics of structures internal to the organism. These procedures have enabled Dumitrescu (1978b) to claim that his laboratory has produced "reproducible images representing functional and pathological states of the investigated subject for all parts of the body."

Dumitrescu sees the human body as electrically sensitive and self-regulating. Electronography, he feels, can record dysfunctions in self-regulation. It can also enable researchers to observe "energy transfer" between human subjects and between the body and its environment. Thus Dumitrescu holds the position that electronography's potentials have only begun to be tapped. This stance is challenged by medical researchers who, instead, have turned to computerized axial tomography—the CAT scanners now used in hospitals throughout the world (Swets et al., 1979). Based on the physics of how X rays pass through differing body parts, the CAT scanners distinguish soft tissues and organs, spotting abnormalities by producing television images shaded according to the density of the tissue. When the developers of CAT scanning were awarded the Nobel Prize in 1979, the Nobel committee declared, "No other method within X-ray diagnostics has led to such remarkable success in such a short time." However, the CAT scanner's price—up to seven hundred thousand dollars —prohibits its use in many parts of the world. Perhaps electronography would be capable of filling the needs of this market.

Pictures of Electrons

I discovered another unique use of electrophotography during my 1979 visit to Hungary. Lajos Vetoe, a dental surgeon living in Balatonfuered (a town on Lake Balaton, Hungary's "Inland Sea"), told me that he had used electrophotographs in his work since 1976. Much to his surprise, he was able to diagnose many types of dental disease with electrophotography as well as if he had used more expensive equipment and more time-consuming procedures. For this assessment, he used an extracted tooth or tooth portion.

For example, he was able to detect the declining metabolism of the lower molars. He suspected that tooth decay reduces the electrical activity of the tooth's dentine (or ivory); thus the corona differs from that of a healthy tooth. Further, Vetoe suggested that the electrical activity of dentine decreases the resistance to acid and to bacterial penetration into the enamel.

In the case of pulpitis—the decay of the tooth's pulp or interior —Vetoe again was able to make a correct diagnosis with electrophotography. The pulpitis condition could be seen as a foglike emission on the electrophotograph; the dentine showed up as a dark background.

The most dramatic difference was found in comparing living and dead molars. Vetoe proposed that teeth, like other bodily organs, have a characteristic electrostructure that is disturbed in the course of disease. This disturbance is observable through electrophotography and is associated with circulatory problems, loss of liquids, evaporation, temperature decline, broken nerves, and/or swelling of the gums.

On one occasion, Vetoe photographed a decaying tooth that was missing its crown or top portion. However, a "phantom" of the crown appeared when the picture was developed. Vetoe observed this effect in 1976. It was his first and last "phantom"; in 1979 he told me that the phenomenon had never repeated itself.

The diagnostic uses of electrophotography pioneered by Vetoe, Dumitrescu, and others may not become more widespread until greater control is exerted over the two dozen variables that can affect the results. In addition, there is still no consensus over the exact nature of the Kirlian effect. In 1975, Victor Adamenko defended his thesis for a Scientific Candidate degree; it was titled, "Investigation of Image Formation by Means of High-frequency Electrical Discharge." His conclusion was challenged by M. K. Romanovsky, a physicist who served as a participant in Adamenko's examination. Romanovsky insisted that the electrons themselves are responsible for the darkening of the photographic emulsion during electrophotography.

Adamenko replied that the Kirlian effect is more complicated than Romanovsky suggested. The background can be provided by ultraviolet light and visible light, but the images themselves are produced by the "cold electron emission" or electron traces that interact with the positive ions present in the discharge in gaseous form. The positive ions, according to Adamenko, provide focusing. Thus electrophotographs differ from pictures taken by electron microscopes: The latter provide dead images, since cells are killed in the high vacuum produced.

Adamenko (1974) arrived at his conclusions by observing that in any electrical discharge, electrons and ions are both present. The discharge is accompanied by a wide spectrum of electromagnetic radiation, X-ray radiation, radio waves, infrared light, ultraviolet light, and light in the visible spectrum. Adamenko eliminated the role of radio waves and infrared light by noting that photographic film is not sensitive to them. He used a special luminescent screen in some experiments that demonstrated that visible light did not play an important role in the resulting image. X-ray radiation was ruled out by similar processes.

A special kind of film, insensitive to ultraviolet light, was used, and the corona was still obtained. An aluminum cover was then placed over the luminescent screen; this cover was opaque to ions but transparent to electrons. The corona was again produced, thus demonstrating that electrophotographs basically are pictures of an electron discharge. This is the basic fact, according to Adamenko, that allows the experimenter to examine the dynamics of the life process and to use electrophotography in medical diagnosis.

In 1974, a paper was delivered at the Parapsychological Association that substantiated the fact that Kirlian images were the results of an electric field (Burton, Joines, and Stevens, 1975). The authors asked "whether or not Kirlian photography should continue to be classified as a paranormal event." They concluded that Kirlian images may be explained in terms of our existing knowledge of electrical corona.

However, the Soviet researchers never claimed that electrophotography was a parapsychological phenomenon, nor did most of the American scientists who became involved in the work. The claims came from American journalists who confused the Kirlian corona with the "aura" purportedly seen by psychic sensitives. Once scientific data had produced alternative explanations, many newspapers ran articles that Kirlian photographs had been "debunked." What had really been disproved was the fantasy created by the media, not by science.

In the meantime, some legitimate researchers became wary of working with electrophotography because of its occult connotations. This was an unfortunate development, as the electrical photographs of Semyon Kirlian may still have much to teach humanity about its potentials.

References

Adamenko, V. G. [The riddles of high-frequency bioelectronics.] *Tekhnika Molodezhi,* Oct. 1974.

————. Memories of Semyon Kirlian. *International Journal of Paraphysics,* 1979, *13,* 3–14.

Belov, I. [Torches, illuminating the unknown. *Literary Gazette,*] Oct. 1960.

Bergman, J. An aura of mystery *The Saturday Evening Post,* Oct. 1979

Borún, K., and Manczarski, S. [*Parapsychology Today.*] Warsaw: Iskry, 1977.

Boyers, D. G., and Tiller, W. A. Corona discharge photography. *Journal of Applied Physics,* 1973, *44*(3), 102–12.

———. The color in Kirlian photography—fact or artifact? *Functional Photography,* May 1976.

Burton, L.; Joines, W.; and Stevens, B. Kirlian photography and its relevance to parapsychology research. In J. D. Morris, W. G. Roll, and R. L. Morris (eds.), *Research in Parapsychology, 1974.* Metuchen, N.J.: Scarecrow Press, 1975.

Dakin, H. S. *High-voltage Photography,* 2nd ed. San Francisco: Washington Research Center, 1975.

Davis, M., and Lane, E. *Rainbows of Life: The Promise of Kirlian Photography.* New York: Harper/Colophon, 1978.

Dick, W., and Gris, H. Soviets are diagnosing diseases with photos of invisible energy. *National Enquirer,* April 23, 1975.

Dumitrescu, I. F. Electronography. *Electro/78 Conference Record.* New York: Institute of Electrical and Electronic Engineers, 1978. (a)

———. Electronography: A scanning method for the electromagnetic exchanges between the human body and the electric environment. A paper presented at the Veterans Administration Hospital, Bronx, New York, 1978. (b)

———. [*Electronography: Electrographic Methods in Biology.*] Bucharest: Editura Stuntifica n Enciclopedica, 1979.

Dumitrescu, I. F.; Golovanov, N.; Golovanov, G.; and Eugen, C. Letter. *Psychoenergetic Systems,* 1977, *2*, 308–14.

Edelberg, R. Response of cutaneous water barrier on ideational stimulation. *Journal of Comparative and Physiological Psychology,* 1966, *71*, 28–34.

Edelson, E. Aura phenomenon puzzles experts. *The Smithsonian,* Apr. 1977.

Eidson, W. W., and Faust, D. L. Kirlian photography: An update. In L. J. Kaslof (ed.), *Wholistic Dimensions in Healing: A Resource Guide.* Garden City, N.Y.: Doubleday, 1978.

Golvin, V. The Kirlian effect in medicine. *Medical Science Gazette,* Aug. 11, 1976.

Graff, E. International Kirlian Research Association: 1980 status report. *IKRA Communications,* Winter, 1980.

Gris, H., and Dick, W. *The New Soviet Psychic Discoveries.* Englewood Cliffs, N.J.: Prentice-Hall, 1978.

Hubacher, J., and Moss, T. The "phantom leaf" effect as revealed through Kirlian photography. *Psychoenergetic Systems,* 1976, *1,* 223–32.

Jodko-Narkiewicz, J. Cited in: [Photography serves physiology.] *Kraj,* Mar. 1896.

Kirlian, S. D., and Kirlian, V. K. [Photography and visual observation by means of high-frequency currents. *Russian Journal of Scientific and Applied Photography and Cinemaphotography,*] 1961, *6,* 397–403. Available from the Clearing House for Federal Scientific and Technical Information, Arlington, Va. 22151. Report AD 299–666. Also in S. Krippner and D. Rubin (eds.), *The Kirlian Aura.* Garden City, N.Y.: Anchor Books, 1974.

————. [*In the World of Wonderful Discharges.*] Moscow: Zhanie, 1964.

Konikiewicz, L. W. Kirlian photography in theory and clinical application. *Journal of the Biological Photographic Association,* 1977, *45,* 115–34.

Krippner, S. Biological applications of Kirlian photography. *Journal of the American Society of Psychosomatic Dentistry and Medicine,* 1979, *26,* 122–28.

Krippner, S., and Rubin, D. *Galaxies of Life: The Human Aura in Acupuncture and Kirlian Photography.* New York: Gordon & Breach, 1973.

Krippner, S., and Rubin, D. *The Kirlian Aura.* Garden City, N.Y.: Anchor Books, 1974.

————. Preliminary investigations of Kirlian photography as a technique in detecting psychokinetic effects. *International Journal of Paraphysics,* 1977, *11,* 69–73.

Krivorotov, V. K.; Krivorotov, A. E.; and Krivorotov, V. K. Bioenergotherapy and healing. *Psychoenergetic Systems,* 1974, *1,* 27–30.

Leonidov, I. Russians photograph life—and death. *Fate,* Sept. 1962.

Lvov, V. [Reckoning with simpletons.] *Vechernii Leningrad,* Mar. 27, 1974.

Montandon, H. E. Psychophysiological aspects of the Kirlian phenomenon: A confirmatory study. *Journal of the American Society for Psychical Research,* 1977, *71,* 45–50.

Monteith, H. Photographing the life field. *Fate,* June 1974.

Moss, T. *The Probability of the Impossible.* Los Angeles: Tarcher, 1974.

————. Electrical photography: An historical controversy. *IKRA Communications,* Fall 1978.

Moss, T., et al. Health and disease in plants as seen through Kirlian photography. *Psychoenergetic Systems,* 1979, *3,* 33–45.

Moss, T., and Johnson, K. Radiation field photography. *Psychic,* July 1972.

Musial, Z., and Wolniewicz, B. Psychotronics as neo-occultism. *International Journal of Paraphysics,* 1977, *11,* 30–41. (Originally published in Poland in 1973.)

Omura, Y. Acupuncture, infra-red thermography, and Kirlian photography. *Acupuncture and Electrotherapeutics Research: The International Journal,* 1976, *2,* 43–86.

Ostrander, S., and Schroeder, L. *Psychic Discoveries Behind the Iron Curtain.* Englewood Cliffs, N.J.: Prentice-Hall, 1970.

Pehek, J. O.; Kyler, H. J.; and Faust, D. L. Image modulation in corona discharge photography. *Science,* 1976, *194,* 263–70.

Poock, G. K., and Sparks, P. W. An image intensification technique for motion picture Kirlian photography. In S. Krippner (ed.), *Psychoenergetic Systems.* New York: Gordon & Breach, 1979.

Reeves, C. T. Use of Kirlian photography in fatigue assessment. A report prepared for the Safety Engineering Graduate Program and Texas A&M University Graduate Center, U.S.A.M.C. Intern Training Center, Red River Army Depot, Texas. Unclassified technical report ADA 026349, 1975.

Ryzl, M. Training the psi faculty by hypnosis. *Journal of the Society for Psychical Research,* 1962, *41,* 234–52.

Stepanov, P. [Diagnosis by electrical discharges. *Medical Cadres,*] Apr. 14, 1976.

Swets, J. A., et al. Assessment of diagnostic technologies. *Science,* 1979, *205,* 753–59.

Tiller, W. A. The light source in high-voltage photographs. In S. Krippner and D. Rubin (eds.), *The Energies of Consciousness: Explorations in Acupuncture, Auras, and Kirlian Photography.* New York: Gordon & Breach, 1975.

————. A comment. *Psychoenergetic Systems,* 1976, *1,* 232–34.

Vetoe, L. [Photography of tooth sections in a high-voltage, high-frequency electric field. *Hungarian Dental Review,*] 1978, *71,* 272–73.

Vilenskaya, L. [Radiant phantoms.] *Tekhnika Molodezhi,* Oct. 1974.

Weberman, A. J. Mind control: The story of Mankind Research Unlimited, Inc., *Covert Action,* June 1980.

Zielinski, L. *Russia and Poland.* In E. J. Dingwall (ed.), *Abnormal Hypnotic Phenomena: A Survey of Nineteenth-century Cases,* Vol. 3. London: J. & A. Churchill, 1968.

Zinchenko, V. P., and Leontiev A. N. [Parapsychology. *Great Soviet Encyclopedia,*] 3rd ed., Vol. 19. Moscow: Sovietskaia Entsiklopedia, 1974. English translation published in New York by Macmillan, 1978.

CHAPTER 9

Problems of the Unconscious

> . . . Man has acquired unprecedented power over the material world. While bringing numerous inestimable blessings to our generation, this power has at the same time imposed great responsibility on us. Man shall be incapable of rationally controlling the world of things until he has learned to control himself. . . . Hence, the great importance of the problem of the unconscious. . . . At the present time, study of this problem undoubtedly acquires a serious social significance.
>
> F. V. Bassin and A. E. Sherozia
> (1979, pp. 31–32)

Soviet personality theory has its fundamental bases in the philosophical concepts of dialectical materialism of Karl Marx, Friedrich Engels, and V. I. Lenin, and in the neurophysiological findings of I. P. Pavlov. Its practical applications as well as its experimental research approaches have been largely guided by the work of A. S. Makarenko (1951), an educator who, in the 1920s, had remarkable success in restructuring personalities and rehabilitating delinquent youth. As a result, the guiding principles of contemporary Soviet personality theory and Makarenko's dicta are:

1. Personality can most effectively be developed and maintained in, by, and for the collective.
2. The collective is the principal factor in the development of personality.
3. One can study children while teaching them, and teach the children while studying them.

A major research tool in Soviet personality procedures is the "transforming experiment" that changes the phenomenon while studying it, as when new treatment techniques are tested with juvenile offenders or emotionally disturbed patients. Other research approaches include human typology studies based on Pavlov's conditioned-reflex theories, and the study of the theory of "set" developed by the Georgian school of psychology. This latter movement was headed by D. N. Uznadze and is seen by many Soviet psychologists as the key to understanding unconscious processes. Meticulous laboratory studies have also been carried out on the development of speech, thought, perception, and attention as influenced by "set" (Brozek, 1962).

In 1976, I received an invitation to Tbilisi, capital of the Georgian Soviet Socialist Republic (SSR). Tbilisi State University planned to host an International Symposium on the Problem of Unconscious Mental Activity. I accepted the invitation, and sent a copy of my paper "Psychophysiology, Converging Operations, and Alterations in Consciousness." In the paper, I cited data from biofeedback, dream, and meditation research to demonstrate how psychophysiological monitoring could be combined with verbal reports to investigate consciousness. These findings, I wrote, confirmed I. P. Pavlov's assertion that the human organism is an integrated whole; as such, the entire organism participates in the conscious experience (Krippner, 1978, pp. 658–67).

In addition, I traced the use of psychophysiological monitoring back to the days of Alexander the Great. The Roman historian Plutarch wrote about the strange events that occurred in the household of one of Alexander's ablest generals, Seleucus. Shortly after he had married a woman named Stratonice, Seleucus' young son, Prince Antiochus, fell ill. Many physicians attended the young prince, but to no avail; indeed, Antiochus announced that he was about to die. Finally the celebrated Greek physician

Erasistratos was summoned. After his examinations detected no bodily disease, Erasistratos concluded that the prince was suffering from an affliction of the mind—one tentatively diagnosed as "love sickness." Since Erasistratos took the position that mind and body are closely related, he decided to observe the prince's reactions to his visitors. Plutarch described how Erasistratos would spend day after day in the young man's chamber, and if any of the beauties—male or female—of the court entered, he would study Antiochus' reactions. Whenever the prince's stepmother, Stratonice, came to see him, Antiochus would display sudden sweats, palpitations of the heart, stammering speech, helplessness, stupor, and pallor. When General Seleucus was informed of the physician's diagnosis, he dissolved his marriage to Stratonice, sent her away, and his son recovered.

A Birthday in Georgia

The Symposium was postponed twice and finally rescheduled for October 1979. All participants were asked to submit new papers. This time I wrote about "Access to Hidden Reserves of the Unconscious Through Dreams in Creative Problem-Solving." I delivered the paper in Tbilisi on October 4, my forty-seventh birthday.

I told the assembled scientists that "conscious" (as meaning "inwardly sensible or aware") first appeared in the English language in 1620. "Consciousness" (or "the state of being conscious") appeared in 1678, and "self-consciousness" (or "consciousness of one's own thoughts") in 1690 (White, 1960, p. 43).

Even before these words were used, humans had some understanding that mental activity outside their waking consciousness did exist. William Shakespeare died long before the word "unconscious" first appeared in English. However, several passages in his plays give witness to Shakespeare's understanding:

> My mind is troubled, like a fountain stirred;
> And I myself see not the bottom of it.
> (*Troilus and Cressida,* Act III)

Sleep that knits up the ravell'd sleeve of care,
The death of each day's life, sore labour's bath,
Balm of hurt minds, great nature's second course,
Chief nourisher in life's feast.

(*Macbeth,* Act II)

Suspicion always haunts the guilty mind;
The thief doth fear each bush an officer.

(*King Henry VI, Part III,* Act V)

The word "unconscious" first appeared in English in 1751 and in German by 1776. It was used in the writings of Coleridge, Goethe, Schiller, and Wordsworth. Fyodor Dostoevski, the Russian novelist who died in 1881, anticipated Freud with his penetrating insights into unusual mental processes. Dostoevski's vivid sense of the harmonies and cacophonies of the unconscious are illustrated in a passage describing a dream from his novel *The Idiot:*

> These obvious absurdities and impossibilities with which your dream was overflowing . . . you accepted all at once, almost without the slightest surprise, at the very time when, on another side, your reason was at its highest tension. . . . And why, too, on waking and fully returning to reality, do you feel almost every time, and sometimes with extraordinary intensity, that you have left something explained behind with the dream, and at the same time you feel that interwoven with these absurdities some thought lies hidden, and a thought that is real, something belonging to your actual life, something that exists and always has existed in your heart. It's as though something new, prophetic, that you were awaiting, has been told you in your dream. [p. 455]

Montague Ullman (1965) has described four creative aspects of dreaming: the element of originality, the joining together of disparate elements into new patterns, the concern of the dreamer with important symbols, and the reaction of participating in an involuntary experience. Ullman has noted that the final product can be banal or ecstatic but "it is an act of creation to have the dream in the first place." Dmitri Mendeleev, Camille Saint-Saëns, and Leo Tolstoy were among the creative persons who sometimes derived inspiration from their dreams (Krippner and Hughes, 1977, pp. 106–26).

There are a number of examples that demonstrate creative problem-solving in dreams using "hidden reserves" of the unconscious. Elias Howe had worked unsuccessfully for several years to invent a lockstitch sewing machine:

> . . . Howe made the needles of his early failures with a hole in the middle of the shank. His brain was busy with the invention day and night and even when he slept. One night he dreamed . . . that he was captured by a tribe of savages who took him a prisoner before their king. "Elias Howe," roared the monarch, "I command you on pain of death to finish this machine at once. . . .
>
> Try as he would, the inventor could not get the missing figure in the problem over which he had worked so long. . . . He saw himself surrounded by dark-skinned and painted warriors who formed a hollow square about him and led him to a place of execution. Suddenly he noticed that near the heads of the spears which his guards carried, there were eye-shaped holes! He had solved the secret! What he needed was a needle with an eye near the point! He awoke from his dream, sprang out of bed, and at once made a whittled model of the eye-pointed needle with which he brought his experiments to a successful close. [Kaempffert, 1924]

Giuseppe Tartini, the composer who invented the modern violin bow, dreamed that the devil had become his slave. In the dream, he gave the devil a violin and, to his surprise, Lucifer played "a sonata of such exquisite beauty as surpassed the boldest flights of my imagination." After Tartini awoke, he recalled the music as best he could; the result was "The Devil's Sonata," his most famous composition (Porterfield, 1941, p. 9).

Richard Wagner, describing his opera *Tristan and Isolde* to a friend, wrote, "For once you are going to hear a dream, a dream that I have made sound. . . . I dreamed all this; never could my poor head have invented such a thing purposively" (Hock, 1960).

Robert Louis Stevenson learned early in his life that he could dream complete stories and that he could even go back to the same dreams on succeeding nights to give them different endings. Later, he trained himself to dream plots for his novels and short stories. He wrote that his dreams were produced by "little people" who "labor all night long," and "set before me truncheons of tales upon their lighted theatre." Stevenson's short story *The Strange Case of Dr. Jekyll and Mr. Hyde* came to him in a dream after two days of failing to come up with a satisfactory plot by conscious deliberation (Woods, 1947, pp. 871–79).

Jean Cocteau (1952, pp. 81–82) dreamed he was watching a play about King Arthur; Cocteau later noted that it was "an epoch and characters about which I had no documentary information." The dream was so challenging that Cocteau was led to write his play *The Knights of the Round Table*. He concluded, "The poet is at the disposal of his night. His role is humble, he must clean house and await its due visitation" (p. 82).

Similar examples exist in scientific endeavors. Niels Bohr, the physicist, dreamed he was sitting on a sun composed of burning gas while planets attached by their filaments revolved around him. Interpreting the sun as symbolizing a fixed center around which electrons revolved enabled Bohr to conceive a new model of the atom (Van de Castle, 1971, p. 2).

Reserves of Memory

In my presentation, I mentioned Georgian psychologist D. N. Uznadze and how an understanding of his theory of "set" could be useful in understanding aspects of the creative dream. Uznadze held "sets" to be the most important elements of unconscious activity, forming the key components of goal-directed behavior.

Uznadze and his followers held the position that "set" involves changes in the functional condition of the nervous system; often not apparent, they play an important role in the dynamics of succeeding conscious experiences. "Set" theory, for example, might explain the emergence at night of answers to the problems that had occupied Elias Howe for several years. In a similar fashion, Robert Louis Stevenson came to rely on his dreams for inspiration. Others have been taken by surprise by the wealth of information given them in dreams: Tartini's dream contained music that, he claimed, "surpassed the boldest flights of my imagination"; Wagner wrote "never could my poor head have invented such a thing purposively"; and Cocteau's dream involved "an epoch and characters about which I had no documentary information." In all these cases, the insight of the unconscious could be understood on the basis of "set" theory. Unconscious "sets" can fulfill the role of a bridge to tap one's reserves of memory (Kupriyanovich, 1970). In so doing, "set" theory makes it unnecessary to view the conscious and unconscious as two completely separate realms, allowing psychology to understand the unity of central nervous system phenomena.

I ended my presentation by drawing the audience's attention to the symbol that served as the emblem of the Symposium—a centaur that appeared on our badges, programs, proceedings, posters, and on the curtain in back of the speaker's podium. The half man, half beast was portrayed shooting a demonic face in his own tail. My translator, Vladimir Verovacki, a Yugoslav psychology stu-

Fig. 2 Emblem, International Symposium on the Problem of Unconscious Mental Activity, Tbilisi, USSR, 1979, with Symposium title in Russian, English, and Georgian.

dent who had come to Tbilisi with me, had conducted some research in the local library and discovered that the centaur was taken from an A.D. 1188 Georgian astronomical treatise, being a symbol for the month of November. I said that the centaur reflected medieval religious superstition and an irrational fear of the unknown; by shooting at his own tail, the centaur was in fact attempting to destroy an element of his own unconscious. The importance of this inner element has been demonstrated many times: Howe's savage king stimulated the invention of the lockstitch sewing machine; the devil in Tartini's dream composed part of his sonata. The savage and the devil were parts of the creators themselves, perhaps the parts most responsible for their creative processes. To kill or suppress these aspects of our unconscious is to destroy a vital part of ourselves.

George Reavy (1964), in his Introduction to the work of Soviet poet Yevgeny Yevtushenko, wrote, "There is something about the poet and his poetic utterance that has a terrifying effect. . . . It is as though poetry were an irrational force which must be bridled and subjugated, and even destroyed" (pp. x–xi). Peter Ilich Tchaikovsky was driven by his creative forces throughout his life. As a child, he was once found in bed, weeping. "The music! The music! Save me from it," he sobbed, striking his head. "It's in here and it won't let me rest!" (Anon., 1964).

Rollo May (1975, p. 91) has pointed out how creativity brings out new meaning, new forms, and a reality that was not present before. This process can be viewed as threatening, but it should be integrated rather than destroyed, encouraged rather than suppressed. "Set" theory can help disclose the association between the conscious and the unconscious, thus making creativity less threatening and uncovering its roots.

Walking in the Dark

The Symposium had been organized by the Georgian Academy of Sciences and Tbilisi State University in conjunction with the Déjerine Psychosomatic Institute of Paris. The organizing committee was headed by A. S. Prangishvili (of the Georgian Academy's Institute of Psychology), A. E. Sherozia (of Tbilisi State

University's Department of Philosophy and Psychology), F. V. Bassin (of the USSR Academy of Medical Sciences), and V. S. Rotenberg (of the First Moscow Medical Institute). Bassin, a student of A. R. Luria and an expert on Freud, recalled my 1971 lecture at the Institute of Pedagogical Sciences. Rotenberg, a colleague of Vladimir Raikov (for example, Rotenberg, Raikov, and Andreev, 1978), spoke knowledgeably about American psychology and expressed interest in research data concerning hemispheric brain functions—particularly such right-hemispheric functions as music, form perception, and divergent thinking. He had received a doctoral degree in medical science in 1979 after writing his dissertation on dream theory.

In their opening presentation, Bassin and Sherozia (1979) traced Soviet investigation of the unconscious back to several nineteenth-century Russian physicians such as M. Y. Mudrov, G. A. Zakharin, and A. A. Ostroumov, who reported that "unaccountable feelings" of their patients often related to the development of disease and the restoration of health. Later, N. I. Pirogov observed similar phenomena in surgery, and I. M. Sechenov spoke of "dark, vague sensations" that eluded the awareness of his patients.

I. P. Pavlov repeatedly spoke of the mixture of the conscious and the unconscious that could be observed in everyday life. Pavlov likened the psychologist to a person walking in the dark with a lantern that lights up only small sections of the way, leaving vast areas of terrain unexplored.

In the 1920s, D. N. Uznadze began his work at Tbilisi State University. Uznadze's basic idea was that the relation between any stimulus affecting a human being and the behavioral response evoked by this stimulus is never direct. On the contrary, it is always mediated by the psychological "set" of the responding subject. Unconscious mental activity serves to prepare the organism for a response and to regulate that response once it is elicited; thus the unconscious is an inevitable agent in one's "set." At the International Congress of Psychology, which I attended in Tokyo in 1972, a Soviet psychologist had pointed out:

> The error of previous researchers lies in their seeking for the trace
> of perception in memory rather than in the state of the subject,

where the trace of a preceding stimulus could be detected. It is "set" that constitutes such a state. [Grigolava, 1972]

The approach initiated by Uznadze has been applied to many areas: the conscious formation of goals but the inability to attain them due to unconscious "sets," the development and maturation of belief systems, the selective character of perception in which some objects are not sensed accurately as a result of one's "set," and individual differences in fear, panic, suspicion, affection, sympathy, etc. Bassin and Sherozia concluded that not only can individual "sets" be unconscious, but also the laws governing "sets" are unconscious. Therefore, ignoring the existence of unconscious mental activity and disregarding this factor as a determinant of behavior leads to a distortion of the understanding of a person's mental life, especially in medicine and education.

Several psychologists maintain that nonverbal thought is important in the unconscious determinants of "set." Dreams involve preverbal thought and can be understood, according to the Soviets, from the vantage point of a person's conscious attitudes and goals. This is an example of one's conscious thought illuminating the unconscious instead of the more frequently cited instances of unconscious material explaining conscious behavior.

Repression and Sublimation

Nancy Rollins (1978), an American psychiatrist, pointed out that both "set" theory and psychoanalysis utilize the concept of the unconscious. For Freud, however, the "energy" responsible for psychological phenomena was generated internally; in "set" theory, the individual assimilates "energy" from the environment and transfers it to an internal need.

Rollins observed that the Rorschach inkblots and similar psychological techniques can be used to measure one's "set." Similar instruments can be used to study defense mechanisms—those procedures used by people to protect themselves against unwelcome psychological information. One such defense mechanism is repression, a refusal to allow threatening psychological information to come to the surface. Repression plays an important part in human behavior, according to the psychoanalysts. For the "set" theorists, however, repression is not a central issue but can be explained by understanding one's "set." Sublimation is another defense mechanism, one that Freud regarded as more mature than repression because sublimation transforms a socially unacceptable drive to a socially acceptable one. Both the psychoanalysts and the "set" theorists feel that some types of creativity could be the results of sublimation; for example, an artist might paint nude bodies rather than acting out his or her sexual fantasies directly.

Freud saw defense mechanisms as originating in early psychosexual experiences. To the proponents of "set" theory, defenses can change during life as one's personal "sets" are restructured. Accordingly, the significance and meaning of an unpleasant situation (such as separation, frustration, loneliness, disability) can be changed if the individual's social setting is altered. Separation from a loved one may have been a traumatizing event in childhood but it need not remain so if it later occurs in a different social context. A person's response to the same stimulus may be completely opposite if one's "set" has changed.

Uznadze insisted that people are not slaves of a given situation; behavior is not permanently conditioned by traumatic experiences. People are social beings and in the context of social life they develop the ability of "objectification" that Uznadze held to be the most characteristic feature of humanity. Because people can "objectify," a "set" that has been directly conditioned by a given situation can be relegated to a minor role in one's life. As a result of objectification, the object is perceived as a thing and becomes a part of consciousness. No longer is the person simply reacting to the object; the old "set" exists in a displaced form and a more important role is assumed by "objectified reality," which is the basis for the appearance of a new "set."

People can act, not only impulsively as most animals do, but also in a voluntary manner. This activity was designated by Uznadze as the "second plane" of the mind's operation as contrasted with the "first plane" of impulsivity.

In personal relationships, the formation of emotionally positive "sets" in relation to another person is facilitated if that person becomes the object of active care. "Set" theorists maintain that love must be active in order to be long-lasting. In education, A. S. Makarenko stressed active attitudes on the part of teachers.

Uznadze and his followers placed great importance upon the way that social rituals, rites, and traditions can organize "sets." This was held to be especially true in regard to the strong relationship between "set" and symbolization. Thus, Rollins pointed out, one's "set" would have an important impact on the content and feeling tone of dreams and other altered states of consciousness.

Rollins told the Symposium audience that she found F. V. Bassin's treatment of symbolism inadequate. Bassin, for example, rejected the idea that a symbol could have a latent meaning, because—in Rollins' opinion—to admit this was to imply some concept of repression. In discussing a dream, Bassin (1968, p. 329) had used an example of a man about to part with his wife who was standing with him at the fork in the road. Although Bassin interpreted this image as implying separation, Rollins added that it could instead symbolize decision making or commitment to a course of action.

Rollins pointed out that Freud and Uznadze recognized dreams as having psychological meaning and that unrealized intentions from the recent past often operate during sleep. Both recognized the role of primitive thought modes and the role of symbolization in dreaming. Both were committed to the construction of a comprehensive system of scientific psychology. And both found certain phenomena of everyday life to be manifestations of the unconscious—slips of the tongue, automatic behavior, artistic productions, and children's play.

In concluding her brilliant presentation, Rollins lauded the contributions of Soviet psychology, which include the development of a positive theory of consciousness that spells out a synergistic relationship between conscious and unconscious processes. A. E. Sherozia (1979) has applied general systems theory to the study of personality, postulating a holistic, tripartite system: consciousness, unconscious activity, and "set." He has also allowed for other unconscious mental activity besides "set."

A similar position was taken by E. D. Wittkower of Canada's McGill University. A specialist in psychosomatic illness, Wittkower (1960) placed the discussion of human unconscious activity within the framework of general systems theory. Proponents (for example, Miller, 1978; Ruttenber, 1979) of this approach describe how biological and social systems are organized and operate at hierarchical levels: cells, organs, organisms, groups, organizations, societies, and supranational systems. Wittkower saw no basic disagreement between "set" theory and psychoanalysis because, by and large, they act within different hierarchies: "set" theory primarily at the organic level and, psychoanalysis at the group level. Although Wittkower's premise was, to me, somewhat oversimplified, I was pleased that he had introduced general systems theory into the discussion, echoing a longtime interest of Sherozia.

Responding to Questions

Speaking for the psychoanalytic contingent, Léon Chertok called the conference a "breakthrough." Director of the Déjerine Psychosomatic Institute of Paris, Chertok recalled that Freudian psychoanalysis was condemned by Soviet authorities as unscientific in the early 1930s. The new position, that Freud was a pioneer in exploring the unconscious, was a dramatic turnaround. Howard Shevrin of the University of Michigan Medical Center agreed, observing that "for the first time, Western psychoanalysts and scientists interested in the unconscious were able to meet and exchange views with their Soviet colleagues." He continued:

> The Soviet psychotherapist can, and often does, display a great fund of wisdom, skill, and empathy in trying to get the patient to understand and overcome the causes of his misery or neurotic behavior. Yet no amount of confidence and trust can get at what the patient is not aware of himself. For that we require those psychoanalytic techniques that can enable the patient to discover the conflicts hidden in his unconscious by re-experiencing them within the framework of the patient-doctor relationship. [Astin, 1979]

I agreed with this evaluation of the conference's importance although I regretted that alternative approaches to the unconscious were not adequately represented. Hans Ansbacher, an American psychologist, devoted an entire paper to the work of Alfred Adler, while a Soviet psychologist compared Uznadze and Carl Jung. I briefly introduced Adler's and Jung's dream theories in my presentation, but both pioneers deserved far more attention. In addition, other points of view in psychology were virtually ignored, among them the behavioristic, cognitive, Gestalt, humanistic, and transpersonal approaches. Even so, the conference was a monumental success and the audience paid rapt attention to the speakers from a dozen different countries in Europe and North America.

It was difficult for me to attend all the sessions of the Symposium because Soviet psychologists would stop me on the way into the auditorium and ask me questions. I had not mentioned parapsychology in my formal address, yet most of the queries centered on that topic. Indeed, on the final day of the Symposium, I was unable to enter the auditorium and hear any of the discussions because I had so many questioners with whom to interact. For example, I was asked, "Did you know that there are copies of all your books in Moscow's Lenin Library?" "Does the right hemisphere of the brain process telepathy and clairvoyance?" "What do you think of Professor Hasted's work with children who claim to bend metal?" "Do the Filipino healers actually remove impurities from the body without surgery?" "How do you explain reincarnation?" "Did you know that our scientists have photographed visual hallucinations?"

I replied that there was some evidence that the cerebral cortex's right hemisphere is more active than the left hemisphere during ESP tasks (Braud and Braud, 1975) and that John Hasted (1977) was engaging in some carefully controlled work with children who attempt to bend metallic objects through PK. Both lines of research, however, were preliminary and need to be carefully replicated. Regarding the Filipino healers, I was intrigued by my observations of their work but would want an interdisciplinary team of scientists, physicians, and magicians to conduct a careful study of them. As for the documented cases concerning memories of other people's life events (Stevenson, 1977), I noted that these phenomena—if authentic—could be explained in ways other than reincarnation. For example, Carl Jung postulated the notion of a "collective unconscious" that contained information about everyone who had ever lived. Perhaps through hypnosis or dreams a person could gain access to some of this information, especially if it coincided with problems being faced in the individual's personal life. A similar explanation could be given on the basis of Karl Pribram and David Bohm's "holographic paradigm" of an "enfolded order" in the universe where all information was potentially available to everyone. These explanations were challenging and exotic but did not demand that one accept the position that one was continually being reborn carrying memories of the past life into the present one.

I had read about the innovative photography experiments conducted in the city of Perm by G. P. Krokhalev (1979), a psychiatrist who had asked subjects to stare at a black-and-white negative image for fifteen seconds under intense electrical illumination. The lights were turned off and the subject stared at a sheet of film for seven seconds. When the film was developed, an image could be seen dimly but clearly. In this manner, photographs of geometric forms, numerals, and faces were obtained. The phenomenon was explained on the basis of electromagnetic waves radiating from the retinas creating visual forms in space, reminiscent of holographic images. I observed that this work was extremely imaginative and deserved replication in other laboratories. However, I expressed doubt that hallucinations could be produced this way because, in my opinion, hallucinatory images were created in the brain rather than in the retinas.

One example given me concerned an alcoholic who hallucinated pillars surrounding him; between the columns were faces of his relatives. When told to stare at the film, the patient concentrated on these images. When the film was developed, it was said to show a clear picture of a pillar as well as dim forms resembling faces. In addition to his attempts to confirm his photographs of visual hallucinations, Krokhalev has recently initiated attempts to objectify auditory hallucinations.

Reserves of Personality

Once Verovacki and I reached Tbilisi, we were joined by James Hickman and by Mary Payne, his research associate in a California-based project on mind-body relationships. Hickman had been to the USSR with me in 1972, attending the informal parapsychology meetings in Moscow, and had also participated in the 1973 Congress of the International Association for Psychotronic Research in Prague.

Hickman and Payne had stopped in Czechoslovakia to see Zdeněk Rejdák, who reported that psychotronic research was continuing to develop in his country. One of the most promising developments involved placing a psychic sensitive in an electromagnetic field, similar to the procedure that I had observed in Warsaw during my 1973 visit. In neither Warsaw nor Prague had controlled experiments been done—studies, for example, that would place one group of alleged psychic sensitives in an electromagnetic field and another group in a similar setting without the current being turned on. If the second group *believed* that they would be more effective in the electromagnetic field, the belief alone could account for the enhanced results on ESP tests. Another worthwhile comparison would be to test alleged sensitives in strong and weak fields to see if different scores would result. Until a variable (such as an electromagnetic field) is varied and manipulated, one cannot make statements inferring cause and effect in parapsychology or in any other behavioral science.

V. N. Pushkin, my host at the Academy of Pedagogical Sciences in 1971, was on the program, and I was eager to see him again. He and Alexander Dubrov had written a book on parapsychology that was scheduled for publication in 1981 by Plenum Press in New York. Since my last visit to the USSR, Pushkin had also published a brief article concerning his work with Boris Ermolaev, a film producer who had the purported ability to suspend objects in midair.* As Pushkin (1973) described this process:

> . . . Every time we began the experiments with Ermolaev, there was a "warming up" phase in which he moved distant objects without touching them. After that, he would hold his hand over cards which had been placed on the table, face down. With great accuracy, Ermolaev would name the suit (e.g., Hearts, Spades)

---

* Another PK subject, tested by Larissa Vilenskaya (1979), reportedly raises wooden rods from the floor without touching them. The subject, Elvira Shevchuk, lives in Kalinin, between Moscow and Leningrad.

and numerical designation (e.g., Ace, Nine, Queen) of each card. At this point, the most important part of the experiment would begin. Ermolaev would lift up an object (e.g., a tennis ball), squeeze it between his palms, and slowly move his hands apart. On many occasions, the object would remain suspended in space. The distance between Ermolaev's hands could extend as far as twenty centimeters (about eight inches) and the object would still remain suspended. Further, it was noted that the greater the surface of the object, the longer it remained suspended in the air. . . . [p. 55]

Pushkin began to discuss the phenomenon with Dubrov, who had hypothesized that living systems are capable of creating and controlling gravitational waves. Naturally, I was interested in these reports, as well as somewhat skeptical. I was looking forward to talking to Pushkin and encouraging him to write a descriptive and technical article covering his work with Ermolaev in the depth it deserved.

Unfortunately, Pushkin was ill and could not attend the Tbilisi symposium. Shortly after I returned to the United States, I learned that Pushkin had died of cancer. We all mourned his passing but were grateful that, before his death, he had edited another book, *New Data on the Latent Abilities of Human Personality*. A historic volume, this book placed psychic phenomena within the larger context of such latent reserves of the human potential as accelerated learning, communication between twins, and creativity.

The news was better concerning Yuri Nikolayev, director of the fasting program for schizophrenics that Hickman and I had observed in 1972 at Gannushkin State Hospital in Moscow. He had retired, but his innovative treatment program continued to attract attention from other countries and had been copied or adapted in many clinics or hospitals.

In 1979, the Fourth International Congress on Psychotronic Research was held in São Paulo, Brazil. One of the Soviet participants, F. N. Romashov, described his use of Nikolayev's fasting treatment with seventy-three patients suffering from gastrointestinal diseases. Fasting was combined with electroacupuncture, physical therapy, massage, and gymnastics. Romashov reported that forty-two patients demonstrated remarkable improvement, twenty-nine moderate improvement, and that three showed no change. In none of the cases did complications or aggravations develop. Among other diagnostic and monitoring techniques, iridology was used. (Iridology is a controversial method of determining patients' conditions by observing the iris of their eyes, especially discolorations, spots, and rings. If the human organism operates in a way resembling a hologram, information from one area could be reflected in the condition of another area. Romashov reported that he has investigated twenty-three hundred individuals using iridology in an attempt to verify the validity of this procedure.)

Schizophrenia was a frequently mentioned topic at the Tbilisi Symposium. A. D. Zurabashvili (1975) spoke of a "personological" approach to psychotherapy with schizophrenics, tracing the connections among work, duty, and morality. "Personology" emphasizes both the integrative and the evolutionary capabilities of human personality. Work therapy is one of the most effective psychotherapeutic methods; it mirrors Leo Tolstoy's observation that a mental wound heals from within if it is externally stimulated by the "life force." Zurabashvili insisted that psychotherapy be humane, because even in the most serious cases of schizophrenia some traces of love and good survive.

Valentina Zavarin of the Langley Porter Neuropsychiatric Institute in San Francisco used "set" theory to study the language of schizophrenics. She found that schizophrenics demonstrate a typical language pattern. A schizophrenic might refer to a violin as a "fiddle," or a "musical instrument," not recognizing the difference in levels of abstraction. Other schizophrenics may speak only in rhymes or may scrupulously avoid certain words. A difficulty with one concept, due to an unhappy personal experience, may generalize to others, or "irradiate," as the proponents of "set" theory term the process.

Adamenko Revisited

Victor Adamenko attended the conference, having been assigned to cover it for *Izvestiya,* an official Soviet publication. He showed us his latest patent—a visual display system for Kirlian photography that he had developed with the Kirlians before their death. He noted that it would be possible for another inventor to adapt the device and obtain a patent in a foreign country. We hoped that this would be possible but informed Adamenko that there was little interest in the Kirlian effect on the part of American technology and medicine.

Adamenko's work with Alla Vinogradova had continued, although her busy schedule as a child psychologist prevented her from devoting much of her time to developing her unusual abilities further. In 1972, Hickman and I had seen Vinogradova move objects across a table without touching them. At that time we concluded that she had developed the skill to control the electrostatic field produced by rubbing her hands, rubbing the object, or using a table and target object that would be conducive to producing the electrostatic effect. Even though we did not consider the phenomenon psychokinetic in nature, we were intrigued by the process and felt it was worthy of further study.

Adamenko showed us photographs depicting Vinogradova's recent work with E. T. Kulin (1973), a biologist in Kiev whose specialty is the study of human electrical fields. He had measured Vinogradova's electrical field, finding it far more powerful than that of the average person. He discovered that the strength of her field decreased when she was tired or indisposed.

In an effort to determine whether her ability to move objects was entirely explainable through the electrostatic effect, Kulin asked Vinogradova to swim in a pool before attempting to move objects. She complied—and was still able to move cylinders and other items across a table without touching them. However, Kulin measured her bodily field after she emerged from the swimming pool and found that there had been very little decrease. Thus the results are still inconclusive, although he noted that he had never observed a bodily field powerful enough to account for the power needed to move the type of objects used by Vinogradova. Adamenko further stated that in his opinion electrostatic effects were often components of PK but were not essential to it.

The conversation switched to Nina Kulagina, and we learned that she continued to participate in a variety of scientific tests in various Soviet laboratories. In one laboratory she reportedly had been able to bend a laser beam by mental concentration alone. In addition, she had worked with hospitalized patients under conditions where her healing ability was carefully monitored.

Adamenko also had been assigned to join us in Alma-Ata for our meetings with A. S. Romen and Victor Inyushin. Adamenko commented that very few foreign scientists had ever taken the time to visit that remote part of the USSR but that he was pleased to hear of our decision to go there. He was also looking forward to attending a medical conference in the Latvian SSR where he, Vinogradova, and Edward Naumov would be discussing possible medical applications of parapsychology.

One of the most eloquent addresses of the Symposium was given by V. P. Zinchenko, co-author of the historic article on parapsychology in *Questions of Philosophy*. In his talk, Zinchenko spoke of Freud's pioneering work on the unconscious and how Freud saw the mind as "unbound in time and space." Zinchenko related this concept to Soviet studies in memory; from a psychological point of view "past" and "future" are difficult to distinguish because memory is not only a trace of a past event, but also a precondition for the realization of future actions. Zinchenko (1968) has developed a model of information processing to help explain such related concepts as visual imagery, problem-solving activity, and creativity.

Zinchenko and A. N. Leontiev (1974) had written the entry on parapsychology for Volume 19 of the *Great Soviet Encyclopedia,* describing it as the study of "forms of perception by a mode of information transmission that cannot be explained by mechanisms of the known sense organs" and "corresponding forms of action of living matter on physical phenomena taking place outside the organism without the intermediary of muscular force." They pointed out that parapsychology's development "is hindered by mystics and charlatans." However, they also observed there are unusual "phenomena that actually exist but are not yet scientifically clarified by scientific psychology and physics." Zinchenko and Leontiev recommended that the mystics be demystified, that the charlatans be exposed, and that the valid phenomena be studied by existing disciplines, as there is no basis for developing parapsychology as a separate field.

Vassilchenko Revisited

G. S. Vassilchenko had attained his goal of establishing sexology as an independent discipline since I had last seen him in 1972. He had become director of the Department of Sexual Pathology in the Scientific Research Institute of Psychiatry of the Russian SFSR Ministry of Health. Vassilchenko had also supervised the preparation of a sex manual for medical professionals (Vassilchenko, 1977).

Vassilchenko gave me a copy of the manual, noting that it discussed the analysis of sexual disturbances. A general systems theory approach was used, allowing for the interaction of psychological, neurological, and hormonal factors with one's urogenital apparatus. Because sexual functioning involves both conscious and unconscious activity, "set" forms the psychological correlate of the link between the two (Vassilchenko, 1978). Since behavior is mediated by one's immediate "set," sexologists need to examine the individual's "set" in cases of sexual dysfunction. They may find that the problem rests not in one's intellectual attitude toward sex, but in one's unconscious attitudes, motivations, or expectancies.

Vassilchenko had described several types of sexually compatible pairs, again basing his work on general systems theory. Vassilchenko summarized for me his advice to couples who could not have children: "If they are unable to direct their sexuality for procreation purposes, they should not be dismayed; they can still enjoy the recreational benefits." And in compiling data from the people he studied, Vassilchenko concluded that the earlier one's sex life begins, the longer it is likely to last. Vassilchenko's work on couples is important because the lack of attention given to relationships between two people had always struck me as a major deficit in Soviet applications of psychology and psychiatry.

Vassilchenko (1977) spent one chapter of his book discussing sex in the larger context of love. He observed that love involves deep feeling, caring, intent to help, and "togetherness" between people on personal, social, spiritual, as well as biological levels. He quoted an ancient Indian verse from the *Upanishads:*

> There are three sources of attraction
> In the love of human beings;
> They are spirit, mind, and body.
>
> Mutual attraction of spirits
> Gives birth to friendship.
>
> Mutual attraction of minds
> Gives birth to respect.
>
> Mutual attraction of bodies
> Gives birth to desire.
>
> The combination of all three
> Gives birth to love. [p. 177]

In line with his use of general systems theory, Vassilchenko defined love as "a complex dynamic system based on intellectuality, emotions, and will power," and noted that it consists of a multitude of variables. In contrast to the temporary feelings of desire, "true" love's deep feelings enable the relationship to be one of fulfillment and wholeness. In "true" love, one often denies the personal ego's needs and becomes transformed through union with another.

Vassilchenko told us he had used Greek terms to delineate several types of love. *Eros,* or "being in love," involved desire, often sexually toned. For example, Pierre and Natasha, in Leo Tolstoy's novel *War and Peace,* demonstrated *eros.* This type of love can include social and spiritual as well as sexual elements. *Philia* is love based on friendship; it involves social connections but is determined by personal choice. *Philia* need not have a sexual component and is illustrated by the smoking-club friendships in Herman Melville's novel *Typee.*

Storge is love based on affection, such as the tenderness among family members or even toward pets. Mr. Pontifex in Samuel Butler's novel *The Way of All Flesh* is shocked that his son does not love him—but Pontifex had never displayed *storge* toward the boy. *Agape* is altruistic, often sacrificial, love that is self-giving and is not based on need. *Agape* can be patriotic in nature or directed toward nature or to humanity as a whole; Dante wrote that it is "the love that moves the sun and other stars." *Agape* is typically spiritual and impersonal (while *eros* is usually biological, *philia* personal, and *storge* social). The use of the term "spiritual" by Vassilchenko and other Soviet writers refers to feelings of great depth and universality rather than to those associated with organized religion (Averinthev and Spirkin, 1977).

Vassilchenko also mentioned the publication of a sex manual for the general populace, *Four Young Couples* (Khodakov, 1979). Its message that "everything done in bed is acceptable" came as a considerable shock to the more puritanical elements of Soviet society. However, the manual did not take a liberated view of homosexual behavior, which was attributed to incorrect glandular functioning; nor did the book point out that homosexuality is a criminal offense in the USSR, punishable by imprisonment.

The manual reveals that Soviet children do not obtain basic knowledge about sex from either parents or teachers, a contributory factor to the 40 percent divorce rate among married couples. Naum Khodakov, the author of the manual, claims that sexual disharmony is the chief cause of divorce. Not mentioned are two problems I heard cited with frequency: cramped living accommodations and the high rate of alcoholism among Soviet men.

Birth-control pills are difficult to obtain in the USSR, but are more easily available to those who have foreign currency and can purchase them from tourists. Khodakov does not mention the pill but does describe various other methods. Nor does he mention abortion, probably the most frequently used method of birth control in the country (Stern, 1979).

Khodakov concludes that masturbation is not harmful and that most heterosexual practices are necessary and rational, "especially those that cause admiration of your partner and increase sexual desire." One patient described in the book claimed he could only obtain sexual satisfaction if he dressed in women's underwear and if his wife called him by a woman's name while they were making love. Khodakov told the couple, "Go ahead, so long as it makes you happy."

Raikov Revisited

Vladimir Raikov informed us that he had been elected to membership in the Soviet Artists' Union, and showed me his official membership card. In January, he had a gallery exhibit of his work and those of his students whose artistic ability had been enhanced through hypnoproduction. The exhibit was a great success and was well attended. Evaluations had been solicited from 149 people; all but a dozen reactions were favorable (Raikov, 1980b).

Raikov remarked that he had been working with "supermemory" development through deep hypnosis, enhancing his subjects' memory up to twenty times. He had also improved abstract thinking (for mathematics and chess) through hypnosis—a theme discussed by Georgi Lozanov, who showed a film about suggestopedic instruction. I learned from Lozanov that the 1978 UNESCO conference in Sofia had been very helpful to the development of his projects. I also found out that Technika, the Bulgarian trade commission, had signed contracts with American firms that would allow Lozanov to spend several months in the United States teaching the principles of suggestology to American educators. We were both pleased that this important educational innovation would soon be more widely available in the United States.

During March, April, and May 1979, Lozanov had visited the USA to train new instructors and to try out his new language manuals with American subjects. A. J. Lewis (1979) was one of ten educators who studied with Lozanov for four weeks. Lewis stated:

> . . . In approximately 22 lessons of 3 hours duration we learned 2,000 plus lexical units in a new foreign language (Italian), including the basic grammar. Tests showed that we had achieved a passive mastery (ability to read, understand and translate dictation into English) of 90% of the material, and 60–70% of active mastery (use in everyday conversation). . . .

Although all of us were open-minded on the subject, our skepticism grew when we were presented with around 800 new words in a foreign language in our first 3 hour lesson. To our own amazement, subsequent personal experience convinced us that we too are capable . . . of "super learning."

. . . Suggestopedic methods have been used to accelerate learning processes for people of all ages and any subject matter. The U.S.S.R. is reportedly using it to teach languages to some 30,000 guides being prepared for the 1980 Olympics. . . . [p. 4]

Raikov told the Symposium participants about his most complex study to date in which he attempted the use of deep hypnosis to regress adults to infancy. He pointed out that there are three basic groups of hypnotizable individuals: those who retain self-awareness during hypnosis, those who lose this awareness, and those who alternate between the two conditions. Members of the first group recall their entire experience once hypnosis is terminated, those in the second group have complete amnesia, while those in the third group demonstrate a partial amnesia. Members of the first and third groups can usually engage in conversation with the hypnotist, but those in the second group cannot. Some people in the third group described their session as "dreamlike" and reported that they had a "divided" experience in which they observed what was going on; these descriptions were not given by individuals in the second group (Raikov, 1980a).

Raikov presented data from a study of ten students (six males and four females) who were members of the second group—those who demonstrated a capacity for deep hypnosis. All were told that they were infants; they were then asked their age and were requested to open their eyes. None of the subjects answered the request and none opened their eyes. A spreading of the toes when stroked (a response resembling the Babinski reflex, which disappears as the infant matures) appeared in half the cases. When their eyelids were pulled back, uncoordinated eye movements were observed for all ten subjects.

As these behaviors had been observed by Raikov earlier, the possibility existed that he gave unconscious, subtle clues for the subjects to perform in this manner. Therefore, Raikov asked V. S. Rotenberg and B. L. Andreev, two well-known neurologists from the First Moscow Medical Institute, to carry out additional tests.

Rotenberg and Andreev noted uncoordinated eye movements and spontaneous sucking reflexes in all the subjects, the grasping reflex in four, a "crying" without tears in five, movements of the limb extremities in four, the toe-spreading reflex in five, and the foot-bending reflex in six. No subject showed fewer than two of these seven behaviors; one student manifested all of them.

Raikov described one student who previously had shown an ability to enter deep hypnosis. A few minutes after the induction was concluded, the student, who was lying on his back, began to "cry" in a high-pitched voice. His arms bent at elbow and wrist joints. The neurological examination showed that his eyes were moving independently of each other. The grasping and Babinski reflexes were observed, as were sucking movements when the lips were touched. Not all the phenomena occurred for the same length of time; the uncoordinated movement of the eyeballs appeared to last during the entire period of deep hypnosis. When Raikov told the subject he was now an adult, all the infantile behaviors disappeared. Following the termination of hypnosis, the student could recall nothing about the experience.

In a follow-up study, Raikov used two groups of subjects capable of entering deep hypnosis. The subjects in one group were regressed to infancy, and the others were told that they were highly talented actors capable of acting as if they were infants. The subjects in the first group demonstrated many of the infantile behaviors observed by Raikov in his earlier work. Members of the second group became very much involved in their roles as infants. Some sucked their thumbs, some cried, but none exhibited the Babinski-type reflexes, the uncoordinated eye movements, or the behaviors observed with the other group.

The experiences of the two groups differed. When Raikov suggested during hypnosis that they could tell him how it felt to be hypnotized, members of the second group gave simple, concrete responses such as, "I see a man in a white coat," and "I have tiny hands and feet." Members of the first group responded more euphorically, stating, "I could spend my entire life in this state," and "I understand it all; I realize everything." It was my feeling that perhaps Raikov had elicited responses from their "hidden observers" in obtaining answers to these questions.

Ernest Hilgard (1977) had noted that even deeply hypnotized subjects were able to comment upon their experiences and dubbed that part of the psyche making the response a "hidden observer."

In interpreting his results, Raikov recalled the experiments of Wilder Penfield (1975), the Canadian neurologist who found that electrical stimulation of his patients' brains could produce spontaneous recall of early childhood experiences. According to Penfield, the patients' experiences were so vivid they described "reliving" them rather than merely "remembering" them. Penfield suggested that people store their experiences as if they were filmed and tape recorded; under certain changed states of consciousness, these experiences could be replayed.

Raikov surmised that his subjects had lost their infantile responses as they matured. However, the reflexes still remained in a latent condition—one that could be activated by deep hypnosis.

Raikov's report on his work was well received, and his film on age regression was a personal triumph. There was such a huge crowd waiting to see the movie that it had to be shown twice. On film, one could see Raikov inducing hypnosis and the infantile behaviors that resulted. In one case, he told a hypnotized subject that she was five years of age. She began to speak in a childish tone of voice and use gestures that were childlike. When asked to draw a picture of a man, she produced a crude sketch of a person as well as creatures she described as "flying mice." Raikov told her that the mice were going to eat the man; the subject tried to protect him by holding her hands around him, and began to cry. (Later, some of us suggested to Raikov that he could administer figure-drawing tests to hypnotized subjects at different ages of regression; this would be a more objective way of determining the ability of hypnosis to activate the motor memories used in their childhood by his subjects.)

At the conclusion of the film, Léon Chertok, the French psychoanalyst, and I were asked to comment. I mentioned that I had seen Raikov's work firsthand in Moscow. I praised his innovations and remarked that both hypnosis and dreams give clear-cut evidence that the unconscious exists.

Raikov was asked what words he used during hypnotic induction. He replied that the technique differs from person to person;

Raikov intuitively grasps what will be most appropriate and behaves accordingly. "For some," he remarked, "I am very gentle, but for others a stern look and a firm touch are all that are needed."

Another film that aroused considerable interest portrayed an artist's reaction to sensory deprivation. The blindfolded subject was placed in a tub of water. There were no auditory or visual sensations for the duration of the experiment. Soon the subject experienced vivid visual imagery—walking in the forest during a rainstorm, exploring underwater life, being immersed in colorful geometric patterns. Near the end of the experiment, the subject was asked his name and responded,

> The sound of the rain in the autumn,
> The red sun in the silence of the sky.

The reaction to this film was enthusiastic and it was a topic of conversation for several days.

Healers and Artists

During our stay in Tbilisi, we were told that folk healing is widely practiced throughout the USSR and has been the focus of several research studies. It is significant that Soviet parapsychology's bitter critics—Kiatagorsky, Lvov, and the others—have stopped writing articles attacking their nation's healers in recent years. One reason may stem from the reports that we repeatedly heard concerning healers who are called to Moscow in order to treat prominent political and military leaders.

The Georgian SSR allows healers to apply for an official license. Once obtained, the healer can charge money for his or her services. Victor Adamenko introduced us to one of these licensed healers, Juna Davitashvili. Telling us she had taken courses in physiology to better acquaint herself with the human body, Davitashvili proceeded to diagnose my current status of health. She correctly identified my major problem as centering around the abdominal area; however, Adamenko and others knew about my operation for duodenal ulcers some years earlier. She also correctly identified a sore muscle in my left foot, a condition that I had noticed while jogging on the previous day.

Davitashvili then stated that I had "minor problems" of the shoulder, heart, liver, and spleen. However, there was no way to determine the accuracy of this diagnosis because Davitashvili claimed that she was going to heal me. For the next six days, she spent five minutes each afternoon making circular movements around my body with her hands to stimulate the flow of my "healing energies." She also "laid on" hands over the problem areas of my body and initiated a circular massage in an attempt to transfer some of her "healing energy" to me. Did it work? The muscle of my left foot was no longer sore and I resumed jogging. I did not suffer the attacks of diarrhea that bothered some of the foreigners at the conference. However, I informed Adamenko that before-and-after examinations by a physician, as well as long-term follow-up observations, would be useful in attempting to determine the effects of Davitashvili's treatments.

Levan Machaidze, a director of programming for Georgian television, was preparing a documentary on the local healers and asked for my opinion. I began to discuss how many psychosomatic ailments can be ameliorated by treatments by a healer, especially if the client believes in the healer's effectiveness. I observed that the process was based on suggestibility, a phenomenon also utilized in hypnosis. "It is not hypnosis!" proclaimed one of Davitashvili's supporters. "It is a transfer of biological energy!" I did not want to argue the point, but a few minutes later, Davitashvili agreed to attempt to diagnose a newspaper reporter. As soon as she brought her hand near his body, he swayed, and only our prompt action kept him from falling to the floor. Was this suggestibility or the release of too much "biological energy"? I suspected the former but did not press my point. And later, when Georgian television taped my interview, I was asked many questions—but none about the mechanisms of successful healing.

Also appearing on the television documentary was Galina Shatalova, a Moscow physician who practices the "laying on" of hands with many of her patients. Shatalova told me that her attempts to transfer "biological energy" often seem to help the patients more than orthodox treatment involving medicine and drugs.

I told Shatalova that the World Health Organization (WHO) has pledged itself to an ambitious goal—worldwide health provision by the end of the century. To meet this goal, WHO has decided to utilize the services of unorthodox healers. Halfdren Mahler (1977), as director general of WHO, stated:

> The training of health auxiliaries, traditional midwives, and healers may seem disagreeable to some policy makers, but if the solution is the right one to help people, we should have the courage to insist that this is the best policy. . . . [p. 3]

Also present for the television production was Gyorgi Kenchadze, a licensed healer living in Tbilisi. One night we visited Kenchadze's home, one room of which served as his healing clinic. He allowed us to observe him at work as a stream of clients arrived for healing. One woman, a longtime client, told us how helpful her treatments had been over the years. As she approached, he held out his arms. She closed her eyes and fell toward him; he caught her and helped her into a comfortable chair where she remained for nearly an hour. When he revived her, she appeared alert and happy; I observed that her prolonged rest was probably of considerable benefit.

One of Kenchadze's clients was a boy who had flown down from Moscow with his mother. Suffering from a severe case of asthma, the boy appeared nightly for a "laying on" of hands. Kenchadze's technique was quite different from Davitashvili's, as he never worked with a client more than a minute or two, and barely touched his clients instead of making the circular rubbing movements I had seen Davitashvili undertake. Nevertheless, the boy's mother told us that his asthmatic symptoms had completely disappeared and that they were preparing to return to Moscow the following day. I hoped the "cure" would be long-lasting.

The best-known healer in the Soviet Union is Alexei Krivorotov, who worked in Georgia for many years. We were told that he had moved to Krasnador to undergo extensive scientific testing, much of it involving the effect his "laying on" of hands would have upon hospitalized patients. However, one of his sons, Victor Krivorotov, remained in Tbilisi, where he was engaging in work with sick people.

In addition to the "laying on" of hands taught to him by his father, Victor Krivorotov has been asking his patients to keep a personal journal to assist the healing process, especially if their problem is psychological or psychosomatic in nature. According to Krivorotov, emotional difficulties often result when one's experiences and informational input are not integrated and assimilated. Therefore, he has his clients keep a written account of their personal relationships; work, family, and educational experiences, as well as episodes of happiness and joy. From time to time, they summarize each of these five areas of their life. Eventually they have five "chapters" of a book— a volume of their own lives. The process of self-reflection and journal keeping is said to assist their recovery and to prevent the onset of more serious diseases.

Victor Krivorotov is also a talented artist and allowed us to visit his studio. It was filled with beautiful paintings, most of them in the surrealistic tradition. They portrayed many of the themes that Krivorotov used in his healing work: dreams, ecstatic experiences, family unity, and occupational fulfillment.

We also visited the studio of Temo Djeparidze, a Georgian artist of prodigious creative gifts. We surveyed his paintings, commenting that the variety of styles would suggest that this was the work of several people rather than one man. Especially remarkable were Djeparidze's three-dimensional portraits—huge human heads made from papier-mâché, which protruded from the canvas. After we drank a toast to world peace, Djeparidze remarked that art could assist this quest because "it is a language that all people understand." He also expressed the hope that art could "help psychologists love the people who come to them for assistance."

A third artist whose studio we visited was Amiry Kakabadze, the son of David Kakabadze, the late Georgian master whose paintings grace the state art museums in Tbilisi. We were taken on a tour of these exhibits by G. N. Kechkhuashvili, chairman of Tbilisi State University's Department of Philosophy and Psychology. Kechkhuashvili (1978, p. 573) had delivered a paper noting that the work of such contemporary composers as Igor Stravinsky, Sergei Prokofiev, and Dimitri Shostakovitch was originally perceived by many as devoid of any artistic merit. Kechkhuashvili's research had indicated that music appreciation is often based on a tonal fixated "set." When a new tonal structure emerges in music, a new "set" must evolve to enable the listener to enjoy it.

Although Kechkhuashvili did not mention rock music, I felt that its reception in the USSR confirmed his theory. In 1971, rock music was denounced by the authorities as "decadent." By 1979, however, there were rock bands in many of the restaurants I visited. A "folk rock" band from Moscow played at the Symposium banquet. A few weeks after I left the country, Tbilisi was host to the Soviet Union's first rock festival; the musicians were encouraged by government authorities to look to their own musical heritage and not to idolize American and British rock stars.

Etery Andronikashvili, Kakabadze's widow, showed us additional canvases painted by her husband. We were impressed by the wide range of subject matter as well as the variety of his styles, which ranged from realism to abstract expressionism. Amiry Kakabadze's work had progressed in different directions, including theatrical sets, three-dimensional collages, and portraits. The Kakabadze studio also contained several paintings by Georgian primitive painter Niko Pirossmanashvili, whose folk art captured the way of life followed in the nineteenth century. Pirossmanashvili's work has acquired a new popularity due to the wave of nostalgic nationalism evident throughout much of the Soviet Union.

Human Potential

On our final day in Tbilisi, we met Joseph Goldin, a biochemist and cinematographer who described a stunning project of major importance. Goldin had been asked to serve as scientific secretary of the newly formed Commission for the Development of Human Potential* within the USSR Academy of Sciences' Council on Cybernetics. Goldin had been a member of the first suggestopedia class taught by Georgi Lozanov in Moscow. Since that time, Goldin has been interested in the ways that extraordinary human abilities are inhibited by society's expectations.

* An alternative translation would be the Commission for the Maximum Development of Man.

Goldin (1978) told us how he had applied suggestopedic principles to a demonstration with a dozen stutterers. The demonstration took place in a Moscow theater before an audience of eight hundred. Employing suggestopedia in the form of psychodrama, Goldin claimed that all twelve stutterers began to speak fluently. For example, one of the stutterers was a young man who had lived with his parents in the United States, where they served in the diplomatic corps. Thousands of dollars had been spent on speech therapy, but to no avail. However, his speech showed a significant improvement during the demonstration. (I was curious as to whether there was a follow-up; stutterers can often speak fluently when their social setting is altered, as when speaking to pets, to themselves, or as characters in a play. Nevertheless, Goldin's report was extremely provocative.)

While working with the stutterers, Goldin studied reports of purported instantaneous cures over the ages. One common denominator was the use of a collective condition or group-support system. Other commonalities were positive expectations on the part of the afflicted person and careful preparation on the part of the healer, often culminating in a dramatic effect. Goldin combined these factors by preparing a biography of each stutterer, which was read by a physician in the form of a dramatic monologue. The biography led to an exhortation that the stutterer was able to rid himself or herself of the ailment. The resulting catharsis was so powerful that the audience, consisting largely of friends and family members, was emotionally moved as well. When the stutterer began to speak fluently, there were tears as well as cheers from the onlookers.

Goldin told us that the newly formed Institute would stress three areas: the development of "latent reserve creative abilities" (as in suggestopedia), "sociodynamic aspects of collective and individual activity" (as in sports), and psychoenergetics (the study of psi phenomena). Goldin mentioned that he had secured the cooperation of many prominent artists and film makers to assist in his project, as well as leading physicians such as G. S. Vassilchenko and outstanding scientists such as F. N. Romashov. On his return to Moscow he planned to organize suggestopedic foreign-language classes to give airport personnel, traffic controllers, and tourist guides working vocabularies in several languages to prepare them for the crowds attending the 1980 Olympics in their city.

Goldin gave us a copy of the symbol for the Institute: the Tower of Babel emerging from a human head. I recalled that the

Fig. 3 Emblem, USSR Commission for the Development of Human Potential; design modeled after a painting by the Flemish artist Pieter Brueghel the Elder.

biblical account of the tower ended with all the workers speaking different languages, making it impossible for them to finish their task. Goldin expressed the hope that humankind could create a happier ending for this fable and showed me another design in which people of all nations are cooperatively building a huge letter "N." The initial stood for a "New Order," one to be reached through the exploration of human potential. One of Goldin's colleagues has coined the term "anthromaximology," the study of the maximum development of human possibilities, for research in this area.

One afternoon, many of the symposium's 1,400 participants gathered at Tbilisi State University for the unveiling of a bust of Uznadze. A. S. Prangishvili officiated, observing how "set" theory has a fifty-year history and how it explains the synergy between conscious and unconscious mental activity. At that event, and at others, the most excited participants were students who, according to one observer (Astin, 1979), "acted as though their eyes had just been opened." They crowded around the speakers, asking questions and wanting to find out as much as possible. One of the students remarked, "This is a wonderful event. You have no idea how hard we have worked for it and how much we have looked forward to having you here" (p. A7).

As we left Tbilisi, Sherozia observed that the unconscious could now be considered an official part of Soviet science. True, there had been scheduling problems and communication difficulties. But as a Moscow psychologist commented, "When your wife bakes her first cake, you don't criticize her. You are simply happy that she has been able to bake a cake at all."

References

Anonymous. Music that sings. New York: Radio Corporation of America, 1964.

Astin, A. Soviet is wavering in its rejection of Freud's ideas. New York Times, Oct. 9, 1979.

Averinthev, S. S., and Spirkin, A. G. [Love.] Moscow: Medicina, 1977.

Bassin, F. V. [The Problem of the Unconscious.] Moscow: Izdatelstvo Meditsina, 1968.

Bassin, F. V., and Sherozia, A. E. The Role of the Category of the Unconscious in the System of the Present-day Scientific Knowledge of the Mind. Tbilisi: Metsniereba, 1979.

Braud, W. G., and Braud, L. W. The psi-conducive syndrome:

Free response GESP performance following evocation of "left-hemispheric" vs. "right-hemispheric" functioning. In J. D. Morris, W. G. Roll, and R. L. Morris (eds.), *Research in Parapsychology, 1974*. Metuchen, N.J.: Scarecrow Press, 1975.

Brozek, J. Current status of psychology in the USSR. In P. R. Farnsworth (ed.), *Annual Review of Psychology*, Vol. 13. Palo Alto: Annual Reviews, 1962.

Cocteau, J. The process of inspiration. In B. Ghiselin (ed.), *The Creative Process*. Berkeley: University of California Press, 1952.

Dostoevski, F. *The Idiot*. New York: Modern Library, 1942. (Originally published in 1868.)

Goldin, J. Commentary to the "cinematographic report." *Journal of Suggestive-Accelerative Learning and Teaching*, 1978, *3*, 146–50.

Grigolava, V. V. Concerning the perception of stimuli of which the subject has no awareness. In E. A. Faraponova (ed.), *Short Communications Prepared for the Twentieth International Congress of Psychology*. Moscow: USSR Society of Psychologists, 1972.

Hasted, J. B. Physical effects of paranormal metal bending. *Journal of the Society for Psychical Research*, 1977, *49*, 583–607.

Hilgard, E. R. *Divided Consciousness*. New York: John Wiley & Sons, 1977.

Hock, A. *Reason and Genius*. New York: Philosophical Library, 1960.

Kaempffert, W. A. *A Popular History of American Invention*, Vol. 2. New York: Charles Scribner's Sons, 1924.

Kechkhuashvili, G. N. Music and fixated set. In A. S. Prangishvili, A. E. Sherozia, and F. V. Bassin (eds.), *The Unconscious: Nature, Functions, Methods of Study*, Vol. 2. Tbilisi: Metsniereba, 1978.

Khodakov, N. [*Four Young Couples.*] Moscow: Miv, 1979.

Krippner, S. Psychophysiology, converging operations, and alterations in consciousness. In A. S. Prangishvili, A. E. Sherozia, and F. V. Bassin (eds.), *The Unconscious: Nature, Functions, Methods of Study*, Vol. 2. Tbilisi: Metsniereba, 1978.

Krippner, S., and Hughes, W. Dreams and human potential. In H. M. Chiang and A. H. Maslow (eds.), *The Healthy Personality: Readings,* 2nd ed. New York: D. Van Nostrand, 1977.

Krokhalev, G. P. [Objectifying optical hallucinations.] *Psychotronik,* 1979, *1,* 8–18.

Kulin, E. T. [Bioelectric effects on human physiology.] *Proceedings, First International Congress on Psychotronic Research.* Prague: Cevran, 1973.

Kupriyanovich, L. [Reserves of memory.] *Nauka i Zhirn',* 1970, *37,* 65–72.

Lewis, A. J. "Super learning"—a possible solution to our educational problems. *Lozanov Learning Institute Report,* June 9, 1979.

Mahler, H. The Staff of Aesculapius. *World Health,* Nov. 1977.

Makarenko, A. S. *The Road to Life: An Epic of Education,* 3 vols. Moscow: Foreign Language Publishing House, 1951. (Originally published in 1933–35.)

May, R. *The Courage to Create.* New York: W. W. Norton, 1975.

Miller, J. G. *Living Systems.* New York: McGraw-Hill, 1978.

Penfield, W. *The Mystery of the Mind.* Princeton, N.J.: Princeton University Press, 1975.

Porterfield, A. L. *Creative Factors in Scientific Research.* Durham, N.C.: Duke University Press, 1941.

Pushkin, V. N. The autogravity hypothesis as a possible explanation for psychokinetic phenomena. *Socialist Industries,* Sept. 9, 1973. Also published in the *Journal of the American Society of Psychosomatic Dentistry and Medicine,* 1976, *23,* 54–58.

———. [*New Data on Latent Abilities of Human Personality.*] Moscow: Society of Nature Researchers, scheduled for publication in 1981.

Pushkin, V. N., and Dubrov, A. P. *Parapsychology and the New Natural Sciences.* New York: Plenum Press, scheduled for publication in 1981.

Raikov, V. L. Age regression to infancy by adult subjects in deep hypnosis. *American Journal of Clinical Hypnosis,* 1980, *22,* 156–63.

———. [The unconsciously perceived world.] *Teknika Molodezhi,* March 1980.

Reavy, G. Introduction. *Poetry of Yevgeny Yevtushenko*. New York: October House, 1964.

Rollins, N. Consciousness, unconsciousness, and the concept of repression. In A. S. Prangishvili, A. E. Sherozia, and F. V. Bassin (eds.), *The Unconscious: Nature, Functions, Methods of Study*, Vol. 1. Tbilisi: Metsniereba, 1978.

Romashov, F. N.; Velchover, E. S.; and Aleckseeva, A. N. [The combined use of fasting and electroacupuncture in the treatment of gastrointestinal diseases.] *Proceedings, Fourth International Congress on Psychotronic Research*. São Paulo: Society of Psychobiophysical Investigation, 1979.

Rotenberg, V.; Raikov, V.; and Andreev, B. [Hypnosis and hysteria.] *Revue de Médecine Psychosomatique et de Psychologie Medical*, 1978, *20*, 321–25.

Ruttenber, A. J. Introduction to the general system basis of psychoenergetics. In S. Krippner (ed.), *Psychoenergetic Systems*. New York: Gordon & Breach, 1979.

Sherozia, A. E. [*Psychic Functioning, Consciousness, Unconsciousness: Towards a Generalized Theory of Psychology.*] Tbilisi: Metsniereba, 1979.

Stern, M. *Sex in the Soviet Union*. New York: New York *Times* Books, 1979.

Stevenson, I. Reincarnation: Field studies and theoretical issues. In B. B. Wolman (ed.), *Handbook of Parapsychology*. New York: Van Nostrand Reinhold, 1977.

Ullman, M. Discussion. Dreaming—a creative process. *American Journal of Psychoanalysis*, 1965, *24*, 10–12.

Van de Castle, R. L. *The Psychology of Dreaming*. Morristown, N.J.: General Learning Press, 1971.

Vassilchenko, G. S. The apparatuses of afferent synthesis and "end of action outcome" acceptor as physiological correlates of the unconscious in the sexual sphere. In A. S. Prangishvili, A. E. Sherozia, and F. V. Bassin (eds.), *The Unconscious: Nature, Functions, Methods of Study*, Vol. 2. Tbilisi: Metsniereba, 1978.

Vassilchenko, G. S. (ed.). *General Sexopathology: A Manual for Medical Professionals*. Moscow: Medicina, 1977.

Vilenskaya, L. Elvira Sheuchuk. *International Journal of Paraphysics*, 1979, 13, Covers.

White, L. L. *The Unconscious Before Freud*. New York: Basic Books, 1960.

Wittkower, E. D. Twenty years of North American psychosomatic medicine. *Psychosomatic Medicine,* 1960, *22,* 308–16.

Woods, R. L. *The World of Dreams*. New York: Random House, 1947.

Zinchenko, V. P. [Perceptual and mnemonic elements of creativity.] *Voprosy Psikhologii,* 1968, *14*(2), 3–7.

Zinchenko, V. P., and Leontiev, A. N. [Parapsychology. *Great Soviet Encyclopedia*.] 3rd edition. Vol. 19. Moscow: Sovietskaia Entsiklopedia, 1974. English translation published in New York by Macmillan, 1978.

Zurabashvili, A. D. Some clinical problems of ethics in schizophrenia. *Titus Homo,* 1975, *6,* 78–83.

CHAPTER 10

Self-regulation in Kazakhstan

> Some of the changes experienced under self-regulation cannot be achieved by any other means such as hypnosis, drugs, physical agents, etc. . . . But close attention must be given to the construction of formulas. Phraseology should be handled with the same care with which a surgeon wields his scalpel.
>
> A. S. Romen (1972)

In 1978, a world championship chess match was held in the Philippine resort of Baguio City. The reigning champion, Anatoli Karpov, was challenged by Victor Korchnoi, a Soviet defector. Karpov was accompanied from Moscow by a cadre of security officers as well as by Vladimir Zoukhar, a neuropsychologist and hypnotist with purported paranormal skills (Thacher, 1979).

During the match's early games, Dr. Zoukhar sat in the front row of the amphitheater staring at the challenger. Korchnoi donned dark glasses but was still upset. After Korchnoi demanded that Zoukhar be expelled for attempting to hypnotize him at a distance, officials ordered Zoukhar to sit in the back of the hall. It was to no avail; Karpov soon built up a four-to-one lead.

Korchnoi countered by studying headstands with two yogis and bounced back by winning four games. Karpov's aides demanded that the yogis be expelled from Baguio City, and the match officials complied.

Three months after the matches began, the decisive game was played. Dr. Zoukhar walked boldly to the front of the amphitheater and fixed an unblinking gaze in Korchnoi's direction. Again the challenger began to play badly; after five hours, he sealed his last play and rose from the table a beaten man. Later, Korchnoi declined to sign his game card as a protest against the "intolerable conditions under which the games have been played."

It is unlikely that Zoukhar possessed any paranormal powers; his mere presence could have upset Korchnoi and affected his game. However, the publicity given to the incident raised questions as to how far parapsychological research had infiltrated the Soviet sports scene.

East German Sports Schools

In the 1976 Olympics, Soviet athletes won more gold medals than representatives from any other country (Shteinbakh, 1980). The United States placed third. East Germany placed second; its women swimmers, for example, won eleven of the thirteen gold medals awarded. I visited East Berlin in 1973 and found out that many of the country's future athletes are identified as early as kindergarten; some are sent on to special sports schools that begin at the fourth grade. Special dietary and exercise programs are initiated to facilitate the development of these future champions.

There has been some conjecture that East German athletes are injected with anabolic steroids to help develop their muscles; a Bulgarian weight lifter lost his Olympic medal in 1976 when traces of steroids were found in his urine following a medical examination. The East Germans hotly deny this accusation, claiming that extensive training is responsible for the prowess of their champions (Amdur, 1978).

The Leipzig Institute of Sports is the East German sports laboratory. It extends over fourteen acres and employs some nine hundred people, of whom half are scientists. Kurt Tittel, the director, informed a visiting reporter:

What is special about our training? We have pushed the science of nutrition to its highest level; it must be different according to the sports practiced. Drugs? This is ridiculous. They are harmful to the body and do not produce better performance. [Katz, 1977]

According to the November 1976 issue of *Track and Field News,* East German weight lifters receive "mental training sessions" once or twice a day that consist of hypnosis, autosuggestion, and similar procedures. Dance or ballet is scheduled daily, as are injections of vitamins B_1, B_6, B_{12}, and C. The athletes take vitamin E every third day as well as such minerals as calcium and iron. Gerovital is administered every other day. I had learned about this substance in Romania; a procaine derivative, Gerovital is used to retard aging and enhance a sense of well-being. The training program also makes use of films, massage, and a plotting of physical and psychological "highs" and "lows." Caffeine tablets are administered before training sessions, while relaxation and re-generation exercises follow training sessions and each competitive event.

There are sixteen sports schools in East Germany where promising students are sent if they have obtained satisfactory grades and have obtained parental consent (Katz, 1977). In addition to the academic curriculum, students receive fourteen hours of sports training a week. Sports facilities include indoor stadiums, playing fields, skating rinks, and tracks. Johannes Rech, vice president of the East German Sports and Physical Culture Work Federation, told reporters that participation in sport was a guaranteed constitutional right; 60 percent of the population engages in athletic activities. Future champions are identified early and work with expert trainers from various disciplines (Katz, 1977).

One discipline that is not utilized in this training is parapsychology; East German scientists and journalists take a more hostile position on ESP and PK than those in any other country I visited in Eastern Europe. One article (Spickermann, 1975) appearing in the official newspaper of the East German Communist Party noted that "astrologers, clairvoyants, and prayers for health currently experience increasing success in the capitalist countries." The article continued:

> Lacking a scientific world view, and without Marxism-Leninism, many people in the capitalist countries face social, economic, and political changes, quite helpless and confused. Particularly in moments of crisis, social theories offered by the ruling class prove to be useless, providing no answers to the pressing questions of life. Many seek an escape from this frustration by turning toward a mystical belief in miracles. . . . Mysticism, is after all, well suited to distract the masses from important and substantive economic and political questions.

The article ends by praising Professor Otto Prokop of Humboldt University's Institute of Legal Medicine in East Berlin. It is claimed that Prokop and his collaborators have unmasked such "occult undertakings" as "thought photography" and "life emanations" as frauds.

Sports Politics

The adventure of sports provides people with an opportunity to cultivate and reshape their bodies and, in so doing, to explore the limits of human possibility. Sports point toward human transformation as well as the discovery of practical ways to improve education, cure disease, and lengthen life.

In addition, sports can be a useful political and diplomatic technique to gain prestige. Andrew Strenk (1979) identified East Germany as the forerunner in the field of "sports politics," observing that the country has invested about 2 percent of its annual gross national product in athletics. Some state organizations, such as the Free German Labor Federation, have contributed 10 percent or more of their budgets to the East German sports program.

The results have been spectacular. By the time of the 1976 Montreal Olympics, East Germans had won 340 world and 263 European titles as well as 92 gold medals in Olympic events. This success paved the way for international diplomatic recognition. Guenther Heinze (1973), vice president of the East German Sport and Gymnastic Federation, noted:

East German Sport did its part in obtaining recognition internationally. . . . Sport led the way in increasing the international prestige of our socialistic republic and led to its diplomatic recognition by a majority of the world's nations. [p. 874]

The United States once refused to issue visas to East German athletes to compete in America but changed its position when these athletes attained prominence.

The Soviet Union also spends immense sums on athletics, with contributions coming from such diverse sources as the state insurance fund, trade unions, consumer cooperatives, the police, the military, governmental agencies, and sports societies (Strenk, 1979). In addition to its emphasis on international competition, the USSR encourages participatory sports on other levels. Reportedly, there are over 5 million athletes in the USSR, 220,000 sports clubs, 6,000 sports schools, 57,000 gymnasia, 2,000 ski centers, 500 swimming pools, and 400 stadiums catering to children. Moscow alone claims 1,525 gymnasia, 237 tennis courts, and 41 swimming pools—all available for public use.

Sports facilities are widely used by the elderly, who comprise an important part of the Soviet labor pool and remain active much longer than is common in America. The National Commission on the Artificial Prolongation of Human Life has studied the effects of magnetized food on subjects including the USSR's reported 19,000 centenarians. (By contrast, the United States has 9,400 centenarians out of a population of 214 million, only 40 million less than that of the USSR.)

The importance of sports in prolonging life is exemplified by Alexander Mikulin (1977), who wrote a book while in his eighties on active longevity. The 100,000 copies printed sold out in a week. Mikulin was the third person to be given the title "Hero of Socialist Labor" for work in engineering. The plane that flew from Moscow to the United States in 1937, breaking a world record, had a Mikulin engine, as did the best Soviet attack planes in World War II and the first Soviet jet MIG airplanes. In 1943 he was elected a member of the USSR Academy of Science, earning the prestigous title of "Academician."

During World War II, Mikulin overworked himself and became seriously ill. While in the hospital, he began to plan ways to regain his health. The regimen he developed includes running every day and taking a sauna every week; the procedures induce sweat, which eliminates body poisons. Active sports are also recommended, as are massage, a sensible diet, increased water consumption, and a regular schedule of work and rest.

Mikulin has stated that laziness is an enemy that will weaken the resolve of participants in his program. He has observed:

> Thousands of people have died prematurely . . . only because they were too lazy to go through a cycle of physical exercises every morning. To win health and a happy old age, you must find or cultivate in yourself the will to overcome laziness. [Kadzhaya, 1979]

Mikulin has invented a "health machine" resembling the apparatus used indoors by rowers to develop the muscles used in rowing. He recommends using this machine only five or six minutes per day, combining it with other parts of his health program.

Mikulin has emphasized that sports enhance the "quality of one's life," which is a more important goal than sheer athletic proficiency. There are also reports of Soviet athletes who enter into altered states of consciousness during their sports activities. Yuri Vlasov, the champion Soviet weight lifter, told Robert Lipsyte (1975), a reporter:

> At the peak of tremendous and victorious effort . . . while the blood is pounding in your head, all suddenly becomes quiet within you. Everything seems clearer and whiter than ever before, as if great spotlights had been turned on.
>
> At that moment you have the conviction that you contain all the power in the world, that you are capable of everything, that you have wings. There is no more precious moment in life than this, the white moment, and you will work very hard for years just to taste it again. [pp. 280–81]

The Soviet sports champion Vasily Alexeyev, the first human to lift a 500 pound weight over his head, imagines seeing himself lifting weights just before making the attempt (Elliott, 1980; Murphy and White, 1978). Track stars often picture their destination while they are running, and imagine it is receding into the distance whenever they want to increase their speed.

The United States Olympic Committee, while not making an effort in these areas that matches those of East Germany and the

USSR, has instituted a few programs in biofeedback training and mental practice at Squaw Valley, California, and other training centers. Some American sports teams have worked with psychologists to improve their attitude, concentration, and determination, as well as specific athletic skills utilizing approaches such as biofeedback, hypnosis, meditation, relaxation, and visualization. One psychologist, Lee Pulos, has helped the Canadian National Women's Volleyball team by having them practice both mentally and physically. For example, he told one player to imagine a particular shot several hundred times until she visualized vividly. Then, when the image was well established, the athlete began to practice that shot on the court, bringing her body into alignment with her inner vision. Periods of physical practice alternated with periods of mental practice until the athlete clearly imagined what she wanted to do, and then did it to her and the coach's satisfaction (Murphy and White, 1978, pp. 152–53).

Richard Suinn, a psychologist at Colorado State University, developed an imagery program and used it successfully with the U.S. ski team. Barbara Kolonay later applied it to free-throw shooting and conducted a thorough investigation of its effectiveness at New York's Hunter College (Lauck, 1978). Kolonay's procedure involved two parts: a relaxation segment and an imagery segment. For the latter portion of the training, each player would sit in a straight-backed chair, close his eyes, then imagine the exact details of going to the free-throw line, being handed the ball, hearing the crowd, feeling the weakness in his body, breathing heavily, shooting the free throw, and seeing it go through the basket.

There were eight teams involved in Kolonay's test—two of which served as control groups. The other six teams were informed that they were receiving the entire process (that is, fifteen ten-minute sessions during the last half of the season), although only two of these teams actually did. Two received just the relaxation procedure, two others only the imagery. The two control teams dropped slightly in their free-throw percentage during the test period. The two using relaxation alone improved from 67 to 69 percent; the two using imagery from 69 to 71 percent; and the two using both procedures from 68 to 75 percent. Some individual players, such as Columbia University's Ricky Free, improved as much as 15 percent. In analyzing these results, several psychologists concluded that imagery builds confidence. In addition, electromyograms taken of the athletes have indicated that the muscles actually perform the exact motion imagined.

Hypnosis has also been used advantageously by American athletes. W. L. Howard and J. P. Reardon (1978) of Ohio State University studied the effect of hypnosis on the weight-lifting abilities of two subjects. They had the hypnotized athletes rehearse weight lifting, paying special attention to the movements involved. By using time distortion, the athletes slowed down their movements, mentally rehearsing even the most minute details of the event. Both subjects demonstrated enhanced performance, perhaps because the neuromuscular pathways involved in weight lifting were activated. However, the experimenters also suggested the possibility that mental practice activates the specific neurological components of the brain involved in the movement being rehearsed. Either alternative would support the position of "set" theory that the psychoneurological components underlying an activity can be set up in advance, thus facilitating and directing the event.

Other American approaches to the psychology of sports include slow-motion photography and computer analysis of an athlete's performance, applied kinesiology (the study of human movement), and the study of such personality traits as motivation and the need for achievement. Marvin Clein, director of the Human Performance Laboratory at the University of Denver, has improved the skills of many Olympic contenders as well as those of other athletes (Backes, 1978). Clein has observed, "I didn't invent the scientific approach to sports performance. I didn't even pioneer in it. The Eastern European countries did, particularly the Russians—and who do you think has been winning most of the Olympic medals in recent years?"

Apples in Asia

In October 1979, James Hickman, Mary Payne, Vladimir Verovacki (our translator), and I arrived in Alma-Ata, capital of the

Kazakh Soviet Socialist Republic.* Our Intourist guide had pointed out that the USSR, which occupies nearly one sixth of the globe's populated areas, is comprised of fifteen republics (or states). The largest of these is the Russian Soviet Federated Socialist Republic, which includes such cities as Moscow, Leningrad, and Novosibirsk. The second largest is Kazakhstan, an Asian republic that borders China. "Alma-Ata" means "Father of the Apple" in the Kazakh language, and the four of us had the opportunity of buying this large, delicious fruit in the local markets.

Hickman and Payne are members of the Transformation Project, which is engaged in the exploration of exceptional bodily functioning: the ways in which it takes place, the characteristics of people who report it, and the exercises that facilitate its development (Hickman, Murphy, and Spino, 1977). Initiated by Michael Murphy, cofounder of California's Esalen Institute, the Transformation Project had long been interested in the work of Dr. A. S. Romen; Hickman and Payne had come with Verovacki and me to Alma-Ata to ask him about his work with psychological (or "psychic," in the sense of involving the psyche) self-regulation. Romen, who holds a degree in medical science and works with patients at the Psychiatric Clinic of State Hospital No. 2 in Alma-Ata, enthusiastically described his research. Victor Adamenko had flown in from Moscow to cover the meetings for *Izvestiya*. Also present was Victor Inyushin, whom Hickman and I had met during our trip to Moscow in 1972.

I recalled that as an undergraduate, I had been told by my psychology professors that it was impossible for human beings voluntarily to control the functions of their autonomic nervous systems (which is composed of both sympathetic, or arousing, and parasympathetic, or calming, systems). Therefore, the reports that yogis could alter such autonomic functions as heartbeat rate, blood flow, and body temperature were branded absurd. However, the biofeedback data that began to emerge in the early 1960s verified what the yogis had claimed for centuries (for example, Basmajian, 1963).

In biofeedback, an instrument attached to the human body

* Just before we left Tbilisi, the soccer team from Liverpool, England, had stayed in our hotel. They were soundly trounced by the Tbilisi team in a game that drew far more attention than our Symposium on the unconscious.

gives a continuous record of one or more of the subject's physiological processes so that he or she might alter those processes directly. If someone wants to lower his or her pulse, for example, a record of it is presented as a sound, a light, or a moving line on a graph. By watching the record, the subject gradually learns what thoughts, images, feelings, moods, muscular contractions, and other factors are associated with the pulse fluctuations. With this growing awareness, the subject can learn to modify his or her physiology so that the pulse drops or rises at will. Biofeedback can also be used to help people control their blood pressure, brain waves, muscular tension, stomach acidity, and several other bodily processes (Green and Green, 1977).

However, patients do not have to rely on electronic devices to regulate body functions. Neither the yogis nor the Zen meditators used machines, nor do practitioners of such contemporary approaches as autogenic training, progressive relaxation, or self-hypnosis.

William Tiller (1972) reported that the Moscow Medical Institute has been making extensive use of autogenic training with its patients. Their research studies involved five groups of exercises for the relaxation of the muscular system, the cardiovascular system, and thermal regulation. It was discovered that the patient needs to find the body position (for example, lying, sitting) that puts the least stress on the physical system before proceeding. It was also found that it was not necessary to produce a feeling of warmth in the entire body; the feet, hands, and arms were the most important areas for the direction of warmth sensations.

These phrases were used in one exercise:

My right arm becomes warmer and warmer. (The subject is asked to imagine the arm in warm water.) I feel the warmth extend in waves from my hand to my shoulder. I have the pleasant feeling of warmth in my arm.

To induce relaxation, different suggestions were used:

My right arm is relaxed. (If there is tension, the subject is asked to tense the muscles, then relax them.) My right arm is becoming heavier and heavier. (The subject is asked to imagine the arm being filled with lead.) My right arm has become heavier. (This

procedure is carried out with the left arm and with both legs.)
Now my entire body is relaxed.

If done in the morning, this exercise is sometimes followed by
one that supposedly enables the subject to become active and
alert:

> The feeling of heaviness in my arm is ceasing. Now it has ceased
> completely. My breathing is deep and regular. I feel full of power
> and energy. (The subject is asked to imagine some sort of activ-
> ity.)

For cases of hypertension, these phrases are often used:

> I am getting calmer and calmer.
> Now I am quite calm.
> My heartbeat is regular.
> My breathing is calm and regular.

These statements are repeated mentally three times, with fifteen-
second intervals between repetitions. After three months of utilization, only one repetition usually is needed.

Mastering Breathing

Romen (1973) studied these techniques extensively, eventually
developing his procedure of psychological self-regulation, which
he defines as "a directed purposeful regulation of the various actions, reactions, and processes of the organism realized by means
of its own mental activity . . ." (p. 5).

An initial impetus for Romen's work in the 1950s was the search
for ways cosmonauts could control their psychophysiological
processes while in space. In expanding these practices, Romen
(1970) observed strict scientific procedures, using only healthy
subjects who had never attempted self-regulation of any sort and
avoiding suggestion as to the end results. Romen standardized his
conditions and only gave the subjects explanations at specific
points in their training.

Training in self-regulation consists of four basic exercises:

1. The experiencing of calm and muscular relaxation and the mastery of the breathing rhythms. Mastery of this exercise is reached when subjects experience clear sensations of immobility and heaviness in their musculature and a free breathing rhythm without tension.
2. The experiencing of warmth in separate parts of the body, primarily in the arms, chest, abdomen, and head. Mastery of this exercise is reached when subjects experience clear sensations of warmth in the suggested areas, confirmed with the use of electrothermometers.
3. The experiencing of coolness in separate parts of the body, and the contrasting sensations of warmth and coolness in different parts of the body simultaneously. Again, mastery of this exercise is reached when subjects experience clear temperature sensations, which are validated with electrothermometers.
4. The experiencing of mastery of the heart rhythm. First, subjects learn to count their heart beats mentally, and then to increase or to decrease their heart rate on command. Mastery of this exercise is reached when subjects can noticeably alter their heart rhythm.

The trainings were conducted in small groups of three to eight persons, both under a physician's supervision and independently. The sessions initially lasted ten minutes, but were reduced to three, four, or five minutes as the training progressed. Each new exercise was practiced for from five to eight days, two or three times a day; complete mastery of the four exercises took from ten days to five weeks, with the average being from three to five weeks.

After the exercises were thoroughly mastered, simple self-suggestion formulas were taught and practiced. All formulas were spoken mentally with the eyes closed. Toward the end of every session the trainees suggested to themselves that they would achieve greater success in their next session's task.

Upon ending their session, subjects were taught to breathe calmly and deeply and to perform light stretching movements, beginning with the legs and extending through the whole body. They would then suggest feelings of energy and lightness to themselves, shake their arms, and open their eyes. Sometimes visualizations were also employed, such as imagining an energizing shower or a cool rubdown.

Submergence and the Self

One of Romen's studies involved the investigation of visual afterimages, images that continue to be seen after the eyes are closed. Prior to this time there had been two general sets of theories concerning visual afterimages—one explaining the images as changes in receptor elements of the retina, the other explaining the images in terms of the functional state of the central nervous system, specifically in the visual apparatus of the cerebral cortex. The results from the studies were mixed; in forty-nine experiments, the duration of afterimage increased under the influence of self-suggestion, while in twenty-two experiments the duration of images decreased. Therefore, neither theory was confirmed; indeed, both may have some validity.

Romen's work led him to describe three stages of depth of self-suggestion or "self-suggested submergence"; these correspond approximately to American rating scales of depth of hypnosis:

1. Light. A weakly expressed state of calm and immobility in which the environment is easily perceived, distraction during training is observed, and the subject sometimes has difficulty in concentrating on the assignment.
2. Medium. Attention is concentrated on a narrow range of imagery, the surroundings are periodically perceived unclearly, suggested sensations such as calm and muscular relaxation are pronounced, and the trainee has no desire to change the body position.
3. Deep. All self-suggested sensations are clear, consciousness is narrowly focused, there is often amnesia for the experience, and when self-control is lost there can be a transition into sleep.

Romen believes that these stages may be used to explain and to evaluate the duration of the imagery flow. As the state of self-suggestion becomes deeper the changes in duration of flow of images become greater, and in the third stage, the duration of the afterimage is shortened or disappears completely.

During self-suggestion, subjects often experience peculiar psychological and physiological phenomena; these individual reactions vary widely. Romen calls these reactions "psychic" (using the term "psychic" to mean "mental" rather than "paranormal"). Some of these phenomena include: clear visual images and the experience of being in another place, compulsive and/or automatic flow of thoughts, passive arousal of memories that are sometimes accompanied by visual images, and separation from one's personality with distortion of the body image. Occasionally "derealization" occurs in which the surroundings of the room become unclear, unreal, or indistinct, as if covered by a veil. Romen (1973) observed that these sensations appear suddenly during self-suggestion and disappear when training is continued or when self-suggestions of discontinuation are given.

Much of this work resembles the biofeedback training practiced in the United States; however, in the Soviet Union, greater emphasis is placed on the individual and on his or her capacity for purposeful, directed self-regulation. Instruments are seen as adjuncts to provide verification of abilities developed psychophysically. Emphasis is repeatedly laid upon the development of the person's capability for self-observation and self-regulation.

Possibly the simplest exercise mastered by Romen's subjects is learning to control skin temperature; after training, a majority of subjects tested were able to raise or lower the temperature in their hands at will, from three to four degrees centigrade. After a period of time, participants found that they could exercise this ability at will—even while not in a "submerged" state. This ability was developed in eight to twelve days of daily practice. The greatest changes were achieved not by those with initial strong imagery or heightened psychosomatic shifting, but by those who practiced their assignments regularly.

Romen (1973) reported that beginning in 1959, studies were conducted on subjects' abilities to influence their own psychosomatic functioning. These abilities included partial and general catalepsy (rigid immobilization of muscle groups), automatic movements involving writing and speech (including glossolalia or "speaking in tongues"), and isolated contraction of the abdominal muscles. Romen found that not only could trainees induce partial catalepsy in their limbs, but also that all twenty-one of his subjects in one study could achieve the "cataleptic bridge"—suspending their bodies rigidly between two chairs.

In the experiments on glossolalia, initially placid subjects began moving their heads, developed chewing movements, and began speaking nonsense syllables. Some trainees reported "feeling as if they had no tongue," being "absent from their bodies" (what is known in the United States as "out-of-body experiences"), or that their "mouth acted separately from their head and body" (Romen, 1976). These experiences were sometimes accompanied by partial or complete amnesia.

Romen considers self-suggested automatic actions as being akin to naturally occurring "automatism" (or automatic movement), which is sometimes accompanied by "systematic deliriums of haunting and influence" (Lewis, 1976). These are very similar in form to "spirit writing" as performed by supposed mediums, and to some of the *kriyas,* automatic movements among Yoga practitioners purportedly caused by the rising of the "kundalini energy." Romen's automatisms, however, are produced synthetically in the laboratory; while they cannot be deemed paranormal or pathological, they may be useful in shedding light on some of their exotic cousins.

One study was conducted in which self-suggestion was applied to Yoga exercises involving the isolated expansion and contraction of abdominal muscles. Normally these exercises required several months to master; using self-suggestion, trainees learned the exercises in from five to ten days. The subjects practiced the exercises while rhythmically inhaling and exhaling, and visualizing and self-suggesting the results. None of the control subjects were able to contract single striate muscles of the abdomen; the self-suggestion trainees were able to perform this difficult exercise in any position—lying, sitting, standing, or in the "lotus" posture.

Learning During Sleep

One area in which suggestion has been applied for years is the area of learning. One intriguing question is whether or not one can learn while asleep. Like the related work in suggestology and suggestopedia, sleep learning (or "hypnopedia") is based on Pavlovian theory. I. P. Pavlov believed that the cells of the cerebral hemispheres are exceedingly sensitive and are thus subject to damage from excessive strain. Protection is afforded them by the inhibitory process that cuts off the acceptance of stimuli into the cortex from time to time. Sleep is a form of protective inhibition; Pavlov held that sleep is internal inhibition that is widely irradiated, extending over both hemispheres as well as the lower brain centers. However, sleep inhibition may be partial rather than total. During the transition from wakefulness to sleep, or in such altered states of consciousness as those induced by hypnosis, suggestion, or relaxation, one part of the cortex may be in a state of sleep inhibition while the other part may be awake. Suggestopedia and hypnopedia take advantage of this phenomenon and utilize it for learning.

K. I. Platonov (1959), basing his work on Pavlovian theory, studied a brain-injured subject who was unable to learn efficiently because he could not shut out irrelevant stimuli while awake. Partial sleep, however, seemed to inhibit these stimuli, thus focusing and strengthening the stimuli presented in a learning task. This procedure was replicated by Cecelia Pollack (1962) with a nonreading, brain-injured boy. He was taught, through an auditory blending method, two lists of words of equal difficulty; one list was also presented while he was in a state of partial sleep. The latter list of words was learned more accurately, and Pollack concluded, "The results of the study indicate that learning of auditory material does occur during partial sleep" (p. 107).

Researchers at the Ukrainian Academy of Sciences in Kiev have pioneered in hypnopedia, discovering that the most effective teaching period is in the half hour before the subject falls asleep and in the half hour that follows (Shabad, 1966). American researchers (Simon and Emmons, 1955) found much the same thing, noting that the period of time in the morning just before wakefulness was also propitious. These two periods are referred to as "hypnagogic" and "hypnopompic" states by sleep researchers; Soviet researchers typically give their subjects a "set" that they will absorb the material during this period of time. But as sleep deepens, the brain's processing of auditory material changes, making it difficult for the sleep learner to assimilate complex verbal material.

Because theta brain waves predominate during the hypnagogic and hypnopompic states, Thomas Budzynski (1977) and other American biofeedback researchers have taught people to produce theta in the laboratory. Budzynski has reported:

> One client was a graduate student who had failed a Spanish-language exam and was so anxious about taking it a second time that he was unable to study at all. [We] made a Spanish-English tape which included suggestions that the client would be able to study effectively and remember the material. After hearing the tape twelve times under twilight state conditions, the student was able to study without anxiety and passed the exam easily. [p. 41]

Elmer and Alyce Green (1977, pp. 140–49), at the Menninger Foundation, initiated a ten-week biofeedback training program for combined alpha and theta brain waves with college students and found that it tended to facilitate creative imagery. A book containing knowledge was one recurring image; another was a wise old man in the form of a teacher or physician.

Romen told us that he and his colleagues began investigating hypnopedia in 1960 using two groups who were tested in the morning on material presented during the night. In one group, the subjects were read to while they were asleep, while in the other group the subjects were awakened and then read to; neither group recalled very much material.

At this point, Romen introduced self-regulation; following training, the subjects put themselves into deep relaxation and gave themselves a "set," telling themselves that in the morning they would be able to recall the new material (Lewis, 1976). After they went to sleep, materials with both scientific and emotional content were read to them. Following the training period, subjects were able to recall 70 percent of the material read to them. Furthermore, they could remember the material for a considerable length of time afterward; one trainee reportedly was able to remember materials from the experiment some eight years later.

An article in *Northern Neighbors* (December 1965) was highly critical of American companies making "learn while you sleep" recordings, stating, "This effort of 'free enterprise' to cash in on basic Soviet discoveries is highly questionable. . . ." It was pointed out that the method of playing a record by a student's bedside was found to be useless. The tapes need to be in a separate room where they can be monitored by an instructor. The voice frequency and range must be within a narrow range, as must the number of words spoken per minute. In the morning, the lesson of the previous night is reviewed for thirty minutes, then subjects are fully awakened by light music. It is noted that the subject must have a strong emotional desire to learn if the training is to be successful; if motivation is present, average learners as well as advanced learners can do well with hypnopedia.

Controlling Body Functions

The role of blood-sugar metabolism is a controversial topic in both the United States and the USSR. One school of thought holds that blood-sugar imbalance is responsible for a great deal of mental illness, but neither American nor Soviet physicians regularly administer the glucose tolerance test that measures the cycle of sugar utilization in the body (Hoffer and Walker, 1978, p. 44). Romen discovered that the existing studies demonstrated poor controls—taking blood samples at different times, ignoring the fluctuation of cycles in individual subjects, not accounting for subject anxiety prior to injections, etc. Romen (1970) claimed to correct these oversights in his work. For example, blood samples were taken several times before and after food intake and at identical times during a twenty-four-hour period. All possible measures were taken into account to control spontaneous fluctuations. Then a series of studies was undertaken to determine the effect of emotions connected with the act of taking blood samples to determine blood-sugar levels. When subjects experienced anxiety or fear, or reacted in negative ways, their blood-sugar level increased. When they were calm or relaxed, the fluctuations were insignificant. Thus the supreme importance of taking into account the effects of emotions on blood-sugar levels was established.

In subsequent experiments, subjects self-suggested themselves into the "submergent" state, then actively imagined that they were eating sweets. At frequent intervals thereafter, their blood-sugar levels were measured. Data demonstrated that the trainees were able to influence their blood-sugar levels in this way. Sharp decreases of blood sugar occurred in 53 percent of the subjects after five to thirty minutes of the imagined eating of sweets; in some cases, this was accompanied by hypoglycemia (a condition where the blood-sugar level is sustained below the normal level). In the other subjects, increases of blood-sugar level were found. These results established that voluntary, directed influence could be exerted over blood-sugar levels. Romen indicated that if control could be exercised over as subtle a function as glycemia, there is no bodily limit to what the mind could influence. Writing about the different fluctuations observed in his subjects, Romen (1970) hypothesized that in those cases in which directed self-suggestion is accompanied by increased activity of the adrenosympathetic system, activity would be increased in the liver; this would lead to an increase in blood sugar. When self-suggestion is accompanied by an increase of parasympathetic activity, the pancreas would be activated, the insulin level increased, and glycemia lowered.

Romen also conducted studies in which trainees experienced pain with and without self-regulation (Lewis, 1976). Painful stimuli were inflicted upon the subjects with a spinal injection needle administered to different parts of the body. In a total of 101 studies, most subjects achieved immediate lowering of pain sensitivity through the efficacious use of self-suggestion. After further training of 10 days or less, they were able to achieve complete analgesia (local loss of feeling), and 14 of the trainees were able to experience full anesthesia (total loss of feeling throughout the body). Nine subjects had their upper arms and hands punctured through entirely. On several others, minor surgery and dental work were performed without the use of anesthesia.

The subjects who experienced anesthesia differed from the others, strongly believing in the possibility for directed self-suggested influence on the organism. This indicates that full anesthesia is not explainable by duration of training alone, since six persons achieved full anesthesia immediately without any prior special preparation, while the other eight were trained for from three to five days.

In one set of experiments, the galvanic skin response (a measure of skin electricity), pneumogram (a recording of air pressure produced by breathing), and an electrocardiogram were taken in the normal state and after various bodily parts were subjected to pain. In one selected subject, punctures in the right arm resulted in a feeling of acute pain and pronounced changes of the galvanic skin response, depth of breathing, and heart rhythm. Upon experiencing anesthesia induced through self-regulation, no pain was experienced during puncturing; no significant changes of the pneumogram or electrocardiogram, and no galvanic skin activity were observed during this time. In a further experiment, the same subject self-suggested a sensation of pain; his galvanic skin response became more pronounced, while the depth of breathing and heart rhythm changed more dramatically than during the actual administration of punctures!

Romen considers that the experiments with analgesia and anesthesia establish that sensitivity to pain can be considerably heightened or lowered by directed self-suggestion. These findings demonstrate the impact of self-suggested action on the organism and have great theoretical and clinical value for understanding the mechanism of various sensory disorders and their therapy. Practical applications range from dentistry to dueling, from medicine to the martial arts, and from training cosmonauts to training patients to produce anesthesia.

Self-suggestion, Sports, and Hypnosis

Vital to success in athletics is control over psychological functions formerly believed to be "unconscious" such as one's self-image and degree of confidence. Here, according to Romen (1976, 1977, 1979), suggestion can play a major role. Self-suggestion can be used in related aspects of training: to visualize and obtain desired results in practice, to combat anxieties and fears, to imbue the athlete with confidence, to "role play" successful competitions, to prevent "prestart fever" and nervousness, and to provide athletes with a way to rest deeply before and between meets. Self-suggestion is also used to obtain very specific results, such as decreasing sensitivity to pain, preventing sunstroke and/or freezing, stabilizing movement and improving coordination, increasing speed of perception and reaction time, and stabilizing body cycles when moving across different time zones.

Two research studies in particular performed by Romen and his associates have had direct application to athletics. It has been known that reaction time is a function of many variables, including individual personality traits, condition of health, training, age, sex, level of fatigue, environmental factors, drugs, weather, etc. Whether or not self-suggestion could be utilized to improve reaction time was unknown.

In one experiment, the subjects sat in front of a movie screen; when a light flashed on the screen, they reacted by pushing a button connected to an electrochronometer. Reaction times were measured first while the subjects were in their normal state and then while in a self-suggested state of relaxation. While in the latter state, trainees suggested to themselves that they would react faster to the light stimulus on the screen. It was found that the subjects were able to accelerate their reaction times through the use of self-suggestion, primarily through self-suggesting calmness and relaxation. When trainees self-suggested an acceleration of reaction speed, a decrease in reaction time resulted, probably because of the anxiety and tension involved in "trying too hard."

Another study involved the influence of self-suggestion on visual perception speed. Simple geometric shapes (for example, squares and circles) with one distinctive sector were projected on a screen one at a time using an electrical optical tachistoscope. An "erasing image" was utilized to minimize the possibility of afterimages. Visual-perception speed was measured according to the minimal exposure time of a shape necessary to identify it; optimal exposure was defined as the shortest period in which a subject could correctly identify the figure and location of the distinctive sector several times consecutively. In 59 experiments, some 2,838 different images were used. Three groups were tested: a control group, a group that self-suggested calm and relaxation, and a group that self-suggested attention and focus. The calm and relaxed group experienced a decrease in visual-perception speed (as compared to the controls), while the self-suggested attention group experienced an increase in visual-perception speed, an ability apparently more amenable to conscious willing than the manual reaction time attempted in the experiment with the movie screen. According to Romen, this discovery is being applied in industrial work, aviation, and space, as well as in athletics.

Since the 1950s, there has been an increase in the number of Soviet studies in the use of suggestive techniques in education, medicine, psychology, and related fields. Indeed, hypnosis and suggestion have been used widely in Europe, beginning with Anton Mesmer's "animal magnetism," to the turn-of-the-century schools of J. M. Charcot and Pierre Janet, to Emile Coué's "Every day in every way I am getting better and better," to J. H. Schultz's autogenic training. In the USSR, K. I. Platonov's (1959) handbook for physicians, *The Word as a Physiological and Therapeutic Factor,* has been reprinted many times and translated into English.

Romen (1963, 1968, 1972) has followed in this tradition; well known are two conference proceedings he edited: Volumes 1 and 2 of *Psychic Self-Regulation,* published in 1973 and 1974. However, Romen believes that self-suggestion is greatly superior to hypnosis. In comparing the two, he observed that:

1. Successful regulation of autonomic functions can only be achieved with about 10 percent of subjects in hypnosis.
2. Hypnotic procedures are more difficult to apply and require the presence of a hypnotist, while self-suggestion methods are easier and more accessible to people who might benefit from them.
3. In hypnosis the subject is very passive; in self-suggestion he or she takes an active role. Indeed, this is probably the most important feature of self-suggestion vis-à-vis hypnosis.
4. Certain electrobioluminescent phenomena can be obtained with self-suggestion that are not obtainable with hypnosis, nor with the actual stimulus itself.
5. On the other hand, it is apparent that hypnosis is more effective in certain types of therapy; its use is dependent on the patient and the particular condition being treated.

Self-suggestion is a major therapeutic modality in the Soviet Union today; it is applied to a large number of conditions, as it may be used to heighten and improve many capabilities and performances. Probably the first and major application of self-regulation is to enable the subject to create in himself or herself a state of calm and relaxation. Many patients experience chronic anxiety, worries, or pains, both physical and psychological; the simple ability to experience relaxation and peace of mind, even if only for a few minutes, is a welcome relief to these people, as well as a powerful healer in its own right. Given sufficient relaxation and rest, many mental disorders and conflicts begin to resolve and heal themselves spontaneously. The achievement of this state of calm and relaxation is basic to the healing of any disorder, mental or physical.

Self-suggestion is used as an adjunct in the therapy of various kinds of neurotic states such as anxiety neuroses, compulsions, obsessions, and phobias; in the treatment of character disorders; to help prevent recidivism with chronic alcoholism, cigarette smoking, and drug abuse; in the prevention of epileptic seizures; in treating insomnia and helping subjects to experience deep, refreshing sleep; in treating various sexual disorders (for example, impotence, frigidity, premature ejaculation); in treating warts, itching, and skin disorders; in helping asthmatics to breathe regularly and deeply; and in alleviating various types of creative blocks.

Nontherapeutic uses of self-suggestion include enabling people to fall asleep and awake at will, improving one's health and resistance to disease, using "self-induced sensory deprivation" to increase awareness of one's internal body organs and functions, regulating cyclical bodily functions and thus improving work efficiency and attention during night work, preventing jet lag, improving memory, learning foreign languages faster and with greater retention, and training actors, singers, and musicians. Self-suggestion is also used in the training of athletes and cosmonauts, in neutralizing the effects of drugs and alcohol, in improving one's self-image and the ability to get along with others—in short, in improving and enhancing just about any human function or ability desired.

Other Investigators, Other Projects

Applications of self-regulation have been made by other Soviet authors in such areas as education (Schwartz, 1971), insomnia (Mirovsky, 1973), longevity (Dilman, 1972), mental health (Belayev, Lobzin, and Kopilov, 1977; Gumenok and Schertis, 1978), memory training (Nagorny, 1972), relaxation (Belayev, 1973; Richednikov, 1971), and stuttering (Lubinskaya, 1970). One book that incorporated principles of self-regulation, *The Art of Being Yourself* (Levy, 1977), became a best seller. V. M. Dilman's (1972) popular book of living a longer life described "overcoming aging by physiological self-regulation."

I. P. Ivanov (1974) worked with athletes, teaching them self-regulation and recording their sleep-dream cycles, stress patterns, and work habits. Once these data had been collected, Ivanov produced an individualized profile. Based on this profile, the athlete and the trainer worked together to mobilize the organism's "reserve capacities."

"Intellectual self-regulation" was the topic of a study reported by S. E. Zlochevsky (1974), which utilized principles of "set" theory. Before sleep, subjects were asked to summarize results of the day's intellectual work and produce a plan for the following day. The majority of those participating in the three-week experiment reported observable benefits. They could remember facts better, concentrate more easily, formulate ideas more coherently, and write more fluently. In the latter instance, subjects claimed success in producing poetry, prose, scientific papers, and journalistic articles.

Leonid Rothstein (1977), an émigré from the USSR, has developed a self-regulation program for use in psychotherapeutic settings. He has patients concentrate on their fear or obsession, then quickly shift to another subject. A patient repeats this procedure several times until it becomes easy and simple. They may then reduce the fear by saying, "I am perceiving everything calmly. My fear is going away." Sometimes Rothstein's patients

experience unusual states of consciousness during these procedures and may even report instances of clairvoyance or precognition.

Detecting "Energetic Fields"

An application of self-regulation to psychic ability has been made
by Barbara Ivanova (1974, 1977), whom I met in 1971 and
1972. Sometime later, she claims to have been forced into premature retirement from her position as an interpreter and teacher of
languages at the Moscow State Institute for International Relations, possibly because she was too outspoken, especially on such
controversial topics as life after death (Ebon, 1978).

Ivanova observes that relaxation techniques have always been
available. The Yakuts, a Siberian ethnic group, sit down in the
shade of a tree and shave a rod before making an important decision. This practice enhances calmness and concentration. In a
similar manner, Ivanova practices relaxation techniques before
she begins a healing session. After obtaining a "self-harmonizing
state" of her own body, Ivanova activates a "mutual energy field"
by which she can send "healing irradiations" to a sick person. The
distances between Ivanova and the people she attempts to heal are
not important, she feels. But when the sick persons are present,
she will often teach them self-regulation to put them into a receptive state of mind.

Ivanova's healing sessions are divided into three phases. In the
informational phase, she speaks with her clients, explaining her
theories, telling them what to expect, and assisting them to relax.
The experimental phase consists of the creation of the "mutual
energy field," and the evaluation phase analyzes the experiences
of the indisposed persons. For Ivanova, this phase is very important, as it provides feedback for the healer and support for her clients. This three-phase procedure is used by Ivanova for both individual and group healing.

Larissa Vilenskaya (1976) worked closely with Ivanova in
Moscow and conducted a study in which she employed subjects

with no previously identified psychic gifts. She taught them to observe "energetic fields" purportedly produced by healers between
two fingers of their hands. Before long, they not only claimed that
they were observing the "fields" produced by the healers but also
were correctly naming the colors that the healers later said they
had been evoking. Before long, the subjects were detecting someone's "field" by feeling warmth, a "prickly" sensation, or "resistance," as if the "field" were dense. The prior development of
"skin vision" by subjects was reported by Vilenskaya to be useful,
though not mandatory for this task.

Vilenskaya conducted several studies with her subjects. In one,
she and E. V. Kordyukov, a physician, used a highly sensitive
magnetometer to compare the intensity of magnetic fields during
calmness, physical stress, and emotional stress. The magnetic field
of both hands varied as the four subjects went from one condition
to the other. Vilenskaya observed:

> . . . if the subject is prepared to perform healing, the intensity of
> the hand's magnetic field increases. At the same time, if a person
> just contracts the muscles of the arm, the intensity of the field
> decreases rapidly. . . . Using the Kirlian photography technique
> . . . , whenever a person is under intellectual stress the Kirlian
> aura decreases. Moreover, we have just found that electrical
> stimulation of the acupuncture points . . . also diminishes the
> magnetic field of the hand. . . . [p. 76]

During attempted healing, a decrease in the magnetic field of
the patient was detected. Not only was the patient relieved of
pain, but also the magnetic field of the patient's right hand
dropped markedly within three minutes. Vilenskaya concluded
that a normal human organism "has no tendency toward radiation
of energy; on the contrary, an ill person or a healer emits much
more energy. A healer does so in a controlled manner, a patient
in an uncontrolled manner" (p. 78).

Vilenskaya also claimed to have investigated the influence of
healers upon fifty cucumber seeds, noting that the effect was more
pronounced in the first few days after germination than in the following days. However, the weight of the plants was greater than
that of the plants in the control group even at the end of the
twenty-four days when the experiment was terminated. Vilens-

kaya's experience with both plants and people convinced her that the optimal healing time was between five and fifteen minutes.

After completing those research projects, Vilenskaya emigrated to Israel, where she hoped to continue her parapsychological investigations. Since I had last seen her in 1972, she had also conducted research with psychological tests at the Institute for General and Pedagogical Psychology, as well as independently pursuing her interest in parapsychology.

Both Ivanova and Vilenskaya mentioned Yoga as well as self-regulation as valuable adjuncts to healing. But in 1973, a Soviet sports commission issued a statement discouraging the study of Yoga because it encouraged withdrawal and self-absorption. Bridge (the card game) was discouraged at the same time. However, Yoga is still practiced in "health groups" (Uccusic, 1977) such as those for whom Ivanova and Vilenskaya gave lectures, and there are indications that the Soviet press is beginning to take a favorable look at Yoga (for example, Katkov, 1980).

Martial arts classes exist in various parts of the Soviet Union, with an emphasis on judo. Indeed, in the 1976 Olympics, Soviet athletes took two of the three judo titles in the lighter weight classes where the Japanese have traditionally reigned supreme. Soviet athletes have also gained prominence in gymnastics: Alexander Tkachev and Nelli Kim, for example, gave impressive performances in the 1979 World Gymnastics championships.

In 1974, V. B. Gorsky used self-regulation in his training program with adult gymnasts, obtaining striking results after only ten sessions. He found that self-regulation exercises worked most effectively if suggestions of strength were alternated with one or two minutes of relaxation exercises to relieve fatigue. The gymnasts who completed the sessions reported that they felt better prepared for the sports event.

The Only Privileged Class

Gorsky (1974) also used self-regulation with ten fourth-grade children who were interested in studying gymnastics. Some of the subjects had so little suppleness or strength that they could not even complete one pullup on the horizontal bar. In executing the program, Gorsky used a preparatory exercise, saying to the children, "I am peaceful. All is calm. . . ." This was followed by such statements as "I am heavy. I am weak." Subsequently came such statements as "I am warm. . . . I am light. . . . I am resilient. . . . I feel strong." If they complained about the heavy sensation, pupils were told that the heaviness would leave once their strength appeared. This exercise was repeated but with the suggestion of coldness rather than heat. Similar instructions were given when the subjects were standing and walking. They also were given relaxation exercises while they were standing. The results showed an enhanced capacity for gymnastic training for all the pupils, including those who were not exceptionally supple or strong. Gorsky concluded that children who are motivated to learn gymnastic skills should not be rejected if they are too weak.

Gorsky's concern for children is typical of the attention given them by various professional workers in the Soviet Union. Nancy Rollins (1972), the psychiatrist we met in Tbilisi, is one of the few American experts on Soviet child psychiatry—a subject that she had investigated during a previous visit. From her and from several others, we had heard about the extensive network of childcare facilities in the USSR: Some 13,000 children's clinics and 1,200 children's sanitoriums enable 13 million Soviet children to have regular medical checkups. There are 120,000 preschool establishments in the USSR (over 2,000 in Moscow alone); furthermore, the 1977 Soviet Constitution requires ten years of education for all its young citizens.

We also heard about the new All-Union Research Center of Mother and Child Health, which coordinates nationwide research in the area. The Center was built from the proceeds of the Communist Subbotnik—a day of unpaid work marking the centennial of Lenin's birth. Research in child care is carried on at twenty-four institutes throughout the country.

Children are referred to as "the only privileged class in the Soviet Union" (Ovchinnikova, 1979, p. 29). Moscow has 150 children's libraries, 140 music schools, 12 junior forestries, and 5 children's cafes. If children show ability in the arts or sciences, they can enroll in a music school (from the first grade) or an art school (from the fifth grade). In addition, there are two types of specialized secondary schools: art, music, and dance on the one hand, and special-subject schools on the other. At the latter, students can study biology, chemistry, mathematics, physics, or foreign languages; a youngster who shows an aptitude for such a subject can enroll in a local school with parental permission. For the former, gifted children are sought out in all parts of the country, and those selected may attend schools outside of their localities (Borzym, 1974).

In 1973, Nadya Pavlova won the International Ballet Contest. She had grown up in a small town in the Ural Mountains where she was a member of the amateur ballet club at her school. She and other children performed before a group of teachers from the ballet school connected to the opera and ballet theater in the city of Perm. As a result, the school officials offered Pavlova an opportunity to study with them (Ovchinnikova, 1979). This type of identification also enables children to attend the celebrated school of the Kirov Ballet in Leningrad, which was the topic of a popular English-language documentary film, *The Children of Theatre Street*.

Moscow *News Information* of September 18–21, 1979, carried an article about School No. 20 in Dushanbe in the Tadzhik SSR, where children are taught singing, dancing, Tadzhik folk art, and modern music. In addition, films, art, and literature (both prose and poetry) are incorporated into the curriculum. These activities are said to "help develop a harmony of reason and feelings in children—the basis of a fully fledged individual." Handicapped children are attended to as well; in Novosibirsk, in the Russian SFSR, there is a school for children suffering from curvature of the spine, where the children do all their studies lying in specially constructed beds. They also are given corrective calisthenics, massage, and physiotherapy.

Novosibirsk is also known as a "science city" because of its twenty-two research institutes and the large proportion of scientists who live there. The average age of the residents is thirty-five; as scientists meet and marry other scientists, they have children who often manifest an interest in scientific fields. These children attend special schools for the development of their talents, and the schools have aroused some controversy. One position holds that gifted youngsters should be educated with ordinary boys and girls; to do otherwise is "elitist" and deprives other children of the stimulation bright children provide. Others assert that it is unfair for talented youngsters to have anything less than superior education. When I was told about this controversy, I remarked that the same debate has gone on in the United States since the first classes and schools for gifted children were organized in the 1930s. Whatever the ultimate resolution of this controversy, it is obvious that talent searches for gifted Soviet children are constantly going on and that methods are being devised for the development of their abilities.

Soviet educators frequently quote the United Nations Declaration of Rights of the Child. It states that every boy or girl "shall enjoy special protection, and shall be given opportunities and facilities, by law and other means, to enable him to develop physically, mentally, morally, spiritually, and socially" (Ovchinnikova, 1979, p. 29). The Constitution of the USSR guarantees all children equal rights to education, to health protection, to physical and intellectual development, and to rest and recreation. In addition to schools for gifted children, the Soviet Union provides special schools for the deaf, the hard of hearing, the blind, the partially sighted, the speech handicapped, and the brain damaged (Gallagher, 1974; Holowinsky, 1977).

The Soviet Union also identifies children who appear to be gifted in athletic ability, sending them to the 2,230 government-sponsored sports schools in various parts of the country. In addition, there are over 2,000 sports schools sponsored by trade unions. The best known of the state schools is the Children's Sports School in Moscow, which enrolls 350 future champions. Marat Rankov, in an interview with the *International Herald Tribune* (February 15, 1978), observed that the youngest children at the school are 7. There are 14 coaches and a great array of sports equipment. Rankov observed one 8-year-old, Valentina Shkoda, working on the bars, beams, and mats of the gymnasium:

> Valentina Shkoda . . . carries herself with the indications of strength and the poetry of motion that mark a champion. . . . When she makes a mistake . . . she is reprimanded by one of her coaches. She begins her routine again, the delicate motions of the hands, the gentle tilt of the head, the tiny leg pointed arrow-straight—going into a somersault off the beam, a perfect landing,

a smile. Valentina does this three hours a day, six days a week for the better part of the year. If the school succeeds, and if Valentina succeeds, you will see her on television during some future Olympic competition.

Two months before my arrival in the USSR in 1979, the Spartakiad was held in Moscow. Held once every four years, the two-week-long series of games was to serve as a rehearsal for the 1980 Olympics. The Spartakiad featured ten thousand Soviet athletes, sifted from nearly one hundred million entrants over two years of eliminations. For the first time, over two thousand foreign competitors were included, some of them American athletes (Pavlov, 1979).

Many of the Soviet participants at the Spartakiad were products of the nation's sports schools. Also at the event, the official 1980 Summer Olympics symbol, a beguiling bear cub named Misha, made its debut.* We saw Misha at souvenir stands in each hotel we visited. The Misha pins, emblems, and toys reminded us of the importance given to sports in the Soviet Union. They also reminded us of the value of self-regulation—a process through which individuals may gain greater control over their own functioning. The work of Alexander Romen thus serves as an important key, opening the door to the development of human potentials.

References

Amdur, N. Drug "fever" in world sports. San Francisco *Chronicle,* Nov. 22, 1978.

Backes, C. J. The science of athletics. *TWA Ambassador,* Jan. 1978.

Basmajian, J. V. Control and training of individual muscle units. *Science,* 1963, *141,* 440–41.

* Despite President Carter's boycott of the Moscow Olympics, James Hickman returned to the USSR in 1980 to present a paper at the First World Congress on Sports and Society. Held in Tbilisi in July, the conference was sponsored by the International Council of Sport and Physical Education.

Belayev, G. S. [*Autogenic Training: A Manual for Professionals.*] Leningrad: Medicina, 1973.

Belayev, G. S.; Lobzin, V. S.; and Kopilov, I. A. [*Psycho-Hygiene and Self-Regulation.*] Leningrad: Medicina, 1977.

Borzym, I. [The gifted individual: Problems of development and rearing.] *Psychologia Wychowarwcza,* 1974, *17,* 600–16.

Budzynski, T. Tuning in on the twilight zone. *Psychology Today,* Aug. 1977.

Dilman, V. M. [*Why Does Death Occur? A Biological Essay.*] Leningrad: Medicina, 1972.

Ebon, M. Iron Curtain ESP. *Human Behavior,* Nov. 1978.

Elliott, L. Alexayev, Soviet superstar. *Reader's Digest.* Feb. 1980.

Gallagher, J. J. *Windows on Russia: United States-USSR Seminar on Instruction of Handicapped Children.* Washington, D.C.: Department of Health, Education, and Welfare, 1974.

Gorsky, V. B. [Utilizing psychic self-regulation techniques in training beginning gymnasts.] In A. S. Romen (ed.), [*Psychic Self-Regulation,*] Vol. 2. Alma-Ata: Kazakh State University, 1974.

Green, E., and Green, A. *Beyond Biofeedback.* New York: Delacorte Press, 1977.

Gumenok, H. M., and Schertis, B. M. [*The Psycho-Hygiene of Sports Activities.*] Kiev: Higher Education, 1978.

Heinze, G. [East German sport.] *Theorie und Praxis der Koerperkultur,* 1973, *22,* 874.

Hickman, J. L.; Murphy, M.; and Spino, M. Psychophysical transformations through meditation and sport. *Simulational Games,* 1977, *8,* 49–60.

Hoffer, A., and Walker, M. *Orthomolecular Nutrition.* New Canaan, Conn.: Keats, 1978.

Holowinsky, I. Z. Training of defectologists and special educators in the Soviet Union. *Journal of Special Education,* 1977, *11,* 469–71.

Howard, W. L., and Reardon, J. P. Anxiety reduction, self-concept modification and facilitation of neuro-muscular performance via cognitive restructuring and hypnosis. Paper presented at the annual meeting of the American Society of Clinical Hypnosis, St. Louis, 1978.

Ivanov, I. P. [Toward optimization of sportsmen's psychological state.] In A. S. Romen (ed.), [*Psychic Self-Regulation,*] Vol. 2. Alma-Ata: Kazakh State University, 1974.

Ivanova, B. By-products of psi. *International Journal of Paraphysics,* 1977, *11,* 117–18.

———. [Healing at a distance.] *Metapsichica,* Jan.–June 1974.

Kadzhaya, V. Academician Alexander Mikulin's "Health Machine." *Soviet Life,* Sept. 1979.

Katkov, A. Yogis—What the scientists say. *Moscow News,* Jan. 6, 1980.

Katz, P. East Germany's athlete factory. San Francisco *Sunday Examiner and Chronicle,* Apr. 10, 1977.

Lauck, D. The science of psyching. *Sky,* June 1978.

Levy, V. [*The Art of Being Yourself.*] Moscow: Knowledge, 1977.

Lewis, A. J. Influence of self-suggestion on the human organism. In A. J. Lewis (ed.), *A Report.* Los Angeles: Garret Research, 1976.

Lipsyte, R. *Sportsworld.* New York: Quadrangle/New York *Times* Book Company, 1975.

Lubinskaya, C. M. [*How to Use Psychic Self-Regulation to Treat Stuttering.*] Moscow: Education, 1970.

Mikulin, A. [*Active Longevity.*] Moscow: Physical Culture and Sports Publishing House, 1977.

Mirovsky, N. [*Psychotherapy for Insomnia.*] Kharkov: Kharkov Psychiatric Institute, 1973.

Murphy, M., and White, R. A. *The Psychic Side of Sports.* Reading, Mass.: Addison-Wesley, 1978.

Nagorny, V. A. [*Gymnastics for the Brain.*] Moscow: Soviet Russia Publishers, 1972.

Ovchinnikova, I. *The Privileged Class.* Moscow: Novosti Press Agency, 1979.

Pavlov, S. Sports for everyone. *Sputnik,* July 1979.

Platonov, K. I. *The Word as a Physiological and Therapeutic Factor.* Moscow: Foreign Language Publishing House, 1959.

Pollack, C. Sleep-learning as an aid in teaching reading to a brain-injured boy. *Journal of Mental Deficiency Research,* 1962, *6,* 101–7.

Richednikov, A. C. [*Muscle Relaxation.*] Moscow: Physique and Sports, 1971.

Rollins, N. *Child Psychiatry in the Soviet Union: Preliminary Observations.* Cambridge, Mass.: Harvard University Press, 1972.

Romen, A. S. [*The Influence of Autogenic Training on Some Vegetative and Psychic Processes.*] Alma-Ata: Kaparanda, 1963.

―――. [*The Influence of Self-Regulation on Psychophysiological Processes.*] Taskhent: Uzbek Ministry of Health, 1968.

―――. [*Self-Suggestion and Its Influence on the Human Organism.*] Alma-Ata: Kazakh State University, 1970.

Romen, A. S. (ed.). [*Psychoneurology, Psychiatry, and Psychology.*] Alma-Ata: Kazakh Ministry of Health, 1972.

―――. [*Psychic Self-Regulation,*] Vol. 1. Alma-Ata: Kazakh State University, 1973.

―――. [*Psychic Self-Regulation,*] Vol. 2. Alma-Ata: Kazakh State University, 1974.

―――. [*Psychoprophylaxis and Psycho-Hygiene in Sports.*] Alma-Alta: Mektep, 1976.

―――. [*Psychic Self-Regulation in Sports.*] Alma-Ata: All-Union Scientific Research Institute of Physical Culture, 1977.

―――. *Proceedings, Southern European Congress for Sports Psychology.* Varna, Bulgaria: Nauka, 1979.

Rothstein, L. S. Autogenic phenomena and their application to self-regulation. Private communication (San Diego), 1977.

Schwartz, I. E. [*Suggestion in Pedagogical Process.*] Perm: Perm State Pedagogical Institute, 1971.

Shabad, T. 1,000 sleeping Russians "study" English. New York *Times,* Jan. 5, 1966.

Shteinbakh, V. *The Soviet Contribution to the Olympics.* Moscow: Novosti Press Agency, 1980.

Simon, C. W., and Emmons, W. H. Learning during sleep. *Psychological Bulletin,* 1955, *52,* 328–42.

Spickermann, A. [Ideological questions: Parapsychology—the latest irrational fad.] *Neves Deutschland,* Feb. 8–9, 1975.

Strenk, A. What price victory? The world of international sports and politics. *Annals of the American Academy of Political and Social Science,* 1979, *445,* 128–40.

Thacher, M. Tactics in the chess wars. *Human Behavior,* May 1979.

Tiller, W. A. Autogenic training in the USSR. *Journal of Paraphysics,* 1972, *6,* 155–58.

Uccusic, P. Private communication (Vienna, Austria), 1977.

Vilenskaya, L. V. A scientific approach to some aspects of psychic healing. *International Journal of Paraphysics,* 1976, *10,* 74–78.

Zlochevsky, S. E. [Ways of realizing psychological potential of intellectual self-regulation.] In A. S. Romen (ed.), [*Psychic Self-Regulation,*] Vol. 2. Alma-Ata: Kazakh State University, 1974.

CHAPTER 11

Acupuncture by Laser Beams

We know that every living organism is a system that radiates energy, thus creating a field around itself. But we know little about the organism's energy network, especially during telepathy when two organisms appear to interact at a distance. . . . A living organism can be described as a "biological field" or "biofield." . . . The biofield has a clear spatial formation and is shaped by several physical fields—electrostatic, electromagnetic, acoustic, hydrodynamic, and quite possibly others still inadequately explored.

Victor Inyushin (1977)

Free medical service is one of several economic advantages guaranteed to Soviet citizens under the provisions of the Constitution along with housing, education, and employment. These benefits are at the heart of the USSR's definition of human rights. Soviet physicians, about 70 percent of whom are women, administer the most massive system of national health care ever known. There are about twenty-five doctors to every ten thousand people (compared to twenty per ten thousand in the United States). Life expectancy is said to average seventy years in the Soviet Union, and the number of hospital beds is ten per thousand people (compared with nine per thousand in the United States).

The system has its flaws; to achieve quantity, the quality of treatment sometimes suffers. Hospital sanitation is spotty; anesthetics and modern equipment are often unavailable; many advanced drugs need to be imported; dentistry is old-fashioned. Pioneering heart research is done in one hospital while, in another, a man is transfused with incompatible blood until he nearly dies. Artificial plastic lenses are implanted into eyes, but a Muscovite who breaks her glasses often cannot get new ones for months. A black market exists for both medical goods and services (Shipler, 1977). The Soviet goal is lifetime health care for everyone, and any enterprise that ambitious is bound to have defects.

Soviet medicine works best at keeping people healthy; the backbone of this preventive system is a paramedic named the "feldsher." Feldshers (or field surgeons) were innovations introduced by Peter the Great. Today they study medicine for two to four years; like medical corpsmen in the U.S. military services, they stand between a nurse and a physician on the professional scale.

The feldshers, most of them women, work at the physician's side or on their own in the rural areas where doctors are scarce. They conduct routine physical examinations, administer immunization programs, give emergency first aid, and foster sanitation and hygiene (Shipler, 1977).

The best medicine for the Soviet worker is often to visit a health resort. Nowhere is the "health vacation" more widely practiced than in the USSR. There are special spas for each ailment (for example, arthritis, tuberculosis, heart conditions—which have increased in number, along with cancer, with the rise in Soviet affluence), but most are designed just to relieve the weary. Trade unions generally pay 70 percent of the cost for a health resort. While there, the patient embarks on a therapeutic program of mineral baths, warm mud packs, electrosleep treatments, daily walks, body-building workouts, vitamin and mineral supplements, and special diets that reduce consumption of animal fats and increase the use of fresh vegetables.

One of the most popular springs in the USSR is located in the health-resort city of Pyatigorsk. Thousands of people each day drink a warm cup of the hydrogen sulfide mineral water at the spa. In the same city, water is piped in that is so radioactive it must be diluted before people can bathe in it. After a bath in a hot tub of this water, the patient enters a lounge where he or she can listen to piano music while gazing out at the snow-capped peaks of the Caucasus Mountains. An American visitor to the health spas reported:

> . . . Although medical care is controlled completely by the state, many individual physicians and clinics are free to experiment with and practice virtually any form of natural healing they believe to be worthwhile. . . . Natural therapy in the Soviet Union exists as a *supplement* to ordinary medical care, and so there is no real conflict between the approach which emphasizes drugs and the approach favoring physical and nutritional medicine. Then again, since the state ultimately has to foot the medical bill for all 260 million Soviet citizens, there is, I think, a realization that ultimately it is a lot cheaper to have people taking mineral water baths and vitamins than to dispense millions of tranquillizers and muscle relaxants—which in America are used for practically the same purposes.
>
> . . . I didn't realize how bureaucratic, how authoritarian . . . our own health care system is . . . until I experienced firsthand the diversity of belief and practice which is permitted in the Soviet Union. [Bricklin, 1978, p. 37]

An example of this diversity is the use of herbal medicine in the USSR. Several excellent books are available describing medicinal plants that grow there, together with the illnesses they have been found to ameliorate. *Herbal Plants of the USSR* (Alexeev et al., 1971) and *The Popular Medical Encyclopedia* (Bakuleff and Petroff, 1965) are widely consulted.

A Network of Points

This diversity is also illustrated in the way that acupuncture was incorporated into Soviet medicine in the 1950s following a trip to China by Nikita Khrushchev. Twenty years later, acupuncture facilities were functioning in all the major cities and industrial centers of the USSR (Vogralik, 1972). Soviet scientists had also made remarkable progress in analyzing, defining, and explaining some of acupuncture's properties (Krippner, 1974).

According to classical Chinese theory, there are 12 meridians running on either side of the body that represent the bodily organs as well as 2 additional meridians in the front and back (Kajdos, 1974). Arrayed along this network of meridians are hundreds of acupuncture points—741 according to some practitioners, even more according to others. Unlike many of their American counterparts who refused to take this "life energy" system seriously, Soviet physicians attempted to put these notions to practical use. In one application, 61 tobacco smokers were given 4 weekly acupuncture treatments consisting of a 15-minute stimulation of 8 points in the ear. Two thirds of the subjects reported a noticeable reduction in the pleasurable taste sensation of tobacco following their first treatment. At the end of the program, 19 had stopped smoking completely and 31 had reduced their habit to 5 cigarettes or less per day (Mitrofanova et al., 1976). In addition, researchers in the USSR tried to identify and measure the physiological properties of these pathways and points. It is conjectured that connections exist among all parts of this electrical network, which possibly acts as an organizing and cohering force for other bodily systems. It may conduct information about developing pathology to surface points where the information can be detected by Kirlian photography and other procedures that measure the electrical properties of acupuncture points and meridians—properties such as voltage and current resistance, which vary with the organism's state of health.

At Expo 67 in Montreal, the Soviets exhibited the tobiscope, an instrument that measures the electrical conductivity between a point on the skin and a built-in reference point (Drabnika, 1969; Hill, 1977). It was this device that Adamenko demonstrated for me in 1971, locating points of high electrical conductivity and low skin resistance that roughly correspond to the network of acupuncture points mapped out by the Chinese physicians some five thousand years earlier. Although there are now several instruments more sophisticated than the tobiscope, it is important historically.

The tobiscope consists of a bridge circuit so arranged as to be balanced by normal skin resistance and unbalanced when making contact with an acupuncture point. The electrical signal due to the imbalance is applied to a direct-current (DC) amplifier, which boosts the signal so as to activate a light bulb located in the front portion of the device. In other versions of the tobiscope, the signal activates an audio speaker or a meter, which provides some type of measurement. The device is held in one hand (making contact with the metallic base), and the point is applied to the skin of the subject, while the other hand of the operator is in contact with a different portion of the subject's skin. Thus an electrical circuit is made from the base of the tobiscope through the body of the operator, along the body of the subject, to the tip of the tobiscope and, via internal connections, back to the base of the device. Moving the point over the skin, a variety of point locations are found that cause the light to be activated. These points are areas of low electrical resistance on the skin; one also finds a network of such points on animals and, to a lesser degree, on plants.

The skin must be dry if the tobiscope is to be effective. The DC resistance between any two acupuncture points on the body differs by less than a factor of two, suggesting that almost all of the resistance is embodied in the thin layer of epidermis at the skin surface. A similar range of resistance variation occurs due to emotional charge, mental concentration, hypnotic induction, and light excitation (Tiller, 1972).

Adamenko (1970) once performed a healing experiment with acupuncture meridians (pathways that are said to connect the points) utilizing the semiconductor effect. (A semiconductor is a substance whose electrical conductivity at a normal temperature is intermediate between that of a metal and an insulator.) One often finds, when measuring the resistance between symmetrical points on the left and the right sides of the body, that the resistance is quite different in the forward direction than in the reverse direction. If a person is healthy relative to the acupuncture meridian, the resistance will be the same. If the person suffers an illness in the body organs associated with that meridian, one will find a difference in resistance. Adamenko asked a folk healer to project "energy" with his hands located a short distance from the client. The difference in the client's resistance lessened but the healer's meridians became temporarily unbalanced in the process. Some observers interpret these findings to support the notion of an "energy" transfer to the client, but I suspect that expectancy on the part of the healer and the client might produce the dramatic results. In any event, the procedure is simple enough that it can be replicated by other investigators.

Folk healing may be one of several ways to stimulate acupuncture points and balance meridians. Soviet practitioners also use chemical stimulation, manual massage, electrical stimulation, and laser beams. Adamenko altered the electronic circuit of the tobiscope so it could be used to identify and measure properties of the meridians. He has also measured acupuncture points and pathways with Kirlian photography and with the biometer—a hand-held device that gives a reading on a meter indicating the strength of the electrical current in the bodily area being studied (Adamenko, Kirlian, and Kirlian, 1974). In addition, V. A. Puschov (1972) has described an apparatus for the detection of acupuncture points that works on alternating current. Its dual-electrode system enables it to measure the difference in skin resistance between the acupuncture point and the area surrounding it. The skin surface being investigated is covered with a chemical solution that assists the accuracy of the reading.

Many of these Soviet devices were studied and replicated by Americans who had been to the USSR (for example, Moss, 1979; Tiller, 1974); researchers in other parts of the world also developed similar devices (for example, Motoyama, 1977). Applications have also been made to research concerning altered states of consciousness. Adamenko (1970) found dramatic changes in electrical conductivity of the acupuncture system during hypnosis. Although he has not related his data to acupuncture, American investigator L. J. Ravitz (1962) has reported correlates of hypnosis and the body's electromagnetic field.

Data Transmission in the Body

Robert Becker, a prominent American medical researcher, and his colleagues (Becker et al., 1979) also found electrophysiological correlates of acupuncture points and meridians.

Earlier work had been conducted by H. S. Burr (1973), a Yale University biologist who set out to understand body electricity by measuring the difference in voltage between two points on the surface of living organisms. Abnormalities in these voltage measurements were found to give advance warnings of cancer in one study; in another, high voltages correlated with psychological feelings of well-being, while low voltages were associated with negative moods. It was also discovered that wounds would change the voltage measurements which could serve as useful indices of healing rates. Among female subjects, the voltage measurements were found to be helpful in determining the precise moment of ovulation, since this event is preceded by a steady rise in voltage, which falls rapidly after the egg has been released.

Becker was familiar with this work as well as the theories of Albert Szent-Györgyi (1960), the Nobel Prize-winning scientist who speculated that cells and other biological components might have electronic solid-state properties. (Electronic equipment such as transistors and crystals that can control current without the use of moving parts are referred to as "solid state" devices. Semiconduction, which Adamenko felt characterizes his healing data, is a property of solid-state electronics.) To Szent-Györgyi, the human cell is similar to a miniaturized computer, and the laws of solid-state physics govern the cell's actions. Becker reasoned that if Szent-Györgyi were correct, life processes would be regulated by the body's solid-state properties such as semiconduction. And if this were so, externally generated electromagnetic levels could be used for healing.

Over the years, Becker conducted research that confirmed his hypothesis. He found that externally generated electromagnetism could stimulate bone growth and regenerate tissue. For example, Becker knew that a salamander would regenerate a leg if it were severed. By studying the "current of injury" flowing between the damaged tissue and the healthy area, Becker noted that the current flowed away from the damaged area toward the healthy tissue. By reversing the flow of current from healthy to damaged areas, Becker healed skin ulcers and burns. He speeded up the healing of fractured bones with implanted electrodes. He applied current to a frog's stump—and the leg grew back. Later, Becker

(1972) obtained partial limb regeneration in a rat (including bone and muscle) by applying the appropriate kind of current.

Szent-Györgyi proposed that solid-state mechanisms could play a role in living organisms. If so, current would be carried by electrons, and the body's cells and tissues would possess semiconductivity. Such diseases as cancer represent a breakdown in the operation of the bodily computer.

Szent-Györgyi has also hypothesized that there is a pool of electrons continually available as well as a chain of atoms with approximately equal but increasing ionization potentials. Thus there could be a chain of electron transfer reactions in which the electrons would "flow" to the atoms with a higher ionization potential. This process could form the substrate for biological semiconduction.

Becker uncovered a primitive control system in the human body that is semiconductive in nature. Its primary function is sensing injury and effecting repair. The DC electronic signals of the system are generated and distributed by the perineural cells that flank the central nervous system. Pain transmission is one of the functions of the DC electronic-data transmission system in the perineural cells, specifically the Schwann and glial cells.

Becker's acupuncture research revealed to him the practical implications of this network. Acupuncture points are sites of DC potentials and serve, with the meridians, as a primitive data-transmission and control system. As such, they are vitally important in healing—a circumstance understood long ago by the ancient Chinese practitioners. Two Soviet researchers, L. A. Pirozyan and V. M. Aristarhov (1969), also demonstrated the existence of semiconductivity in cell membranes. Victor Inyushin and his colleagues put this knowledge to practical use, stimulating acupuncture points with light from laser beams.

Laser Light

In 1924, Albert Einstein received a paper from Indian physicist S. N. Bose that described light as a gas consisting of photons (Forward, 1979). This "photon gas" was unusual, for the particles in it did not obey the common-sense statistical laws that billiard balls do. If one randomly rolls a number of balls on a frictionless billiard table, sooner or later they will all end up in one pocket or another. In repeated trials, it would be found that all the balls had an equal probability of falling into any one of the pockets. But if the billiard balls behaved like photons, one would discover that if one of the pockets already had a ball in it, the rest of the balls would have a tendency to fall into that pocket. In fact, the more balls already in a pocket, the more likely another ball would choose to join its identical mates. There is no force or attraction involved in this effect; it is a statistical tendency that causes photons to travel together. This is the principle, mathematically expressed by Bose and Einstein, underlying the functioning of a laser.

Although Einstein did not invent the laser, his work laid the foundation. It was Einstein who pointed out that stimulated emission of radiation could occur. He used his photon mathematics to examine the case of a large collection of atoms ready to emit a photon at some random time in a random direction. If a stray photon passes by, the atoms are stimulated by its presence to emit their photons early. More remarkably, the emitted photons go in the same direction and have exactly the same frequency as the original photon. Later, as the small crowd of identical photons moves through the rest of the atoms, more and more photons will leave their atoms early to join in the subatomic parade (Forward, 1979).

To invent the laser, technical problems had to be overcome and reflecting mirrors added to facilitate the stimulated emission. The acronym LASER stands for Light Amplification by Stimulated Emission of Radiation—based on Einstein's concepts concerning the emission.

In 1964, the Nobel Prize in physics, for laser development, was jointly awarded to N. G. Basov and A. M. Prokhorov (members of the Soviet Academy of Sciences) and C. H. Townes, a Columbia University scientist. The laser phenomenon had been independently discovered during the 1950s in both countries. In the United States, for example, Townes had found that the light of a flashbulb caused the molecules of certain rare earth crystals to emit in turn a burst of powerful, concentrated light. In 1960, the first operational laser was developed at Hughes Aircraft using a synthetic ruby crystal. Reports of laser action in a number of other systems followed, and soon there were chemical and electrical lasers employing various gaseous, liquid, and solid substances. Soviet scientists once used a vodka tonic, while Americans successfully tried Jell-O. In each case, the molecules of the substance oscillate and emit light at a certain frequency. Laser light may be coaxed out of the substance if stimulated with energy (light, electrical discharge, etc.) of the right frequency.

The effect of light on living organisms has been well known for many years. For example, white light is essential to photosynthesis (the formation of carbohydrates in the chlorophyll-containing tissues of plants), while red light has little effect on this important process. Blue and violet light can suppress life activity; ultraviolet light can tan—or burn—one's skin. Laser light is the most powerful light on earth. Ordinary light is diffuse; it is made up of electromagnetic waves oscillating at many different frequencies diffused in many different directions. Laser light, on the other hand, is coherent (with all the waves in phase with each other) and monochromatic (oscillating at only one frequency). Because it does not fan out like the beam of a flashlight, laser light can be focused and aimed.

Light Drills and Scalpels

Since their invention in 1960, lasers have proved invaluable in such varied fields as metallurgy, communications, and photography. In one use, the laser acts as the illuminating system of a microscope. As lasers emit only monochromatic, coherent light, images of much higher quality can be obtained. Researchers at the Ukrainian SSR's Academy of Sciences reported building a "holographic" microscope apparatus using lasers for photographing tissue-culture cells (Gamaleya, 1977). Their original medical application, in both the United States and the USSR, was as "scalpels of light"—cutting damaged tissue with an edge finer than that of any knife (Taratorkin and Lazarev, 1979). Another application uses lasers as "light drills," evaporating tissue rather than burning through it. Both of these medical uses have utilized the laser's capacity for carefully controlled destruction of living material such as skin tumors and tattoos.

Inyushin, on the other hand, has explored stimulation through lasers rather than destruction. By directing monochromatic red light or monochromatic polarized red light on the skin, into the eyes, or into acupuncture points, he claims to have succeeded in stimulating tissue regeneration, assisting recovery from disease, and affecting various psychological and physiological functions (Inyushin and Chekorov, 1976).

The mechanics of this action are based on the fact that atoms exist at different energy levels. When they absorb energy, they rise to a higher energy level; returning to the lower energy level, they give off energy often in the form of a photon—an elementary "light particle." If stimulated with energy of a specific frequency, certain materials will first absorb that energy and rise to a higher energy level; on dropping back to the lower energy level they will emit light energy that is both monochromatic and coherent, a light that can be amplified and focused.

In practice, most lasers consist of a light-emitting medium (for example, ruby crystal, gases such as argon or helium and neon), a source of energy to excite the medium (for example, a xenon flash lamp), and two mirrors, one of which is partially transparent, that face each other and enclose the medium. In a ruby laser, for example, the flash lamp will first emit a burst of white light. Some of this light is absorbed by chromium atoms in the ruby; the atoms rise to a higher energy level and then emit monochromatic red light as they "fall back" to their original energy level. The part of the red light that strokes the two end mirrors is reflected back and forth many times (for example, it oscillates) before exiting through the partially transparent mirror as a focused, amplified, monochromatic, coherent beam of light.

Lasers are classified according to the kind of material they use as the light-emitting medium. Gas lasers use rare inert gases like argon, xenon, or helium and neon. Optically pumped solid lasers use crystals or rare-earth elements (for example, ruby, sapphire, or neodymium); they are "pumped" with light to stimulate the coherent emission of photons. Semiconductor lasers emit light when an electrical current is passed through certain semiconductor materials. There are also liquid, dye, and chemical lasers.

Inyushin's work with lasers is only one series of medical applications made by Soviet scientists. One application is its use in dentistry (Korytinyj, 1979). In another application, laser radiation is concentrated into a microscopic beam that can damage certain parts of a cell while leaving others untouched, providing a powerful method of studying cell composition. A variation of this procedure involves focusing the laser on a cell part to induce its vaporization. The vaporized material is then subjected to spectral analysis, a method of determining component elements of a sample by breaking down its light into component wave lengths (or spectrum).

The laser microbeam also may be focused on a certain area of the cell to study its light-absorption properties. Pigmented parts of a cell absorb only specific wave lengths of light; it is thus possible by varying the laser-wave length to study light absorption in a selected part of the cell while leaving the rest of the cell intact. Because of the extremely short duration of the beam, no significant conduction of heat energy takes place to other structures within the cell.

Z. G. Beyasheva and B. A. Bekmuhambetova (Gamaleya, 1977) have studied the action of red polarized light, white polarized light, and helium-neon laser light on humans. The different types of light were directed into the eyes of the subjects; an EEG (electroencephalogram) was monitored on the frontal and occipital lobes of the brain. The researchers found that red and white polarized light increased the amplitude of the frontal EEG, and suppressed the occipital EEG. Helium-neon irradiation caused a total suppression of all EEG rhythms, demonstrating the potential powerful effects of lasers on living organisms.

Other Soviet researchers have applied the use of a laser microbeam together with a spectrometric technique of blood analysis. Laser rays were focused into a beam and directed onto dry whole blood, either crystallized or on a cotton fabric surface. Using this method, they recorded sixteen different elements in the composition of the blood. Blood samples from different persons were then able to be differentiated on the basis of their content of trace elements (Gamaleya, 1977).

In another series of experiments, Soviet scientists studied the effects of monochromatic polarized red light on the healing of wounds. Identical skin wounds were inflicted on both ears of rabbits; one ear was irradiated and one was not. Within a period of three hours, there was an obvious change in the irradiated tissue: The wounds treated by laser eventually healed faster than the nonirradiated ears (Gamaleya, 1977).

Soviet biologists have studied the effects of low-intensity helium-neon laser light on the regeneration of bone fractures. The subjects for the experiment were seventy-two dogs whose skulls were broken under anesthesia. Regeneration was studied on the radium bone (in the skull), which either demonstrated partial cleavage or a complete fracture. Irradiation of the wound was performed with a helium-neon laser; it was reported that the fractures of the laser-treated dogs healed much more quickly (Inyushin and Chekorov, 1976).

Helium-neon laser irradiation of boils has been highly successful, even for those that have persisted for ten years or more. The typical daily treatment originally lasts for thirty seconds, increasing slightly over time and concluding after about a month, at which time the boil usually has disappeared. Helium-neon laser treatment for burns has been attempted at the Kazakh SSR Clinical Hospital, with a reported 50 percent decrease in the duration of the healing period. Laser irradiation has also been applied to the treatment of cerebral palsy, skin transplants, and spinal-cord ailments (Inyushin and Chekorov, 1976).

Resonance, Bioplasma, and Self-regulation

Soviet scientists have theorized that the effect of laser light upon tissue might be thermal (or heat-oriented) in nature; accordingly, they increased the temperature of radiation but found that an inhibition of the regenerative processes took place. They tried varying the frequency of the laser light being used and found no distinct stimulating effects in other parts of the red spectrum, confirming the notion that the healing effect takes place only at specific frequencies.

Inyushin (1978) disagrees with the thermal explanation, taking the position that this stimulation of growth occurs through *resonance*. Resonance is a phenomenon in wave mechanics where the peaks and troughs of waves in a medium are in phase with a stimulating agent. Normally, waves are out of phase, and the different merging frequencies tend to "dampen" or cancel each other out. In resonant phenomena, with the peaks and troughs "aligned," the strength of the wave continues to build and, because it has almost no resistance to itself, is more powerful while using up less energy.

Inyushin believes that the basic matrix resonating on the action of monochromatic, coherent radiation is the electrically charged subatomic particles that are associated with living organisms. Laser light initiates the wave action; bioplasma is the wave medium. At the resonant frequency, this low-intensity light reinforces, or augments, the natural wave pulsation of bioplasma, thus stimulating the organism's own healing action naturally. Inyushin suggests that the growth activities of the organism are directed by "biofields"—the "energy fields" within and around an organism of which bioplasma is one component. Laser irradiation acts to stimulate the "biofield," thus acting on energy systems rather than on physical structures.

Inyushin found the concept of acupuncture points and meridians consistent with his viewpoint on resonance. He named his laser acupuncture device the "biostimulator" and conjectured that laser acupuncture works by creating a resonant stimulation of bioplasma in the meridians. Thus laser acupuncture can stabilize, stimulate, or restore the organism's bioplasma. For Inyushin, disease basically reflects a disturbance in the bioplasmic balance of the body. In other words, there are few localized ailments—instead, disease usually involves the entire organism (Inyushin and Chekorov, 1976, p. 14). The patient should be treated "as a bioenergetic whole"; the energy reserve can be utilized in its fight with an ailment once it is stimulated by laser acupuncture. This holistic point of view needs to permeate medicine:

A completely new field of directed regulation of the bioenergetic state of the organism is being discovered. The resonance bioeffects induced by radiation force us to create new concepts about the living organism as being a whole, in which the energetic processes lie at the foundation of all manifestations of life. [Inyushin and Chekorov, 1976, p. 7]

This holistic position was supported by A. S. Romen in his work with self-regulation. He told us that subjects trained in self-regulation could use this process to inhibit the electrical conductivity of their acupuncture points when they were stimulated by a laser. In addition, they could inhibit the effects of alcohol, drugs, heat, and cold (Romen and Inyushin, 1968).

An earlier visitor to Alma-Ata, biophysicist Scott Hill from the University of Copenhagen, commented on these findings, noting:

> The self-regulatory abilities of the body are really responsible for the many healings of medical science. No drug can cure an illness, unless the body's own mechanisms are functioning in the correct way. Therefore, we may consider that all illnesses, and all healings, are due to some aspect of the systems that control biological self-regulation. [Hill, 1979]

Some Soviet information theorists (Avramenko et al., 1976) have observed that acupuncture data indicate a new source of body information. The human brain appears to manage this material as part of the organism's self-regulation processing. Further, this information appears to be universal; its understanding will affect people's ability to control their behavior and improve their health. The information theorists suggest an expansion of research in psychophysics—the study of relationships between physical stimuli and sensory events.

Approaching this problem from the standpoint of general systems theory, Soviet physiologist P. K. Anakhin (1973) observed that "the brain is a keyboard on which hundreds of millions of different melodies—acts of behaviour or intelligence—can be played" (p. 195). However, not one of the features of brain activity considered to be a typical indicator of intelligence appeared suddenly during the evolutionary process. All these properties were present "with the first beginnings of life; all of them, already at that time, formed part of life's dynamic physiological structure." Living beings had to adapt themselves to the space-time continuum of nonliving matter in order to survive.

Dreaming is another vital aspect of brain activity, and many proponents of a holistic approach to health and disease see the dream process as a mechanism of body-mind integration. During the Nazis' siege of Leningrad, Vasili Kasatkin vowed that if he survived, he would examine the nature of dreams. The young physician had noticed the frequency of dreams about food during the siege. When someone reported a series of dreams about other topics, they often pointed to symptoms of an illness that did not develop until a few days later. Kasatkin later became head of a dream-research unit of the Neurological Surgical Institute in Leningrad. His book *The Theory of Dreams* (Kasatkin, 1972) reports data from over eight thousand dreams that demonstrated that they could warn of an impending illness. For example, one man dreamed of being buried underneath a collapsing building; he was later hospitalized for hypertension. A woman who dreamed that she was crawling through a narrow passage that closed in on her later was diagnosed as tubercular.

These dreams, of course, are not precognitive but indicate that the human body is so sensitive that it notes changes before the person involved becomes consciously aware of them. The data demonstrate the unitary nature of bodily function, and how this unity is typically overlooked despite the information it has to offer.

The Bioluminescence Cycle

At another level of bodily functioning, the phenomenon of bioluminescence is ignored by most scientists, being regarded as merely an exotic facilitator of sexual attraction and intraspecies communication among primitive forms of life (Herring, 1978). Soviet researchers, however, have studied bioluminescence—light emission resulting from the body's use of oxygen—not only in connection with acupuncture but also as an important diagnostic clue. In one study, twenty-two healthy people, twenty-nine patients suffering from tuberculosis, and twenty-seven patients with malignant lung tumors were studied. Ten measures of bioluminescence of each person's blood serum were taken. The intensity of radiation was measured by photomultiplier tubes; averages for each person were computed as well as averages for the three groups. It was discovered that the tubercular patients showed a higher level of luminescence than the healthy subjects and that the patients suffering from lung cancer showed a lower level. The investigators suggested that malignancies might introduce "extinguishing" elements into the blood that tend to reduce the intensity of luminescence (Shpolyanskaya et al., 1975). No reason was given for the high luminescence of tubercular patients.

In another Soviet study, the characteristic twenty-four-hour cycle in bioluminescence disappeared with cancer patients. However, in those successfully treated by surgery, the cyclic pattern returned (Inyushin and Inyushina, 1972).

Inyushin (1978) discovered a twenty-four-hour fluctuation in the electrical conductivity of the acupuncture points; the minimum conductivity was observed at 2:00 A.M. and the maximum at 6:00 P.M. These data suggested that acupuncture treatments are most effective in the evening, when the conductive systems of the organism possess a large reaction capacity.

Inyushin (1968) also investigated the bioluminescence (that is, light emission) of eight areas on the skin of fifteen subjects both before and during gas laser radiation on the mouth. Seven of the eight areas were points around the chin, ear, eye, and jaw, traditionally used in needle acupuncture of diseased teeth. The eighth area was not an acupuncture point but a reference point in the cheek. Bioluminescence was measured with a Kirlian device and a photomultiplier tube. The results were dramatic: Both before and during gas laser radiation, the acupuncture points all showed greater bioluminescence than the control point; further, a significant decrease in bioluminescence was observed in four of the seven acupuncture points during the radiation. Inyushin repeated this experiment three times, always obtaining similar results.

In further studies of the bioluminescence of acupuncture points, again using such devices as photomultiplier tubes, Inyushin (Inyushin and Inyushina, 1972) discovered not only that acupuncture points are more luminescent than other skin areas, but also that there is a rhythmic twenty-four-hour luminescence cycle that can be influenced by meteorological factors. For example, A. K. Podshibyakin, an electrophysiologist at the Kiev Institute of Physiology, found that when solar flares explode from the sun, there is an almost instantaneous change in the electrical potential of acupuncture points. (The bioluminescence of acupuncture points was confirmed in 1974 by Gary Poock, a faculty member of the U. S. Naval Postgraduate School in California, but he did not examine the correlation with solar flares.) These data reflect holism; in discussing Inyushin's work, Guy Playfair and Scott Hill (1978) remark that human beings, like all living creatures, are electromagnetic systems in electromagnetic environments from which they cannot isolate themselves:

> Ours is not a universe of isolated parts; we are made of the same raw material as the rest of it, and we respond to the same forces that drive and shape it all. Star and skin are in regular contact. [p. 326]

A further application of this holistic model is the Soviet use of negative ions. Atmospheric ions are held by some Soviet researchers to have a significant effect on human performance. Their observations indicate that negative ions normalize subjects under stress, while positive ions have debilitating effects. In 1950, a special committee to study ion therapy was organized in the Pavlov Institute of Physiology, USSR Academy of Science (Vasiliev, 1958). Since that time, considerable research has been carried out suggesting that the presence of negative ions in the environment creates conditions favorable for the maintenance of health. In addition, their appearance appears to enhance the performance of athletes, reduce blood pressure, and alleviate arthritic and rheumatic conditions.

There are other factors that need to be investigated. For example, the quantity of positive ions increases during the submergence of nuclear submarines. Since cosmic radiation produces atmospheric ionization, cosmonauts probably receive a substantial dosage of air ions. High-voltage electrical equipment also ionizes the air. Falling barometric pressure and hot, dry seasonal winds pack the air with positive ions, while waterfalls and running water produce negative ions (Krueger and Smith, 1960)—a fact that has determined the location of several Soviet health resorts. In surveying the data, M. C. Diamond (1980) concluded that negative air ions can influence the chemical content of the brain but warned that some commercial negative-ion generators produce too much ozone to be safe. She also noted that the specific processes by which negative ions affect behavior are not completely understood.

At the Control Center

During our stay in Alma-Ata, Hickman, Payne, Verovacki, and I spent several hours discussing laser acupuncture with Inyushin and his associate, Olga Zorina, who uses the technique in a children's hospital. Inyushin told us that two conferences on laser technology had been held in the USSR in 1979, in Kiev and Lvov. Researchers reported that lasers and biological systems seemed to work well together and that medical and technological experts were able to speak in similar terms. An Italian manufacturer was at the meetings and obtained permission to produce ten thousand biostimulators for sale in Western Europe and the United States.

Near the end of my stay, Inyushin informed me that he was trying to obtain the necessary approval from six agencies for a special visit. When the permits arrived, he noted that I was to be the first American and the fourth foreigner to visit the laboratory, which housed his personal office, as well as a dozen divisions that demonstrated the array of research Inyushin supervised.

Joining us was Lidia Kireva, one of Inyushin's research associates, and Vladimir Verovacki, who served as translator. Inyushin and Kireva took us far outside the city limits of Alma-Ata to a country retreat. We walked over a bubbling stream on a small bridge and approached a wooden building flanked by gigantic whale bones. On the door was posted a sign in both the Russian and Kazakh languages: Chairman, Department of Biophysics, Kazakh State University.*

As we entered the building, we were greeted by three large colored photographs of Soviet President Leonid Brezhnev, Pre-

---

* Inyushin's affiliation is sometimes given as Kirov University. Actually, the complete name of this institution is "Kazakh State University, named after S. M. Kirov." Kirov was a Soviet revolutionary who died mysteriously in 1934.

mier Aleksei Kosygin, and Yuri Andropov, head of the Committee for State Security. On another wall was a chart listing Inyushin's research projects throughout Kazakhstan. The control center—appearing on the chart's top—was the building we had just entered.

Inyushin's office contained a map of Kazakhstan; the locations of all Inyushin's laboratories and projects were identified and differentially coded as to whether the focus was agriculture, medicine, space science, or basic research.

Another room contained a display, divided in half, with examples of electrical radiation (or electrochemiluminescence) on the right and examples of natural radiation (or biochemiluminescence) on the left. The right side displayed photographs of the Kirlians, Adamenko, and a series of electrical photographs, while the left showed materials of mitogenic radiation and other forms of bioplasma. One photograph depicted a portable laser apparatus carried from field to field by a truck. In another, one could identify a rotating laser apparatus in a cornfield. Both devices were used in attempts to increase crop yield. A graph portrayed the extension of laser applications in agriculture from 1 hectare (2.5 acres) in 1971 to 10,000 hectares in 1979.

Inyushin's headquarters contained several divisions with such names as the Laboratory of Photochemistry, the Laboratory of Photoenergetics of Plants, the Laboratory of Spectral Analysis, the Laboratory for Biostimulation with Resonance, and the Laboratory for Quantitative Analysis of the Kirlian Effect. In the latter laboratory, attempts were being made to understand the complexities of Kirlian photography through quantification. Inyushin showed us a Kirlian device that utilized fiber optics—glass filaments that carry the light produced by the corona discharge to a photomultiplier tube where it can be measured. The data are registered on a chart recorder so that moment-by-moment fluctuations can be noted. The process occurs in an artificially created argon and helium atmosphere because these elements provide an environment stable enough to prevent weather changes that affect luminosity. This atmosphere also reduces the chance that the observed light might come from the electrodes or from the gas produced by the spark—factors overlooked by most American researchers.

The Kirlian effect produced in this laboratory can be observed under a microscope and recorded on videotape. I told Inyushin about American efforts along these lines: Rodney Ross' (1974) noncontact Kirlian device using a microscope, Gary Poock's (1979) use of imagery-processing techniques to quantify the Kirlian effect on the basis of the colors produced, and his image-intensification technique to make films of the effect (Poock and Sparks, 1979). Russell Targ and Jonathan Cohen (1974) developed a system for making video records of corona discharges, demonstrating that with some subjects, changes in the Kirlian fingerprint are associated with alterations in consciousness rather than artifacts introduced by finger pressure or movement.

Another laboratory contained a huge Tesla coil, unique in the USSR. It was part of a gigantic Kirlian device that was connected to a television screen. Inyushin had told us that bioplasma, consisting of subatomic particles, is quickly destroyed by the Kirlian process. The device in this laboratory, however, allows one to see the bioplasma before it is destroyed and to record it on videotape.

In another laboratory, mitogenic radiation (supposedly a form of bioplasma) was being photographed. Inyushin described how he would place the root of a plant a short distance away from a piece of unexposed film in a totally darkened room. After three hours, the developed film would portray the root. Inyushin showed me several photographs of cucumber, wheat, and rye roots in which the details were sharp and clear. Ultraviolet radiation is said to be the chief component of mitogenic radiation; thus stimulation of the plant with an ultraviolet laser can increase the amount of mitogenic radiation available for study.

"Energetic Bodies"

Inyushin claimed that he and Romen had been able to train people, through self-regulation, to control their skin bioluminescence. Some had gone on from that point to concentrate on plants from another room; the density of the mitogenic radiation sometimes increased, producing a bright spot on the film that—according to

Inyushin—provided a dramatic datum supporting the reality of psi. Inyushin advanced the theory that living organisms are "energetic bodies" interacting with fields of energy in their local and cosmic environments. Some people can be trained to utilize this energy to heal themselves, to heal others, and to interact at a distance with other organisms. Therefore, self-regulation may be closely linked with unusual healing, ESP, and PK phenomena.

I offered a possible example of this interaction. Douglas Dean (1975) had studied the water treated by healers through a "laying on" of hands and found that some of the water was no longer hydrogen-bonded. The same results were observed when magnets were placed in the water for thirty minutes, suggesting that the healers' effect was similar to a magnetic effect. Inyushin told us that he had conducted a similar study in 1968, obtaining identical results. He added that he obtained better results when he studied the degree of light polarization in the water.

We also discussed PK experimentation and I mentioned that I had heard about a Soviet investigation in which a metal spiral, suspended by a silk thread, reportedly was rotated by the intense gaze of psychic sensitives. However, I noted that this type of experiment could not be considered valid unless the target object was enclosed in a sealed container to prevent thermal currents, air drafts, and other forces from moving the object. I suggested that a better target object would be a laser beam and told Inyushin that several attempts had been made to deflect or modulate laser beams by American psychics; two of them, Ingo Swann (1975) and Karen Getsla (Grotta, 1978), had already claimed success. Inyushin agreed with me that this would be a worthwhile line of research and stated that human deflection of laser beams had been successfully attempted in the USSR several years earlier by Nina Kulagina and other psychic sensitives.

Before I left Inyushin's office, he showed me a biostimulator. Touching the flexible tip of it to my little finger, he turned on the laser beam, stimulating an acupuncture point on my finger and producing a vibrant red glow in my hand. As a gift, he gave me several scientific books and monographs and handed Verovacki a copy of *June Without Rain* (Tchernogolovina, 1979), a collection of short stories, one of which is a fictionalized account of Inyushin's research efforts. His gesture of friendship had a touch of irony since much of our tour—and conversation—would be dubbed "science fiction" by critics in both the United States and the USSR (Popovsky, 1979, p. 192).

Expectancy and Healing

In 1976, the Institute of Reflex Therapy was organized in Moscow with the study of acupuncture as its primary focus; by 1979 its work was conducted in fifteen laboratories and clinics. However, the newly organized body soon took an interest in other types of healing, and its director, R. A. Duvenyan, went to the Philippines to observe the controversial folk healers there. Although his visit was mentioned by several scientists during my 1979 stay in the Soviet Union, nobody seemed to know what Duvenyan had concluded.

When I was asked for my impressions, I stated that most, but not necessarily all, of the spectacular effects observed could be due to sleight of hand (Krippner, 1976). There are many ways in which a magician can appear to "open" the body, extract organic material, or produce stones, twigs, and even bits of plastic that were placed there purportedly by means of sorcery. However, most people become so fascinated by the unusual phenomena that accompany the healing sessions that they fail to pay attention to whether or not healing occurs.

To address this issue, Patricia Westerbeke (Westerbeke, Gover, and Krippner, 1977) accompanied sick Americans to the Philippines on three occasions in 1973 and 1974. One questionnaire was given to the patients before they saw any of the healers. It asked about the nature of their disease, about personal habits (smoking, drinking, etc.), and about their attitudes (for example, "How much confidence do you have in the ability of the Philippine 'psychic healers' to make you well?"). Another questionnaire was administered after the Americans had seen the healers, and a third was given six months to a year later. Both of these latter questionnaires focused on the amount of help the patients felt they had received.

When the answers to the first two sets of questions were

correlated, there was no relationship between the perceived benefits from the healers and the Americans' consumption of tobacco and alcohol; nor were their sex, age, or religious commitment important factors. However, there were very high (and statistically significant) correlations between the healing patients received and their degree of confidence in unorthodox healers, their reported personal experience with psychic phenomena, and the degree to which they would be willing to change their life to regain their health.

When the answers to the first and the third questionnaires were correlated, many of the same findings emerged. After six months to a year, sex, age, religious commitment, and tobacco or alcohol consumption were unrelated to long-term change. Strongly related to improvements in the patients' physical or mental condition was their confidence in unorthodox healing, reported personal experience with psychic phenomena, and their willingness to change their lives. The amount of help they felt immediately after the healing session was related to long-term improvement, as was the sensation of "energy" experienced at the time of the healing session.

In summary, the Americans' attitudes appeared to be instrumental in determining the amount of help they obtained from the folk healers. There is a temptation to criticize these healers because of the role played by the expectation of their clients. However, the same observation must be made of Western medicine. Physicians have always known that their ability to inspire expectant trust in a patient partially determines the success of treatment. A physician can give a sugar pill to a patient who thinks he or she is receiving a powerful medicine, and the patient will frequently get well. This "placebo effect" is so strong that a survey of research by F. J. Evans (1974) revealed that the ingestion of placebo "medication" can significantly reduce pain and suffering in approximately one out of every three patients.

When acupuncture first began to gain popularity in the United States, many investigators attributed its effects to the placebo effect, expectancy, and suggestion (for example, Chaves and Barber, 1974). Although these factors probably play a role in acupuncture, just as they do in orthodox medicine, the electrophysiological correlates of acupuncture points indicate that additional processes are occurring. The research data demonstrate this as well. Scientists (Stewart, Thompson, and Oswald, 1977) at the University of Edinburgh conducted a study to determine if acupuncture could reduce pain under conditions that ruled out suggestion. Twelve volunteers were selected and underwent an experience in which heat was applied to their skin. They were told to push a button when the pain became intolerable. In one condition, no acupuncture was used. Another condition used traditional acupuncture treatment, while in a third, the needles were inserted into skin areas that were not acupuncture points. When the acupuncture points were used, subjects took more than twice as long to reach the pain threshold as when no acupuncture was used. Pseudoacupuncture proved to be effective—but less so than the genuine method, demonstrating that suggestion plays a role in pain reduction with acupuncture but is not the entire explanation.

An even more comprehensive study was reported by J. A. Stern and his associates (1977). Pain was produced either by pressure applied to the twenty subjects' left arms or by immersion of the left-hand fingers in ice water. Reduction of each type of pain was attempted by hypnosis (induced by videotape to insure standardization), electrical stimulation of acupuncture points following needle injection, similar stimulation of skin areas that were not acupuncture points, injections of morphine and diazepam (a tranquillizer), and oral administration of aspirin and a placebo. A pain rating report was given by each subject every fifteen seconds during the five-minute pain periods. Hypnosis proved to be the most effective pain-reduction agent followed by morphine and acupuncture (which was more effective for the pain induced by pressure). None of the other four procedures was effective; when the subjects were divided into good and poor hypnotic subjects, the former were found to obtain more pain relief from hypnosis, morphine, and diazepam. Poor hypnotic subjects actually reported an increase in pain when under the influence of diazepam than under the nondrug condition. The researchers concluded, "Hypnotic suggestibility does not account for the effectiveness of acupuncture stimulation . . ." (p. 192).

The role of "brain opiates," such as enkephalin, in alleviating pain has recently been explored (Marx, 1979). Acupuncture can stimulate their release into the nervous system, but so can suggestion. In either event, enkephalin (which resembles morphine) blocks nerve signals on their way to the higher brain centers, where they would be experienced as pain. Pain researchers, both Soviet and American, realize that pain is often beneficial, as it can warn a person of a developing disease. Therefore, pain reduction needs to be selective, and the procedure should be practiced by qualified experts.

This cautionary note pervaded my discussions about innovations in medicine with Soviet physicians and scientists. It is an easy matter to become excited and enthused when discussing advances in the healing professions. But this enthusiasm must always be tempered by concern for the welfare of patients. Sick people are not guinea pigs to be poked, stuck, or drugged without a great deal of evidential data that the novel treatment will help rather than hurt them. The Soviet constitutional guarantee of free medical service is indeed praiseworthy. The ingenuity and dedication of its practitioners will determine how soon that image will become reality.

References

Adamenko, V. G. Electrodynamics of living systems. *Journal of Paraphysics,* 1970, *4,* 113–20.

Adamenko, V. G.; Kirlian, V. K.; and Kirlian, S. D. Detection of acupuncture points by the biometer. In S. Krippner and D. Rubin (eds.), *The Kirlian Aura.* Garden City, N.Y.: Anchor Books, 1974.

Alexeev, V. E., et al. [*Herbal Plants of the USSR*] Moscow: Misl, 1971.

Anakhin, P. K. The forming of natural and artificial intelligence. *Impact of Science on Society,* 1973, *23,* 195–212.

Avramenko, R. F., et al. [Information energy and the theory of wave psychophysics.] In V. G. Nikiforov and V. N. Pushkin (eds.), [*Electroacupuncture and Problems of Energy-Information Control of Human Activity.*] Moscow: USSR Ministry of the Coal Mining Industry, 1976.

Bakuleff, A. N., and Petroff, F. N. (eds.). [*The Popular Medical Encyclopedia,*] 4th ed. Moscow: Bolshaya, 1965.

Becker, R. O. Stimulation of partial limb regeneration in rats. *Nature,* 1972, *235,* 109–11.

Becker, R. O., et al. Electrophysiological correlates of acupuncture points and meridians. In S. Krippner (ed.), *Psychoenergetic Systems.* New York: Gordon & Breach, 1979.

Bricklin, M. Natural healing behind the Iron Curtain. *Prevention,* Sept. 1978.

Burr, H. S. *The Fields of Life.* New York: Ballantine, 1973.

Chaves, J. F., and Barber, T. X. Acupuncture analgesia: A six factor theory. *Psychoenergetic Systems,* 1974, *1,* 11–20.

Dean, D. The effects of "healers" on biologically significant molecules. *New Horizons,* 1975, *1,* 215–19.

Diamond, M. C. Uppers and downers in the air. *Psychology Today,* June, 1980.

Drabnika, S. The tobiscope. *Sputnik,* Sept. 1969.

Evans, F. J. The placebo response in pain reduction. In J. J. Bonica (ed.), *Advances in Neurology.* Vol. 4. New York: Raven Press, 1974.

Forward, R. L. Einstein's legacy. *Omni,* Mar. 1979.

Gamaleya, N. F. Laser biomedical research in the USSR. In M. L. Wolbarsht (ed.), *Laser Applications in Medicine and Biology,* Vol. 3. New York: Plenum Press, 1977.

Graff, E. S. Kirlian electrography as a clinical diagnostic tool. *Laboratory Management,* May 1978.

Grotta, D. A monograph on the persistence of psychic manifestations at Drexel University. *Philadelphia Magazine,* Dec. 1978.

Herring, P. (ed.). *Bioluminescence in Action.* New York: Academic Press, 1978.

Hill, S. Acupuncture research in the USSR. *International Journal of Paraphysics,* 1977, *11,* 10–11.

————. Biophotons and biophysical effects of ultraweak EM radiation. *International Journal of Paraphysics,* 1979, *13,* 65–82.

Inyushin, V. M. [Study of electrobioluminescence of acupuncture points with and without the action of laser radiation.] In B. A.

Dombrovsky et al. (eds.), [*Bioenergetic Questions—and Some Answers.*] Alma-Ata: Kazakh State University, 1968.

——. Bioplasma: The fifth state of matter. In J. White and S. Krippner (eds.), *Future Science.* Garden City, N.Y.: Anchor Books, 1977.

——. [*Elements of a Theory of the Biological Field.*] Alma-Ata: Kazakh Ministry of Higher and Special High School Education, 1978.

Inyushin, V. M., and Chekorov, P. R. [*Biostimulation Through Laser Radiation and Bioplasma.*] Alma-Ata: Kazakh State University, 1975. English translation, Copenhagen: Danish Society for Psychical Research, 1976.

Inyushin, V. M., and Inyushina, T. P. [On the investigation of some electrobioluminescence properties of plants, animals, and man.] In B. N. Tarusov et al. (eds.), [*Ultraweak Luminescence in Biology.*] Moscow: Nauka, 1972.

Kajdos, V. [*Acupuncture: With Metal and Fire.*] Prague: Pressphoto, 1974.

Kasatkin, V. N. [*The Theory of Dreams.*] Leningrad: Medical Edition, 1972.

Korytinyj, D. L. [*Laser Therapy and Its Application to Dentistry.*] Alma-Ata: Kazakhstan Press, 1979.

Krippner, S. Acupuncture in the Soviet Union. *Journal of the American Society of Psychosomatic Dentistry and Medicine,* 1974, *21*, 91–97.

——. Psychic healing in the Philippines. *Journal of Humanistic Psychology,* 1976, *16*, 3–31.

Krueger, A., and Smith, R. The biological mechanisms of air ion action. *Journal of General Physiology,* 1960, *43*, 533–40.

Marx, J. L. Brain peptides: Is substance P a transmitter of pain signals? *Science,* 1979, *205*, 886–89.

Mitrofanova, N., et al. [The acupuncture needle vs. the tobacco habit.] *Techika Molodezhi,* Oct. 1976.

Moss, T. *The Body Electric.* Los Angeles: J. P. Tarcher, 1979.

Motoyama, H. Physiological measurements and new instrumentation. In G. W. Meek (ed.), *Healers and the Healing Process.* Wheaton, Ill.: Theosophical Publishing House, 1977.

Pirozyan, L. A., and Aristarhov, V. M. [The possible energy

mechanisms accompanying the appearance of biopotentials. *USSR Academy of Science News, Biology Series,*] Jan. 1969.

Playfair, G., and Hill, S. *The Cycles of Heaven.* New York: St. Martin's Press, 1978.

Poock, G. K. Statistical analysis of the electrobioluminescence of acupuncture points. *American Journal of Acupuncture,* 1974, *2,* 253–57.

———. A numeral quantification technique for Kirlian photographs. In S. Krippner (ed.), *Psychoenergetic Systems.* New York: Gordon & Breach, 1979.

Poock, G. K., and Sparks, P. W. An image intensification technique for motion picture Kirlian photography. In S. Krippner (ed.), *Psychoenergetic Systems.* New York: Gordon & Breach, 1979.

Popovsky, M. *Manipulated Science.* Garden City, N.Y.: Doubleday, 1979.

Puschov, V. A. [The registration of electroconductance of acupuncture points.] In Romen, A. S. (ed.), [*Some Questions of Biodynamics and Bioenergetics in the Healthy and Ill Organism: Biostimulation by Laser Radiation.*] Alma-Ata: Kazakh State University, 1972.

Ravitz, L. J. History, measurement, and applicability of periodic changes in the electromagnetic field in health and disease. *Annals of the New York Academy of Sciences,* 1962, *98,* 1144–1201.

Romen, A. S., and Inyushin, V. M. [Some data on voluntary influence on electrobioluminescence.] In B. A. Dombrovsky et al. (eds.), [*Bioenergetic Questions—and Some Answers.*] Alma-Ata: Kazakh State University, 1968.

Ross, R. Cold electron emission patterns due to biological fields. In S. Krippner and D. Rubin (eds.), *The Kirlian Aura.* Garden City, N.Y.: Anchor Books, 1974.

Shipler, D. K. Soviet medicine mixes inconsistency with diversity. New York *Times,* June 26, 1977.

Shpolyanskaya, A. M., et al. Differences in biochemiluminescence intensity of blood serum in tuberculosis and lung cancer. *Psychoenergetic Systems,* 1975, *1,* 67–68.

Stern, J. A., et al. A comparison of hypnosis, acupuncture, morphine, Valium, aspirin, and placebo in the management of experimentally induced pain. In W. E. Edmonston, Jr. (ed.), *Conceptual and Investigative Approaches to Hypnosis and Hypnotic Phenomena*. New York: New York Academy of Sciences, 1977.

Stewart, D.; Thompson, J.; and Oswald, I. Acupuncture analgesia: An experimental investigation. *British Medical Journal*, 1977, Part 1, No. 6053, 67–70.

Swann, I. *To Kiss Earth Goodbye*. New York: Hawthorn, 1975.

Szent-Györgyi, A. *Introduction to a Submolecular Biology*. New York: Academic Press, 1960.

Taratorkin, V., and Lazarev, B. Scalpel, laser beam, and ordinary deafness. *Sputnik*, Sept. 1979.

Targ, R., and Cohen, J. Kirlian video photography. SRI Project 3194–3. Menlo Park, Calif.: Stanford Research Institute, 1974.

Tchernogolovina, G. [*June Without Rain*.] Alma-Ata: Jazushi, 1979.

Tiller, W. A. A technical report on some psychoenergetic devices. *ARE Journal*, 1972, 7, 81–94.

———. Some energy field observations of man and nature. In S. Krippner and D. Rubin (eds.), *The Kirlian Aura*. Garden City, N.Y.: Anchor Books, 1974.

Vasiliev, L. L. Atmospheric ions and health. *Punja Medical Journal*, 1958, 7, 270–73.

Vogralik, V. G. [Exaggerated hopes and realistic possibilities.] *Zdorovye*, July 1972.

Westerbeke, P.; Gover, J.; and Krippner, S. Subjective reactions to the Filipino "healers": A questionnaire study. In J. D. Morris, W. G. Roll, and R. L. Morris (eds.), *Research in Parapsychology, 1976*. Metuchen, N.J.: Scarecrow Press, 1977.

CHAPTER 12

Personality, Bioplasma, and Holographic Patterns

> There is no need of any great penetration to see from the teaching of materialism . . . the omnipotence of experience, habit, and education, and the influence of the environment. Man is a natural being. As a living, natural being he is . . . endowed with the natural capacities and vital powers of an active natural being. . . .
>
> Karl Marx (in Easton and Guddot, 1967, p. 176)

Leonid Brezhnev (1976) once spoke about the need for Soviet psychologists to demonstrate loyalty to the teachings of Marx and to develop criticisms of other psychological concepts. Soviet psychologists justify their emphasis on a correct philosophical, dialectical-materialist orientation, and their struggle against "bourgeois idealist" or "vulgar materialist" personality theories, by maintaining that there cannot be valid practice without a proper philosophical base. Soviet personality theorists also maintain that the work of all scientists, including themselves, is based on a matrix of philosophical concepts, explicit or implicit, and that this matrix determines the direction that scientific research takes. For the Soviet personality theorist, one such basic philosophical question is the relationship of mind and matter. This point of view is typified by the following formulation of V. N. Myasishchev (1958), a leading exponent of materialist personality theory:

Without a scientific, materialist psychology, it is impossible to solve the problem of psychogenesis and psychotherapy. Modern Soviet psychology is developing on the foundation of the general theory of dialectical and historical materialism and on the foundation of the teachings of I. P. Pavlov. It takes as its point of departure the sociohistorical and natural historical understanding of man. . . . Man is not only an object, but a subject, whose consciousness reflects reality and at the same time transforms it. [pp. 7–8]

In the United States, personality theorist Gardner Murphy has taken an analogous position:

Perhaps the most prevalent attitude of contemporary psychologists is to regard the problem [of the relationship of mind and matter] as outside the scope of psychology as at present defined. This attitude, however, very naturally means in practice a refusal to admit that any such problem exists. This again turns out upon closer examination to mean among many psychologists that the answer to the problem is quite simple, and that philosophy has made itself much trouble over many unproductive and unreal problems. When we turn to ask what this simple and obvious answer is, we find persisting, without great alteration, a variety of answers prevalent in the nineteenth century, indeed, a number of them prevalent in the ancient world. [Simon, 1957, p. 3]

The "Transforming Experiment"

Soviet personality theorists insist that the basic philosophical problems of psychology must be solved before constructive experimental work can get under way. That they are philosophical materialists is often stated explicitly in their writings; but they make certain to distinguish their Marxian philosophic position from "vulgar" or "mechanistic" materialism. The Soviets point out that Marxian-oriented psychology is not simpleminded and reductionistic. On the contrary, it can subsume the most unusual forms of human behavior and experience, presenting a structure in which they can be understood (for example, Macovski, 1977).

Soviet personality theorists claim that the incidences of neurosis, juvenile delinquency, crime, and drug addiction are much lower in the USSR than in the United States. They state that the "New Soviet Man" demonstrates concern for the common welfare, pride in the achievements of the collective, cooperativeness, patriotism, and a respect for work, rather than self-aggrandizement.

Other evidence cited as validating Soviet personality theory is A. S. Makarenko's achievement in dramatically restructuring the personalities of several thousand delinquent youths through the influence of the peer collective. These successes exemplify the type of experimentation and validation that is most prevalent in Soviet psychology—the "transforming experiment."

An enormous literature has been written about the "transforming experiment," in which individual personalities are assessed in the process of experimental efforts to change personality and behavior in a specified, desired direction. Similarly, it is held that assessment for purposes of vocational guidance is best accomplished by longitudinal observation of the child and young person in their natural settings, rather than by vocational aptitude testing. However, there has been a renewal of interest in the past few decades in the use of tests and questionnaires in assessing vocational aptitudes and motivation (Lomov, 1966), as well as the use of tests to help determine student placement in special schools (Wozniak, 1976, p. 126). Intelligence tests are considered useful in some cases but only show what knowledge has been acquired, not how the knowledge was obtained. Currently, Soviet psychologists hold that the inherited and acquired aspects of mental ability form an indissoluble whole and that the family and school are important determinants of children's talents (Leites, 1979).

A. S. Makarenko (1951) made a significant impact on Soviet personality theory and practice. His major work, *The Road to Life,* is cited in practically all Soviet writings on personality development as well as in books on education and childrearing. In 1920, Makarenko was assigned to rehabilitate children left homeless by the 1917 Revolution and the civil war that followed. In the course of his successful work in rehabilitating young delinquents, he developed a set of theories about personality development that became keystones for Soviet personality research and educational practices. Makarenko held that the moral foundation of the child's personality is the result of assimilating forms of social behavior occurring in the course of a child's relations in a collective school, camp, or commune. No valuable properties of a child's personality can be cultivated without the experience of a collective.

This position became apparent to American psychologist Uri Bronfenbrenner (1970); after visiting several Soviet schools, he concluded:

> . . . The results of this inquiry indicate that the rather different Soviet approach to the upbringing of the young is not without significance for our own problems. . . . Perhaps we have reached the point of diminishing returns in allowing excessive autonomy and in failing to utilize the constructive potential of the peer group in developing social responsibility and consideration for others. . . . What is called for [is] . . . greater involvement of children in responsibility on behalf of their own family, community, and society at large. [pp. 164–66]

A major emphasis in the application of personality theory has been on rearing and educating the "New Soviet Man." Therefore, the large bulk of research and application has been in day nurseries, nursery schools, kindergartens, children's homes, and schools. In the day nurseries connected with factories, to which working mothers bring their infants at the age of two months, one can observe nurses massaging, exercising, and verbally stimulating their charges. Several infants usually are placed in one playpen to encourage early socialization. There they are exposed to novel, stimulating, and colorful toys; the "orienting reflex" is often observed as an infant focuses on a new toy. However, the toy is sometimes moved so that the infant's attention can be refocused on the other infants.

Stress is laid early on social ownership. Children are taught to engage in criticism and self-criticism for the good of the collective, and to build a self-upbringing and self-disciplining collective (Rahman, 1973).

Person and Environment

In 1888, I. P. Pavlov began to study the physiology of digestion in animals. Pavlov elucidated the neuromechanisms regulating digestive activity and, in 1904, received the Nobel Prize for his work.

In his experiments with the salivary response to foods, Pavlov observed a phenomenon that at first he considered a nuisance—the dog salivated not only in response to the introduction of food into its mouth, but also to a variety of neutral stimuli such as bells, which coincided temporally with feeding. A systematic study of this learning process led to Pavlov's formulation of unconditioned and conditioned reflexes (Razran, 1971).

Contemporary Soviet personality theory continues to draw heavily on the heritage of Makarenko, Marxist philosophical works, and the conditioned-reflex theory of Pavlov. The majority of Soviet personality theorists have been associated with pedagogical institutes and the Academy of Pedagogical Sciences. Beginning in the late 1950s, there has been a progressive expansion of personality studies into areas other than pedagogy (or education), and a broadening of their theoretical and experimental bases. There has also been an increasing willingness to acknowledge that the teachings of Makarenko, Marx, and Pavlov, while seminal, are not in themselves sufficient to cover so complex a phenomenon as human personality.

After the 1917 Revolution, the majority of the younger personality theorists set themselves the task of developing a new Soviet psychology of personality. Since Marxism contends that all aspects of a society, including its science, are based upon economic relationships and that science serves the interests of the ruling class, these psychologists had to free themselves of "bourgeois influences" to found a science of personality that would reflect the interests of the new "ruling class," the working people. Thus science was to serve the new society and the "New Soviet Man" (Bauer, 1952).

L. S. Vygotskii (1962) is highly regarded for his original formulations about language and his experiments in personality development. Vygotskii's work was continued by two distinguished pupils, A. R. Luria (1969) and A. A. Leontiev (1977) until their deaths in the late 1970s. Vygotskii is credited with originating the sociohistorical-origin theory of higher human mental functions and was the first to demonstrate the Marxist thesis of the sociohistorical nature of human consciousness (Ziferstein, 1977). Vygotskii held the position that the major determinant of personality is the place one occupies in the system of social relationships and the activities one carries out within that context. Both Vygotskii and Luria were interested in tracing how human behavior originates in simple reactions to stimuli and slowly comes under control of the symbol system of language.

Soviet personality theorists generally view the theories of Carl Rogers (1959) and Kurt Lewin (1935) favorably because they pay greater attention than most non-Soviet psychologists to the effects of the social environment on the development of personality. Further, they study the personality from a holistic viewpoint. The Soviets credit Lewin with refuting mechanistic concepts in psychology and demonstrating that the process of association takes place only when it is a necessary link in a series of activities directed toward the satisfaction of a person's needs.

Gestalt psychology was also praised because its concept of holism was considered compatible with the philosophy of dialectical materialism. Curiously, psychoanalysis was considered "progressive" in the 1920s because of its methodological application of historical materialism. By the 1940s, however, psychoanalysis fell under attack for its excessive emphasis on early experience (Rubinshtein, 1946). In recent Soviet writings on personality theory, criticisms of Freudian psychoanalysis have been moderated. It is held that psychoanalysis created an illusion that it had finally discovered an objective method for uncovering the deep, hidden roots of human experience. Since there was a need for a scientific conception of personality and for an adequate research methodology, the psychoanalysts unjustifiably broadened the conclusions at which they had arrived. While many of the data obtained by the psychoanalytic method were true, the interpretation of these facts was invalid.

Soviet theorists generally applaud the efforts of Alfred Adler and Carl Jung to move away from Freud's interpretation of human personality and to find a place in theory for the social factors in personality development. They also note that Jung was correct in stressing the enormous power of moral strivings, but incorrect in seeing them as having an innate or divine origin.

Soviet theorists are critical of such neo-Freudians as Erich Fromm, Karen Horney, and H. S. Sullivan, although they acknowledge that their theories generally have a clearly defined social direction. The social criticism of the neo-Freudians is regarded as naïve and ineffectual, not going far enough in its critique of "bourgeois" institutions.

Because Soviet psychology closely interfaces with the political system, the ensuing control may have been responsible for the slow growth of the field. For example, the official psychological journal, *Voprosy Psikhologii,* did not appear until 1955. The Association of Soviet Psychologists, sponsored by the Academy of Pedagogical Sciences, was not organized until 1957. Only in 1968 did the Council of the Ministers of the USSR approve the offering of Ph.D. degrees in psychology through Soviet universities (Brozek and Slobin, 1972).

However, there is evidence that Soviet psychologists are freeing themselves of rigid adherence to dogma. Joseph Wortis (1962) found some personality theorists of the opinion that dogmatism hinders the solving of scientific problems in an atmosphere of free discussion among competent specialists. In addition, there is an increased interest in unconscious mental processes and in the emotional aspects of personality. "Set" theory is seen by many as a fruitful approach to the exploration and understanding of unconscious processes.

In addition, psychologists in the USSR have taken an optimistic position about the person's relationship to the physical and social environment. They hold that:

1. The individual can know the true nature of the environment, and the true nature of his or her own physical and social functioning.
2. This knowledge can give a person the power to change his or her material and social environment—and self—for the better.
3. There is a continuous reciprocal—or dialectical—interaction

between the person and the environment. By improving the environment, one makes possible one's own self-improvement, and by improving oneself, one furthers the improvement of the environment.

4. The plasticity of the individual's brain and personality makes positive changes possible at all ages.

5. The individual's "higher" social, ethical, and moral needs are more compelling than his or her "lower" animal needs.

6. In the process of upbringing, these "higher" needs can be used to inculcate socially desirable character traits in children.

7. This process of "correct" upbringing can be continued by individuals themselves—who can also improve their society.

8. A collective society provides optimum conditions for the improvement of humankind.

The unlimited plasticity of the human personality, even at a mature and advanced age, is assumed, and heavy emphasis is placed on those areas of personality theory applicable to child rearing and education, vocational guidance, motivation of workers, improvements in industrial productivity, and the mental health of the masses.

Creativity and Brain Functions

Soviet scientists see mental processes as functions of the brain, the highest form of organic matter. Psychological activities are not localized, but are products of functional cortical systems that develop as a consequence of the organism's interaction with the environment. Damage to a localized area of the cortex need not produce permanent loss of a function because it is possible, by appropriate training, to organize a new functional cortical system that will successfully carry out this activity.

Research by A. R. Luria (1973) in neuropsychology demonstrated that a given psychological activity may be performed by one of several of the brain's cortex systems. For four decades, Luria worked with brain-damaged patients, correlating results of his cleverly designed bedside tests with neurological reports. Luria (1979) separated behaviors into their component parts, then attempted to use the spare "working" systems of the mental apparatus to provide a "replacement" for portions of the cortex that had been destroyed. He viewed the brain as a "working constellation," a point of view resembling that of Karl Pribram, with whom he co-edited a book on the brain's frontal lobes (Pribram and Luria, 1973). This portion of the brain is basic to the regulation, feedback, and control of human conscious activities, all of which are developed through speech and language.

In Soviet brain physiology, plasticity is believed to be the outstanding property of nerve cells, especially those of the brain's cerebral cortex. When a portion of the cortex is destroyed by disease or accident, the function associated with the lost cells often can be regained as other areas of the brain take over that function. This capacity of the brain to restructure itself is believed by Soviet scientists to be based on a plasticity in the nerve cell itself. For example, scientists in the USSR have crisscrossed the leg nerve and the digestive nerve of a dog, finding that the dog will eventually recover its normal walking ability (Peat, 1976, p. 9).

Pavlov saw the force of nature at work in the organism as a whole and in the individual cell, both of which seem simultaneously present in one another. Nature is miniaturized, and it materializes at the very core of being, in its smallest parts. It opens, inwardly, into an internal universe as extensive as the macrocosmic, external one. (Again, this concept resembles Pribram's holographic concepts; in every section of a hologram there exists a miniature duplicate of the entire picture.) Pavlov viewed the whole organism as conscious. However, a psychology which studies isolated behavioral reactions can easily ignore the issue of consciousness. This is not true of Soviet psychologists who, carrying Pavlov's work forward, view consciousness and behavior as a unity, with consciousness formed during practical activity and revealed in the course of that activity. H. S. Kostyuk (1970) pointed out that the psychological riches of an individual are dependent on the riches of one's interaction with the environment. Luria (1966) postulated that:

> The behavior of an animal, however complex, is the result of two factors: inborn tendencies, on the one hand, and direct, individual experience, formed in the course of conditioned-reflex activity, on the other. In contrast to this, the conditions in which a human being is formed include yet a third factor . . . : the assimilation

of the experience of mankind in general, which is incorporated in objective activity, in language, in the products of work, and in the forms of social life of human beings. [p. 22]

In general, Soviet psychology treats creativity as an essential human trait, part of one's need for self-realization through productive work. Imagery is considered to be the basis of creative intelligence (Kabanova, 1971), while emotions are thought to be another component of inventive behavior, and are viewed as part of the image-forming process (Tikhomirov and Vinogradova, 1970). In the United States, studies of the brain tend to focus on motor movements, since these phenomena are easily observable. The Soviets, however, view sensory functioning as being the most important aspect of the nervous system and as constituting the essential organizing process of the brain. Therefore, the Soviet concept of behavior implies orientation and coordination. This process involves the interaction of three types of imagery: an image of the space in which the behavior is to occur (this activity being centered in the brain's occipital and parietal lobes), an image of the position of the limbs and general body posture (centered in the temporal lobes), and imagery of the sequence in which the behavior will take place (centered in the frontal lobes). Thus the organism has a model of behavior based on images of the space in which it will act, of the body's relation to this space, and of the sequence by which it intends to attain the goal. It is by means of this "intentional imagery" that one can control one's own behavior, as in self-regulation activities.

L. L. Vasiliev (1966) suspected that human creative abilities had much in common with psi faculties. V. M. Bekhterev (1973) made an attempt to explain human creativity from a reflexological point of view. Creativity is basic to all human beings because exploration is the most basic reflex of the organism (Tikhomirov, 1969, 1975). Often called the "orienting reflex," this concept dominates the Soviet attempt to understand creativity and similar aspects of human behavior (Sokolov, 1961).

In the "orienting reflex," every part of the organism participates The image is at the reflex's center; Soviets who work with children suggest that an image emerges early in learning, controlling the subsequent functioning of the motor system that develops into a "habit" (Peat, 1976, p. 26).

There can be no behavior without orientation, as a general understanding of the environment is necessary to control one's own behavior (Javrishvili, 1978). Marx observed how people were degraded by work that lacked meaning for them; today, Soviet researchers claim to have found that workers are more productive when they understand the part they play in production—in other words, after their "orienting reflex" has been taken into consideration (Peat, 1976, p. 27). Thus the "orienting reflex" is always a growth reflex, since it allows the organism to change in the process of learning. To create is also to re-create ourselves.

The "orienting reflex" is known to exist in fish, turtles, and birds as well as in mammals. Its four characteristics are its central integration, its exclusivity (that is, it is the only activity present at a given time), its adaptational effect for the organism, and its inclusion of feedback. All these characteristics emphasize its holistic nature and its importance in the development of human potentials.

Some see memory mechanisms as antitheses of creativity, but to P. I. Zinchenko (1968),* they are essential to problem solving. Further, memory is not only a trace of a past event but, more importantly, a precondition for the realization of future actions (Tikhomirov, 1975).

Intelligence is also associated with creativity and is seen as a conglomerate of psychological abilities that become evident when an individual is engaged in various activities (Yurkevitch, 1974). Soviet psychologists take the position that it is impossible to measure intellectual potential as an entity independent of experience and education.

Poetry and Pacing

Accounts of the creative process by Soviet poets reveal the principles enunciated by psychologists in the USSR. For example, Irina

* P. I. Zinchenko is not to be confused with V. P. Zinchenko, coauthor of the 1973 paper on parapsychology in *Questions of Philosophy*.

Snegova (1976) reflects the importance of the growth process in creativity at the ending of her poem *Elegy:*

> A craftsman cannot ever cease creating,
> Or he lets slip the secret of his art. [p. 118]

Andrei Voznesensky (1979), USSR State Prize laureate, reveals the relation between creativity and activity in an autobiographical account:

> I create my poems by pacing the room or, more exactly, my pacing creates me. As I walk I feel the rhythm of the streets, of my own inner turmoil, of the crowd or the forest, almost . . . subconsciously. That was how I wrote my *Parabolic Ballad.*
>
> Why did the highway ending in the night sky dictate to my army boots my *Lament for Two Unwritten Poems?* Why did the blizzard that arose during the evacuation settle in my child memory to howl out the rhythm of *Goya?* Why did the roll and pitch of a ship's deck on the Black Sea whisper to my feet the broken lines of *Oza?*
>
> I don't know. My feet do. [p. 148]

Voznesensky's poem in honor of the Soviet ballerina Maya Plisetskaya evokes vivid imagery:

> . . . There are geographical,
> Temperature and magnetic poles.
> Plisetskaya—she's the pole of magic.
> She whirls the audience into
> The vigorous hole of the
> Thirty-two fouettés
> Of her temperament.
> Enchanting, she whirls on,
> Releasing no one. . . .
> Even her silence is the mad
> Shouting silence of expectation,
> The actively tense silence
> Between lightning and thunder. . . . [pp. 164–65]

Vasili Solovyov-Sedey, winner of the Lenin Prize and composer of popular songs such as "Moscow Evenings," was stationed in Leningrad during the Nazi siege in 1941. Resting after a day of work at the docks, he noticed a group of singing sailors. Wondering if they would ever return to their homes, Solovyov-Sedey wrote "Evening at the Roads," a song that began, "Farewell, beloved city." A few days later he performed it before his fellow composers, but the song met with derision and rejection.

Solovyov-Sedey left Leningrad just before it was blockaded, traveling to the Ural Mountains, where he joined a concert group that entertained soldiers. In 1942, he performed "Evening at the Roads" in a small dugout at the war front. The soldiers enthusiastically asked for a repeat performance, and another. Soon the song was played over the radio, became popular, and stimulated concert invitations from all over the front. Solovyov-Sedey (1979) remarked:

> What led to such an abrupt change in my song's destiny? The fascist hordes had been defeated near Moscow and swept back from a large territory previously occupied by them. Confidence in a speedy return to the temporarily abandoned cities and towns was supported by the military successes of the Soviet army. "Evening at the Roads" fitted in with the people's mood. [p. 75]

In other words, a change in "set" produced a change in the appreciation of Solovyov-Sedey's song.

Stalinist Oppression

According to Soviet psychology, creativity emerges from a person's interaction with the environment. If favorable social conditions are necessary for the maximum development of humanity's possibilities, it would also be true that unfavorable conditions would erect barriers to creativity. Even so, the ability of the creative individual to triumph over adversity is demonstrated by such figures as Boris Pasternak, Alexander Solzhenitsyn, and Andrei Sakharov; each of these Nobel Prize winners in his own way survived conflicts with governmental authorities.

One of the most illustrative examples of Joseph Stalin's oppression and its effects on creativity is the life of Dmitri Shostakovich. In his memoirs, the great composer describes how artists had to behave in order to survive:

An artist whose portrait did not resemble the leader disappeared forever. So did the writer who used "crude words." No one entered into aesthetic discussions with them and asked them to explain themselves. Someone came for them at night. That's all.

These were not isolated cases, not exceptions. . . . It did not matter how the audience reacted to your work or if the critics liked it. All that had no meaning in the final analysis. There was only one question of life or death: How did the leader like your opus? [Volkov, 1979, pp. 95–96]

As Shostakovich was not able to vent his anger in words, he claims to have done so in his music. The Fifth Symphony was meant to describe the composer's moral stress; his Seventh Symphony's so-called invasion theme had less to do with the Nazi attack than with the Stalinist terror. The Thirteenth Symphony was intended as a protest against anti-Semitism, and his Fourteenth evoked the horrors of the Gulag prison camps (Volkov, 1979, pp. xxx, xxxi, xxxiv, xxxvii).

During the 1948 Composers' Congress, Shostakovich, along with Aram Khachaturian and Sergei Prokofiev, was condemned for "antipeople formalism and decadence." Eventually, Shostakovich was "rehabilitated" and, in 1966, was awarded the Order of Lenin. In 1971, he received the Order of the October Revolution and served for many years as a deputy in the USSR Supreme Soviet. Even so, he ended his memoirs describing "the bitterness that has colored my life gray" (Volkov, 1979, p. 276).

Nicholas Margineanu (1980), a Romanian social psychologist, was another victim of Stalinist oppression. Margineanu attended lectures by Sigmund Freud at the University of Vienna, studied with American psychologists Gordon Allport, Gardner Murphy, and Edward Thorndike, and wrote several books in Romanian, English, and French. During the Second World War, he was dismissed from his teaching post at the University of Cluj, in Northwest Romania, by the Nazis.

Margineanu welcomed Hitler's defeat, but in 1948, he was again dismissed from the University by the new Communist government and put on trial. He had been acting as vice president of the Romanian Association for Friendship with the United States; upon his arrest he refused to make denunciations of America and was imprisoned by Stalinist agents. During the first few months of their imprisonment, Margineanu and his 356 fellow prisoners lost an average of 40 percent of their body weight. Food from their relatives arrived and the prisoners went to receive it, against the wishes of their guards. Upon returning to their cells, they found that their clothes had been taken. They were forced into a cold room without windows, where they remained naked for three days and three nights, sometimes collapsing into their urine and feces. They were beaten three times a day as an example to other prisoners not to disobey their guards. Nevertheless, the unity of the prisoners was so great, and their determination so strong, that none of them became ill or even caught a cold during this ordeal.

In 1964, through the intervention of another of Thorndike's well-known students, UN Secretary General U Thant, Margineanu was freed. He insisted he had never mixed in politics because "science is like a coquettish girl, it permits no other flirtations."

From these experiences, Margineanu developed the concept of "height psychology," which explores the interactions among human nature, social relationships, and the cultural environment. Margineanu sees life as a drama; along the way, the individual must make critical choices. If these choices are positive, promoting love and joy, human personality will be fulfilled and social justice will be activated. Without these values, personal and social "height" will not be obtained. It is only these superior values that bring to human beings the true significance of their lives. Margineanu recalls that the idea of "height psychology" came to him when he saw the deep peace in the eyes of some of his fellow prisoners, ready for any sacrifice, including death. "In a dictatorship," Margineanu (1980) concludes, "there are only two ways of living —with less hell around you but with conflicts in your consciousness because of accepting its tyranny . . . [or] with complete hell, namely that of the prison, yet with [peace] in your heart because one has remained in conformity with one's own consciousness" (p. 7).

During my 1979 trip to the USSR, scientists and artists were quick to denounce the Stalinist terror and expressed relief that those days were behind them. However, there also appeared to be a nostalgia for the past, especially for the countryside and villages. Plays, novels, and films expressed this feeling; there was even some sympathy shown for the last Russian Czar and his adviser, the lecherous monk Rasputin. A popular song glorified Rasputin, and a movie vividly portrayed his life story. (The film, in which Vladimir Raikov played a featured role, had never been released prior to this time, for unknown reasons.) However, Stalin's picture could be seen in homes and taxicabs of his native Georgia because, despite his monstrous acts, he was still a "native son."

As Communist Party chairman, Stalin felt that he was qualified to evaluate not only artistic works but also scientific projects. In so doing, he rejected classic genetic theories in favor of those formulated by Trofim Lysenko, who believed that the environment could have a direct effect upon the genetic composition of species. Until Lysenko's fall in 1965, those who disagreed with him could only carry out their research in secret.

Stalin was quite interested in biology and agriculture; as the plans he supported failed to produce larger yields, he blamed others and purged many leading Soviet scientists. When the errors of Stalinism were recognized, liberalization occurred. For example, scientists are not permitted to write *samizdat* or "underground" literature, but they are not penalized for reading it. An end to scientific isolation is seen as advantageous in that the scientific and technical advances of other nations can be shared without the expense of duplication (Medvedev, 1978). Soviet-American contacts in the field of psychology have intensified as a result of this decision (Byrnes, 1976). When I was in Tbilisi, I was told of a successful conference on decision making held there earlier in the year between fifteen Americans and two dozen Soviet behavioral scientists. Other Soviet-American seminars were being planned on such topics as psychophysics and psychophysiology. Everywhere I went, I was asked if I could facilitate joint conferences as well as exchanges of students and scholars. However, these scientific exchanges were curtailed by President Carter in 1980 following the arrival of Soviet troops in Afghanistan. I took issue with this action, agreeing with an editorial in *Science* that stated, "We should not lose contact with some of the best elements of Soviet society, a group that . . . may have a significant influence on future developments in the Soviet Union. . . . In times of political tensions, we should extend collaborations, not cut them back" (Weisskopf and Wilson, 1980, p. 711).

Bioplasma and the "Biofield"

Contemporary Soviet personality theorists continue to adhere to the Marxian ideas that human consciousness is a reflection of the single material reality. Scientific theories, they say, can and must become more accurate reflections of this reality. Only a dialectical materialist philosophy can assure such a "correct" scientific understanding.

However, material reality is extremely complex and cannot be understood by a simplistic, one-dimensional approach. Western personality theory has a number of useful formulations to offer as well. It is in keeping with the tenets of dialectical materialism to employ a multiplicity of approaches and tools, including those available in the West.

Gardner Murphy and J. K. Kovach (1972), writing about psychology in the USSR, describe "the magnitude of its existing and potential impact on the entire body of modern psychology," pointing out that it is "not a closed system" (p. 377). Although Soviet research projects in accelerated learning, hypnotically stimulated creativity, and parapsychology are not part of mainstream behavioral science in the USSR, they do demonstrate an openness to unusual phenomena. Another example of this innovative posture is the concept of bioplasma.

Scientists recognize solids, liquids, gases, and plasmas as the four states of matter. Plasmas are mixtures of subatomic particles, chiefly ions, which are negatively charged electrons and positively charged nuclei. Plasmas can be produced when individual atoms are ionized, resulting from electrons being forced away from their nuclei at high temperatures. Some plasmas are characterized by high temperatures; a candle flame is a plasma, and the aurora borealis, ball lightning, and the sun all consist of plasma. Other plasmas exist at low temperatures; in both cases, charged particles are present, but they have a higher velocity (and less interaction) in the high-temperature plasmas (Adamenko, 1971). Plasmas are used in physics to achieve nuclear fusion and may someday assist in the development of alternative energy sources. In Novosibirsk, devices are being developed that would raise plasma temperatures to the level of the sun, using the heat for energy.

Bioplasma, the hypothesized fifth state of matter, along with plasma, is a "particle soup." In it, free protons, free electrons, and ions (all subatomic particles existing with no nuclei) coexist without a definite molecular structure. Inyushin (1971) has pointed out that bioplasma was first described and named by V. S. Grischenko in 1944. It is said to exist around and within living organisms; bioplasma does not reach the extreme temperatures of plasmas because living organisms have solid-state properties, such as semiconductance. However, in both plasma and bioplasma, the electrons have been "stripped off" the nuclei of the atoms.

A living organism can be described as a "biological field" or "biofield," a field being a region consisting of lines of force that affect each other. This "biofield," according to Inyushin, has a clear spatial formation and is shaped by fields such as the electrostatic, electromagnetic, acoustic, and hydrodynamic. The "biofield" is said to be enhanced by breathing exercises and is adversely affected by tobacco smoke. It is also held that psychic healing, to be effective, must facilitate a positive change in the "biofield" which, in turn, produces a change in the body of the person being treated.

Bioplasma represents one of the components of a living organism's "biofield." As a result, it is difficult to measure or observe bioplasma in isolation from one or more of the other fields (Inyushin, 1970). Due to the equivalence of positive and negative particles in bioplasma, it is more stable than other components of the "biofield" and affords a structure to the "biofield."

The equivalence of positive and negative particles produces an equilibrium that is probably important in the maintenance of an organism's health. Bioplasma is constantly being renewed by the chemical processes within the cells, especially those occurring in the mitochondria—tiny rod-shaped bodies in the cells' cytoplasm. Mitochondria contain many cell enzymes, particularly those involved in the citric acid cycle; Inyushin believes that transfers of electrons from one cell to another occur along the mitochondria.

In addition to the bioplasmic particles reportedly produced by processes in the mitochondria, there is a direct absorption of charges from the environment. The lungs play an important role in the absorption of environmental charges. In the interplay between organism and environment, some bioplasmic particles are absorbed from external sources, while others are radiated into space in the form of "microstreamers" (channels of bioplasmic particles traveling through the air) and "bioplasmoids" (fragments of bioplasma that have broken away from the organism).

Wlodzimierz Sedlak (Sedlak, 1975; Wolkowski, Sedlak, and Zion, 1978), a Polish biologist, has proposed a model of the bioplasmic body that he sees as the basis of electronic processes, chemical processes (such as the release of enzymes), and as the carrier of all information within an organism. For Sedlak, life can be viewed as an electromagnetic phenomenon generated in a medium of protein semiconductors. The biochemical processes familiar to traditional biochemistry take place within this bioelectric medium. "One should think," he proposes, "of metabolism in terms of transformation of energy rather than of matter." The nature of life, therefore, ultimately can be understood through the concepts of plasma and electromagnetic fields. Sedlak and his associates organized a successful conference on the topic of bioplasma at Catholic University in Lubin, Poland, during 1973.

Romanian biologist Eugen Macovski (1977) also has described the semiconducting properties of living organisms. He holds that life is electromagnetic in nature; ions released in metabolism maintain the stability of the organism's "biostructure." This "biostructure" organizes plants and animals, directing their growth and development. Macovski sees the "biostructure" as providing a missing link in Inyushin's theories; the "biostructure" is composed largely of bioplasma, but together with the organism's cell division and molecular structure, it generates bioplasma as well.

Genady Sergeyev (Sergeyev, Shushkev, and Gryaznukhin, 1972) claims to have developed a "bioplasma detector" that can measure alterations in the "bioplasmic field" at distances up to ten feet. He reports recording fields of up to ten thousand volts per centimeter in the area occupied by a target object with no indication of an electrical field between the object and the subject who is attempting to influence it through psychokinesis. Sergeyev (1976) believes that PK is a laserlike polarization of bioplasma and refers to it as a "biolaser effect." Individuals who can create this effect to influence another person adversely are often said to have "the evil eye."

The critical elements of this device are two silver plates and a barium titanate crystal which, when polarized, divides different types of light from one another and sends them in different directions. When he used this device with Kulagina, Sergeyev reported finding a bodily emission of bioplasma (chiefly from the cerebral cortex) when she attempted PK (Sergeyev and Kulagin, 1972).

When he left the Soviet Union after a study tour in 1971, an acquaintance of mine was given a device that was purportedly a bioplasma detector, as well as the blueprints for the device. Unfortunately, the equipment was badly damaged in a taxicab accident while he was being driven to the airport, and the machine reached the United States in virtually inoperable condition. What of the blueprints? Engineers who have studied them admit that the device should be able to detect strong bodily electric or magnetic fields but suspect that so-called bioplasma is a more complex phenomenon—one that the device may not be sensitive enough to measure. In the meantime, Adamenko (1971) suggests that the presence of bioplasma, if it exists, could be detected with a Geiger counter.

The validity of the bioplasma hypothesis is controversial both inside the USSR and in other parts of the world (Van Hasselt, Van Immerseel, and Klijn, 1974; Volkenshtein and Klimontovich, 1979). Some biophysicists doubt that the substance could maintain itself under the temperature and pressure conditions that characterize living organisms because plasma typically exists at very high or very low temperatures and extremely low densities. However, Inyushin has cited several types of experiments that he believes have validated his concept.

Bioplasma can be indirectly studied with Kirlian photography. In experiments with rabbits, it was noted that the corona discharge varied greatly whenever the rabbit was frightened or in pain. The intensity of the reaction increased twofold or threefold at the moment of an electric shock, but there was a return to the corona's ordinary size in a few minutes. By introducing a sensor into the rabbit's brain, an intensity of radiation ten times greater than that observed on the skin and muscles was noted. These experiments, and others like them, suggest that the accumulation of bioplasma is most intense in the brain; less bioplasma is found in connecting tissues and in body organs. In human beings, bioplasmic activity purportedly is found in the center of the spinal cord and at the fingertips as well as in the brain (Inyushin, 1977).

Because the Kirlian corona consists largely of an artificially created field (with which bioplasma may interact briefly before it dissipates), other techniques have been developed. In bioluminescence (the emission of light from an organism from causes other than high temperatures) bioplasma may play a key factor. Inyushin (1977) attempted to inhibit the luminescence of geranium leaves by placing them in a solution of a chemical known as methylene blue. Another group of leaves was not chemically treated and was used as a control. Luminescence decreased to 19 percent of that of the control leaves—perhaps because methylene blue is a strong acceptor of free electrons, one of the components of bioplasma. Additional procedures to study bioplasma are being developed with liquid crystals and lasers; for example, Inyushin suspects that bioplasma is the critical mechanism in acupuncture meridians that enables stimulation of an acupuncture point to affect a distant point of the body.

Mitogenic radiation (a radiation said to be emitted by living cells during cell division) is felt to be one of the major types of bioplasma along with infrared radiation, sound waves, and biogravity waves. The proponents of mitogenic radiation claim that it is produced by cell division (mitosis) and can stimulate the division of other cells (Gurvitch et al., 1974). The best-known studies along these lines were those conducted by V. P. Kaznacheev and his colleagues (1973) with two tissue cultures, separated by quartz dividers, in Novosibirsk. When toxic agents were introduced into one culture, the cells in the other culture also began to die, producing a "mirror effect." The earlier studies by A. G. Gurvitch failed to be confirmed in Western Europe and the United States; however, a partial replication was reported by Australian chemists (Quickenden and Que Hee, 1974). Gurvitch's work is very influential among Inyushin's circle; Gurvitch's notion that light resonance in tissues can stimulate cell division laid the groundwork for laser application in agriculture.

When we visited Inyushin in Alma-Ata, James Hickman and I

gave him a copy of a master's thesis written by D. R. Callahan (1976) at the University of North Carolina's Department of Bacteriology and Immunology. Callahan searched for mitogenic radiation in bacteria, tissue cultures, and yeast but found none; he concluded that "no mitogenic radiation exists in any of the systems studied." Inyushin took the thesis with him, and the next day told us that the instruments Callahan used made it unlikely that he would have been able to detect the radiation. (A similar opinion was rendered by Kaznacheev when Hickman met with him in Novosibirsk a few days later.)

Hickman and I pointed out that if the original report had only contained more details, the "mirror effect" would have stood a better chance of being replicated in the United States. It is generally agreed that ultraviolet radiation can destroy or mutate cells, probably because it is absorbed by DNA (nucleic acid) (Jagger, 1964). However, skepticism has been expressed at the distances involved and the "mirroring" said to take place. We told Inyushin that if more data were available, bioplasma would be taken more seriously and additional work could be undertaken. We were told (as we had been informed before) that Soviet scientific reports are admittedly brief, but not because it is the policy to withhold information. Rather, there was a paper shortage following World War II that set the precedent of short articles. Further, communication among Soviet scientists is both frequent and easily accomplished, thus there is no need to cover material that has already been passed on orally; indeed, many of the papers we read were reports from conferences and symposia. Finally, no amount of descriptive material could substitute for a visit to a laboratory and participation in an actual experiment.

This is the procedure that had been followed in 1976 when Scott Hill visited Alma-Ata. Inyushin had arranged a demonstration that would verify the existence of both bioplasma and psi (Playfair and Hill, 1978, pp. 319–21). Hill was shown a double-walled metal room serving as a Faraday cage, permitting no electromagnetic radiation to enter except the light from the helium-neon laser used in the experiment. Inside the cage, on a table and intersecting the laser beam, stood a plant, the experimental "subject"; outside the cage was the experimental "agent," a cat. The animal was placed in a metal box with only its head visible and was connected to an electrical stimulator outside the cage through electrodes attached to its ears.

After a stable baseline of transmitted light had been recorded from the plant leaf, the cat was put inside the cage with the plant while the leaf tracing continued. Then, at a signal from Inyushin, a technician applied fifty volts in short pulses across the cat's ears, causing it considerable distress. The cruel treatment of the cat seemed to affect the plant as well; Hill reported that the level of light detected as the amount of light transmitted through the leaf increased, indicating less fluid in the leaf and a resulting greater transparency and more transmitted light.

Inyushin claimed to have conducted similar experiments with a human as "agent" or even another plant as "agent." He explained the results in terms of bioplasma, the shape, form, and extent of which could be controlled by the "agent." A similar explanation has been given of psychic healing, PK, and telepathy by Inyushin and his colleagues.

The final proof Inyushin (1979) gave for the existence of bioplasma was the noncontact photograph I had observed in his laboratory. Clear images of plant roots were obtained in complete darkness without direct contact with the film. Dead plants are unable to leave such an image on the film. One advantage of the bioplasmic concept is its ability to offer an explanation of psi phenomena and other unusual characteristics of living systems. Another is its ability to do this within a Marxian materialistic framework.

Germ and Soma

Inyushin conceives of bioplasma as breathing "in one rhythm with the cosmos"; it is the matrix of the "biofield"—a "frozen hologram" (Playfair and Hill, 1978, p. 316). In the holographic process, a record is made of interfering waves; if the record is then illuminated by any of the original waves, an image is produced replicating the original information. This is a powerful tool insofar as any bit of the original is sufficient to recover the entire informational record.

Two different types of bioplasma may be responsible for programming the development of an organism as well as maintaining it once it has developed; Inyushin refers to these as "germ bioplasma" and "soma bioplasma." Germ bioplasma (allegedly found in DNA molecules) has a higher density of electrons than soma bioplasma, according to Inyushin; in addition, it has a wave structure that is more stable. As the major component of the biofield, it initiates cell division. The wave structures of a dividing cell are said to generate a holographic pattern containing information about the division. With each subsequent development of germ bioplasma, more complex holograms are generated containing additional information. Soma bioplasma, which has a greater degree of plasticity than germ bioplasma, generates a holographic pattern that contains information about the mature organism. Soma bioplasma, the highest concentration of which is found in the human brain's gray matter, is more complex than germ bioplasma. As a result, the information contained in its holographic patterns is more complex as well.

If the matrix of an organism's "biofield" is holographic in nature, it contains information not only about that organism itself but about other organisms as well. The wave characteristics of bioplasma enable living organisms to interact at a distance. If space, and even time, present no barrier to information, telepathic, clairvoyant, and precognitive phenomena may occur. Concentrated bioplasma may produce psychokinetic effects in a manner analogous to lightning.

Soviet astronomer and physicist N. A. Kozyrev (1965) holds that time has such characteristics as flow, density, and causal orientation resembling, in a way, the polarization of light. These characteristics are so variable that reciprocal cause-and-effect positions may become reversed. The flow of time as a source of vital processes is especially important in organic life, perhaps enabling one organism to influence another. Time cannot propagate in space; it appears everywhere instantaneously. Again, there are holographic patterns involved that may help explain such phenomena as ESP and PK.

These Soviet attempts to construct holographic models resemble the work of Karl Pribram (1975), who has suggested not only that sensory information is relayed in bits and pieces, to be sequentially reconstructed by neuron interaction, but also that sensory cells can interact so as to form the sort of interference pattern typified by a hologram. Thus brain functioning occurs not only in terms of pathways but also in terms of patterns of neuron firing. Pribram's work generally has been well received in the USSR; his basic idea of diffuse storage of information in the brain is reminiscent of I. P. Pavlov's analysis of each "sensory analysis" system into a nucleus and a peripheral section, and in the concept of "latent reserves," both of which emphasize the diffuse interconnection of fibers from different systems (Peat, 1976, pp. 10–11).

These models of the brain and of the universe are not without their drawbacks. In the case of Inyushin's concepts, one might point out that plasmas are highly unstable. For bioplasma to lay the basis of a "biofield" that organizes and directs life processes, a certain degree of stability would be required. Furthermore, Inyushin does not explain how germ bioplasma initiates cell fission or the timing of this division. If germ bioplasma is stable, why should it split? And if it does split, what governs the timing?

Any meaningful new theory needs to explain the success of earlier theories. Just as Einstein explained classical physics as a special case of general relativity, so must Inyushin explain biochemical data as particular projections of bioplasma and the ensuing wave interactions. Is the biological organism positioned within the bioplasmic sea? Or are pools of bioplasma spatially located within the organism? These are questions that the proponents of bioplasma have yet to answer.

"Bioholography"

Inyushin's most provocative conceptualization is that the bioplasmic wave structure can be described holographically. While Pribram made a holographic interpretation of brain functioning, Inyushin attempted a "bioholographic" interpretation of an entire organism both in its function and in its structure. If Inyushin is correct, an entire organism can be described from information concerning the state of its electrical field; behavioral and medical applications could then be made from this description. It can be held that molecular behavior is reducible to interactions among electrons and nuclei; those in turn may be reducible to basic wave equations (due to the advances made in quantum physics). Thus, in principle, an entire organism can be characterized according to wave equations and, as such, should be replicable holographically from a limited amount of information.

In suggesting medical and behavioral applications of this model, however, Inyushin may be pushing holography beyond its limits. Basically, holography is a technique of processing data, not a mode for analyzing them. It can reconstruct a system but it does not provide for an analytic understanding of a system. While wave equations might be useful in generating a method of reconstructing an organism, they may not be able to handle the complexities involved in analyzing the organisms and their behavior. Millions of waves would be involved as well as millions of interactions.

In much the same way, the model provided by Einstein's theory of special relativity is more encompassing than older models, but it has only a limited bearing on our understanding of physical interactions. Special relativity is most applicable at subatomic levels, while classical physics is still applied to everyday events in the observable physical world. Biochemistry and molecular biology still are able to explain the phenomena of living organisms; if these sciences should stagnate, "bioholography" may be needed.

Until then, Inyushin's model can be viewed as a useful attempt to describe the field effects of living organisms. Further, he has helped to point out that these fields may dramatically affect the organism. Do portions of these fields deserve to be dubbed a "fifth state of matter"? This is a matter of definition. Some scientists would prefer to lump the plasmas together with the gases and deal with only three states of matter. In a similar spirit of reductionism, some would consider the bioplasmic components of fields so ephemeral as to be unworthy of the attention given them by Inyushin.

I believe that the fabric of the universe is woven of a single cloth. But to make sense of the universe, scientists have made arbitrary divisions in this fabric, noting differences in color, texture, and elasticity. Gregory Bateson (1979) has observed, "A world of sense, organization, and communication is not conceivable without discontinuity, without threshold. If sense organs can receive news only of difference . . . then threshold becomes necessarily a feature of how the . . . world is put together" (p. 202). In other words, the bioplasma hypothesis will gain acceptance if it is able to explain data better than any other model, or should data become available that are consistent with Inyushin's explanations of the life process.

If ESP and PK phenomena were to become obvious, rather than obscure, Inyushin would have a framework that could be used for their classification, understanding, and application. Indeed, Soviet psychology stands in a splendid position to explore parapsychological phenomena. From the interest in psi shown by Pavlov, Bekhterev, and Vasiliev, to the statement in *Questions of Philosophy* by Zinchenko, Leontiev, Lomov, and Luria, there is a tradition of cautious openness to ESP and PK that is unmatched by psychological traditions in any other country of the world. In commenting on contemporary Soviet psi researchers, British parapsychologist John Beloff (1979) observes that they are often found wanting in intellectual discipline and restraint, but display exemplary dedication and courage. As their isolation from parapsychologists in other parts of the world disappears, one hopes that their discipline will increase with no diminution of their dedication.

Tomorrow's Science

On my last day in Alma-Ata, I was received by Nikara Bakirovna Abaeva, Minister of Science for the Kazakh SSR and Associate Chairwoman of the Kazakh Presidium (or governing council). I found Abaeva to be one of the most impressive government officials I had met anyplace in the world; her questions were keen, her comments incisive, and her concern for human welfare indisputable.

Adamenko, Romen, and Inyushin joined Hickman, Payne, Verovacki, and me for the reception, as did Romen's wife, Ludmilla, and Lidia Kireva and Olga Zorina, Inyushin's two research associates. I told Abaeva how pleased I was to observe the important role that Soviet women were playing in science and recalled the vital contributions of Valentina Kirlian to the development of electrical photography. In addition, such women as Nina Kulagina and Alla Vinogradova have made themselves available as subjects to researchers studying human possibilities.

Abaeva asked what had motivated us to travel halfway around the world to Kazakhstan. I responded that the visit would have been desirable if only Inyushin or Romen had been in Alma-Ata; but with both of these scientific titans in the same place, the trip became mandatory. In addition, I told of our concern for world peace and how person-to-person contact among scientists could play a small but vital role in that quest.

Romen commented that the problem of psychoenergetics is more important than that of the atom. He observed that nations now have defensive techniques to protect themselves against the atomic bomb—but protection against "psychic warfare" has not been adequately explored. Adamenko countered that psi could never be developed to the extent that it would be a viable weapon, but Romen remained unconvinced. Inyushin said that he did not know what military capacity psychoenergetics might have, but confided it might be just as well that scientists did not discover all the secrets of life.

I told the group about secret psi research in the United States, which—so the story goes—has involved a clairvoyance game. The players were asked to identify the shifts of underground weapons in the secret U.S. missile system. This system would constantly shift missiles from one side to another to make their identification (and destruction) impossible. However, the psychic sensitives were said to have identified the missile shifts correctly and consistently eight out of ten times. Although I was skeptical about the report, I noted that its currency in the United States revealed the concern with strategic uses of psi.

Abaeva was far more interested in the topic of healing and asked me about my recent appearance at the United Nations. I replied that before leaving for the USSR, I had lectured on folk healing to the United Nations Parapsychology Club. In addition, I met with Dr. S. A. Malafatopolous, a project director for the World Health Organization. He told me that their goal is the provision of health-care services to everyone in the world by the year

2000. He also told me that he realizes that there may not be enough physicians available to meet this goal; the only viable alternative is to train folk healers to cooperate with the physicians. Malafatopolous had served the UN for many years in Africa. While there, he decided it was foolish for medical personnel to enter into competition with the local witch doctors and shamans. Instead, he began to forge alliances and to train the native healers. He has continued this work on a broader scale, attaining remarkable success but also encountering opposition from such groups as the American Medical Association.

Inyushin compared the situation to that of the cooperation needed between scientists and artists because the scientists alone will not be able to attain an understanding of reality. He also stressed the need for cooperation among all nations to solve the world's problems. Nothing that Abaeva had founded the Dostoevski Museum in Kazakhstan, he cited the great writer's advice:

> To transform the world, to re-create it afresh, men must turn into another path, psychologically. Until you have become really, in actual fact, a brother to everyone, brotherhood will not come to pass. [Dostoevski, 1952, p. 158]

Abaeva told us that Dostoevski had spent several years in Kazakhstan and that he understood the necessity of providing for all the basic human needs—psychological and emotional as well as physical and material. Abaeva concluded our meeting by predicting that the study of the untapped possibilities of human beings will play an important role in the science of the future. But this science will become a reality more quickly if Soviet and American scientists will work together and share information.

As we left for the airport, Lidia Kireva gave me a basket of the huge red apples for which Alma-Ata is renowned. It was a splendid conclusion to my visit. I left the Soviet Union inspired by the new image of the person I had encountered and the new areas of science I saw being developed. Finally, I realized that this goal would be reached more rapidly if the world's researchers would follow the advice of Nikara Abaeva and work together for the benefit of all humanity and for the development of tomorrow's science.

References

Adamenko, V. G. Seminar on the problem of biological plasmas. *Journal of Paraphysics,* 1971, *5,* 105–13.

Bassin, F.; Prangishvili, A.; and Sherozia, A. How the unconscious is manifested in creativity. *International Journal of Paraphysics,* 1979, *13,* 99–113.

Bateson, G. *Mind and Nature.* New York: E. P. Dutton, 1979.

Bauer, R. A. *The New Man in Soviet Psychology.* Cambridge, Mass.: Harvard University Press, 1952.

Bekhterev, V. M. *General Principles of Human Reflexology.* New York: Arno Press, 1973. (Originally published in 1917.)

Beloff, J. Book reviews. *Journal of the Society for Psychical Research,* 1979, *50,* 181–84.

Brezhnev, L. I. In [Twenty-fifth Congress of the Communist Party of the USSR and tasks of Soviet psychology.] *Voprosy Psikhologii,* 1976, *22*(2), 3–8.

Bronfenbrenner, U. *Two Worlds of Childhood: U.S. and U.S.S.R.* New York: Russell Sage Foundation, 1970.

Brozek, J., and Slobin, D. (eds.). *Psychology in the U.S.S.R.: An Historical Perspective.* White Plains, N.Y.: Arts & Sciences Press, 1972.

Byrnes, R. F. *Soviet-American Academic Exchanges, 1958–1975.* Bloomington: Indiana University Press, 1976.

Callahan, D. R. A study of bioluminescence in bacteria and other systems. Unpublished Masters thesis, Department of Bacteriology and Immunology, University of North Carolina, Chapel Hill, N.C., 1976.

Dostoevski, F. M. *The Brothers Karamazov.* Chicago: Encyclopaedia Britannica, 1952. (Originally published in 1880.

Easton, L., and Guddot, K. (eds.). *Writings of the Young Marx on Philosophy and Society.* Garden City, N.Y.: Doubleday, 1967.

Gurvitch, A., et al. [*The Energetic Basis of Mitogenic Radiation and Its Recording on Photomultipliers.*] Moscow: Medicina, 1974.

Holowinsky, I. Z. Contemporary Psychology in the Ukrainian Soviet Socialist Republic. *American Psychologist,* 1978, *33,* 185–89.

Inyushin, V. M. [Laser light and living organisms.] Alma-Ata: Kazakh State University, 1970.

————. Biological plasma of human and animal organisms. In Z. Rejdák et al. (eds.), *Symposium of Psychotronics.* Downton, Wiltshire: Paraphysical Laboratory, 1971.

————. Bioplasma: The fifth state of matter. In J. White and S. Krippner (eds.), *Future Science.* Garden City, N.Y.: Anchor Books, 1977.

————. [Bioplasma—it's a reality! *Engineering and Science,*] May 1979.

Jagger, J. Photoprotection from far ultraviolet effects in cells. In J. Duchesne (ed.), *The Structure and Properties of Biomolecules and Biological Systems.* New York: Interscience, 1964.

Javrishvili, T. D. [*Electrical Activity of the Conscious Brain.*] Tbilisi: Metsniereba, 1978.

Kabanova, E. N. The role of the image in problem-solving. *Soviet Psychology,* 1971, *9,* 346–50.

Kaznacheev, V. P., et al. [Intercellular interactions at a distance. *Chemistry,*] 1973, *46,* 17–23. An extensive discussion of these experiments appears in Chapter 7 of [*Progress in Biological and Medical Cybernetics*] edited by A. L. Berg and S. N. Brajnes, Moscow: Medicina, 1974.

Kostyuk, H. S. [Engels and problems of psychology.] *Voprosy Psikhologii,* 1970, *16*(6), 3–17.

Kozyrev, N. A. An unexplored world. *Soviet Life,* Nov. 1965.

Leites, N. Kids' talents: Inherited? *Soviet Life,* Dec. 1979.

Leontiev, A. A. [*Activity, Consciousness, Personality.*] Moscow: Izdatelistro, 1977.

Lewin, K. *A Dynamic Theory of Personality.* New York: McGraw-Hill, 1935.

Lomov, B. F. [*Man and Technology: Studies in Engineering Psychology,*] 2nd ed. Moscow: Izdatelistro Sovietskoye Radio, 1966.

Luria, A. R. *The Human Brain and Psychological Processes*. New York: Harper & Row, 1966.

———. The neuropsychological study of brain lesions and restoration of damaged brain functions. In M. Cole and I. Maltzman (eds.), *A Handbook of Contemporary Soviet Psychology*. New York: Basic Books, 1969.

———. *The Working Brain*. New York: Basic Books, 1973.

———. Basic approaches used in American and Soviet clinical neuropsychology. *American Psychologist*, 1977, *32*, 959–68.

———. *The Making of Mind: A Personal Account of Soviet Psychology*. Cambridge, Mass.: Harvard University Press, 1979.

Macovski, E. [*The Nature and Structure of Living Matter*.] Bucharest: Editura Academiei Republicii Socialiste, 1977.

Makarenko, A. S. *The Road to Life: An Epic of Education*, 3 vols. Moscow: Foreign Languages Publishing House, 1951. (Originally published in 1933–35.)

Margineanu, N. Depth and height psychology: Self-realisation in self and society. *Association for Humanistic Psychology Newsletter*, March, 1980.

Medvedev, Z. A. *Soviet Science*. New York: W. W. Norton, 1978.

Murphy, G., and Kovach, J. K. *Historical Introduction to Modern Psychology*, 3rd ed. New York: Harcourt Brace Jovanovich, 1972.

Myasishchev, V. N. [Some problems of the theory of psychotherapy.] In M. S. Lebedinskii (ed.), [*Problems of Psychotherapy*.] Moscow: Medzig, 1958.

Peat, R. *Mind and Tissue: Russian Research Perspectives on the Human Brain*. Claremont, Calif.: Khalsa Publications, 1976.

Playfair, G. L., and Hill, S. *The Cycles of Heaven*. New York: St. Martin's Press, 1978.

Pribram, K. H. [*Languages of the Brain*.] Moscow: Progress, 1975.

Pribram, K. H., and Luria, A. R. (eds.). *Behavioral Electrophysiology of the Frontal Lobes*. New York: Academic Press, 1973.

Quickenden, T. I., and Que Hee, S. S. Weak luminescence from the yeast *Saccharomyces cerevisiae* and the existence of mitogenic radiation. *Biochemical and Biophysical Research Communications,* 1974, *60,* 764–70.

Rahman, L. *Soviet Psychology: Philosophical, Theoretical, and Experimental Issues.* New York: International Universities Press, 1973.

Razran, G. *Mind in Evolution: An East-West Synthesis of Learned Behavior and Cognition.* Boston: Houghton Mifflin, 1971.

Rogers, C. R. A theory of therapy, personality, and interpersonal relationships, as developed in the client-centered framework. In S. Koch (ed.), *Psychology: A Study of a Science,* Vol. 3. New York: McGraw-Hill, 1959.

Rubinshtein, S. L. [*Foundations of General Psychology,*] 2nd ed. Moscow: Uchpedgiz, 1946.

Sedlak, W. The electromagnetic nature of life. *Proceedings, Second International Congress on Psychotronic Research.* Paris: Institut Metaphysique International, 1975.

Sergeyev, G. A. [*Biorhythms and the Biosphere.*] Moscow: Department of Natural Science, Moscow State University, 1976.

Sergeyev, G. A., and Kulagin, V. V. Psychokinetic effects of bioplasmic energy. *Journal of Paraphysics,* 1972, *6,* 18–19.

Sergeyev, G. A.; Shushkev, G. D.; and Gryaznukhin, E. G. The piezoelectric detector of bioplasm. *Journal of Paraphysics,* 1972, *6,* 16–18.

Simon, B. (ed.). *Psychology in the Soviet Union.* London: Routledge & Kegan Paul, 1957.

Snegova, I. Elegy. In R. Kazakova (ed.), *The Tender Muse.* Moscow: Progress, 1976.

Sokolov, E. N. Reflex receptor mechanisms. In N. O'Connor (ed.), *Recent Soviet Psychology.* New York: Liveright, 1961.

Solovyov-Sedey, V. A composer looks at his life. *Sputnik,* Sept. 1979.

Tikhomirov, O. K. (ed.). [*Psychological Investigations of Artistic Creativity.*] Moscow: Medicina, 1969.

———. [*Psychological Investigations of Creative Activities.*] Moscow: Nauka, 1975.

Tikhomirov, O. K., and Vinogradova, Y. E. Emotions in the function of heuristics. *Soviet Psychology*, 1970, *8*, 198–203.

Van Hasselt, P.; Van Immerseel, W.; and Klijn, J. A. J. Kirlian photography: The myth of bioplasma. *Medikon*, Apr. 1974.

Vasiliev, L. L. Can we control inspiration? *Soviet Life*, Mar. 1966.

Volkenshtein, I. M., and Klimontovich, N. [Biosplasma—myth or reality? *Engineering and Science*,] Mar. 1979.

Volkov, S. (ed.). *Testimony: The Memoirs of Dmitri Shostakovich*. New York: Harper & Row, 1979.

Voznesensky, A. My path to poetry. *Sputnik*, Sept. 1979.

Vygotskii, L. S. *Thought and Language*. Cambridge: MIT Press, 1962. (Originally published in 1934.)

Weisskopf, V. W., and Wilson, R. R. United States-Soviet scientific exchanges. *Science*, 1980, *208*, 711.

Wolkowski, Z. W.; Sedlak, W.; and Zion, J. The utility of bioelectronics and the bioplasma concept in the study of the biological terrain and its equilibrium. *International Journal of Paraphysics*, 1978, *12*, 51–62.

Wortis, J. A. A "thaw" in Soviet psychiatry? *American Journal of Psychiatry*, 1962, *119*, 586.

Wozniak, R. H. Intelligence, Soviet dialectics and American psychometrics: Implications for the evaluation of learning disabilities. In S. A. Corson and E. O. Corson (eds.), *Psychiatry and Psychology in the USSR*. New York: Plenum Press, 1976.

Yurkevitch, V. S. [Individual differences in self-regulation and the ability to learn.] *Voprosy Psikhologii*, 1974, *20*(4), 84–95.

Ziferstein, I. Soviet personality theory. In R. J. Corsini (ed.), *Current Personality Theories*. Itasca, Ill.: F. E. Peacock, 1977.

Zinchenko, P. I. [Perceptual and mnemonic elements of creativity.] *Voprosy Psikhologii*, 1968, *14*(2), 3–7.

Afterword

This is a highly personal work, whose special values extend in two directions: subject matter and geography. Stanley Krippner's professional and private interests are extraordinarily multifaceted; his contacts are global, reflecting a geographical variety that matches his academic versatility. In earlier writings, notably the autobiographical *Song of the Siren,* Dr. Krippner provided an overview of his research and travels; the particular value of the present volume is its focus on impressions and studies that are specifically linked to several visits to the Soviet Union and the Warsaw Pact countries.

Throughout his career, Krippner has succeeded in maintaining a careful balance between open-mindedness and solid professional standards. This attitude has opened doors for him—and kept them open!—that might have remained closed to someone with a more rigid approach to the concepts and methodology found in the USSR and other countries of Eastern Europe. Dr. Krippner's mixture of tolerance and caution is well reflected on the following pages. A visit to the Soviet Union, and some of its academic circles, is also a visit into the mind and personality of Stanley Krippner. When he addresses his audience, often in the first person, the reader has the feeling of being involved in a conversation —almost hearing the sound of the author's voice. This is, of course, particularly true to those who have attended Dr. Krippner's lectures, participated in his seminars, or observed him as he answered questions from students.

In dealing with the delicate and not always clear-cut subjects of Soviet research, Krippner practices alert observation and a reportorial manner. He is not completely detached from the people or subject matter with which he deals, but manages to maintain a cordial courtesy. This courtesy stands him in good stead when he finds himself forced to comment on some of the apparent short-comings he encounters. Thus, when he observes that Soviet exper-imental methods may lack certain controls, or that their published reports on experiments often fail to contain all the details neces-sary for an adequate comprehension or replication of such tests, he notes that historical and environmental factors appear to con-tribute to such limitations.

All in all, Krippner's role is that of the informed, sympathetic, courteous scholar-traveler who delights in exotic encounters but is not distracted by them; who tells foreign inquirers of U.S. research projects but is more interested in listening than in talk-ing; who is fascinated by novel ideas and techniques but relates them, as it were, in a low voice and with an appropriate caveat here and there.

In an age of rampant specialization, Dr. Stanley Krippner's wide range of interests gives him a unique role. As Faculty Chair-man of the Humanistic Psychology Institute in San Francisco, he is in a position to maintain his long-standing contacts in such areas as child psychology, creativity, parapsychology, and other specialties within psychology, psychiatry, education, and re-lated fields. *Human Possibilities* begins with an inquiry into novel techniques that have emerged in the Soviet Union. Inasmuch as Krippner was one of the pioneers in the study of dream telepathy, it is appropriate that parapsychology should surface in several chapters, notably those dealing with psychokinesis.

It is altogether fruitful, I believe, that Krippner has juxtaposed parapsychological elements with other concepts that might be de-scribed as either psychological or extra-psychological. In dealing with the photographic processes developed by Semyon Kirlian, for example, it is not clear, nor need it be, whether the phenomena in question can be categorized as parapsychological. Hypnosis, for example, was a special area of interest to psychic researchers in the nineteenth century, whereas its uses and mechanisms today belong in several disciplines.

Krippner's comments on fasting therapy are a good illustration of his technique, which observes with keen interest without neces-sarily endorsing everything that is seen. The insight one gathers

under Dr. Krippner's guidance coalesces eventually into an odd
déjà vu experience. Much of what is encountered, though novel
and venturesome, has an air of nineteenth-century experi-
mentalism about it—even when it is as futuristic as "acupuncture
by laser beams." Marxist ideology is ever present, if only in the
influence that the concepts of I. P. Pavlov, electromagnetism, and
certain mechanistic views of the human brain exert over much of
Soviet psychology and psychiatry.

The post-Stalin generation of Soviet scientists, men and women
of Krippner's own generation, are obviously keen to advance
ideas that go beyond the orthodoxies of yesteryear. The Soviet
Union, however, which is consistently interested in scientific and
technological advances abroad, seems oddly ambivalent in regard
to permitting some of its scientists to keep up with the work and
personal views of colleagues abroad. The erratic nature of simple
postal communications in the USSR, to which Krippner occasionally refers, is a case in point.

In his own work, Stanley Krippner shows some of the agreeable
patterns that remind us of the nineteenth-century world traveler
who gave us an informal but informed account of fascinating facts
and impressions from faraway places, made vivid by the personality of the narrator. By straddling some of the attitudes and man-
ners of the nineteenth and the twentieth centuries, Krippner has
provided us with intriguing views and challenging insights.

New York, New York   Martin Ebon

Index

A. A. Uktomskii Physiological
    Institute, 35
Abaeva, Nikara Bakirovna, 324–26
Abortion, 216
Academy of Pedagogical Sciences, 7,
    13, 25, 302, 304
  first lecture on parapsychology at,
    1–4, 8–12, 202
  full name of, 2
Acupuncture, 5, 18, 65, 98–99
  Adamenko on, 271, 272–73
  bioluminescence and, 283–86
  bioplasma and, 318
  in China, 270, 271
  data transmission in the body,
    273–75
  healers (healing) and, 272–73
  Kirlian effect and, 271, 273, 287–88
  laser beams and, 18, 268–97
  meridians of the body and, 271, 272,
    273
  placebo effect and, 99, 291–93
  self-regulation and, 282
Acupuncture points, 270–73, 275,
    291–92
Adamenko, Victor, 4–5, 8, 12, 15, 17,
    19, 23, 45–46, 180, 211–13, 221–22,
    241, 287, 324, 325
  on acupuncture, 271, 272–73
  on basic phenomena, 32
  on bioplasma, 314–15, 317
  electrophotography and, 170–72,
    174, 177–78, 179, 188–89, 211–12,
    273
  exhibition of PK, 20–22
  on healers (healing), 177, 274
  motion picture by, 20, 22, 23
Adler, Alfred, 206, 207, 303–4
Afghanistan, 313
Afterimages, 245
Agricultural Scientific Research
    Institute, 179
Albert, M. L., 158
Alcoholism, 108, 111, 216, 255
Alexander the Great, 195
Alexeev, V. E., 270
Alexeyev, Vasily, 238

Allport, Gordon, 311
All-Union Research Center of Mother
    and Child Health, 260
Amdur, N., 234
*American Journal of Clinical
    Hypnosis,* 117
American Medical Association, 326
American Psychological Association,
    23, 25
American Society for Psychical
    Research, 4
Anakhin, P. K., 282
Andreev, B. L., 218–19
Andronikashvili, Etery, 225
Andropov, Yuri, 287
Anesthesia, self-regulation and, 251–52
Ansbacher, Hans, 206
Anthromaximology, 228
Antiochus, Prince, 195–96
APA Monitor, 25
Aristarhov, V. M., 275
Art of Being Yourself, The (Levy),
    256
Association for Humanistic
    Psychology, 14, 20, 87
Association of Soviet Psychologists,
    304
Astin, A., 206, 228
Astronauts, 11
Austria, 140
Avramenko, R. F., 282

Babaian, E. A., 8
Bach, Johann Sebastian, 133–34
Backes, C. J., 240
Bakirov, A. G., 58, 59–60
Bakuleff, A. N., 270
Barber, T. X., 291
Barzak Education Institute, 163 *n*
Barzakov, Ivan, 163
Basmajian, J. V., 241
Basov, N. G., 276
Bassin, F. V., 194, 202, 203, 205
Bateson, Gregory, 323–24
Bauer, R. A., 302
Beatles, the, 19, 159
Beck, A. T., 91

Beck, Robert, 68
Becker, Robert, 65, 66, 273–75
Bekhterev, V. M., 16–17, 104–5,
    115–16, 140, 307, 324
Bekhterev Institute, 96
Bekmuhambetova, B. A., 279
Belayev, G. S., 256
Beloff, John, 324
Belov, I., 174
Benítez-Bordón, R., 135
Bergman, J., 173
Bernat, Anna, 167–68
Beyasheva, Z. G., 279
Bieliauskas, V. J., 92
Bioenergetic fields, 57
Bioenergetic healing, 3–4
"Bioenergotherapy and Healing"
    (Krivorotov, Krivorotov, and
    Krivorotov), 177
Biofeedback, 10, 241–42, 249
Biofields, the, 314–20, 321
    Inyushin on, 268, 281, 315
Bioholography, 322–24
Biolaser effect, 317
Biological plasma, see Bioplasma
Bioluminescence, 283–86
    self-regulation and, 288–89
Bioplasma, 17, 314–24
    acupuncture and, 318
    Adamenko on, 314–15, 317
    emission of, 317–18
    as the fifth state of matter, 315
    germ, 321–22
    Inyushin on, 315, 318–21, 322
    Kirlian effect and, 317–18
    laser beams and, 281–82, 288
    the mitochondria and, 315–16
    PK and, 316–17
    soma, 321–22
Biostimulators, 289
Bird, C., 65, 66
Bird, Lois, 58–59
Birth-control pills, 216
Black market, 36, 269
Blau, F. A., 72–73
Blindfolds, 5
Blood-sugar metabolism, 250–51
Body radiation, 168–69
Boguslavsky, M. G., 37
Bohm, David, 208
Bohr, Niels, 199
Bolshoi opera and ballet, 6–7, 8
Borún, Krysztof, 166
Borzym, I., 261
Bose, S. N., 275–76
Bowers, K. S., 104
Boyers, D. G., 190
Bradna, Jiri, 56–57
Brain

creativity and brain functions, 305–8
electromagnetic fields and, 62–66
evolution of, 63–64
Luria on, 305–6
microwaves and, 65
Pribram on, 156–58
rehabilitation from injuries to 12–13,
    14
solar magnetism and, 64
Brain/Mind Bulletin, The, ix
Brain neurotransmitters, 84
Brain opiates, 292–93
Brainwashing, 133
Braud, L. W., 207
Braud, W. G., 207
Brenner, D., 66
Brezhnev, Leonid, 27, 286, 298
Bricklin, M., 270
Bronfenbrenner, Uri, 301
Brown, D. P., 82
Brozek, J., 13, 195, 304
Brueghel, Pieter, the Elder, 227
Budzynski, Thomas, 249
Bulgaria, 123–34, 142–43, 161–63
Bulgarian Ministry of Public
    Education, 124
Bulgarian National Commission for
    UNESCO, 124
Bulgarian National Opera Company,
    127
Burchinal, M., 137
Burr, H. S., 274
Burton, L., 179, 189
Butler, Samuel, 215–16
Byrnes, R. F., 313

California, University of (Los
    Angeles), 72
Callahan, D. R., 319
Canada, 137–38, 271
Carter, Jimmy, 263 n, 313
CAT scanners, 186–87
Cephalization, 63–64
Chall, J. S., 155
Chamberlain, John, 56
Chaplin, Charlie, 111
Charcot, J. M., 254
Chaves, J. F., 291
Chekorov, P. R., 278, 280, 281–82
Chen, C., 75
Chertok, Léon, 206, 220
Chess match (world championship),
    233–34
Chijov, V., 33, 36
Children in the USSR, 259–63
Children of Theatre Street, The
    (documentary), 261
Children's Sports School, 262–63
Child Study Center, 123

China, acupuncture in, 270, 271
Chinese Communist Party, 75
Chlorpromazine, 91
City Lights (motion picture), 111
Clairvoyance, 5, 18, 19, 72, 167, 325
  proposed term for, 2–3
Clein, Marvin, 240
Cocteau, Jean, 199, 200
Cohen, Jonathan, 288
Coleridge, Samuel Taylor, 197
Collectives, personality theory and,
  95–96, 195, 300, 301–2
Commission for the Development of
  Human Potential, 225–28
  emblem for, 227
Commission for the Study of Mental
  Suggestion, 105
Committee of Applied Cybernetics, 58
Composers' Congress (1948), 311
Conditioning, 9–10, 302
Consciousness, 196
  altered state of, 111–13, 163
  Leontiev on, 13–14
  Lozanov on, 162
  Marxism on, 13, 314
  Pavlov on, 306
  subsystems of, 161–64
Cook, S. A., 61
Cooper, Linn, 151
Cosmonauts, 11, 243, 255, 285
Cott, Allan, 87, 89, 91
Coué, Emile, 254
Creativity
  brain functions and, 305–8
  dreams and, 197–201
  environment and, 310–14
  hypnosis and, 104, 106–8, 118, 217
  intelligence and, 308
  poets, 308–10
  set and, 199–201
  sleep and, 115
  sublimation and, 204
Crime, 300
Czechoslovakia, 55–56, 167, 209
  1973 Conference in, 54–76
Czechoslovakian Scientific Technical
  Association, 54

Dadashev, Tofik, 6, 58–59
Dahl, Nikolai, 104
Dante, 216
Dartmouth College, 155–56
Davidson, Richard, 2, 4–10, 15, 32, 33,
  107–9
Davis, Mikol, 179
Davitashvili, Juna, 221–22, 223
Dean, Douglas, 289
Déjerine Psychosomatic Institute, 201,
  206

Demikov, V. I., 37
Department of Technical
  Parapsychology, 2, 26, 27
Dermo-optical effect, *see* Skin vision
"Devil's Sonata, The" (Tartini), 198,
  199, 201
Diamond, M. C., 285–86
Dick, W., 45, 46, 58, 75, 176, 183
Dilman, V. M., 256
Divorce, 216
Djeparidze, Temo, 224
Dmitrov, Georgi, 126
DNA, 319, 321
Dorofeev, J. F., 13
Dostoevski, Fyodor, 197, 326
Dostoevski Museum, 326
Dowsing, 5, 18, 24, 59–61
  proposed term for, 3
Drabnika, S., 271
Dreams, 75–76, 207–8, 282–83
  creativity and, 197–201
  as preverbal thought, 203
  telepathy and, 10–11
  the unconscious and, 196–201, 203,
    205
Dream Studies and Telepathy
  (Krippner and Ullman), 32
Dream Telepathy (Ullman, Krippner,
  and Vaughan), 3 *n*
Drug addiction, 8, 111, 300
Drugs, 95, 110–11
  suggestions and, 123
  in treatment of schizophrenia, 91
Dubrov, A. P., 54, 58, 62, 66, 209, 210
Dumitrescu, I. F., 166, 183–87, 188
Duplessis, Yvonne, 5 *n*
Duvenyan, R. A., 290
Dynamic psychotherapy, 95

East German Sport and Gymnastic
  Federation, 236
East German Sports and Physical
  Culture Work Federation, 235
East Germany, 139, 150–51, 234–37
Easton, L., 298
Ebers papyrus, 103
Ebon, M., 67, 76, 257, 332–34
Edelberg, R., 181
Edelson, E., 170, 173
Educational hypnosis, 123–24
Eidson, W. W., 181
Einstein, Albert, 275–76, 323
Electroencephalograms (EEG), 114,
  279
Electroluminescence, 186
Electromagnetic fields, 24–25, 61
  the brain and, 62–66
  ESP and, 167, 209
  in evolution, 62–64

glial cells and, 65
immune system and, 64
nature of life and, 316
Electromagnetic Fields and Life
    (Presman), 60–61
Electromagnetic radiation, 65
    telepathy and, 105
Electromyograph (EMG), 56–57
Electronography, 183–87
Electrons, pictures of, 187–89
Electrophotography, 169–89, 325, 333
    Adamenko and, 170–72, 174, 177–78,
        179, 188–89, 211–12, 273
    apparatus for, 171
Electrosleep, 81–83
Electrosone 50 experiments, 81–83
Electrostatics, 20–22
    healers (healing) and, 176–77
Elegy (Snegova), 309
Elliott, L., 238
Emmons, W. H., 248
Engels, Friedrich, 75, 111–12, 194
Enkephalin, 84, 292–93
Environment, creativity and, 310–14
Erasistratos, 196
Erickson, Milton, 151
Ervin, Frank, 92
Esalen Institute, 2, 22, 241
ESP, *see* Extrasensory perception
    (ESP)
Eugen, C., 184
European Congress of Hypnosis in
    Psychotherapy and Psychosomatic
    Medicine, 139
Evans, F. J., 291
"Evening at the Roads"
    (Solovyov-Sedey), 310
Evening Leningrad, 37
Evolution
    of the brain, 63–64
    electromagnetic fields in, 62–64
Experimental Commission on
    Hypnotism and Psychophysics, 105
Experiments in Distant Influence
    (Vasiliev), 105
Expo 67 (Montreal), 271
Extrasensory perception (ESP), 10, 25,
    62, 65, 74, 76, 207, 289, 321, 324
    electromagnetic field and, 167, 209
    emotional factors in, 61
    hypnosis and, 167–68
    low-frequency waves and, 72
    lunar cycle and, 19
    Naumov on, 15–16
    the *Nautilus* experiment, 15–16
    proposed term for, 2
    spontaneous, 19
Eye-roll test, 109–10

Fabricated Miracles (Lvov), 37
Fahler, J., 38, 40, 41–42
Fasting treatment for schizophrenia, 5,
    16, 87–92, 210–11, 333
Fate, 169
Faust, D. L., 181
Feldshers, 269
Fészek Club, 158
Field dependence, 82–83
Field independence, 82–83
Fischer, R., 111
Fluorescence, 71–72
Foley, C., 104
Forward, R. L., 275–76
Foulkes, R. A., 61
Foundation for Research on the
    Nature of Man, 4
Four Young Couples (Khodakov), 216
France, 138
Frank, J. D., 84
Franklin, Benjamin, 103
Free, Ricky, 239
Free German Labor Federation, 236
Freud, Sigmund, 141, 197, 202, 203,
    311
    personality theory and, 303, 304
    on the unconscious, 203, 204, 205,
        206, 213
Friendship, love and, 215
Frigidity, 98, 99
Fromm, Erich, 304
Funding, 4
Füredi, Eva, 158–60

Gallagher, J. J., 262
Gamaleya, N. F., 277, 279, 280
Gardner, Martin, 32–33, 38
Gateva, Evilina, 139
*General Principles of Human
    Reflexology* (Bekhterev), 17
Georgian Academy of Sciences, 201
Germ bioplasma, 321–22
Gerovital, 235
Gestalt psychology, 303
Getsla, Karen, 289
Glial cells, electromagnetic fields and,
    65
Goethe, Johann Wolfgang von, 197
Goldin, Joseph, 225–27
Goleman, D., 157
Golovanov, G., 184
Golovanov, N., 184
Golvin, V., 182
Gorky Medical Institute, 98
Gorsky, V. B., 259–60
Gorvatsevich, S. V., 37
Gover, J., 290
Graff, E., 173
Grateful Dead, the, 11, 19

Gravitational waves, 66
Great Britain, 160
Great Soviet Encyclopedia, 177, 213–14
Green, A., 242, 249
Green, E., 242, 249
Greenberg, Ira, 123
Gris, H., 45, 46, 58, 75, 176, 183
Grischenko, V. S., 315
Grotta, D. A., 289
Group Hypnotherapy and Hypnodrama (Greenberg), 123
Group therapy, 95–96
Gryaznukhin, E. G., 316
Guddot, K., 298
Gumenok, H. M., 256
Gurvich, A. G., 68, 69, 70
Gurvitch, A. G., 177, 318

Hall, Spencer, 111–12
Hansel, C. E. M., 106
Harari, Carmi, 14, 15, 19, 23, 24
Hargitai, Peter, 151–53, 159
Harris, Robert, 15
Harvalik, Zaboj, 61
Hasted, John, 207
Hawaii, University of, 9
Head state, the, 63–64
Healers (healing), 3–4, 17–18, 57–58, 96, 103, 123, 175–77, 207, 325, 326
  acupuncture and, 272–73
  Adamenko on, 177, 274
  electrostatics and, 176–77
  expectancy and, 290–93
  holistic approach to healing, 57
  Kirlian on, 176, 177
  magnetic field and, 257–59
  Naumov on, 177
  self-regulation and, 257–59, 289
  television documentary on, 222–23
  the unconscious and, 221–24
  Yoga and, 259
  Zezulka on, 57–58
Health-care system in the USSR, 92–93
Health vacations, 269–70
Height psychology, 312
Heinze, Guenther, 236–37
Hemodialysis, 92
Herbal medicine, 270
Herbal Plants of the USSR (Alexeev), 270
Herbert, Benson, 35, 36, 40, 41, 42, 43, 45
Herring, P., 283
Hickman, James, 14, 16 *n*, 21 *n*, 208–9, 212, 240–41, 286, 318–19, 324
  motion picture made by, 18–19, 20
Hilgard, E. R., 116, 220
Hill, Scott, 271, 282, 285, 319–20

Hines, W., 92
Hock, A., 198
Hoffer, A., 86, 250
Holland, J. A., 92, 93
Hollon, S. D., 91
Holography, 157
Holowinsky, I. Z., 262
Homosexuality, 216
Hong Kong, 15
Honorton, Charles, 10, 48, 49, 50
Horney, Karen, 304
House of Culture (Czechoslovakia), 54
House of Friendship (USSR), 24, 34
Houston, Jean, 7
Howard, W. L., 240
Howe, Elias, 198, 199, 201
Hubacher, John, 178–79
Hughes, W., 197
Humanistic Psychology Institute, 333
Human rights, vi–viii, 268
Hungarian Ministry of Culture, 147, 158, 163
Hungarian Scientific and Technical Societies, 147, 148, 151, 160 *n*, 163
Hungary, 139, 147–64
Hung Chi, 75
Hypnagogic state, 248–49
Hypnopedia, *see* Sleep learning
Hypnopompic state, 248–49
Hypnoproduction
  adverse effects from, 116–17, 118
  limitations of, 110–11
  sleep and, 115
  three elements in, 113–15
Hypnosis, 5, 72, 103–21, 207, 217–21
  creativity and, 104, 106–8, 118, 217
  educational, 123–24
  ESP and, 167–68
  imagination in, 104
  pain and, 292
  Pavlov on, 103, 115
  rhythm and, 151
  role playing in, 104, 106–8, 110
  self-regulation and, 254
  set and, 109–10
  sports and, 240
  See also Suggestopedia
Hypnotic Induction Profile, 109–10

Idiot, The (Dostoevski), 197
"Image Modulation in Corona Discharge Photography" (Pehek, Kyler, and Faust), 181
Immune system, electromagnetic fields and, 64
Impotence, 98, 99
India, 15, 123
Institute for Biophysics, 24

Institute for Brain Research, 105
Institute for Soviet-American Relations, 24
Institute of Defectology, 2
Institute of Developmental Physiology and Physical Education, 2
Institute of General and Educational Psychology, 2
Institute of Philosophy, 13
Institute of Physiology, 13
Institute of Psychiatry, 98, 214
Institute of Psychology, 13
Institute of Reflex Therapy, 290
International Association for Psychotronic Research, 76, 166, 209
International Congress of Applied Psychology, 13
International Congress of Psychology, 14, 15, 23, 202–3
International Congress on Psychotronic Research, 5 n, 54–76, 210
International Council of Sport and Physical Education, 263 n
International Herald Tribune, 262
International Journal of Clinical and Experimental Hypnosis, 117
International Journal of Paraphysics, ix
International Kirlian Research Association, 173, 180
International Meeting on the Problem of Bioenergetics and Related Areas, 16–22, 25
International Society of Hypnosis, 117
International Symposium on the Problem of Unconscious Mental Activity, 195–228
emblem of, 200–1
Intourist, 1–2, 18, 19, 20, 241
displeasure shown by, 22
shakeup in officials of, 23–24
Inyushin, T. P., 284
Inyushin, Victor, ix, 17, 23, 213, 241, 324, 325, 326
on biofields, 268, 281, 315
on bioplasma, 315, 318–21, 322
laser beam experiments, 278–90
Iowa State University, 124, 134–37
Iran, 15
Iridology, 211
Ivanov, I. P., 256
Ivanov, N. V., 81, 96
Ivanova, Barbara, 257, 259
Izvestiya, 211, 241

Jagger, J., 319
Janet, Pierre, 254
Jänicke, Klaus, 139

Japan, 15
Jarovinsky, Alexander, 147
Javrishvili, T. D., 308
Jodko-Narkiewicz, Jacob, 169
Johnson, Kendall, 173
Joines, W., 179, 189
Journal of Paraphysics, 35
Journal of the American Society for Psychical Research, 10
Journal of the Society for Psychical Research, 27
June Without Rain (Tchernogolovina), 289
Jung, Carl, 207, 304
Juvenile delinquency, 300

Kabanova, E. N., 307
Kadzhaya, V., 238
Kaempffert, W. A., 198
Kajdos, V., 271
Kakabadze, Amiry, 224–25
Kakabadze, David, 224
Kamensky, Yuri, 8
Kampman, Reima, 116–17
Karl Marx University, 139, 150–51
Karpov, Anatoli, 233–34
Kartashev, A. I., 37
Kasatkin, Vasili, 75, 283
Katkov, A., 259
Katz, P., 235
Kaufman, L., 66
Kazakh State University, ix, 286
Kazanetz, E. P., 93
Kazhinsky, B. B., 17
Kaznacheev, V. P., 16 n, 70, 319
Kedrov, B. M., 115
Keil, H. H. J., 35, 36, 38, 39, 40, 41, 42, 43, 44
Kenchadze, Gyorgi, 223
Khachaturian, Aram, 311
Khodakov, N., 216
Kholodov, Y. A., 58, 62–63, 65, 66, 68
Khromchenko, M., 81
Khrushchev, Nikita, 76, 270
Kilmontovich, N., 317
Kim, Nelli, 259
King, Martin Luther, 8
King Henry VI (Shakespeare), 197
Kireva, Lidia, 286, 324, 326
Kirlian, Semyon, 14, 169–70, 173, 174, 175, 176, 177, 178, 189, 212, 273, 287, 333
education of, 169
on healers (healing), 176, 177
hopes for electrophotography, 179–80
Kirlian, Valentina, 4, 14, 15, 170, 173, 174, 175, 176, 177, 178, 179, 212, 273, 287, 325

Kirlian Aura, The (Rubin and Krippner), 15
Kirlian effect, 4, 14, 17, 19, 20, 166–93, 211–12, 325, 333
  acupuncture and, 271, 273, 287–88
  bioplasma and, 317–18
  body moisture and, 181–83
  body radiation and, 168–69
  phantom leaf effect and, 178–79
  pictures of electrons, 187–89
Kirov, S. M., 286 *n*
Kirov Ballet, 261
Kitaigorodsky, Alexander, 37, 74
Kitaygorodskaya, G. A., 141–42
Klijn, J. A. J., 317
Klimuszko, Czestaw, 167
Knights of the Round Table, The (Cocteau), 199, 200
Kobozev, N. I., 69
Koestler, Arthur, 32
Kogan, I. M., 72–73
Kolodny, L., 38
Kolonay, Barbara, 239
Komitiani, Gregor, 176
Konikiewicz, L. M., 181–82
Kopilov, I. A., 256
Korchnoi, Victor, 233–34
Kordyukov, E. V., 258
Korytinyj, D. L., 279
Kostyuk, H. S., 306
Kosygin, Aleksei, 287
Kovach, J. K., 314
Kozyrev, N. A., 64, 321
Krippner, Stanley, 3 *n*, 10, 11, 15, 25, 32–33, 49, 56, 57, 82, 87, 122, 155, 173, 178 *n*, 184, 197, 271, 290, 332–35
Krivorotov, Alexei, 175–77, 223
Krivorotov, Victor, 177, 223–24
Krivorotov, Vladimir, 177
Krmessky, Julius, 55
Kroger, W. S., 103
Krokhalev, G. P., 208
Krueger, A., 285
Kulagin, V. V., 12, 35, 38, 39, 41, 42, 43, 44, 317
Kulagina, Nina, 12, 17, 32–46, 51, 212–13, 325
  in altering biological systems, 41–42
  in altering moving objects, 40–41
  controversy about, 32–38
  emission of bioplasma by, 317
  motion pictures of, 34, 45–46, 47, 48
  Naumov and, 34, 41, 42, 45
  photographic effects by, 42
Kulin, E. T., 212
Kupriyanovich, L., 200
Kyler, H. J., 181

LaMothe, J. D., 56
Landahl, Christer, 139–40
Lane, Earle, 179
Langans, L. B., 37
Languages of the Brain (Pribram), 156
LASER (Light Amplification by Stimulated Emission of Radiation), 276
Laser beams, 157
  acupuncture and, 18, 268–97
  application of, 277–80
  bioplasma and, 281–82, 288
  experiments by Inyushin, 278–90
  resonance and, 281
Lauck, D., 239
Lazarev, B., 277
Lazurkina, Darya, 76
Learning in New Dimensions, 160 *n*
Legerdemain, 37, 39
Leipzig Institute of Sports, 234–35
Leites, N., 300
Lenin, V. I., 7, 13, 75, 76, 95, 126, 194, 260
  on dialectical materialism, 1
Lenin Prize, 14, 309
Leonidov, I., 169
Leontiev, A. A., 303
Leontiev, A. N., 24, 213–14, 177, 324
  on consciousness, 13–14
Lepak, Edward, 169
Leu-endorphin, 92
Levine, J. D., 84
Levy, V., 256
Lewin, Kurt, 303
Lewis, A. J., 217–18, 247, 249, 251
Licensintorg, 19
Life expectancy, 268
Lipsyte, Robert, 238
Lobzin, V. S., 256
Lomov, B. F., 13, 14, 24, 300, 324
Love
  friendship and, 215
  set and, 215–16
Low-energy waves, 64–65, 72
Lozanov, Georgi, 123–24, 126, 127, 129–34, 137, 141, 143, 153, 155, 161, 217–18, 225
  on accomplishments in suggestopedia, 147
  on consciousness, 162
  cultural differences transcended by, 163–64
  deviations from material of, 160
  on fundamental principles of suggestopedia, 132–33
  on importance of music in learning, 139–40
  on positive expectancy, 138–39

on set, 140
unique aspect of procedures of, 156
LSD, 8, 110–11
Lubinskaya, C. M., 256
Ludwig Voltzmann Institute for
    Learning, 140
Lunar cycle, ESP and, 19
Luria, A. R., 6 n, 12–13, 14, 95, 202,
    303, 324
    on the brain, 305–6
    Naumov and, 24–26
    personality theory and, 305–7
Lvov, Vladimir, 37, 38, 74, 178, 179,
    221
Lysenko, Trofim, 313

Macbeth (Shakespeare), 197
Machaidze, Levan, 222
Macovski, E., 300, 316
Magnetic field, healers (healing) and,
    257–59
Mahler, Halfdren, 223
Maimonides Medical Center, 3, 9, 10,
    14, 35, 47, 94, 123–24
    Dream Laboratory at, 3, 4, 23,
    32–33, 37, 47, 81–83, 166
Maire, L. F., 56
Makarenko, A. S., 194–95
    personality theory and, 300–1, 302
Malafatopolous, Dr. S. A., 325–26
Manczarski, Stefan, 166, 167
Manic-depressive psychosis, 93–94
Mankind Research Foundation, 124,
    174
Man with a Shattered World, The
    (Luria), 12–13
Margineanu, Nicholas, 311–12
Markley, O. W., 18
Martin, D. J., 135
Marx, J. L., 292
Marx, Karl, 13, 95, 194, 302, 308
    on man as a natural being, 298
Marxism, 76, 320, 324
    concept of consciousness in, 13, 314
    interpretation of psychology and, 13
    personality theory and, 299–300, 302,
    303
Masters, Robert, 7
Mastrion, Ronny, 14, 174, 175
Masturbation, 216
Materialism and Empiro-Criticism
    (Lenin), 75
Matkhanov, Guennadi, 131
Matter, states of, 314–15
Maurice Thorez Institute of Foreign
    Languages, 140, 142
May, Rollo, 201
May Day Club, 16, 18
Mecacci, L., 13

Medvedev, Z. A., 313
Melville, Herman, 215
Memory, 6, 157–58
    reserves of, 199–201
Mendeleev, Dmitri, 115, 197
Mental illness, concept of, 93–98
Mentalists, 26, 58–59
Mesmer, Franz Anton, 103, 254
Microstreamers, 316
Microwave ovens, low-energy waves
    from, 64–65
Microwaves, the brain and, 65
Miele, Philip, 124
Mikalevskaya, K. N., 182–83
Mikalevsky, K. I., 182–83
Mikulin, Alexander, 237–38
Milbourne, Christopher, 47
Miller, J. G., 206
Minayev, Nikolaus, 5
Mind of a Mnemonist (Luria), 6 n
Mirovsky, N., 256
Mirror effect, 71, 168–69
Mitchell, Edgar, 11
Mitochondria, bioplasma and, 315–16
Mitogenic radiation, 66–73, 318–19
Mitrofanova, N., 271
Montandon, H. E., 176 n
Monteith, Henry, 173
Morgun, V. F., 156
Morris, L. A., 91
Moscow Medical Institute, 242
Moscow Psychiatric Institute, 87–92
Moss, T., 14, 35, 36, 173, 174, 178–79,
    183, 273
Motion pictures, 5–6, 46, 50, 106–7,
    221
    by Adamenko, 20, 22, 23
    documentary on ballet, 261
    by Hickman, 18–19, 20
    of Krmessky, 55
    of Kulagina, 34, 45–46, 47, 48
    by Raikov, 220
    statebound learning in, 111
    on suggestopedia, 129, 130, 217
Motoyama, H., 273
Mudrov, M. Y., 202
Murphy, Gardner, 9, 10, 23, 299, 311,
    314
Murphy, M., 238, 239, 241
Muscle tension, 6, 56–57
Musial, Z., 167
Music
    learning to, 131–34, 139–40, 150–51
    set and, 224–25, 310
Myasishchev, V. N., 299
*Mysterious Phenomena of the Human
    Psyche* (Vasiliev), 3, 105

Nagorny, V. A., 256

Natadze, R. G., 85
National Commission on the Artificial
    Prolongation of Human Life, 237
National Patent Development
    Corporation, 81
Naumov, Edward, 2, 5, 7, 14, 23, 34,
    67, 69, 104, 213
    arrest and sentence of, 26–28
    dialectical materialism and, 3–4
    on ESP, 15–16
    on healers (healing), 177
    on importance of parapsychology, 4
    on information exchange, 9, 12
    Kulagina and, 34, 41, 42, 45
    Luria and, 24–26
    proposed terminology of, 2–3
Nautilus experiment, the, 15–16
Nepal, 15
Neurological Surgical Institute, 75
New Age Blues (Bossman), 56
*New Data on the Latent Abilities of
    Human Personality* (ed. Pushkin),
    210
News Information, 261
New Soviet Psychic Discoveries, The
    (Gris and Dick), 58
Newsweek, 153
New York *Daily News,* 26
New York State Department of
    Mental Hygiene, 33 n
Nicholson, D. R., 141
Nikolaev, Karl, 8–9
Nikolayev, Yuri Sergeyvitch, 5, 16,
    87–92, 210
    Pavlov and, 89–90
Nixon, Richard, 27
Nobel Prize, 187, 276, 302, 310
Nonspecific stress, 90
Northern Neighbors, 249–50

Objectification
    set and, 119
    Uznadze on, 204
"Objects Moved at a Distance by
    Means of a Controlled Bioelectric
    Field" (Adamenko), 22
Occupational therapy, 95–96
Ochorowicz, Julian, 167
Olympics (1976), 234, 236, 259
Olympics (1980), 218, 226–27, 263
Omura, Yoshiaki, 180
Orienting reflex, 307–8
Osmond, H., 86
Ostrander, Sheila, 9, 15–16, 150, 175
Ostroumov, A. A., 202
Oswald, I., 292
Ouidin coils, 171
Ovchinnikova, I., 260, 261, 262

Overton, D., 163
Owen, A. R. G., 46

Pain
    beneficial aspect of, 293
    hypnosis and, 292
    self-regulation and, 251–52
Palmour, Robert, 92
Paraconscious learning, 129–30
Paradiagnostics, 177
Parapsychological Association, 189
"Parapsychology: Fiction or Reality?"
    (Zinchenko, Leontiev, Lomov, and
    Luria), 24–25
"Parapsychology in the U.S.S.R."
    (Krippner and Davidson), 32, 33
Paris, University of, 138
Parise, Felicia, 47–51
Parker, Shelby, 57
Pasternak, Boris, 310
Patrovsky, V. A., 57
Pavlita, Robert, 55–56
Pavlov, I. P., 7, 13, 17, 75, 105, 123,
    194, 195, 322, 324, 334
    on consciousness, 306
    on hypnosis, 103, 115
    influence of, 94, 97–98, 137
    Nikolayev and, 89–90
    Nobel Prize received by, 302
    personality theory and, 9–10, 299,
    302, 306
    on sleep, 248
    suggestopedia and, 122, 137
    on the unconscious, 202
Pavlov, S., 263
Pavlov, Volodya, 75
Pavlova, Nadya, 261
Payne, Mary, 208–9, 240–41, 286, 324
P. B. Gannushikin Memorial Hospital,
    16, 87–92, 93, 96, 210
Peat, R., 65, 306, 308, 322
Pehek, J. O., 181
Penfield, Wilder, 220
Pepperdine University, 124
Personality theory, 194–95, 298–308
    collectives and, 95–96, 195, 300,
    301–2
    creativity and brain functions, 305–8
    environment and creativity, 310–14
    Freud and, 303, 304
    Luria and, 305–7
    major emphasis in, 301
    Makarenko and, 300–1, 302
    Marxism and, 299–300, 302, 303
    Pavlov and, 9–10, 299, 302, 306
    physical and social relationship in,
    304–5
    reserves of personality, 208–11
    set and, 304

the transforming experiment,
299–302
Peter the Great, 269
Petroff, F. N., 270
Petukhov, V. G., 67, 68, 69
Phantom leaf effect, 178–79
Philipov, E. R., 141
Philipov, Elizabeth, 124
Photomultiplier tubes, 68, 70
Photon gas, 275–76
Pillar, Kathy, 147–48
Piller, Katja, 139
Pirogov, N. I., 202
Pirossmanashvili, Niko, 225
Pirozyan, L. A., 275
PK, *see* Psychokinesis (PK)
Placebo effect, 83–85, 91
  acupuncture and, 99, 291–93
Plasmas, 314–20
  nature of life and, 316
Platonov, K. I., 248, 254
Playfair, Guy, 285, 319, 320
Plisetskaya, Maya, 8, 309
Plutarch, 195–96
Podshibyakin, A. K., 284–85
Poetry, 308–10
Poland, 166–69, 209
Polish Society of Technology, 166
Pollack, Cecelia, 123, 124–25, 137, 248
Polyclinic Medical Center, 181–82
Polytechnical University, 139
Poock, G. K., 172, 285, 288
Popovkin, Viktor, 12
Popovsky, M., 290
Popov Society, 72
Popular Medical Encyclopedia, The
  (eds. Bajuleff and Petroff), 270
Porterfield, A. L., 198
Prangishvili, A. S., 201, 228
Pratt, J. G., 33–34, 35, 36, 39, 40, 42,
  44–45, 50, 62, 74, 76
Pravda, 33–34, 124
Precognition, 19, 46
  proposed term for, 3
Presman, A. S., 11, 60–62
Pribram, Karl, 65, 208, 306
  on the brain, 156–58
  holographic models of work of,
  321–22
Prichard, R. A., 135
Prokhorov, A. M., 276
Prokofiev, Sergei, 311
Prokop, Otto, 236
Psi particles, 67–70
Psychedelic Art (Masters and
  Houston), 7–8, 12
*Psychic Discoveries Behind the Iron
  Curtain* (Ostrander and
  Schroeder), 9, 15, 25, 175

Psychic Self-Regulation (ed. Romen),
  254
Psychoanalysis, 303
Psychoenergetic phenomena, 3
Psychoenergetic Systems, 177
Psychokinesis (PK), 4–5, 8, 12, 32–51,
  65, 74, 207, 209–10, 212, 289, 321,
  324
  Adamenko's exhibition of, 20–22
  bioplasma and, 316–17
  devices and distances, 55–58
  lingering effect of, 50
  proposed term for, 3
  USSR endorses study of, 25
Psychological Society of the USSR, 24
"Psychophysiology, Converging
  Operations, and Alterations in
  Consciousness" (Krippner), 195
Psychotronic generators, 55–56
Psychotronics, 54–58, 209
Pulos, Lee, 239
Puschov, V. A., 273
Pushkin, Dr. V. N., 2, 7, 8, 12, 209–10
Pushkin Institute, 140

Que Hee, S. S., 318
Questions of Philosophy, 24, 28, 74,
  213, 308 *n*, 324
Quickenden, T. I., 318

Rachmaninoff, Sergei, 104
Racle, Gabriel, 137–38
Radiation
  body, 168–69
  electromagnetic, 65, 105
  mitogenic, 66–73, 318–19
  telepathy and, 105
  ultraviolet, 69, 70, 71, 319
Radio, low-energy waves from, 64–65
Rahman, L., 302
Raikov, Vladimir, 5, 7, 12, 85, 103,
  106–10, 112–15, 116, 117–19, 202,
  217–21, 313
  motion picture by, 220
Rand, Pamela, 163
Rand Corporation, 174
Randi, James, 33 *n*
Rankov, Marat, 262–63
Rasputin, Grigori E., 313
Rational psychotherapy, 95
Ravitz, L. J., 273
Razran, G., 302
Reardon, J. P., 240
Reavy, George, 201
Rech, Johannes, 235
Reeves, C. T., 175
Reflexology, theory of, 16–17
Regelson, Lev, 27

Rejdák, Zdeněk, 35, 36, 37, 39, 40, 43, 166
on psychotronics, 54, 58, 209
René Descartes University, 138
Repression, 203–6
set and, 204
Research Institute of Suggestology, 124
Resonance, laser beams and, 281
Rhine, J. B., 4
Richednikov, A. C., 256
Rig-Veda, 123
Road to Life, The (Makarenko), 300
Rocard, Y., 61
Rogers, Carl, 303
Rogo, D. S., 42
Role playing, 85
in hypnosis, 104, 106–8, 110
in suggestopedia, 159, 162
Rollins, Nancy, 203, 205, 260
Romania, 183–87
Romanian Association for Friendship with the United States, 311
Romanian Ministry of the Chemical Industry, 183
Romanovsky, M. K., 188
Romashov, F. N., 210–11, 226
Romen, A. S., ix, 213, 233, 241–54, 263, 282, 288, 324, 325
Romen, Ludmilla, 324
Roots of Coincidence, The (Koestler), 32
Ross, Rodney, 288
Rossman, Michael, 56
Rotenberg, V. S., 202, 218–19
Rothstein, Leonid, 256–57
Rubin, D., 14, 15, 173, 178 n
Rubinstein, S. L., 303
Russian Academy of Sciences, 13
Russian Journal of Scientific and Applied Photography and Cinemaphotography, 173
Ruttenber, A. J., 206
Ryzl, M., 36, 167–68

Saféris, Fanny, 138
Saint-Saëns, Camille, 197
Sakharov, Andrei, 310
Saturday Review, 33
Schertis, B. M., 256
Schiefelbein, S., 64
Schiller, Johann von, 197
Schizophrenia
drugs used in treatment of, 91
fasting treatment for, 5, 16, 87–92, 210–11, 33
personological approach to, 211
set and, 85–87, 211
as an umbrella category, 90, 93
varying concepts of, 93–94

Schroeder, Lynn, 9, 15–16, 150, 175
Schultz, J. H., 254
Schuster, Donald, 124, 134–37, 140
Schwartz, I. E., 256
Science, 181, 313–14
Scientific American, 33
Scientific method, key hallmarks of, 73
Sechenov, I. M., 202
Second All-Russian Congress, 105
Second All-Union Conference of Marxist-Leninist Research Institutes, 17
Sedlak, Ulodzimierz, 316
Seleucus, General, 195–96
Self-consciousness, 196
Self-hypnosis, 104
Self-regulation, 233–67
acupuncture and, 282
anesthesia and, 251–52
basic exercises for, 243–44
bioluminescence and, 288–89
by children, 259–63
controlling body functions, 250–52
healers (healing) and, 257–59, 289
hypnosis and, 254
pain and, 251–52
Romen on, 233, 241–54, 263, 282, 288
set and, 256
sleep learning and, 247–50
sports and, 234–40, 252–53, 255, 256
Self-suggested submergence, 245–47
Selye, Hans, 90
Sergeyev, G. A., 35, 41, 42, 43, 316–17
Set, 84–85, 195
creativity and, 199–201
hypnosis and, 109–10
love and, 215–16
Lozanov on, 140
music and, 224–25, 310
objectification and, 119
personality theory and, 304
repression and, 204
schizophrenia and, 85–87, 211
self-regulation and, 256
sexual dysfunction and, 214
sublimation and, 204
suggestopedia and, 140–41
the unconscious and, 84, 199–206
Uznadze on, 84, 119, 140, 195, 199, 202–5
Seven Steps Beyond the Horizon (documentary), 5–6, 106–7
Sex in the Soviet Union (Stern), 99
Sexology, 98–99, 214–16
Sex therapy, 98–99
Sexual dysfunction, 5, 18, 98–99, 111
"set" and, 214
Shabad, T., 248

Shakespeare, William, 196–97
Shapiro, A. K., 91
Shatalova, Galina, 222–23
Sherozia, A. E., 194, 201–3, 205, 228
Shevchuk, Elvira, 209
Shevrin, Howard, 206
Shinkarenko, A. J., 13
Shipler, D. K., 269
Shkoda, Valentina, 262–63
Shostakovitch, Dimitri, 224, 310–11
Shpolyanskaya, A. M., 284
Shteinbakh, V., 234
Shushkev, G. D., 316
Simon, B., 299
Simon, C. W., 248
Simurov, A., 124
Skin vision, 5–6, 35–36, 258
Skurlatov, A. P., 5
Sleep
    creativity and, 115
    hypnoproduction and, 115
    Pavlov on, 248
Sleep learning, 123, 247–50
    self-regulation and, 247–50
Sleep therapy, 94–95, 97
Slobin, D., 304
Slow-wave potentials, 65
Smirnov, N. A., 37
Smith, R., 285
Smith, S., 48, 51
Snegova, Irina, 308–9
Society for Neurology, Reflexology,
    Hypnotism, and Biophysics, 105
Society for Psychical Research, 35
Sociohistorical-origin theory, 303
Sokolov, E. N., 307
Solar magnetism, the brain and, 64
Solovyov-Sedey, Vasili, 309–10
Solzhenitsyn, Alexander, 310
Soma bioplasma, 321–22
Song of the Siren (Krippner), 332
Soomere, Ilmar, 19
Soviet Artists' Union, 217
Soviet Life, 81
Sparks, P. W., 172, 288
Spartakiad (1979), 263
Special relativity theory, 323
Spickermann, A., 235–36
Spiegel, D., 109
Spiegel, Herbert, 109–10
Sports, 241 n, 262–63
    hypnosis and, 240
    self-regulation and, 234–40, 252–53,
    255, 256
Stalin, Joseph, 76, 310, 311, 313
Stalinist oppression, 310–14
Statebound learning, 111–13, 163
Stavish, M., 137
Stefánsky, L. E., 167

Stelazine, 91
Stepanov, P., 182
Stern, J. A., 292
Stern, Mikhail, 99, 216
Stevens, B., 179, 189
Stevenson, I., 207
Stevenson, Robert Louis, 115, 198–99
Stewart, D., 292
Storfer, B., 38
Stoyanov, Produn, 132
Strange Case of Dr. Jekyll and Mr.
    Hyde, The (Stevenson), 115, 199
Stravinsky, Igor, 224
Strenk, Andrew, 236, 237
Strong, F. F., 174
Sturva, Melov, 22
Sublimation, 203–6
    creativity and, 204
    set and, 204
Suggestion, laws of, 123
Suggestive-accelerative learning and
    teaching (SALT), 134–37
Suggestology and Altered States of
    Consciousness, 124
Suggestopedia, 122–64, 226–27
    accomplishments in, 147
    differences in receptivity to, 158
    fundamental principles of, 132–33
    key to effectiveness of, 162
    learning to music, 131–34, 139–40,
    150–51
    mechanized form of, 140 n
    motion pictures on, 129, 130, 217
    Pavlov and, 122, 137
    role playing in, 159, 162
    set and, 140–41
    suggestions vs. drugs, 123
    suggestopedic operetta on, 127–29
Suinn, Richard, 239
Sullivan, H. S., 304
Sunspots, 64
Superlight elementary particles, 69–70
Swann, Ingo, 18, 289
Sweden, 139
Swets, J. A., 186
Szentgyörgvári, Artur, 160 n
Szent-Györgyi, Albert, 274, 275

Tal, Mikhail, 118
Taratorkin, V., 277
Targ, Russell, 288
Tart, Charles, 73, 161
Tartini, Giuseppe, 198, 199, 201
Tass, 67
Tbilisi State University, 195, 201–2,
    224, 228
Tchaikovsky, Peter Ilich, 7, 201
Tchernogolovina, G., 289
Teaching machines, 143

Technical University, 147–48, 163
Technology for Youth, 20
Telepathy, 8, 19, 25, 47, 72, 73, 105, 268
  dreams and, 10–11
  electromagnetic radiation and, 105
  proposed term for, 2
Television
  documentary on healers (healing), 222–23
  low-energy waves from, 64–65
  suggestopedic operetta on, 127–29
Tesla, Nikola, 169
Tesla coils, 169, 170, 171, 174, 288
Thailand, 15
Thant, U, 312
Theory of Dreams, The (Kasatkin), 283
Thioridazine, 91
Thompson, J., 292
Thorndike, Edward, 311, 312
Tikhomirov, O. K., 307, 308
Tiller, William, 14, 46, 173–74, 179, 180, 242, 272, 273
Time, 38, 153, 156
Time as a participant in physical processes, 64
Time-lapse photography, 18
Tittel, Kurt, 235
Tkachev, Alexander, 259
Tobiscope, the, 271–72
Togliatti University, 140
Tolstoy, Leo, 197, 211, 215
Torrey, E. Fuller, 86–87, 92–93
Toth, Robert, 66–68
Townes, C. H., 276–77
Track and Field News, 235
Transformation Project, 241
Transforming experiment, the, 299–302
Tristan and Isolde (Wagner), 198, 199–200
Troilus and Cressida (Shakespeare), 196
Tserkover, E., 58
Tsipko, A., 110
Twenty-second Congress of the Communist Party, 76
Typee (Melville), 215

Uccusic, P., 259
Ukrainian Academy of Sciences, 248, 277
Ullman, Montague, 3 *n,* 11, 32, 35, 36, 41, 42, 43, 46, 47, 48, 123
  on creative aspects of dreaming, 197
Ultraviolet radiation, 69, 70, 71, 319
Unconscious, the, 194–232
  Bassin on, 194, 202, 203, 205
  dreams and, 196–201, 203, 205

Freud on, 203, 204, 205, 206, 213
healers (healing) and, 221–24
nonverbal thought in, 203
Pavlov on, 202
repression in, 203–6
set and, 84, 199–206
Sherozia on, 194, 202, 203, 205, 228
sublimation in, 203–6
Uznadze on, 199, 202–3, 205
United Nations, 8, 312, 325–26
United Nations Declaration of Rights of the Child, 262
United Nations Educational, Scientific, and Cultural Organization (UNESCO), 124, 131, 132, 143, 217
United Nations Parapsychology Club, 325
Universe Book Club, 175
Upanishads, 215
U. S. Air Force, 173, 174
U. S. Army Medical Intelligence Information Agency, 56
U. S. National Institute of Mental Health, 92
U. S. Olympic Committee, 238–39
USSR Academy of Sciences, 13, 24–25, 202, 225, 237, 276, 285
USSR State Committee for Inventions and Discoveries, 70
Uznadze, D. N., 84, 119, 140, 195, 207, 228
  on objectification, 204
  on set, 84, 119, 140, 195, 199, 202–5
  on social activities, 204–5
  on the unconscious, 199, 202–3, 205

Vacations, health, 269–70
Van de Castle, R. L., 199
Van Hasselt, P., 317
Van Immerseel, W., 317
Vasiliev, L. L., 3, 17, 35–36, 62, 105–6, 285, 307, 324
Vassilchenko, G. S., 5, 18, 98–99, 214–16, 226
Vaughan, A., 3 *n,* 11
Velkovskiy, I. Z., 141
Verovacki, Vladimir, 200–1, 208, 240–41, 286, 289, 324
Vetoe, Lajos, 187–88
V. I. Lenin State Pedagogical Institute, 140
Vilenskaya, Larissa, 1, 2, 4, 7, 12, 15, 42, 183, 209 *n*
  on healers (healing), 257–59
Villoldo, A., 57
Vinogradova, Alla, 5, 8, 12, 15, 17, 20–22, 45–46, 177–78, 212, 325
Vinogradova, Y. E., 307

Virginia, University of, 4
Visual-perception speed, 253–54
Vlasov, Yuri, 238
Vogralik, V. G., 98, 270
Volgyesi, F. A., 84
Volkenshtein, I. M., 317
Volkov, S., 311
Voloshanovich, Alexander, 93
Voprosy Psikhologii, 304
Voznesensky, Andrei, 309
Vyacheslavovich, Vyschoslav, 140 *n*
Vygotskii, L. S., 302

Wagner, Richard, 198, 199–200
Walker, M., 250
War and Peace (Tolstoy), 215
Watkins, Anita, 50
Watkins, Graham, 50
Way of All Flesh, The (Butler),
   215–16
Weberman, A. J., 174
Weisskopf, V. W., 314
Westerbeke, Patricia, 290
Western Hemisphere Conference on
   Kirlian Photography, 14, 173
White, L. L., 196
White, R. A., 238, 239
Whitton, J. L., 61
Wilhelm, J. L., 68
Williamson, S. J., 66
Williamson, T., 60
Wilson, R. R., 314
Winnykamen, Fauda, 138
Witkin, H. A., 82
Wittkower, E. D., 205–6
Wolf, Josef, 56
Wolkowski, Z. W., 316
Wolniewicz, B., 167
Woods, R. L., 199

*Word as a Physiological and
   Therapeutic Factor, The*
   (Platonov), 254
Wordsworth, William, 197
Working Group on Suggestology as a
   Learning Methodology, The,
   124–43
World, 32
World Congress on Sports and Society,
   263 *n*
World Health Organization (WHO),
   223, 325
Wortis, Dr. Joseph, 9, 13, 304
Wortz, E. C., 66, 72
Wozniak, R. H., 300

Yevtushenko, Yevgeny, 201
Yoga, 123, 233–34
   healers (healing) and, 259
Yuri Gagarin school, 124–34, 142–43
Yurkevitch, V. S., 308

Zachariev, Zachari, 132
Zakharin, G. A., 202
Zavarin, Valentina, 211
Zdorovye, 98
Zemke, R., 141
Zezulka, Josef, 57–58
Zielinski, L., 167
Ziferstein, I., 81, 95, 96, 97, 303
Zinchenko, P. I., 308
Zinchenko, V. P., 15, 24, 177, 213,
   308 *n*, 324
Zion, J., 316
Zlochevsky, S. E., 256
Zorina, Olga, 286, 324
Zoukhar, Vladimir, 233–34
Zurabashvili, A. D., 211

Dr. Stanley Krippner is recognized throughout the world for his distinguished work in many new, untapped areas of scientific study. Currently the Faculty Chairman of the Humanistic Psychology Institute in San Francisco, Dr. Krippner has also served as President of the Association for Humanistic Psychology, and as Director, from 1964 to 1973, of the Dream Laboratory at Maimonides Medical Center, in New York. In 1972 he chaired the First Western Hemisphere Conference on Acupuncture, Kirlian Photography, and the Human Aura. A noted author as well as scientist, he has written, edited, or coauthored several books in such areas of human behavior as dream studies, parapsychology, and healing. These works include *Dream Telepathy, The Realms of Healing, Song of the Siren,* and *The Kirlian Aura.*